NETWORKING CD-ROMs

The Decision Maker's Guide to
Local Area Network
Solutions

Ahmed M. Elshami

American Library Association
Chicago and London 1996

Cover design by Richmond Jones

Text design and composition by Publishing Services, Inc.

Printed on 50-pound Glatfelter, a pH-neutral stock, and bound in
10-point C1S cover stock by Edwards Bros., Inc.

The paper used in this publication meets the minimum requirements of American
National Standard for Information Sciences—Permanence of Paper for Printed
Library Materials, ANSI Z39.48-1992. ⊚

Library of Congress Cataloging-in-Publication Data

Elshami, Ahmed M., 1936–
    Networking CD-ROMs : the decision maker's guide to local area
  network solutions / Ahmed M. Elshami.
       p.   cm.
    Includes bibliographical references and index.
    ISBN 0-8389-0670-2
    1. Local area networks (Computer networks) 2. CD-ROMs.
  TK5105.7.E47 1996
  004.5'6—dc20   95-40315

Printed in the United States of America.

00 99 98 97 96   5 4 3 2 1

*As I always do, I would like to thank
my wife, Enaam, and my children
for their encouragement and patience*

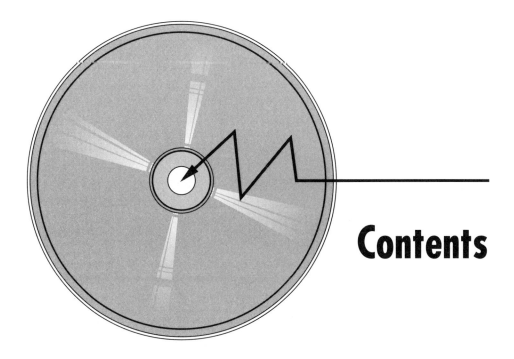

Contents

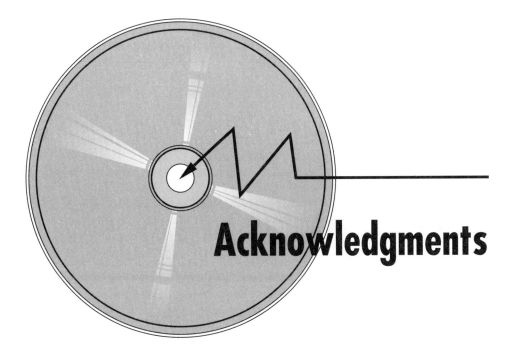

Acknowledgments

I am grateful to the following colleagues, who offered comments on sections of the text of this book:

Jacqueline Hanson, reference librarian, University of California Library, San Diego, California, and Joe Lucia, systems librarian, LaSalle University, Bethlehem, Pennsylvania.

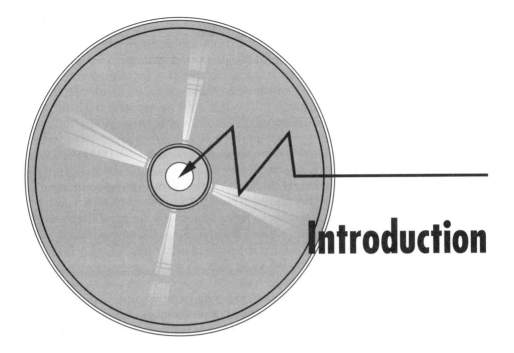

Introduction

The real technology imperative of the late nineties is not computation, but communication. The need to communicate, share data, access computing resources, search remote databases, send messages, and share expensive peripheral devices has made local area networks (LANs) one of the major fields in the computer industry. PC networks are becoming larger, more capable, and more complex. Their primary role is the sharing of information. Today, network users can access centralized information files, exchange messages, and even run programs remotely. PC networks have become the central nervous system of today's business world. Libraries also must embrace the opportunity posed by the explosion in information technology.

In libraries, information is presented to users in many formats: paper, magnetic disks, films, microforms, slides, video, laser discs, audiotape, etc. Making the information stored on CD-ROM (compact disc read-only memory) accessible to a computer is, in fact, an extension of the library concept. Rather than being stored as printed material on shelves or on magnetic disks, the information is stored on laser discs and it is accessed within the library premises. CD-ROM became popular in the second half of the 1980s as a wide variety of materials were published in CD-ROM format. More than 10,000 titles are available on CD-ROM, including directories, dictionaries, encyclopedias, handbooks, indexes, books, periodicals, computer applications and software, clip art collections, photo albums, games, training and educational material, movies, and others. The use of CD-ROM databases in organizations has resulted in a sharp decline in the number of expensive online bibliographic searches. As a result of the popularity of CD-ROMs, many libraries continue to add CD-ROM databases and workstations for patron use. However, in a busy library, the concept of having one database searched by one user at a time became unacceptable because of the cost involved. Consequently, the well-known trio—one CD-ROM disc/workstation/user—proved to be an uneconomical scenario after all. The problems of users handling the discs were also a source of annoyance. Many solutions were suggested. They ranged from administrative (e.g., collecting users' IDs, requiring that they sign forms and make reservations in advance to use a CD-ROM workstation, buying more than one copy of some databases, assigning library staff to handle the CDs, and forcing a search time limit) to technical solutions (e.g., buying CD-ROM drives with locking mechanisms, dedicating workstations to run specific databases, using passwords to access the databases, hiding the directories of the computers in CD stations, and using CD-ROM caddies). By the end of the 1980s, the concept of sharing and adding more security to these valuable sources of information began to emerge. Onto the scene came CD-ROM networking, and along with it came a trail of other ambitious services, such as using Internet functions for remote access to library online catalogs, electronic mail, newsgroups and listserves. Users started to access mainframes and share printers, software applications, and computing utilities. Other services have been added, including dial-in and dial-out capabilities for remote connection. As computers interact with each other, problems involving operability between hardware of different platforms and compatibility between equipment and hardware have emerged.

Who Needs This Book?

Today, computers are not only becoming part of local area networks, they are also being incorporated into enterprise- or campus-wide applications. Consequently, networked computers enable users in geographically dispersed areas to share information as if these users were in one location. As a result, yesterday's standalone computers are now connected to today's electronic highways. Because CD-ROM networks are in fact networks that have the capability of sharing CD-ROMs, one cannot explain CD-ROM networking without explaining computer networks. Furthermore, because of the complexity of networking and of maintaining an effective CD-ROM service, this book is not intended to be exhaustive on the subject. Rather, the book tries to point out the issues involved in creating a CD-ROM network by presenting the basics of networking and the CD-ROM networking solutions available. Thus, the book is written for anyone who has to deal with the issues of networking CD-ROMs or adding a CD-ROM service through an existing network. The author has tried to look at these issues from the perspectives of

> anyone who has no experience with networks but is considering sharing CD-ROMs on a network
>
> an administrator who is considering networking CD-ROM workstations
>
> those familiar with networks who want to know what CD-ROM networking solutions are available for a specific network
>
> anyone who needs to know the issues involved in providing a CD-ROM service through a network

To accomplish this task, the first chapter tries to explain the basic concepts behind PC networks. The concepts are presented and explained briefly in order for the user to develop a quick grasp of network technology. This chapter can be used as a concise reference for most of the network issues discussed in the literature. While the second chapter provides the basics and standards of CD-ROM and other optical technologies, the third chapter helps in selecting CD-ROM drives. Since not every network operating system supports the sharing of CD-ROMs, chapters 4 through 7 will identify network operating systems that have CD-ROM networking capability, as well as those that do not have this capability but use third-party CD-ROM solutions.

Because most of the CD-ROM network products are being developed for Novell's NetWare networks, chapter 5 discusses the NetWare Loadable Module (NLM) approach utilized with Novell's NetWare network operating system. Chapter 6 presents CD-ROM networking solutions for other LANs, such as Banyan's VINES, UNIX, and Macintosh. Chapter 7 highlights the issues that will concern you in your development of a CD-ROM network.

Chapter 8 presents important issues, such as type of CD-ROM licenses, viruses, and security issues. Chapter 9 deals with how to select network servers. Chapter 10 deals with the fundamentals of memory usage and provides ways to avoid the problems associated with limited random access memory (RAM) space. Chapter 11 provides information about network standards, specifications, and network components of many network architectures.

The terminology has been simplified and a glossary has been added for the user to consult. The appendixes provide information about products and their vendors. The reader must realize that the prices given for some products are approximate and can change along with vendor addresses and telephone numbers.

A New Role

Reference librarians have felt the impact of CD-ROM technology the most. With the help of technicians, reference librarians assume a new role as they integrate and blend network searching into reference-desk activities. In a LAN environment, the hands-on and the one-to-one interaction becomes more obvious and has more impact on the users in the area of training. Reference librarians transfer their expertise to the users while they pace among workstations offering their assistance. Also, bibliographic instructions to users include more training on how to survive in the LAN environment and utilize the new service effectively.

LANs are gradually imposing major changes on librarianship. They have changed the flow of information, especially in the area of speed. Before a LAN, a library user would search the online public access catalog (OPAC) for some titles, go to another section of the library to search a database on a standalone CD-ROM station, then move to another location to use a computer application, such as a word processor. After installation of a LAN, a user would access all these sources and accomplish all computing activities from a single workstation.

In libraries, however, automating services requires an integrated automated system that would combine circulation, cataloging, OPAC, interlibrary loan, acquisitions and serials control, reference services, access to mainframes and Internet, searching databases in the library as well as in other institutions, and allowing library users to access information resources using communication facilities. Since accessing the information resources of a library does not have to happen only from inside a library, planning a LAN in the library should take into consideration the library's parent organization and the total networking environment of a library. This way, users can have the information at their fingertips, in the right form, when they need it, no matter where they are.

Although LANs take a lot of money and patience to set up and maintain, the benefits outweigh the cost and effort. Today, in the age of information superhighways, rather than asking whether or not to network, libraries and other organizations should ask themselves *when* to network.

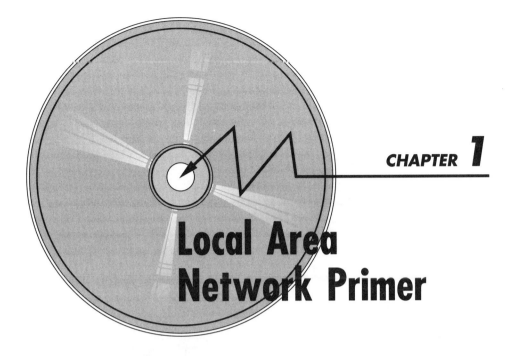

CHAPTER 1

Local Area Network Primer

During the sixties and early seventies, a computer environment consisted of large and very expensive mainframe systems residing in environmentally controlled rooms and run by highly experienced staff. Mainframes were manufactured by such companies as IBM, Burroughs, Control Data, Honeywell, and Univac. Users could access mainframes through "dumb" terminals that depended on the processing power of the mainframe. Terminals were attached directly to mainframes by expensive cabling systems. At that time, the computing environment allowed multiple users to share the computing resources of the host mainframe. Terminals had some capability of receiving and transmitting messages, and equal access to peripheral devices such as printers and modems. Because all computing activities were controlled from one place, this environment was labeled as *centralized computing* (fig. 1–1).

In the 1970s and 1980s, minicomputers established themselves as cost-effective systems for departmental use. This environment continued until around 1980, when the personal computer (PC) was introduced in the market. Even before IBM introduced the IBM PC in 1981, Apple computers were manufactured in large quantities. Together they changed the computing environment forever. Not the overall features and functionality, but rather the processing power of the mainframe was capsulized and brought to the desktop. Still, a mainframe can handle huge amounts of input/output (I/O), online transaction processing, security, data integrity, and management functions compared to the desktop computer. However, most desktop computers, especially the super-servers (desktop PCs with multiple processors and vast amounts of memory), have almost the memory, storage, and processing power of minicomputers.

In businesses as well as educational institutions and others, there was always a problem with the PC, because any application was available to just

1

Terminals

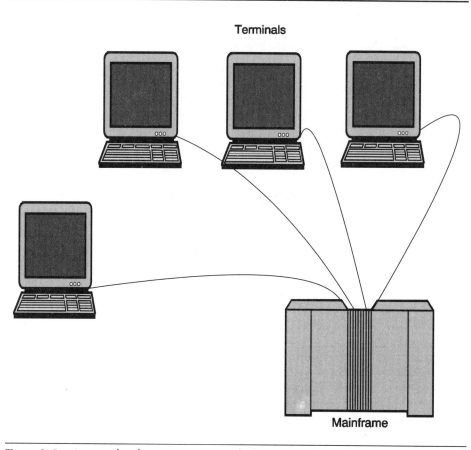

Mainframe

Figure 1–1. *In centralized computing, terminals depend heavily on the processing power of the mainframe.*

one user at a time. However, for the first time since the introduction of the mainframe, the centralized computing environment seemed to lose ground to the newcomer, the microcomputer. Users assumed control of their software and hardware applications. In the history of computing, this was a period of transition. Individually, users were able to run applications, enter data, and print reports on local printers. But there was no computing resource, nor was there multiple-host sharing. PCs were attached to mainframes by cables, and they used software emulators to turn them into regular dumb terminals. But the file transfer rate between the mainframe and the PC was very slow. To transfer data between two separate computers, data were copied to floppy diskettes, which were then delivered by actually walking them to another office—thus creating a network that was humorously termed *sneakernet*.

The concept of local area networks (LANs) was developed at the same time PCs were introduced into the market. A LAN facilitated connections among PCs as well as between PCs and mainframes. In the beginning, few people knew the secrets of PC networking, and so the costs of installing and maintaining LANs were very high. Today, because networks are well established and equipment is mostly standardized (and lower in price), many companies offer a lifetime warranty on their network products.

In practice, networks connect more than personal computers, as they are capable of connecting telephones, videos, and alarm systems. In fact, any situation where data need to be transferred, a LAN can be very useful. Consequently, the term *network* denotes a controllable system of data communications that ties together independent devices such as computer hardware and computer peripherals (e.g., hard disks, printers, CD-ROM drives, etc.), communications devices (e.g., modems, fax machines, etc.), and software resources for the purpose of sharing and transporting information efficiently and economically by electronic means. The information that needs to be shared and transported includes data, text, graphics, animation, and audio. The most important aspect of a LAN is that each computer connected to the LAN remains able to function as a standalone computer.

LAN Fundamentals

To connect computers together, you need cables, connectors, network interface cards (NICs), and a network operating system. A NIC fits inside your computer and enables you to send information to and receive information from other computers through the cabling system. A network can include a few computers within a single department or many computers in several departments within your organization. Networking can be simple or complex, depending on the particular needs of your organization. For example, small offices can link a few computers to share data and printers among users.[1] With medium-size networks, devices such as routers and gateways are needed to link computers in offices across town or across the country. Large networks enable users to access data throughout the world from any number of minicomputers, mainframes, or remote LANs.

Basically, when two or more computers are connected together to share their computing resources, they form a LAN. When two LANs are connected, they make an *internetwork*. When several LANs in one building or campus are connected, the result is a *facility-wide* or *campus network*. When a cluster of buildings of one corporation is interconnected within a geographic area that spans the area of a city or a county (about 50 square miles), the result is a *metropolitan area network* (MAN). When LANs that belong to one corporation are connected over large distances that span one country or more, the result is an *enterprise network*. When LANs that belong to multiple corporations span one country or more, the result is a *wide area network* (WAN). MANs, enterprise networks, and WANs usually communicate through some type of remote link, such as the telephone system or a *public data network* (PDN).

To describe groups of computers, some use the term *domain*, while others use the term *workgroup*. A workgroup can be either a group of users who are physically located in one place and connected by the same local area network, or a logical grouping of users who are scattered throughout an organization but connected to the same LAN. Users in a workgroup usually share documents, applications, electronic mail, and system resources. A resource, however, is an item such as a directory, printer, hard disk, or CD-ROM drive that you and others can share.

The computer that is primarily used to provide shared resources is known as a *network server*. Depending on its size, a network may need more than one server. The three basic types of servers are file, print, and communication servers. While *file servers* provide services to network users, they also provide management functions for network administrators. Servers usually store network operating systems, utilities, and users' programs and data. A file server provides management functions for the files system and for security and user access, and data protection functions and reliability. The *print server* manages print jobs by holding them in a print queue, then releasing them to designated printers. *Communication servers*, however, provide communication channels for the users of a LAN to access outside remote computing resources. They also allow remote users to dial into the network from their homes or other remote locations.

The term *workstation*, on the other hand, is a general term that denotes a computer attached to networks and does not provide shared resources for other network users. The term is now used generically to refer to systems attached to networks. Similar terms exist, such as stations, nodes, and clients. Although the term "node" can be applied to any device connected to the LAN, a node must be intelligent to handle the communications control functions. So, a computer is a node, but a CD-ROM drive attached to a server on a LAN is not a node because it is not as intelligent as a computer. The term *client*, however, assumes a client-server relationship in which the client workstation is the front-end system where users access data and interact with back-end servers (fig. 1–2). The client is a user who typically runs an application in order to access data from a server over a network connection.

In the client-server relationship, the front-end application runs in the memory of the user's workstation. It displays screens and provides user prompts. The user creates queries for the back-end system, which in turn takes the query statements sent over the network and processes them, searching for data, sorting data, or providing other services. When the back-end server has completed the client's request, it returns the result to the client. You can think of the back-end system as an "engine" that performs the major data processing functions. Thus, the retrieval client runs on the user's workstation, while the search engine operates on the back-end server. This approach ensures a balanced workload between the clients and the server.

Networks permit the sharing of computing resources. The basic elements of the computing resources include: software (e.g., professionally developed, user-written, or off-the-shelf applications), peripherals (e.g., printers, modems, fax modems, CD-ROM drives, hard disks), information (e.g., text files, databases in optical or magnetic format, multimedia), and services (e.g., electronic communication by establishing data and mail links).

Generally, the term network applies to any multiuser system that connects computers together for sharing applications, peripherals, and real-time information.[2] In a network, the networking equipment is located wherever the users are located, but the computing resources are physically scattered or distributed. This "decentralized," or "distributed," computing has evolved from centralized and client-server computing. It is basically client-server computing

Workstations

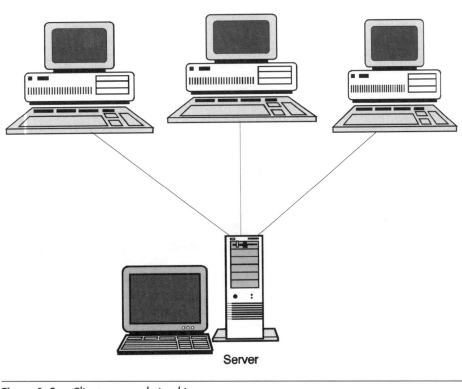

Server

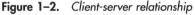

Figure 1–2. *Client-server relationship*

where data are not located in one server, but rather in many servers (fig. 1–3), and these servers might be at geographically dispersed areas connected by WAN links.

The result of distributed computing is a *virtual network*, which is a collection of workgroups, departmental networks, and enterprise networks that appear to the end user or client application to be easily accessed whole. Although this distributed database, which is a collection of data spread across many computers, is stored in multiple physical locations, it appears as one logical, centrally managed database. This configuration provides users timely and flexible access to information and optimizes the use of computer processing power. Furthermore, it allows more control over the safety and integrity of the data.

In the most basic sense, a user using a Macintosh computer in a departmental library, for example, can send a request to search a CD-ROM database that runs under a Novell network in the main library and is accessed through a PC. This user does not necessarily know where the database is located or who is managing it.

Because only the dumb terminals were replaced by intelligent computers, both mainframes and minicomputers can coexist in a microcomputer network environment. It is just the concept of centralized computing that is fading

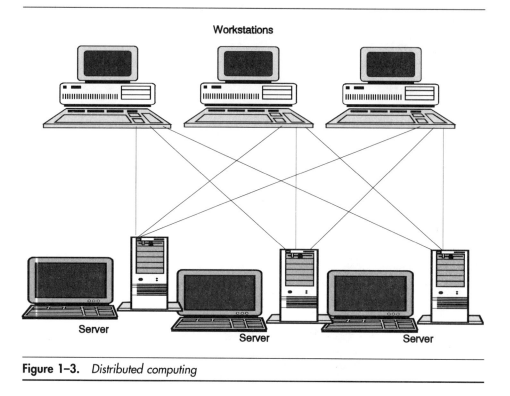

Figure 1-3. *Distributed computing*

away as mainframes and minicomputers are being integrated into—not replaced by—computer networks. Mainframes are crucial in efficiently running large applications such as a national library cataloging system, an online bibliographic service, an airline reservation system, or banking operations that use online transaction-processing software.

Types of Networks

Networks can start small before they grow with an organization. The following is a description of the types of networks that might exist in the workplace.

Network Segment, or Subnetwork

Known also as a *subnetwork,* a *network segment* is a linear cable that is composed of one or more sections of cable. This linear cable is attached to the network interface card (NIC) in the file server. You can virtually attach CD-ROM servers, workstations, printers, and other devices to that cable. All nodes on that segment should be able to receive the same data signal. Actually, you can establish a LAN using one or more network segments.

Local Area Network (LAN)

A local area network (LAN) connects computers in a workgroup, department, or building. A LAN is always physically limited by its topology. The communication of a LAN is basically confined to a moderately sized geographic area—e.g., a single office, a single floor, an entire building, or a group of very close buildings. Some LAN topologies allow the maximum length of the cable to reach almost 10 kilometers. LANs do not use any government-regulated telecommunications facilities such as AT&T, ITT, or local telephone companies.

Facility-Wide Network

Also known as a campus network, a facility-wide network interconnects individual LANs in different buildings within an organization, a campus, or industrial park area. Like LANs, facility-wide networks do not use any government-regulated telecommunications facilities.

Metropolitan Area Network (MAN)

Another type of networking technology is known as metropolitan area networks (MANs). MANs link a cluster of buildings of one organization together within a geographic area that can extend to about 80 kilometers. MAN services use some type of communications service such as a local telephone company, public data network (PDN), a local exchange carrier (LEC), a cable company, or other suppliers. A MAN is smaller than a wide area network (WAN) but larger than a LAN. A MAN can support a variety of services, such as LAN-to-LAN connections, private branch exchange (PBX) connections, direct station attachment, and mainframe connections. A typical MAN is built with microwave systems and/or fiber-optic cable.

Wide Area Network (WAN)

Networks that tie together users that are spread widely over a large geographic area—often crossing the geographic boundaries of cities or states, or encompassing the entire globe—are called wide area networks (WANs). A WAN links the computers outside of an organization's properties (buildings or campus area) and crosses the public areas that are regulated by local, national, or international authorities. Because WANs span intercity, interstate, or even international borders, links are made with public and private telecommunications facilities. If public facilities are used, a WAN utilizes local exchange carriers (LECs), long-distance interexchange carriers (IXCs), and carriers at the remote sites. Typically, the public telephone network forms links among remote sites, but an organization can install its own WAN links by installing microwave, satellite, or other communication technologies.

In WANs, public telecommunications facilities such as AT&T, ITT, MCI, or local telephone companies are used to provide users with access to the processing and data storage capabilities of faraway computing facilities. An example of a WAN is the Internet, which connects thousands of organizations around the globe. LANs typically communicate at higher speeds than WANs since they use copper or fiber-optic cables, which can achieve a moderate speed of up to 10 Mbits/sec (megabits per second), or 125,000 bytes per second. In contrast to LANs, WANs use carrier services with lower transmission speeds. Carrier services include dial-up phone lines, dedicated lines, and circuit-switched or packet-switched services. The existing transmission speeds for dial-up phone lines using modems range from 1,200 to 28,800 bits per second. Dedicated lines can achieve speeds as high as 2,400 to 56,000 bits per second. A common switched service such as Switched-56 operates at 56 Kbits/sec. WANs that communicate via satellite or microwave link may achieve high-speed communications. However, most WANs use telephone communications via modems that provide speeds of 9,600 baud, while special-purpose telephone lines provide communication rates as high as 57,600 baud.[3] If a leased line is used, this guarantees a continuous open communications channel (no busy signal) at any time of the day at a constant cost rate. Leased lines are used when connecting two or more LANs across a long distance.

Enterprise Network

An enterprise network is an evolutionary step beyond workgroup computing. It interconnects all the computer systems within an organization, regardless of operating system, communication protocols, application differences, or geographic location. It may therefore incorporate LANs, MANs, and WANs. Enterprise networks integrate LANs and other devices that are connected to them (e.g., terminals, computers, media storage, printers), as well as voice and image communications, in all offices of an organization. Because they bring together all network resources and make them available to the organization, enterprise networks are known by the descriptive nickname "umbrella networks." An enterprise network integrates all the systems within an organization, whether they are DOS-based computers, Apple Macintoshes, UNIX workstations, minicomputers, or mainframes. Various techniques are usually employed to integrate these systems so that users can access any resources in a transparent way. Thus, an enterprise network is a typical distributed computing system, where resources and data are located throughout the organization.

In the enterprise network, LANs are connected to WANs by "internetwork devices" (e.g., bridges, routers, or gateways). This interconnection is called the *internetwork*, or the *internet* (spelled with a small "i").

Why Establish a Computer Network?

The goal of building a LAN is to share and transfer information in an orderly manner. Through better management of computer resources, LANs can reduce duplication of information and improve accessibility. Also, users' interaction can be improved through information sharing. Sharing CD-ROM resources is one of the main reasons for installing a LAN in many organizations. Other activities that have been popular since the introduction of LANs into libraries are electronic mail and library forums.

In LANs, because access to many types of information as well as to remote sites is done from a single point, that access is accomplished in less time. LAN users have more control over the information they acquire as they exploit local as well as remote information resources. In educational institutions, these new information resources usually enhance the learning process. An advantage of using LANs in academic environments is that faculty and students do not have to acquire a user ID and password such as those needed to access a mainframe.

LANs also eliminate the need of acquiring multiple copies of the same software package as they allow the sharing of one copy among many computers—depending, of course, on the software copyright as well as the license agreement practiced by the vendor. Software sharing allows many users to access the same application software concurrently. In addition to program and file sharing, users can share other network resources, including printers, plotters, CD-ROMs, and other storage devices.

A network provides a way to create workgroups and help users collaborate on projects, schedules, database updating, and document processing. Networks also have centralized system maintenance since it is done from one central location. On the negative side, while the design of a network is not easy, installing, operating, and managing a LAN in a dependable manner could be more difficult. An active LAN is viewed as a flexible, continually changing and evolving interrelation of resources. But the major elements of a LAN are its information resources, nodes, links, and protocols. Networks need continuous traffic management and fast intervention to recover from traffic failures. In some cases, the failure of one workstation can bring other workstations down. Also, the cost of running cables to connect workstations can be high. In the world of networks, the technology is changing so fast that keeping pace with it could be costly to any organization. Another disadvantage of establishing a LAN is the high cost of administration, maintenance, and upgrades.

Components of a Network

A computer network is composed of hardware and software. The main hardware components of a computer network include computers, network interface cards (NICs) or adapters, and the cabling system that ties the hardware together (fig. 1–4). The software components include server operating systems, communication protocols, and network interface card drivers.

Servers

Literally, any desktop computer in a network can be prepared to function as a server. However, in most LANs, only powerful computers are usually selected as network servers. The function of the computer server is to make the computing resources available to other stations attached to the network. The server is used to store all application software, network operating system (NOS) software, CD-ROM network management software, CD-ROM applications software, communications software, and other utilities' software.

In some situations, a network has multiple computer servers, each performing a different task. For example, one server takes care of file management, a second server directs the print jobs to printers, a third server controls the communication of the network, while a fourth server provides a CD-ROM service. In other situations, all these functions can be assigned to just one network server. In modular network operating systems, such as Novell NetWare (a well-known network operating system with almost a 60 percent share of installed networks), one or more servers can provide some or all of these services, depending on which modules you choose to install in the server.

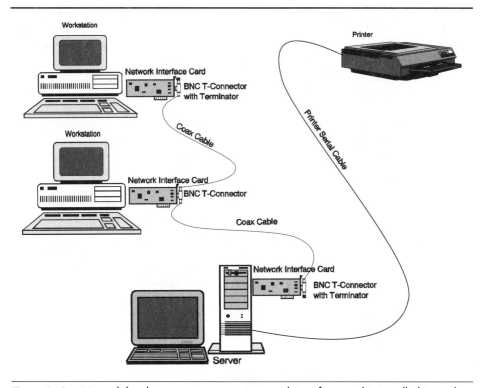

Figure 1–4. *Network hardware components. A network interface card is installed in each server and workstation.*

The server makes all software, hardware, and information resources—as well as print, long-distance links, and communications services—available to other computers on the network. Since it typically has greater microprocessing power, memory, cache, disk storage, and power supplies, it can easily be distinguished from other PCs used as workstations on the network. A network server runs the network operating system, which is special software that forms a shell around the computer's disk operating system (DOS). This shell software filters commands out to the network server before the computer disk operating system can detect them. Microsoft's LAN Manager and Novell's NetWare are examples of network operating systems. In fact, not every server is a physical piece of hardware, as one might think. Some servers actually are software-based servers; the print server and remote e-mail server are examples. There are many types of servers including the following:

File server   Manages operations of the network and provides file storage, retrieval services, and network security. It also controls file access rights.

Print server   Gathers print jobs sent by applications running on PCs, holds them in a queue on the server's hard disk, and feeds them individually to one or more printers attached to the server.

CD-ROM server Manages and controls CD-ROM access to multiple CD-ROM drives.

Directory services server This server holds information about users, servers, and resources on the network.

E-mail server or gateway Provides local or enterprise-wide electronic mail services.

Communications server Provides connection services to mainframe or minicomputer systems, or to remote computer systems and networks via wide area links such as telephone services.

Database server This dedicated system handles user database requests and responses. Typically, a database server follows client-server database access methods. The front-end client and the back-end database split the processing load.

Application server Provides a central storage and access point for applications, simplifying management.

Archive server Backup and archiving can be performed on dedicated devices such as online storage devices, optical disks (where they are available on request), and tape backup systems.

Fax server Provides LAN users with the ability to share the hardware for incoming and outgoing facsimile transmissions.

Video server This server is used for business applications such as video-conferencing, distance learning, and training; it includes a video transfer engine, which manages the continuous and simultaneous flow of video material from the disk drives to remote clients.

Computation server Designed for mathematical applications, a computation server (sometimes referred to as a compute server) is typically implemented on a powerful special-purpose computer that allows a user to perform calculations even though the main program is running on the user's own computer.

Clients or Workstations

The client part of the network operating system software that runs on the workstation redirects network requests from users or applications to servers via the network interface cards and the cabling system. It is through workstations that users can access the information resources of the LAN. Virtually any type of IBM-compatible personal computers, Apple Macintoshes, or UNIX machines can be used as workstations. When selecting workstations, one should keep in mind that in today's networks, most of the processing takes place in the memory of the workstation. The workstation must have the capability required to handle all application programs and services provided to network users. For example, if CD-ROM applications are run through Windows, then only workstations that are capable of running Windows should be selected.

The software that you plan to run has a great effect on the type of computer you choose as a workstation. You have to keep in mind that future software is going to be more complex and demand more computing power. You will need fast computers with large memory capacities.

Computer prices have dropped dramatically in the last few years. In order to use the computer for many years to come, you must consider system upgradability. You should select a computer that can be easily upgraded when you need more memory, hard disk space, or central processing unit (CPU) speed.

Network Interface Cards

Cables are not enough to establish communication among computers in a LAN. Communication is established through a circuit board that fits inside every computer in the LAN. These circuit boards, known as network interface cards (NICs), or controller cards, act as translators. The NICs are responsible for the managing of data transmissions. Communication takes place when stations send and receive signals over the cables via these NICs. The NICs contain programs that format the data into chunks of signals, called packets, for transmission over the LAN. These boards are installed in expansion slots of every computer in the network, including file servers and workstations. There are adapters that can be attached to the parallel printer port of a PC to replace a NIC. Such adapters are good for laptop computers. There are few computers that have network interface cards built-in; you must usually purchase them separately. Each type of network (Ethernet, token ring, ARCNET, and others) requires a specific type of NIC. You have to consult the vendor in order to acquire the right NIC for your network.

The circuitry of the NIC handles the network communication functions. For one computer to send data to another computer, a handshaking process takes place between them. During a handshake, communication parameters are established. Such parameters include transmission speed, data packet size, timeout parameters, and buffer size. Once the communication parameters are established, transmission of data packets begins. When the adapter breaks data into packets, it adds more information to the data packet. For example, it adds to each packet a source address (the address of the computer that initiated the packet) and a destination address (the address of the computer to which the packet is sent).

The way a packet travels across a network depends on the type of the network. In some systems, the packet travels from one station to another. Each station inspects the packet to see if the packet is addressed to it. If not, it passes the packet to the next station in sequence until the right station receives it. In other systems, when a computer sends a packet to another computer, the packet is announced all over the network (like a radio signal). Every station on the network receives the signal, and all the stations know that a packet has been sent out. But because computer addresses are unique, only the addressee accepts the packet.

Cabling System

The communication among computers in LANs takes place over physical channels—e.g., dedicated cables or other communication media like radio waves or infrared beams of light. Such communication channels can support moderate data rates as well as high-speed rates of up to 100 Mbits/sec (megabits per second). In order to establish communication in a network, the cabling system must connect all interface cards installed in all computers in the network. These cabling systems are referred to as *transmission media*. In wireless networks that use radio waves or infrared light, network interface cards use antennas for communication in place of cables. The cabling system includes all the necessary cables and the attachment units needed to attach nodes and other devices to the cable.

Shared Resources and Peripherals

Shared resources and peripherals include the storage devices attached to the server, optical disk drives, printers, plotters, CD-ROM drives, facsimiles, and modems. The types of printers most used on LANs include high-speed dot matrix and laser printers.

Connectivity Devices

Depending on its size, a network might not need any connectivity devices at all. However, when the network starts to grow, it is time to add devices that will enhance its operations. In most cases, a network that spans a small area will work efficiently without the need of any connectivity devices. But when more stations are added and the network grows to serve one or more buildings, or a large geographic area, then connectivity devices are needed. These include repeaters, bridges, routers, brouters, and hubs.

When two LANs are connected to each other, this is known as internetworking. The simplest example of internetworking is the connection of two LANs with intelligent packet-switching devices such as bridges or routers. Packet switches allow traffic to flow between LAN A and LAN B. If the device detects a data packet that is needed to be transmitted from A to B or from B to A, it forwards only that packet and filters all the others. Therefore, connectivity devices can be used to restrict a department or a group of users from accessing specific LANs on the other side of the device.

Repeaters

When a LAN spans a large area, data signals might not be able to reach all workstations. The reason is that data signals tend to travel a limited distance before they degenerate. This is known as *attenuation*. To restore a signal to its original intensity over the extended cable segment, a device called a repeater must be installed. Repeaters regenerate the signal that is sent between two computers on the same LAN running the same network protocols. They are also used to extend the length of the cable to reach faraway offices so that more workstations can be added to a LAN. There is a limit, of course, to the number of repeaters used on one LAN and the length of the cabling system. Repeaters are usually used in a single building. They work primarily on linear cable systems such as Ethernet.

Bridges

If the traffic is heavy in a LAN and there seems a problem in the flow of signals, then the network can be divided into more than one network segment, or subnetwork. These segments can be connected with a device called a bridge. Unlike a repeater, which passes all the traffic to all network segments, the bridge passes only the packets that are addressed from a computer on one segment to a computer on another segment. A bridge can be a standalone device, or it may exist in network servers in the form of another network interface card. Bridges are capable of confining local traffic and transferring only packets destined for other segments over the link.

Routers and Brouters

Although both bridges and routers do exactly the same thing—they examine the addresses in each data packet, then decide to forward it to another LAN or filter it if it does not need forwarding—routers are more efficient than bridges as they have the power to control and manage the connections among networks. If there is more than one path between two computers, each on a different LAN, routers can select the best way to get data from one computer to another. When one path between source and destination fails, routers can pick an alternative route or path. On heavy-traffic LANs, routers can prevent traffic from jamming a network. The brouter is another device that combines the attributes of a bridge and a router. Networks connected by routers can use similar or different networking protocols.

Gateways

A gateway, on the other hand, not only is used to connect networks but is also capable of connecting LANs and WANs that may have entirely different architectures. When two communicating devices on different LANs running different protocols need to communicate (e.g., a PC on a LAN and a mainframe), a gateway must be used to translate among protocols. This device is just a computer that runs special software to establish communications by translating different protocols so that the addressed computer can understand the sender's request and vice versa.

Backbone LANs

When many LANs in one building or in a number of different buildings exist, such as on a campus, they can all be tied together through a central backbone. The backbone LAN (fig. 1–5) is just a collection of small LANs connected together by such internetworking devices as bridges or routers. This allows computers throughout each building to talk to each other. For users, the internetworking devices are transparent. The internetwork appears as one large LAN. Each device connects one or more LANs to the backbone. In a backbone network, each small LAN becomes a subnetwork. Packets are then switched from one LAN to another, depending on their destination. Internetworking devices confine communications on one subnetwork to that subnetwork. However, if a data packet is destined to a different subnetwork in a different build-

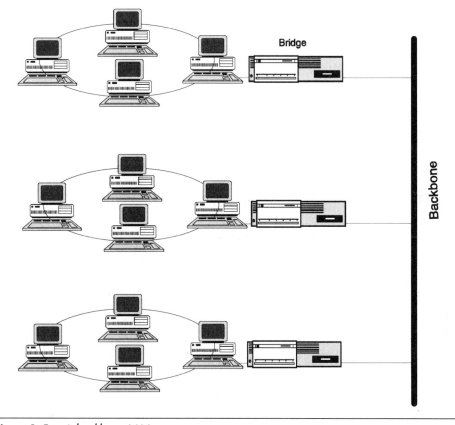

Figure 1-5. *A backbone LAN*

ing, then the internetworking device forwards it to its destination. This will keep the traffic over the backbone LAN to a minimum.

In order to connect the backbone or the campus network to remote LANs owned by the same institution, internetworking devices are used to establish communications and the result is an enterprise network. Still the principles are the same: the internetworking devices pass those packets that are destined to another LAN.

Fiber-optic cable systems such as Fiber Distributed Data Interface (FDDI) are often used for campus backbones. For small networks, servers connected directly to the backbone provide better access for internetwork users than they would if they were attached to subnetworks. In the server-based backbone, servers are equipped with two adapters: one is connected to the backbone to provide connection to other LAN segments, while the other attaches to the local segment.

Hubs and Concentrators

A hub is a central connecting point for cables and serves as the meeting point in a star wiring arrangement. A concentrator is a type of hub. Hubs are typically installed in a department and connect all the computers in that department to one another. Department hubs are then connected to enterprise hubs, forming a hierarchical wiring scheme. Hubs provide repeater functions in networks such as ARCNET and Ethernet 10Base-T. The hub serves as a central place to connect workstations and more easily manage the network. Therefore, on a campus, you can attach each subnetwork to a single hub. This hub device and the cables attached to it form what is known as *collapsed backbone*. Collapsed backbones provide a single connection point for all the subnetworks that are attached to them.

Carrier Services

A carrier is a company that provides telephone and data communication services through such facilities as switching systems, maintenance equipment facilities, and transmission facilities. There are local exchange carriers (LECs) and long-distance carriers, which are known as interexchange carriers (IXCs). A local exchange carrier operates within a specific franchised service area, called a Local Access and Transport Area (LATA). LATAs were created during the split-up of AT&T in 1982. IXCs are carriers that provide long-distance services, such as MCI, US Sprint, AT&T, ITT, ATC/Microtel, and others.

Carriers provide a variety of services to link LANs in different geographic areas together. Depending on the traffic load of your LAN, you may select the type of service that will agree with your network. For example, if traffic is not heavy, you can use an analog circuit switching service that provides dial-up lines through modems with relatively low throughput. Dial-up lines can be used for file transfers, e-mail connections, and remote user access. In this type of service you pay every time you use the service. Single users dialing into a network can use this type of connection.

If you intend to provide temporary connections between a number of different points, you may select digital circuit switching. Circuit-switched services include Switched-56 Services, which operates at 56 Kbits/sec and requires a special channel service unit/data service unit (CSU/DSU) at each site. It is used to handle fax transmissions, backup sessions, bulk e-mail transfers, and LAN-to-LAN connections. The CSU/DSU devices are part of the hardware you need to connect computer equipment to digital transmission lines, such as T1.[4]

Another circuit-switched service is the Integrated Services Digital Network (ISDN), which is offered in specific geographic areas. ISDN is a service that provides digital services on the local cable that runs between your LAN and the switching office. ISDN is predicted as the public telephone and telecommunication interface of the future. It integrates data, voice, and video signals into a digital telephone line. ISDN speeds can reach up to 2 Mbits/sec.

If you expect continuous communications traffic on your LAN, you may select dedicated lines that provide speeds as low as 56 Kbits/sec and as high as 45 Mbits/sec. Dedicated digital services provide dedicated, full-time service between two points. These services, which are leased from a telephone company, require bridges or routers to connect LANs to digital lines.

The standard digital line service is the T1 channel, which provides transmission rates of 1.544 Mbits/sec. If T1 lines are divided into channels for voice or data, T1 is called fractional. T1 can be divided into 24 channels of 64 Kbits/sec bandwidth each. Alternatively, a T3 line can provide the equivalent of 28 T1 lines for users who need a lot of bandwidth. However, if you need to connect simultaneously with many different sites, you may select a fast packet-switching service such as frame relay, Switched Multimegabit Data Service (SMDS), and asynchronous transfer mode (ATM).

Packet-switching services include many types, such as X.25, frame relay, cell switching, and SMDS. X.25 provides remote terminal connections to mainframe systems. While X.25 is not suitable for most LAN-to-LAN traffic because it is slow as it requires a large portion of the bandwidth to handle error checking, frame relay provides a better service than X.25. It is faster and more efficient, which makes it suitable for LAN applications. Your LAN traffic is forwarded through a leased line to the frame relay provider and switched across the network. Frame relay puts user information in variable-length frames that are sent across the network via carrier switches.

Cell-switching networks, namely asynchronous transfer mode (ATM), provide fast packet-switching services. ATM has found wide acceptance in LANs and WANs. ATM can transmit data at megabit- and potentially gigabit-persecond rates. Carriers are installing ATM switches in their own networks. Switched multimegabit data service (SMDS) is offered in selected geographic areas. It is a high-speed metropolitan-area network (MAN) service to be used over T1 and T3 circuits.

Public Data Networks (PDNs) are packet-switching services that provide organizations with leased lines or with dial-up lines. Lines are leased from carriers such as AT&T. Services provided typically include X.25, frame relay, and even ATM. Some of the major PDNs offering these services include: CompuServe Information Services, GE Information Services, Infonet Services, and Tymenet Global Network.

For wide area connection, you may connect your network to the Internet, which provides access to a range of information services, electronic mail services, and connectivity services.

Network Operating Systems

Commonly abbreviated as NOS, a network operating system is responsible for a wide variety of functions, including file services, LAN security, print services, internetwork routing, and network data communications. In addition, a NOS defines how workstations recognize themselves, how data packets are delivered and accepted, how to recover from errors, how to secure the information, and how to start and end a communication.

A NOS is composed of a set of supervisory programs and protocols. Although a network operating system takes control of the operations of the LAN, it does not replace the operating system of the workstation, but rather it coexists with it. While small LANs usually use a DOS-based operating system such as Artisoft's LANtastic, large LANs use a more powerful operating system such as Novell's NetWare, Microsoft LAN Manager, and IBM LAN Server. Most importantly, a NOS must provide support for the disk operating system of the computers used as workstations on the network. Today, there are many computer operating systems, including the following:

MS-DOS (Microsoft Disk Operating System) for IBM PCs and their compatibles

Microsoft Windows (although Windows is considered an operating environment working on top of the disk operating system, many software applications—including CD-ROM applications—are written specifically to run under Windows)

Macintosh System 7 for Apple Macintosh computers

IBM's OS/2 Operating System/2 for 286 computers and higher

UNIX Operating System for UNIX computers

NeXTstep for Intel Processors 3.2

The computer operating system has to be interfaced to the input/output (I/O) bus of each workstation and to the network. For example, Novell uses a proprietary protocol program called IPX (Internetwork Packet eXchange) in its NetWare operating system to do the interfacing. IPX does the actual transfer of data and is responsible for delivering data packets across an internet. IBM developed NetBIOS (Network Basic Input/Output System) protocol for its PCs. NetBIOS is a specification to link a network operating system with specific hardware. Some vendors use their own implementations of NetBIOS.

But the most widely used set of network interfacing protocols when dealing with several different hardware platforms is TCP/IP (Transmission Control Protocol/Internet Protocol). TCP/IP supports the internetworking of dissimilar computer systems. It includes high-level protocols such as Telnet (terminal connection), FTP (file transfer protocol), and SMTP (System Mail Transfer Protocol) for electronic mail services.[5]

A NOS must also provide support for the cabling system used to establish communications on the network. For example, Novell's NetWare network operating system runs on Ethernet topology using coaxial or twisted-pair cables.

Network Environment

The communication and network services are usually established by the network operating system and its associated protocols. Based on that, network operating systems can be divided into two types: peer-to-peer and dedicated-server networks.

Peer-to-Peer

In peer-to-peer, also called decentralized networks, computers are equal. Each computer runs an operating system with built-in networking support that allows it to act as a server and a workstation at the same time. This means that any computer can share its resources with other computers while it accesses any other computer on the network for service. Users can use any computer on the LAN to run the desired network applications. There are many peer-to-peer network operating systems that have built-in support for CD-ROM networking without resorting to third-party software. They include the following: Desk to Desk from CBIS, InvisibleLAN from Invisible Software, LANsmart Network Operating System/LS-300 from D-Link Systems, and Windows for Workgroups from Microsoft. Many peer-to-peer network operating systems are capable of supporting more than 250 workstations.

Advantages of a peer-to-peer configuration:

Resource sharing on peer-to-peer networks allows great flexibility and makes DOS-based networks economical in installations with as few as two PCs. This is due to the fact that these network operating systems can run on any Intel processor in the PC family, even the cheapest and slowest computers such as IBM PC XTs or Model 30s.

For small groups, peer-to-peer systems are simple to install and configure.

Any peripherals attached to any PC as shared devices are easy to use.

Sharing CD-ROM drives is standard in all peer-to-peer networks; there is no need to buy third-party software.

Since a powerful server is not required, the cost of a peer-to-peer network is lower than that of a dedicated server network.

Disadvantages:

In a peer-to-peer network, any user can access the resources on any other computer in the network. While using the resources on the other computer, performance of that computer will suffer.

Peer-to-peer resource sharing typically slows response times and creates administrative problems when files and printers are spread among many servers.

DOS-based peer-to-peer LANs have a low reliability factor. Unlike multitasking LAN operating systems, DOS is an unstable network environment as it tends to crash frequently under heavy traffic.

Unless the network software has some security features to prohibit access to specific hard drives, all users can access any information in any computer on the network.

Most of the NOSes in this group lack sophisticated management tools.

Reporting on the activities of users or the status of resources is inadequate compared to centralized network operating systems.

In peer-to-peer LANs, before accessing another computer, the configuration of each computer on the network would look like this: the floppy drives would be A: and B:, while the hard drive would be C:. When computer X, for example, accesses computer Y, computer Y would look as follows: the floppy drives A: and B: become D: and E:, while its hard drive C: becomes F:.

Because DOS was the first operating system used as the underlying file system, peer-to-peer LANs were called "DOS-based LANs." However, today you can set up peer-to-peer networks running over DOS, OS/2, UNIX, or other operating systems such as Digital's VMS. They can also use networking software based on Microsoft LAN Manager or Sun's Network File System (NFS). In the server, the NOS determines whether the server is dedicated to its service role or also runs local application programs. The NOS resides in the individual PC's memory and divides or "slices" the time of the processor between file services and the standard applications.

In client PCs, the NOS allows network users to access the data and devices on a server through redirector software. This redirector intercepts requests for services from application programs and routes them to the transport-layer software, which can be either NetBIOS or IPX. The transport layer moves the requests to the network interface card (NIC), which transmits the data across the network cabling to the appropriate PC server. Inside the server PC, the NIC and the transport-layer software move requests for service to the file server software, which holds tables of user names and privileges. Once the users are recognized and their program privileges are identified, the file server software passes the calls to the server PC's DOS, retrieves the requested data, and routes the data back to the client PC.

Dedicated-Server Networks

In dedicated-server or centralized networks, all computers have to access one or more specific resource servers for service and information. The network operating system runs on standalone servers and workstations running client software that communicates with the server. In this environment, users cannot run their applications on the file server. Applications can run only on specified workstations. These server-centric network operating systems are more expensive but more powerful than peer-to-peer network operating systems. These network operating systems include the following: LAN Manager from Microsoft, LAN Server from IBM, NetWare from Novell, VINES from Banyan Systems, SCO UNIX from Santa Cruz Operations, and Microsoft Windows NT Advanced Server from Microsoft. At present, only Novell NetWare network operating system versions 3.12 and above have built-in support for CD-ROM networking. In addition, many vendors support CD-ROM sharing on Novell NetWare. The other network operating systems in this category use third-party software to share CD-ROM drives such as: CD Net from Meridian, CD Connection from CBIS, CorelSCSI from Corel Systems, DiscPort from Microtest, OPTI-NET from Online Computer Systems, and SCSI Express from Micro Design International.

Many server-centric network operating systems are capable of supporting more than 1,000 workstations.

Advantages of a dedicated network server:

Server can be located in a secure area.

It is ideal for large networks since the network administrator can exercise a large degree of control over network resources.

Reporting on the activities of users or the status of resources is powerful.

The network operating systems in this category, which are classified as multitasking operating systems, can work on more than one task concurrently.

In addition to power and speed, these multitasking operating systems usually provide important options for flexible, secure, and reliable connections.

Disadvantages:

The cost of using multitasking network operating systems and powerful server PCs is high.

Installation and maintenance is complex.

In order to provide CD-ROM services, the majority of the network operating systems in this category need third-party drivers and software, which may cost more than $1,000. Some network operating systems, such as Novell's NetWare 4.0, provide access to CD-ROM drives without the need for third-party software.

In a server-dedicated LAN, while booting, the server uses its disk operating system (DOS, OS2, UNIX, etc.). Once booted, the network operating system takes control over the disk operating system and becomes the underlying file system. It also takes control over all peripheral hardware attached to the network. Another segment of the network operating system is installed in the workstations to assign them the role of clients.

In the client workstation, requests for service sent by application software (e.g., spreadsheet, database management, and word-processing programs) are intercepted by a software program known as the redirector. This redirector routes certain categories of requests to transport-layer software, which can be either NetBIOS or IPX. The transport layer moves the requests to the network interface card (NIC), which transmits the data across the network cabling. The network server intercepts the requests through its network interface card (NIC). The NIC and the transport-layer software in the PC server move requests for service to the file server software, which holds tables of user names and privileges. Once the users are recognized and their program privileges are identified, the server PC's NOS directs the requests to the appropriate hardware or software to act and provide the service to the client. In this server-based network operating system, the dedicated server does not run local application programs—i.e., users cannot run software applications on the server.

Network Communication Elements

Networks can be described according to the following elements:

- Transmission medium
- Network architecture
- Network type

Transmission Medium

Transmission medium refers to the type of cable used to connect the nodes together. The type of LAN you select determines the type of cables that should be used. For example, a thin Ethernet LAN requires thin coaxial cable, while a star network requires twisted-pair wiring. The common types of network cables include thinnet and thicknet cable, twisted-pair cable, and fiber-optic cable.

Coaxial cable

Coaxial cable, or just "coax," is the traditional network cable. Similar to cable TV cable, coax is capable of transmitting voice, data, and video information at data transfer rates (10 to 20 Mbits/sec). It is also capable of transmitting several signals at once and has some immunity to outside interference. There are two types of coaxial cable: the thin and the thick coax.

Thin coax, also known as thin cable or thinwire, has a small diameter of approximately 0.2 inches. An Ethernet network using thin coax is referred to as cheapernet, thin Ethernet, or just Thinnet.

Thick coaxial, also known as thick cable, thickwire, or standard thick coax, has a diameter of approximately 0.4 inches. An Ethernet network using thick coax is referred to as Standard Ethernet, thick Ethernet, or Thicknet.

Twisted-pair cable

Twisted-pair copper cable is a relatively low-speed transmission medium consisting of two insulated wires twisted around each other over the length of the cable to preserve signal strength. One of the wires is used for the transmission, and the other for the reception of data. Twisted-pair can be shielded or unshielded. Twisted-pair is easier to work with than coaxial cable. New data-grade standards boost data transfer rates over twisted-pair cable up to and above 100 Mbits/sec.

Fiber-optic cable

Fiber-optic cable is a pair of thin strands of glass or plastic surrounded by an insulating fiber. It is capable of transmitting voice, data, and video information. Fiber-optic cable is an excellent choice for building backbones. It is immune to electromagnetic interference and has high security standards. Because it does not emit signals outside the cable, it enables wire tapping to be detected. It uses light pulses to transmit data inside the glass cables at speeds of 100 Mbits/sec and higher.

Wireless methods

Wireless methods allow mobile computing, both indoors and outdoors, depending on the method used. Although the transmission rates are lower than those of wired networks, wireless methods provide convenience and save costs in some cases, since cabling is not required. Wireless networks are suitable for situations where cabling is impossible. Also, it is suitable for temporary locations such as mobile classrooms, mobile health care, spontaneous workgroups, point of sale, inventory control and data collection, trade shows, exhibitions, and special events. Wireless LANs use different technologies, such as infrared, narrow-band (or single-frequency) radio, spread-spectrum radio, and microwave technologies.

Wireless seems to be a cost-effective solution for linking LANs between on- and off-campus buildings, instead of leasing expensive dedicated lines from local phone companies. Some universities are experimenting with wireless for connectivity beyond the confines of buildings and LANs to provide access to their file servers or to the Internet from anywhere on campus and beyond. Basically, wireless networking products fall into two categories: those that use infrared technology (infrared being the same wavelengths used by VCR remote controls) and those that use the Industrial Scientific and Medical (ISM) radio band. The 902 to 928 MHz ISM radio band is not regulated. The 2.4 to 2.483 GHz band is regulated and requires a license from the Federal Communications Commission. Spread-spectrum nodes can be up to 243.8 meters (800 feet) apart in an open environment. These radio waves can pass through masonry walls. However, in a fully closed environment, distances are limited to 33.5 meters (110 feet).

The basic components of a wireless network include the transceiver, which is a transmitter-receiver, also called wireless LAN adapter, transceiver, or wireless modem. These adapters are small boxes that can be plugged externally into the computer's serial port. Some wireless adapters are plug-in cards that can be used for a regular PC or for a laptop's PCMCIA (Personal Computer Memory Card International Association) slot. A transceiver may cost between $295 and $500.

Sometimes you will need a bridge to establish the connection between the wireless network and the wired campus backbone. Radio frequency bridges can connect LANs in buildings up to several miles apart at speeds that match or even exceed that of a T1 line. These bridges can cost about $5,000. A bridge is needed for each side of the connection. A typical bridge is just a regular PC with a WaveLAN card and an antenna to provide the wireless connection.

Network Architecture

The network architecture can be defined in terms of the following important elements: network topology, cable access method, transmission technique, and communication protocols.

Network topology

The layout of the transmission media (cables) that connect the network devices identifies the network topology. The topology identifies how individual workstations are connected together to form the network. Basically, LANs can be configured in three general types of topologies: bus, ring, and star (fig. 1–6).

Linear, or bus, topology

The linear topology identifies a straight cable line that extends from one computer to the next in a daisy-chain fashion. Both ends of the line never meet

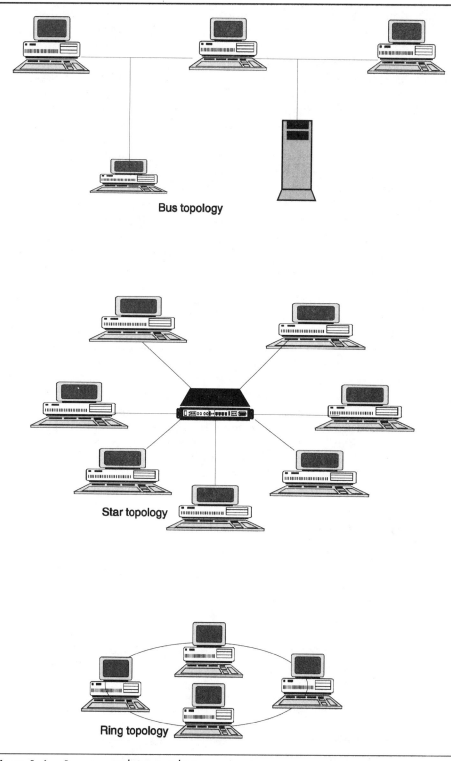

Bus topology

Star topology

Ring topology

Figure 1–6. *Bus, star, and ring topologies*

as each end is terminated with a small device, known as a *resister*. Of all topologies, the bus needs the least amount of wiring, thus bringing the cost down. Adding or removing stations does not shut down the network. However, a break in the transmission media only isolates those workstations located on the downstream side of the break. The bus topology limits the number of stations connected to the cable. To overcome this problem, it is recommended that the LAN be divided into segments and connected via specialized hardware such as repeaters. The bus topology becomes expensive if thick coax cable is used as a backbone. Networks that use bus topology provide throughput that is almost 10 Mbits/sec. Ethernet coaxial networks use linear topologies.

Ring topology

All nodes and other devices in a ring topology are cabled together in a closed loop. A ring network is a network topology that functions by passing data from one network node to the next around a ring until it reaches its destination. Each node receives a message that is passed to it and then, if the message is intended for another node, repeats the signal to the next node. The most common examples are token ring and FDDI (Fiber Distributed Data Interface) networks. Signal speed on a ring network can be 4 Mbits/sec or 16 Mbits/sec. Rings using fiber cables provide throughput greater than 50 Mbits/sec. Since each node is needed to pass the information to the next node, if a node is serviced, it has to be taken off the ring, which will shut down the ring. Another problem with ring topologies is that when a failure occurs anywhere in the ring it shuts down communications throughout the ring. However, some measures such as running a counter ring prevent this from happening. If one ring is down, the other ring will run the communications. The disadvantage of the ring is that there is no central place to monitor the network.

Star topology

A star network is a network physical topology, in which each computer is networked by an individual cable connected to a central wiring device, such as a hub or concentrator. Each computer has a direct path to the hub. The hub not only manages LAN traffic, it also acts as a resource manager to resources shared by the network, such as printers. The 10Base-T network is an example of a star physical topology. Twisted-pair wiring or thin coax cables are usually used in star topologies.

An advantage of the star topology is that a malfunction of any station will affect only this station. Only when the central unit malfunctions will the whole network be down. The star is easy to modify. When a station is added or removed, the rest of the network will not be affected. Also, troubleshooting can be conducted from a central point—the hub. The amount of wiring needed for this configuration exceeds the amount of wiring for a ring or bus topology since each station is connected directly to the central unit.

Star-configured bus has the workstations connected to central hubs in a star topology, then hubs are connected in a bus.

Star-configured ring is a network in which signals are passed from one station to another in a circle (ring), but the physical topology is a star, where stations are attached to central hubs or concentrators.

Cable access methods

Once a workstation is attached to the cabling system, it must gain access to other nodes on the network via the cabling system. The method the workstation uses to gain access to the cabling system is unique to the type of network. Because networks allow only one station to transmit data signals at a time, some methods must be used to control when a station can use the transmission facilities. The cable access methods used most often are Carrier-Sense Multiple-Access with Collision Detection (CSMA/CD) and token passing. While CSMA/CD is used in linear and star topologies, token passing is used in the ring topology.

CSMA/CD is a network access-control mechanism utilized mostly by Ethernet networks. In the CSMA/CD case, a computer will transmit a signal across the entire network at once. Like a broadcast, this signal will be heard by every node on the network. The CSMA/CD allows any station to access the network and transmit information after determining that the network is idle. Actually, before transmitting, a station would check the transmission media to see if other stations are silent and not transmitting. If no other stations are transmitting, that station starts to transmit. If multiple transmissions occur simultaneously, a collision-detection mechanism goes into effect. Once the stations detect the occurrence of a collision, the stations generate a jamming pulse to notify the network that a collision has occurred. Stations then wait a random amount of time before attempting again to transmit. Collisions are normal and do not become a problem except under high traffic levels. CSMA/CD access convention is used in networks such as Ethernet and Apple LocalTalk.

Token passing is a completely different method from CSMA/CD. In order to control traffic and avoid collisions on token ring networks, the controlling computer generates a certain data bit pattern that is continuously transmitted on the ring. This particular bit pattern, called the token, controls the right to transmit. This token is continuously passed from one node to the next around the network. A station must have a token before it can transmit data to the network. When a station is ready to send a message, it has to wait its turn until it receives an empty token to be able to transmit. When an empty token is received, the station captures the token, sets its status to busy, and adds the message and the destination address to it. The message rides the token to its destination. All other nodes continuously read the token to determine if they are the recipient of a message. If they are, they collect the token, extract the message, and return the token to the sender. The sender then removes the message and sets the token status to free, indicating that it can be used by the next node in sequence.

Because only one station can have the empty token at any time, each station is guaranteed a regular opportunity to transmit. This is why token-passing networks are preferred in applications such as manufacturing-process control, in which it is essential to guarantee all stations access to the network, regardless of the level of network traffic. Although the token-passing access method prevents transmission collisions, it is slower than the carrier-sensing method. IBM Token Ring network, FDDI, ARCNET, and token bus networks all use token passing to arbitrate network access.

There are other cable access methods such as Carrier-Sense Multiple-Access with Collision Avoidance (CSMA/CA) and Demand Priority Access Method. CSMA/CA is a variation of the CSMA/CD. Nodes using the CSMA/CA estimate when a collision might occur and avoid transmission during that period. Demand Priority Access Method, which is a new access method for 100 Mbits/sec Ethernet, turns over network access management to a central hub. In this method, workstations request permission to transmit data based on priority, and the hub transmits the highest-priority data first.

Transmission technique

The most common techniques used by the transmission medium for communication in networks are *baseband* and *broadband* transmissions. However, most computer LANs use baseband transmission. An example of a baseband LAN is Ethernet, which uses a bus topology with a CSMA/CD access-control technique.

Because there is no satisfying definition of baseband and broadband, a description rather than a definition will make them easy to comprehend.

A telephone is an example of a baseband device; the frequencies of the electrical waves in the telephone circuitry correspond to the frequencies of the original sound waves. A baseband approach allows transmission by only one attached device at a time. It is like a one-way road with just one lane, where the traffic is moving, but the entire length of the road is used by one car at a time. Thus, the entire capacity of the system's cable is occupied by each transmission, which can be a limitation if an operation must handle large amounts of information. The basic signal is called the *carrier*. When baseband is used, response time decays badly if graphics or pictures are transmitted (real-time video). Because the frequency spectrum (the entire capacity of the road) is used without any frequency division multiplexing (dividing the road into two lanes or more) for a LAN, the use of baseband is somewhat restricted. Ethernet is an example of a baseband network.

Unlike baseband, broadband signaling involves modulation (changing the characteristics of the signal) before transmission. Signals are modulated to take advantage of a communication medium that has a high bandwidth. Broadband networks typically divide the total bandwidth of the communication's channel into multiple subchannels so that multiple types of information can be transmitted simultaneously using different frequencies. It is like dividing the road into more than one lane so that two or more cars can move simultaneously, each in its specific lane. Broadband signaling is used when mixing multiple types of information such as voice and data on a single cable or on multiple cables. If frequency division multiplexing is used, the system is turned into a broadband system. Broadband usually works on the basis of frequency division multiplexing, it effectively can run over larger distances, and it is implemented through protected coaxial or optical fibers. It requires sophisticated design and installation, is more expensive, and is offered by fewer vendors than baseband. The goal of some broadband solutions is to use a single cable to carry several networks. Broadband systems break the capacity of a cable into frequencies, or channels, much like cable television does. Any messages transmitted on a particular bandwidth are assigned to their own channels. Broadband enables users to make transmissions at the same time with different devices.

Communication protocols

Communication protocols are standards that govern the methods by which computers or terminals communicate. They vary in complexity, ranging from Xmodem, a simple file transfer protocol used to transfer files from one PC to another, to the seven layers of the ISO/OSI (International Standards Organization/Open Systems Interconnection) model used as the theoretical basis of many large, complex computer networks. Communication protocols are defined within the context of a layered network architecture. The most common network protocols include the following:

> Apple's AppleTalk
>
> DEC's DECnet (Digital Equipment Corporation)
>
> IBM's SNA (Systems Network Architecture)
>
> The Internet suite, including Transfer Control Protocol/Internet Protocol (TCP/IP)
>
> ISO's Open Systems Interconnection (OSI) model

The dialog between protocol layers includes activities, such as requesting, sending, receiving, acknowledging, or rejecting requests and information. It also includes buffering of incoming data; pausing and restarting transmissions; handling error detection, correction, and retransmission; addressing and routing; and data-packet numbering and sequencing. As long as two systems operate with similar protocols, communication between them can be achieved.

The OSI model was developed by the International Standards Organization in 1977 to standardize computer-to-computer communications. It defines a layered model for an open system environment in which a process running in one computer can communicate with a similar process in another computer if they implement the same OSI layer communication protocols. Figure 1–7 represents the layers of the OSI model.

The model organizes network activities into seven layers with the least complex on the bottom and the most complex on the top. The model is not yet complete. The OSI model was designed to help developers create applications that are compatible across multivendor product lines, and to promote open, interoperable networking systems. According to this model, an open system is a system that obeys the OSI standards and has the ability to communicate with other systems even if these systems are developed by different vendors. In this respect, the OSI model contrasts with proprietary architectures designed to support one vendor's equipment.

Usually, protocols are loaded into a computer as software drivers. An application at the seventh layer interacts with the layer below when it needs to send information to another system on the network. The request is packaged

| Application layer 7 |
| Presentation layer 6 |
| Session layer 5 |
| Transport layer 4 |
| Network layer 3 |
| Data-Link layer 2 |
| Physical layer 1 |

Figure 1-7. *The OSI model*

in one layer and passed down to the next layer, and the process continues. Each layer adds information to the message packet, and this information is read by the corresponding layer in the receiving system's protocol stack. In this way, each protocol layer communicates with its corresponding layer in the other computer system to facilitate communication. The protocol stack encompasses the several layers of software that define the computer-to-computer or computer-to-network protocol. The protocol stack on a Novell NetWare system will be different from that used on Banyan's VINES network, which might be different from that defined by the OSI model.

Product developers use protocol standards to create products that interoperate with other vendors' products. So, a developer working at the physical layer would design products and software drivers that follow the rules defined in that layer. The OSI model divides the network functions into seven connected layers, with each layer building on the services provided by those under it as follows:

1. The Physical Layer deals with the network medium and mechanical components—cables, connectors, and so on. It is responsible for the transparent transmission of bit sequences over different media. Repeaters operate at the physical layer.

2. The Data-Link Layer controls access to the network medium. This layer is divided into the Media Access Control (MAC) and the Logical Link Control (LLC). The MAC controls the traffic on the LAN to avoid data collisions as packets move on and off a network through the network interface card (NIC). The MAC sublayer defines the media access method, which can be either carrier-sense multiple-access/collision-detection (CSMA/CD), token passing, or another Institute of Electrical and Electronics Engineers (IEEE) physical interface. The LLC handles functions such as error control, the logical grouping of information into frames, and the flow control of signals. This layer encodes and frames data for transmission. Bridges operate at this level. The following protocols operate at the data-link layer:

   • High-level data-link control (HDLC) and related synchronous, bit-oriented protocols

- LAN drivers and access methods, such as Ethernet and token ring
- Fast-packet WAN, such as frame relay and ATM
- Microsoft's Network Driver Interface Specification (NDIS)
- Novell's Open Datalink Interface (ODI)

3. The Network Layer handles data routing and switching across the network. Routers operate at this layer. The network layer can look at packet addresses to determine routing methods. The common protocols that work at this level include Internet Protocol (IP), X.25 Protocol, Novell's Internetwork Packet eXchange (IPX), and Banyan's VINES Internet Protocol (VIP).

4. The Transport Layer handles communication across the network. It is responsible for reliable network communication among end nodes. It implements flow and error control and often uses a virtual, or logical, circuit (a dedicated connection) to ensure reliable data delivery. This layer ensures that all data are received and are in the proper order. The non-OSI protocols that can provide connection at this layer include Internet Transmission Control Protocol (TCP), Internet User Datagram Protocol (UDP), Novell's Sequenced Packet Exchange (SPX), Banyan's VINES Interprocess Communications Protocol (VICP), and Microsoft NetBIOS/NetBEUI (Network Basic Input/Output System/NetBIOS Extended User Interface).

5. The Session Layer establishes, coordinates, and maintains session activity between applications, including application-level error control, dialog control, and remote procedure calls.

6. The Presentation Layer handles format, code, and syntax conversion of the data exchanged between two application layer entities.

7. The Application Layer performs network services like file transfer, message exchange, terminal emulation, and electronic mail. Gateways work at the application layer. The protocols that function at this layer include Virtual Terminal (VT), File Transfer Access and Management (FTAM), Distributed Transaction Processing (DTP), Message Handling System (X.400), and Directory Services (X.500).

Network Types

The best known network types are Fiber Distributed Data Interface (FDDI), Ethernet, ARCNET, and token ring. Table 1–1 shows the cable types and their usage in LANs. See chapter 11 for a detailed description of these systems.

Ethernet

Ethernet was developed by Xerox in 1976 to link computers in the Palo Alto Research Center in California. It is capable of supporting as many as 1,024 PCs and workstations. It uses the CSMA/CD access method. Depending on the type of cable used, Ethernet can be designed in two topologies: a bus topology if thin coaxial cable is used, or a star topology if unshielded twisted-pair telephone wiring is used. Ethernet has 10 Mbits/sec throughput and uses a CSMA to access the transmission media. In 1980 the DIX standard was jointly developed by Digital Equipment, Intel, and Xerox (DIX), and became known as

Table 1–1. *Cable types and their usage in LANs*

Cable Type	Network Type			
	FDDI	Ethernet	ARCNET	Token Ring
Coaxial, Thick (RG-11)		X		
Coaxial, Thin (RG-58)		X		
Coaxial, Thin (RG-62)			X	
STP (IBM Type 1)				X
UTP (Voice Grade)			X	
UTP (Data Grade, IBM Type 3, 4)		X	X	X
Fiber Optic	X	X	X	X

the Blue Book Ethernet standard. The Blue Book has evolved into the slightly more complex IEEE 802.3 Ethernet standard, and the ISO 8802.3 specification.

ARCNET

ARCNET (Attachment Resource Computer Network) was developed before Ethernet by Datapoint Corporation in the late 1970s and early 1980s. It uses the token-passing access method on a token bus network topology. In this topology, each star has a hub (fig. 1–8), then the hubs are connected to form a bus (fig. 1–9). Each segment of the ARCNET network supports as many as 256 computers. The computers are assigned number addresses from 0 to 255. The token is passed from workstation to workstation in numerical order. Upon reaching the last workstation, the token loops back to the 0 address, like a ring. Because it lacks high throughput (2.5 Mbits/sec), ARCNET is not acceptable for large networks. Although ARCNET lacks endorsement from the IEEE, it has an American National Standards Institute (ANSI) standard. Several ARCNET vendors are marketing ARCNET Plus, a 20 Mbits/sec version of ARCNET that is compatible with the 2.5 Mbits/sec ARCNET network.

Token Ring

Token Ring was introduced by IBM in 1985. Token Ring network is the IEEE 802.5 standard for a token-passing ring network. The network forms a closed ring that utilizes the token-passing access method at speeds of 4 and 16 Mbits/sec. Workstations in the ring are numbered sequentially. When the token carries a message, the network is busy. The workstation with the next highest number waits for the token to become empty before transacting business. Token Ring uses shielded and unshielded twisted-pair cable. With shielded twisted-pair (STP) wiring, each ring can support up to 256 nodes. With standard telephone unshielded wiring, it can support up to 72 nodes. Although it is based on the ring topology, a Token Ring network uses a star-shaped cluster of up to eight nodes, all attached to the same wire concentrator.

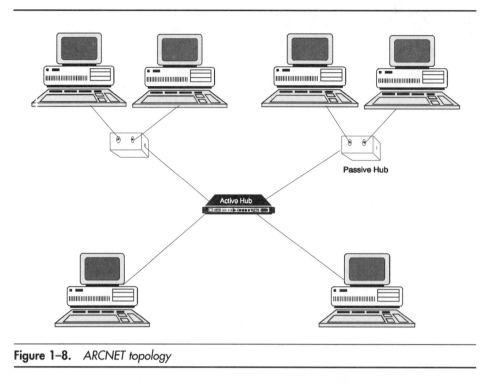

Figure 1-8. *ARCNET topology*

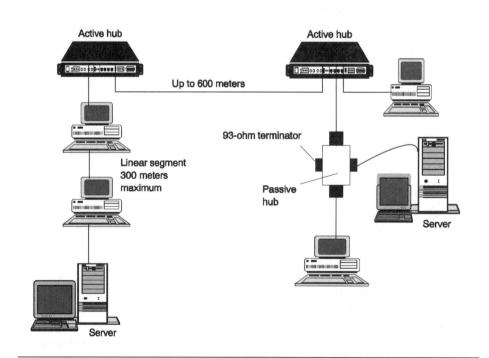

Figure 1-9. *ARCNET active hubs are connected to form a bus.*

Fiber Distributed Data Interface (FDDI)

FDDI is a fiber-optic cable standard developed by the ANSI X3T9.5 committee. It transmits at a speed of up to 100 Mbits/sec over a dual-counter-rotating, token-ring topology (fig. 1–10). If a ring fails, the other ring will keep the network active. An FDDI network using fiber-optic cable can support as many as 500 stations up to 2 kilometers (1.25 miles) apart. Because of its speed, it is a good choice to serve as a backbone linking two or more local area networks, or as a fiber-optic bus connecting high-performance engineering workstations. In the campus environment, bridges connect LANs to the FDDI network. FDDI is suited to systems that require the transfer of large amounts of information, such as medical imaging, three-dimensional seismic processing, oil reservoir simulation, and multimedia with full-motion video. This type of network can also run over shielded and unshielded twisted-pair cabling, known as Copper Distributed Data Interface (CDDI), for short distances.

LocalTalk

LocalTalk is a network wiring scheme used to connect Macintosh microcomputers. These computers come equipped with network interface cards. The wiring for LocalTalk is inexpensive and easy to install. LocalTalk uses the CSMA/CD media access control, where stations are daisy-chained in a bus topology. This LAN protocol defines AppleTalk packet transmission of roughly 230.4 Kbits/sec with a throughput of almost 90 Kbits/sec. Because of its low speed, LocalTalk is suitable for small networks. However, it can be incorporated in enterprise networks.

Before 1989, LocalTalk was originally called AppleTalk. Now, AppleTalk comprises Apple Computer's network architecture, which includes the protocols that operate over the LocalTalk cabling system. LocalTalk is the cabling type, and AppleTalk is the protocol standard, such as IEEE 802.3.

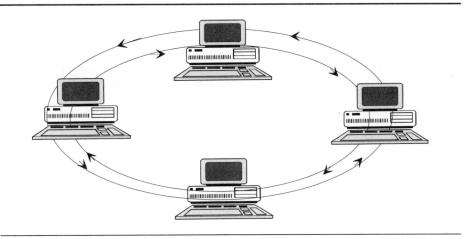

Figure 1–10. *Dual counter-rotating token-ring topology*

Notes

1. A small network is roughly considered to be one with 50 or fewer clients, all running the same operating system. Typically, the users do lots of sharing and printing of files. A medium network would include up to 100 users. Like a small network, such an installation requires file and print services, but these are even more likely to be spread across multiple servers. A medium-size to large network, with perhaps between 100 and 150 users, probably includes a mix of local and remote sites to be connected. Finally, a large enterprise network can span dozens or even hundreds of sites running more than one operating system, with anywhere from 150 to thousands of users.

2. In real-time computing, transactions processing implies that a transaction is executed immediately, as opposed to batch processing, in which a batch of transactions is stored over a period of time, then executed later. The most common examples of real-time computing are banking transaction systems, order entry billing, and airline reservation systems.

3. The speed of data transmission is measured in bits per second (bits/sec). Bauds, on the other hand, are not bits. Baud rates refer to the number of signal changes that occur in one second in a device such as a modem. The name comes from the French telegrapher Emile Baudot, who developed an encoding scheme for the French telegraph system in 1877. Although both terms, *bit* and *baud,* are used in the literature interchangeably, they can mean two different things. If a modem transferred one bit for every signal change, then its bits-per-second rate would equal its baud rate per second. Modern modems can make one baud or signal change equal to two or more bits. Two bits per baud is known as dibit encoding, and three bits per second is known as tribit encoding. In this case, bauds and bits are not equal.

4. T1 is a long-distance, point-to-point circuit providing 24 channels of 64 Kbits/sec, giving a total bandwidth of 1.544 Mbits/sec. You can build your own private network with T1 or T3 lines that make point-to-point connections. You lease a dedicated line from the phone company between each site, then install switching equipment that manages packet traffic among those sites. This is called a private network because your equipment will manage the traffic to each of the leased-line sites. Meanwhile, the local telephone company will serve as a hub for each network within a certain geographic area. T-carrier circuits are leased on a monthly basis, ranging from $3,000 to $20,000. The distance of the lines determines their cost.

   To connect a LAN to a T1 line, you need the following equipment:

   Channel service unit (CSU). The CSU diagnoses and prepares the signals on the line for the LAN, and keeps the line alive if there are problems with the LAN connection equipment.

   Data service unit (DSU). The DSU connects to the CSU, converting LAN signals to T1 signaling formats. Sometimes the CSU and the DSU are included in the same unit.

   Multiplexer. A multiplexer provides a way to load multiple channels of voice or data into the digital line.

   Bridge or router. The bridge or router provides the connection point between your LAN and the T1 line.

   T1 can be used to provide off-campus sites access to computing resources, including CD-ROMs, located in the campus main library. T1 provides a bandwidth of 1.544 Mbits/sec. The standard T1 frame is 193 bits long, made up of 24 eight-bit voice samples and one synchronization bit. It transmits 8,000 frames per second. When a T1 service is made available in single 64 Kbits/sec increments, it is known as *fractional T1.* In Europe, the comparable circuit is known as DS-1, and it has a speed of 2.054 Mbits/sec.

T2, on the other hand, provides up to four T1 channels. It offers 96 channels of 64 Kbits/sec, for a total bandwidth of 6.3 Mbits/sec. T2 is not available commercially, although it is used within telephone company networks.

T3, however, provides up to 28 T1 channels. It can carry 672 channels of 64 Kbits/sec, for a total bandwidth of 44.736 Mbits/sec, and is usually available over fiber-optic cable. It is used almost exclusively by AT&T and the regional telephone operating companies, although certain large corporations are using T3 with digital microwave or fiber-optic networks. In Europe, T3 has been superseded by the CCITT DS-3 designation.

DS (digital signal or digital service) has five levels of common carrier digital transmission service:

DS-0: 64 Kbits/sec, referred to as fractional T1, because it bridges the gap between 56-Kbits/sec direct dial service (DDS) and a full T1 implementation.

DS-1: 1.544 Mbits/sec (T1)

DS-2: 6.312 Mbits/sec (T2)

DS-3: 44.736 Mbits/sec (T3)

DS-4: 274.176 Mbits/sec (T4)

5. You can use Telnet to connect your computer to other computers on the Internet. For example, you can connect your computer to university campuses to search their online catalogs or to chat with other people. The Internet File Transfer Protocol or FTP allows you to transfer programs and files from other computers. With the right computer address, you can literally access any computer on the Internet.

CHAPTER **2**

CD-ROM: The Basics

There are many types of optical media in use today. Each media type has its own characteristics, but all these technologies share one thing—a laser beam that is used to write as well as read data from their shiny surface. Optical data storage media are manufactured in three basic types: CD-ROM (Compact Disc Read-Only Memory), which allows users to read permanently recorded information; CD-Recordable, which allows users to write information permanently on the disc and read that information back; and rewritable, or erasable, which allows users to read, write, and erase information many times. Optical discs have a similar physical construction: very thin layers of plastic and other materials bonded to a wafer-thin adhesive surface.

The Development of Optical Disc Standards

Almost all types of optical discs are descendants of the laser video disk, which was developed at the N. V. Philips Research Laboratories in the Netherlands in the first half of the 1970s. Philips and Sony developed a standard for each compact disc type, and every standard was given a color name for easy identification. Table 2–1 presents the most important types of the optical media and their standards.

The first CD-ROM discs could only store text information. Today, however, the addition of graphics has produced a greater challenge; the result has been the development of standards to handle them. When animation and live motion video with synchronized sound were incorporated onto the disc, even more standards evolved. Today, there is much confusion over which drives can

Table 2–1. *Types of optical media*

Media Type	Recordable	Applications	Format Name
Compact Disc Digital Audio (CD Audio or CD-DA)	No	Entertainment	Physical format: IEC 908 (1980) or Red Book
Compact Disc Read-Only Memory (CD-ROM)	No	Data and software distribution	Physical format: IEC 10149 (1985) or Yellow Book Logical format: ISO 9660 or High Sierra
Compact Disc Interactive (CD-I)	No	Education and entertainment	Physical format: Green Book (1988)
Compact Disc Extended Architecture (CD-ROM XA)	No	Multimedia	Physical format: Extended Yellow Book (1989)
Compact Disc Recordable (CD-R)	Yes	Internal and limited distribution applications such as data archival, archival storage Primary usage: CD-ROM mastering	Logical format: ECMA 168, Frankfurt proposal or ISO 13490 Physical format: Orange Book (1990)
Compact Disc Magneto-Optics (CD-MO)	Yes	Archival storage—will compete with hard drives as the computer primary storage media	Physical format: Orange Book, Part 1 (1990)
Video CD	Yes	Video applications	Physical format: White Book (1993) Complements the physical standards for CD-ROM (Yellow Book) and CD-WO (Orange Book)
Write-Once Read-Many (WORM or CD-WO)	Yes	Archival storage	Physical format: Orange Book, Part II (1990)

ISO = International Standards Organization
ECMA = European Computer Manufacturers' Association
IEC = International Electrotechnical Commission

handle which formats. However, any CD-ROM drive manufactured after 1992 can run the following media: CD Audio (Compact Disc Audio), CD-ROM, CD-ROM XA (CD-ROM Extended Architecture), CD-R (Compact Disc Recordable), and Kodak Photo CD (PCD) discs. Of course, you will need special attachments for a computer to produce sound and graphics. Laser discs are best explained through their color standards.

CD Audio Standard, or Red Book

Introduced by Philips and Sony in 1980, the Red Book standard is considered the foundation of all the other types of compact disc standards. To play a CD Audio, you need a CD player. Since all audio discs are manufactured according to the Red Book standard, all audio compact discs will play in any audio compact disc player. The Red Book specifies that a disc can have up to 99 tracks arranged in a spiral. Information on each track is located in a table of contents found on the innermost track. Each track is divided into sectors. Each sector is 1/75th of a second in length and contains 2,352 bytes of audio data in digital form, in addition to two layers of error detection code and error correction code (EDC/ECC) for each sector. If a laser cannot read the data because of scratches or dirt, the CD player uses the EDC/ECC to re-create the audio signal. An audio CD uses a 60-minute spiral (a 74-minute spiral exists). The player reads data at a rate of 150 Kbytes/sec, or 75 sectors/second.

CD-ROM Standard, or Yellow Book

The Yellow Book, or the ISO/IEC (International Standards Organization/International Electrotechnical Commission) 10149, is the basic physical level standard for CD-ROM format. This standard, introduced by Philips and Sony in 1985, is in fact a redefinition of the Red Book in which two new types of tracks were added to the disc. These are CD-ROM Mode 1, for computer data, and CD-ROM Mode 2, for compressed audio and video/picture data. To run a CD-ROM disc, you need a computer, a CD-ROM drive, and an interface system (a controller card and a cable). In addition to the CD operating system, you will need software for the computer to recognize the CD-ROM drive, in addition to the search and retrieval software.

The Yellow Book used the Red Book standard as a foundation. It used the same sector length (2,352-byte data area), but it redefined it further so that information on the CD-ROM could be accessed randomly instead of playing it sequentially. This feature allows users to search and find the information anywhere on the disc, rather than playing a disc from the very start. Sequential playing is a feature of CD audio players. CD-ROM uses two modes to record data:

CD-ROM Mode 1 redefines the Red Book 2,352-byte data area as:

12 bytes	*4 bytes*	*2,048 bytes*	*8 bytes*	*280 bytes*
synchronization	header information	user data	unused space	error correction and detection codes

CD-ROM Mode 2 redefines the Red Book 2,352-byte data area as:

12 bytes	*4 bytes*	*2,336 bytes*
synchronization	header information	user data

In Mode 1 and Mode 2, the computer uses the first 16 bytes to determine which sector it is reading. In Mode 2, the EDC/ECC has been dropped: the result is that more data can be stored on the disc. Usually discs manufactured in Mode 2 are always in the XA format, which will be explained shortly.

CD-I Standard, or Green Book

Hoping to bring interleaved (i.e., mixed) text, sound, and video to home entertainment systems, Philips introduced the Green Book for CD-I (Compact Disc Interactive) in 1988. CD-I allows the mixing of computer data and compressed audio on the same track. The CD-I standard defines the disc format and the hardware specifics of the player. It also defines the specifics for the microprocessor, memory, operating system, video and audio controllers, and compression methods for audio and video. A CD-I system consists of a stand-alone player connected to a TV set. The sector layouts for CD-I are identical to those of CD-ROM XA.

CD-ROM XA Standard, or Extended Yellow Book

The CD-ROM XA (extended architecture), which was proposed in 1989 by Philips, Sony, and Microsoft, is an extension to the Yellow Book. CD-ROM XA is meant to improve the Yellow Book standard in areas of audio and video capabilities of CD-ROM and to serve as a bridge between CD-ROM and CD-I. CD-ROM XA is, in fact, a subset of the CD-I standard. For example, it borrowed the ADPCM (adaptive differential pulse code modulation) audio compression from the CD-I standard with the option of interleaving audio, video, and computer data. However, a CD-ROM drive that can play an XA disc may not necessarily be able to manage CD-I software. Again, XA redefines a new type of track that combines both the CD Audio of the Red Book and the CD-ROM Mode 1 and Mode 2 of the Yellow Book. It is the most common format for business and entertainment, as it efficiently weaves voice and data on CD-ROM discs in order to optimize synchronized playback.

While Mode 1 includes the EDC/ECC, Mode 2 does not include the error correction capability. Mode 2, however, includes Form 1 and Form 2. These forms refer to two separate audio and video tracks that can be interleaved in Mode 2. Because Mode 1 does not expect interleaved data, Form 1 and Form 2 have no effect on it.

CD-ROM XA Mode 2, Form 1, redefines the 2,352-byte area as:

12 bytes	4 bytes	8 bytes	2,048 bytes	280 bytes
synchronization	header information	subheader information	user data	error correction and detection codes

The eight bytes of subheaders indicate that the disc is of Form 1. The last 280 bytes contain the error detection and correction codes.

CD-ROM XA Mode 2, Form 2, redefines the 2,352-byte area as:

12 bytes	4 bytes	8 bytes	2,324 bytes	4 bytes
synchronization	header information	subheader information	user data	optional EDC

For a drive to be able to read the XA format, the audio recorded as Form 2 must conform to the Adaptive Differential Pulse Code Modulation (ADPCM) audio. This means that the chip on the drive or its controller must be able to decompress the audio signals during the synchronization process. Many drives which are advertised as "XA-ready" are not fully capable of reading XA format until their processor chips include the ADPCM audio component.

CD Recordable Standards, or Orange Book

The Orange Book standard, which was developed in 1990 by Philips and Sony, defines the recordable media. It allows the user to record audio and/or data to the disc (using a special drive) and read the disc on any CD-ROM drive. The Orange Book is composed of two parts: Part I describes a CD-MO (Compact Disc Magneto-Optical) disc, where data can be written, erased, and rewritten like a computer floppy or hard disc; it uses a special type of rewritable storage medium that should not be confused with CD-ROM discs. Part II describes a CD-WO (Write-Once) disc where the data can be written but not erased.

Magneto-Optical (MO)

Magneto-optical storage is a rewritable storage technology. MO platters are a combination of thin film-coated polycarbonate housed in a plastic cartridge. They are mostly used for backup and archival storage. MO discs are removable and interchangeable with one another. Because writing on an MO platter is accomplished through a thermal process with the laser functioning as a heat source, it is crucial to control the laser power accurately.

During the recording of data, a laser beam is focused on a spot on the disc's surface. Since the MO technology is a combination of magnetic and optical storage methods, as the spot is heated sufficiently enough, an electromagnet penetrates the disc to polarize that spot from the other side of the disc. The polarization changes the reflectivity of the spot, which the drive recognizes as a transition. Thus, data can be written and rewritten as many times as required.

The most-used disc sizes are 3.5 inches and 5.25 inches. They offer from 128 Mb to 2 Gb (gigabytes) of storage without compression. In 1993, the capacity of the 5.25-inch disc jumped from 650 Mb to 1.3 Gb and it is expected to double again very soon, while the drive costs about $1,200. The optical media cost about $69. Like a computer hard drive, an MO drive uses a concentric track structure, thus eliminating the need for a variable rotation speed. The speed is almost compatible with the speed of hard drives, which is almost 0.28 milliseconds per rotation. Only when an MO disc is rendered as "read-only" can a CD-ROM drive read that disc.

Multisession CD-Recordable and Applications

While MO is mostly used as an archival storage device, CD-R is used more as a publishing tool. The importance of CD-R is due to its use in premastering the CD-ROMs. They can also be produced in-house and run in CD-ROM drives. Recording data on a CD-R disc in one session produces a single-session CD-R, also known as "track-at-once." A single-session player would assign a lead-in area, write data, then write the lead-out area and table of contents at the end of the session; it will not accept more data after that. However, adding more data in a subsequent session will produce a multisession CD-R, a process that requires the restructuring of the data locations in the directory. At first, all

CD-R discs can display only one session. The reason is that CD-ROM drives originally were programmed to look on these discs for two things: a lead-in command (a point at which to begin reading data), and a lead-out command (a point at which to terminate reading data). Multisession recording, on the other hand, gives each recording session its own lead-in and lead-out areas. In the last session, the player does not assign a lead-out area, but it will create a table of contents.

Because the Orange Book dealt only with single-session recording, nine companies (Philips, Sony, Digital Equipment Corporation (DEC), Kodak, Ricoh, Hewlett-Packard (HP), Meridian Data, Sun Microsystems, and the Jet Propulsion Laboratory) met in 1990 in Frankfurt, Germany, to expand the file organization of the Orange Book to include multisession recording and also discussed the possibility for the standard to support Microsoft Windows NT (New Technology). The Frankfurt File Format (FFF) proposal resulted in a new standard—the ISO 13490 standard.

Acceptance of the Frankfurt proposal has been very slow however, because not all CD-ROM drives can read multisession CDs. Multisession requires a new version of Microsoft CD Extensions (MSCDEX); old CD-ROM drives are not able to read discs manufactured using the new MSCDEX. This second-generation of multisession CD-Rs appeared in 1992. The software for those drives that can read multisession CDs usually continues to look for multiple lead-in commands on the disc after it encounters a lead-out command. However, drives that do not have this capability will read only the first session of a multisession CD-R. Only if the CD-R disc is recorded fully in one session can a single-session CD-ROM drive read all the data on the disc. The number of multisessions is 99, which corresponds to the maximum number of tracks on a CD-ROM. A multisession CD-ROM drive has the ability to read a disc that does not yet have a table of contents. So when buying a CD-ROM drive, you have to make sure that the drive is a multisession drive. Many corporations have made available CD-R discs that were recorded in-house on CD-ROM LANs. The difference between CD-WO and CD-R is that the latter can be read on any CD-ROM drive, while CD-WO needs special readers.

CD-recorders can produce prototypes in CD Audio (Red Book) and CD-ROM (Yellow Book) formats as well as CD-ROM XA and CD-I formats.

Since CD-R discs can be read on CD-ROM drives, a CD-R can be used in libraries to produce bibliographies, databases, and indexes in-house, or even build a kiosk, then make the CD-R available to CD-ROM network users. The National Library of Medicine (Bethesda, Md.), a research library within the National Institutes of Health, produces a monthly medical database on a CD-R disc using a Sony CD-R, then places that disc on a CD-ROM network to be used by researchers. Schools and colleges can place their curricula, names of faculty, telephone directories, community-service information, codes and regulations, and building locations and services on a CD-R to be searched electronically on a CD-ROM network. Data can be copied from the computer hard disk directly to the CD-R disc. This means that graphs can be scanned and saved on a hard drive first before copying them to a CD-R disc. When updating old information on a CD-R disc, new information is recorded at the end on new tracks and old information is rendered unreadable—provided the disc has space to record the new information.

At present, CD-Rs are mostly used for producing samples of CD-ROM databases for testing before premastering CD-ROM discs. Other applications include limited runs of CD multimedia titles for beta testing. Internal policies of corporations and parts catalogs and technical documentation can also be produced on CD-Rs. These discs are useful for archiving, for distribution of corporate databases to branch offices, and for in-house corporate training applications.

In general, CD-R is an economical technology if the number of CD-R copies stays low. For example, CD-ROM duplicators charge $1,500 for 100 discs, while CD-R will be cost-effective for press runs of under 60 discs at $20 per disc.

The CD-R drive uses a high-powered laser to write data on a pregrooved 4.72-inch disk. The pregrooved CD-R medium is made of a polycarbonate substratum, covered with organic dye, then coated with a gold reflective layer (more stable than the CD-ROM's aluminum reflective layer—as the aluminum oxidizes too easily) and a top protective layer of plastic. CD-R's main characteristic is its high data integrity; once data are written, they cannot be overwritten. Also, discs are not affected easily by normal environmental factors, such as heat, dust, and smoke. Another characteristic is that CD-R can be produced in a timely manner without going through the delays associated with producing CD-ROMs. CD-R discs are manufactured in two capacities: a 63-minute disc that holds about 580 Mb, and a slightly more expensive 74-minute disc that holds 650 Mb.

Data are recorded by burning permanent bubbles onto the disc, which will look like CD-ROM pits seen on a disc surface using a high-powered laser. These pits change the intensity of the light reflected from the surface of the disk when a low-powered laser is directed to it. The light intensity is read by a very sensitive photodetector and translated into signals that can be read by computers. There are many CD-R systems available on the market, including dataDisc CDR4X from dataDisc, Personal SCRIBE 1000 from Meridian Data, Philips CD-Recordable from Philips, Pinnacle RCD-202 from Pinnacle Micro, PlayWrite 4000 from Microboards, Quick TOPiX/Windows from Optical Media International, Simpli-CD of Young Minds, and WinOnCD of Philips LMS. Most of these systems can prepare discs in many formats, including CD-ROM, CD-DA (digital audio), CD-ROM XA (sound, text, images, multisession), and CD-I (interactive). Many support premastering and mastering software packages for Windows, Mac, or UNIX. Quadruple-speed CD recorders, which are capable of a 600Kbits/sec transfer rate, are available from many vendors.

The minimum number of components in a typical dedicated CD-R are:

Computer   At least 386-based

Memory capacity   At least 1 Mb if DOS is used, 4 Mb to 8 Mb if Microsoft Windows is used

Hard-disk capacity   1 Gb to 1.5 Gb with a Small Computer System Interface (SCSI—pronounced "skuzzy"), which is a high-speed bus standard used as a transport mechanism to move data between the computer and the interface card

CD-recorder   At least double-speed. Single-speed drives take about 70 minutes to record 650 Mb of data, while a double-speed drive takes about 35 minutes to record the same amount of data. There are quadruple- and sextuple-speed drives on the market. The competition among companies has brought the prices of recorders down to as little as $4,000, including software (prices range between $4,000 and $8,000 compared to 1990's prices, which were over $30,000).

CD-R disc to store data The CD-R disc sells for less than $20 (compared to $200 in 1990).

While recording, a very fast hard disk is required because during the recording process, data are first written from the hard disk to a buffer (a temporary memory storage area) of the CD-R drive, where it is encoded and then transferred to the recordable media (disc). If there is any break in the flow of data to the buffer due to a slow hard disk or any other causes, the buffer suffers from "buffer underrun," which simply means buffer depletion. If this happens, the disc is rendered unusable and the process has to be repeated using a new disc.

Video CD, or White Book

The new DIS 13490 standard provides a specification for the logical organization of data in volumes and files on CD-ROM and CD-WO discs. The new standard was needed to enable recording on and updating of existing CDs and to make it easier for heterogeneous host platforms to access data on CD-ROM and CD-WO discs. DIS 13490 complements the physical standards for CD-ROM (ISO 9660, or "Yellow Book") and CD-WO ("Orange Book"). This format, which has been suggested by the Motion Picture Engineering Group, has been endorsed by Philips and JVC as a new "White Book" standard for video on CD-ROM.

File Structure Standards: High Sierra and ISO 9660

In the CD-ROM industry, there was a severe problem that caused the slow acceptance of CD-ROM technology by many potential users. The first CD-ROM drives lacked universality as they could only read discs produced specifically for them.

What seemed to be needed at the time was a solution to make a CD-ROM disc capable of being read by any CD-ROM drive. This problem motivated the manufacturers of CD-ROMs to meet in 1985 at Del Webb's High Sierra Hotel in Nevada and draft a proposal for a CD-ROM file structure; this became known as the "High Sierra" file structure. After some enhancements, the High Sierra was later approved by the International Standards Organization as the "ISO 9660." The ISO 9660 is not an MS-DOS nor an HFS (Hierarchical File System used mostly by Macintosh computers) file structure, but rather a standard for a CD-ROM file structure. If a drive adheres to the ISO 9660 format, it will automatically read CD-ROMs written to the earlier High Sierra format as well. There is an extension for the ISO 9660 for the UNIX platform, known as the Rock Ridge proposal.

Today, the basic data format for CD-ROMs in the DOS world is the ISO 9660 specification. Although the ISO 9660 is considered universal, other formats do exist. Many companies decided to develop their own formats for their own CDs, such as 3DO, Atari Jaguar, Commodore CD32, SegaCD, Sony MMCD, and Tandy VIS.

The ISO 9660 standard guarantees a file structure that would make a CD-ROM disc work on any CD-ROM drive attached to an IBM or an IBM-compatible PC. Thus, the ISO 9660 standard ensures the interchange-ability of discs, regardless of the drives in which they are used. Although the ISO standard ensures that all drives expect to find a table of contents for a data disc—something known as Volume Table of Contents (VTOC) that tells the CD-ROM drive where, and how, the data are laid on the disc—it did not solve the compatibility problems. For example, indexing and retrieval software, as well as additional search aids, were left to each vendor.

An advantage of the adoption of the ISO 9660 standard is that it became easier for disc publishers to manufacture discs that will work in different plat-forms, such as DOS, UNIX, Macintosh, and other operating system formats.

Because a disk operating system—such as MS-DOS, which runs on IBM and its compatible computers—cannot read the ISO 9660 or the High Sierra file structures, Microsoft developed CD-ROM extensions (MSCDEX) software to allow MS-DOS to read these file formats. Other computer manufacturers developed software to allow ISO 9660 and High Sierra discs to be read by their operating systems, including Apple Computer and Unix Systems.

MSCDEX

MSCDEX overcomes DOS limitations and allows access to CD-ROM discs. The Microsoft Extensions act as a translation utility that translates High Sierra and CD-ROM's ISO 9660 file formats into a DOS file allocation format, so that the PC can read the CD-ROM disc as if it were reading a very large DOS disc. The MSCDEX is included with DOS 6.0 and above. Third-party versions from Meridian and CBIS are also available. MSCDEX is usually shipped with every new CD-ROM drive along with the CD-ROM device driver.

MSCDEX functions include translation of

> High Sierra and ISO 9660 file formats into DOS file allocation format,
>
> provision of a DOS drive letter for CD-ROM access,
>
> and an introduction to the DOS device driver, designated in the CONFIG.SYS file, to access the CD-ROM drive.

Some CD-ROM programs expect MSCDEX software to be present and refuse to run if they do not find the extensions, while others running on a Novell NetWare network load the MSCDEX in a different format, known as a NetWare Loadable Module (NLM). This CD-ROM NLM is usually loaded on a Novell NetWare file server, thus saving at least 32K of the memory of the workstation. Many CD-ROM application software writers have left out the code that makes an application sense the presence or absence of MSCDEX in the system; thus an application will not be tied up to a specific platform, which is assumed to be a PC-DOS.

With MSCDEX loaded, the CD-ROM drive will accept and recognize some DOS commands, such as DIR, COPY, TYPE, etc., but not commands like CHKDSK or SCANDISK because even on a standalone workstation, DOS considers CD-ROM drives as network drives and these commands will not be accepted. Certain CD-ROM networking products such as OPTI-NET (MS-DOS version) cannot establish a connection to CD-ROM drives without the MSCDEX.

The MS CD-ROM Extension is created by a file called MSCDEX.EXE, which is an executable program that works with MS-DOS, version 3.1 or higher. As of this writing, the latest version of the Microsoft MSCDEX.EXE is version 2.23, dated 9/30/93, which is included with MS-DOS version 6.22. All of the DOS-based LAN operating systems with built-in CD-ROM support use MSCDEX.EXE to access the CD-ROM drives. Once the CD-ROM device driver is loaded and a letter is assigned to the CD-ROM drive, and once MSCDEX is loaded, each workstation can see the CD-ROM drive as an extension of its highest drive letter: because the workstation has local drives A, B, and C, the CD-ROM drives will be assigned the next highest drive letters, D, E, F, etc. This is how all workstations on a network can simultaneously access the same CD-ROM drive.

Although the MSCDEX has solved the problem of accessing the CD-ROM drives, it uses a large portion of the computer's conventional memory—about 32K of the precious 640K memory, plus 8K for every CD-ROM drive. After you load network programs and the CD-ROM device driver, MSCDEX, and other software programs, the memory left to run CD-ROM applications will be very limited. This situation is known as "RAM CRAM," which the software installer has to overcome to maintain a reasonable area in the memory to run network application programs.

With the increased number of computers having a local CD-ROM drive, you will encounter a serious problem when trying to access a CD-ROM network. Usually, you will be using a CD-ROM device driver and the MSCDEX.EXE in order to access the local drive. However, you will need a different approach to access the CD-ROM drives on a network, even if the network requires you to load the MSCDEX file. If your organization owns many workstations with the same problem, you have to configure each station in order for these stations to access both the local CD-ROM drives and the CD-ROM drives on a network. Although DOS 6.0 allows multiple configurations for use in these situations, it is really inconvenient to reboot the computer every time you want to switch between the local CD-ROM drive and the CD-ROM network.

On a Novell NetWare network, however, loading the MSCDEX driver in the form of a NetWare Loadable Module (NLM) on the file server and loading the MSCDEX.EXE file on the workstation (provided the device driver for the local CD-ROM drive is already loaded through the CONFIG.SYS file of the workstation) will provide access to both the networked CD-ROM drives as well as to the workstation's local CD-ROM drive with one configuration.

CD-ROM Device Drivers

Computers in general cannot recognize their hardware components (monitors, keyboards, floppy and hard disks, mouse devices, etc.) without software programs known as "device drivers," and CD-ROM drives are no exception. A CD-ROM device driver is usually loaded to make a computer recognize the CD-ROM drive. You have to install the software device driver in the computer. Once installed, the device driver should be loaded first before loading the MSCDEX. Every type of CD-ROM drive requires a specific device driver to establish a communication link between the computer and the CD-ROM drive. For example, Toshiba CD-ROM drives use a Toshiba device driver, while Hitachi drives use a Hitachi device driver and so on. When you purchase a new CD-ROM drive, you will find the driver software on the floppy disk that is usually bundled with the CD-ROM drive.

Usually, in a network, the device driver must be executed while the CD-ROM server begins to boot. This way, the CD-ROM server will recognize the CD-ROM drives attached to it. Once the computer recognizes the CD-ROM drives, it needs the Microsoft Extensions in order to be able to read the ISO 9660 and High Sierra file structures on the CD-ROM disc.

CD-ROM Technology

As the name implies, CD-ROM is a disc, the data on which can be read only. The user cannot write to the disc. The diameter of the disc is 4.72 inches, and its capacity is almost 680 Mb. Depending on the types of data being compressed, this capacity can be increased many times through the use of compression technologies, such as "capaCD," developed by EWB & Associates of California. Unlike the CD-Audio, which runs in a CD-Audio player connected to an amplifier, CD-ROM needs a CD-ROM drive, a CD-ROM interface card and cable, a computer, and software to read the data off the disc and display them in readable form on the computer monitor or in audible form through an acoustic system, which is composed of a sound card, an audio cable, and a speaker system. The master CD-ROM disc is usually manufactured on a glass platter. The master disc goes through many processes until copies are made onto platters made of polycarbonate, a special type of plastic. After the platters are pressed by special equipment, they are covered with other protective layers. The top aluminum layer gives the platter a shiny, reflective surface. The CD-ROM reader uses a very tiny laser beam to read data off the surface of the platter. Depending on the intensity of the reflected light, the microprocessor of a CD-ROM drive decodes the light signals to its original structure, which in turn are passed to a digital device—such as a PC—to be displayed on-screen in a readable format.

CAV and CLV Recording Techniques

There are two techniques to lay out the microscopic pits that represent the data on optical discs (CD-ROM, recordable discs, and rewritable discs). The first method is known as the Constant Angular Velocity (CAV), in which the pits are laid on the disc in concentric tracks resembling the tracks on floppy diskettes. The second method is known as the Constant Linear Velocity (CLV). In this method, the pits are laid out in one spiral track starting from the center of the disc and moving outward. The difference between the CAV method and the CLV method is that on a CAV disc, each ring has the same amount of information on the sectors of the outer portion of the disc as it does on the inner portion. In this case, the rotational speed of the disc is kept constant, but the information on the outer rings is more spread out than on the inner rings, since the number of the sectors per ring is constant.

On a CLV disc, data are arranged sequentially. Each sector or block of data takes up the same amount of physical space on the spiral, resulting in more sectors on the outer part of the spiral than on the inner part. Thus, a CLV disc holds more information than a CAV disc. A CLV drive must spin at constantly changing speeds to ensure that the amount of data passing under the laser reading head is constant. It spins faster on the inside part of the spiral: approximately 1,182 rpm, or 2.65 times faster than on the outside, which spins at approximately 486 rpm. Between the inner and outer tracks, the speed is adjusted as well. Today's CD-ROM drives use this technology, which is known as multispin technology.

CD-ROM vs. Hard Disks

CD-ROMs can store a large amount of information, almost 680 Mb. The fastest CD-ROM drive has an average access time of 250 ms (milliseconds) compared to the average access time of any hard disk of about 18 ms. The reasons why the CD-ROM drives are slower than ordinary hard disks include the following:

1. Because CD-ROM standards were built on CD-Audio standards, manufacturers used the same equipment developed for mastering, pressing, and playing audio CDs. This meant that CD-ROMs have to use the technology of the CD-Audio spiral track. In this design, the data are recorded in sectors. These sectors are arranged in one continuous spiral track. Although this spiral track is ideal for reading large blocks of sequential data, such as music, it is not ideal for random access searching and retrieving of data. The spiral track will result in slower random access times than the concentric tracks used by hard disks. On the hard disk, the sectors can be located faster because they are always found on a given track at a fixed distance from the center.

2. When writing data, hard disks use the CAV encoding scheme. The sectors in this scheme must be placed at maximum density along the inside track of the disc. However, going outward, the sectors must spread to cover the increasing track circumference, leading to "wasted" space between them and within them. For a CAV disc to be read, the disc must be spun at a constant rate of speed.

   To make use of the wasted space, CD-ROM discs use CLV. CLV allows the length of a sector to be constant regardless of its location, whether it is located close to the center or at the outer edge of the disc. This means that the disc must rotate slowly when reading data recorded at the outer edge of the disc, and fast when reading data at the inside of the disc. This technique, which requires a very complicated drive mechanism, slows the drive's random access times while increasing data density over the entire disc.

3. While a hard drive has multiple read heads, a CD-ROM drive has only one laser-head mechanism that spans the entire surface of the disc.
4. Because of their size and weight, laser heads move slower than magnetic heads.

CD-ROM Applications

CD-ROM technology has reached a wide base of users as CD-ROM applications have touched almost every field, such as business, medicine, librarianship, education, and others. Today, an increasing number of CD-ROM applications have targeted homes in the form of video games and educational material. As the CD-ROM market flourishes, CD-ROM drives are becoming an integral part of the computer architecture, like floppy and hard disk drives. Many computer manufacturers are selling their computers equipped with CD-ROM drives.

CD-ROM is hardly considered a data archival tool because of the cost associated with and the time consumed in the premastering and mastering processes. This is contrary to CD-R discs, which can be produced easily and inexpensively, and distributed for use on virtually any CD-ROM drive in any organization.

CD-ROM drives are one of the best ways to provide access to large amounts of information. The discs can cost as little as $1.50 to produce. Information that would take weeks to search and retrieve from paper indexes can be found effortlessly in seconds in CD-ROM. Businesses are using the medium for marketing and marketing research and business reference.

Other types of applications that can be published on CD-ROM include massive font collections, sophisticated commercial text-oriented databases, reference materials, data and knowledge bases, product demonstrations, directories, books, periodicals, educational material, multimedia applications, games, and entertainment programs. Complex topics can be explained and demonstrated through visual text, graphics, animation, and narration. This combination of text, graphics, sound, video, and animation is known as multimedia. Many publishers have just begun exploring the use of multimedia on CD-ROMs. Multimedia is not a specific standard but rather a descriptive term. Multimedia CDs exist for DOS, Macintosh System 7, Windows, and UNIX operating systems.

Law and accounting firms can purchase CD-ROMs with legal cases or current tax information prerecorded. Students use CD-ROMs as a reference tool and in interactive education. Scholars and researchers are able to cut research time and to publish more data than ever. The government is using CD-ROMs for long-term preservation and the archiving of massive amounts of paper and documents. Some organizations are using CD-ROM for signature verification, storage of forms, and handbooks.

The number of software companies that are shipping their software on CD-ROM is increasing. Many companies are distributing their products on CD-ROMs, including Apple Computer, Compaq, Corel Systems, Hewlett Packard, IBM, Microsoft, Novell, Oracle, Sun, and WordPerfect. Software vendors report that producing and shipping applications on CD-ROM is cheaper and more efficient than using standard packages with floppies. Another advantage is that the old problem of software pirating has been greatly reduced with CD-ROM. But the most important advantage is that during installation of the software, you do not have to swap the discs as you usually do when installing the software from floppy diskettes. Therefore, it seems that there is no limit; anything that can be published in any format can just be published on CD-ROM.

CD-ROM Drives and LANs

CD-ROM disk drives are distinct from computer magnetic disk drives as they read data off the CD-ROM disc using a laser beam. CD-ROM drives are usually attached to the computer via a cable and a CD-ROM interface card. The interface card is installed in any empty expansion slot inside the computer. The computer will be able to recognize the CD-ROM drive through two pieces of software: the CD-ROM software device driver and the Microsoft CD Extensions (MSCDEX).

The CD-ROM drive is equipped with a read mechanism, a precise tool that includes many components. The most important parts are the laser diode, the servo mechanism, the lenses, and the beam splitter. The laser diode emits a low-energy beam toward the surface of the disc. The servo motor positions the beam onto the right track by adjusting a reflecting mirror. A lens gathers and focuses the refracted light that is bounced off the mirror and sends it toward a beam splitter, which directs the returning laser light toward another focusing lens. The focusing lens directs the light beam to a photodetector, which converts the light into electrical impulses. The microprocessor decodes and sends these impulses to the host computer as data to be displayed in a readable form.

A CD-ROM drive communicates with a computer through a CD-ROM interface card and a cable. The interface card is installed inside the computer in any empty expansion slot, then is connected to the CD-ROM drive by a cable. Since any computer has only a limited number of expansion slots after a network interface card and other necessary interfaces are attached to the computer server, there will be a very limited number of empty slots to accommodate CD-ROM controller cards. Vendors solved this problem by building towers that are capable of housing multiple CD-ROM drives in cabinets. Each cabinet can hold a large number of drives that are daisy-chained inside the cabinet. These multidrive cabinets can be attached to the server with one controller interface that will occupy just one slot on the motherboard of the computer. Vendors produce these multidisc cabinets as jukeboxes, towers, and CD-ROM server-arrays.

Jukeboxes

Network jukebox technology is an emerging option that can be adopted to provide multiple CD-ROM service to LAN users. Jukeboxes are ideal for very small workgroups that need to access a large number of CD-ROM discs. A jukebox is an external enclosure that contains multiple CD-ROM drives. It has a controller and software that keep track of the discs in each drive. Jukeboxes are equipped with robotic arms and elevator mechanisms to grab discs and insert them into one or more readers (CD-ROM drives), like old music jukeboxes. There is a delay, of course, while one CD is moved away from the head and another is moved into position. Jukeboxes can be attached to network servers or standalone computers. These systems have been designed and targeted for a variety of applications, including document imaging, image and network file archiving, publishing CD-ROM titles, and microfiche conversion.

Some jukeboxes are offered as towers of multiple CD-ROM readers so that many users on a network can access a specific disc without tying up the whole system. There are many jukebox network systems on the market, including Artecon's DSUI series and Dynatek Automation Systems Inc.'s Network CD-ROM devices. Other systems include Pinnacle's Cascade CD 100 and Procom Technology's CD Tower4-DS. Some jukeboxes, like Pinnacle's Cascade CD 100, support discs in Macintosh and IBM PC and compatible CD-ROM, CD-ROM XA, CD-I, Photo CD, High Sierra, and ISO 9660 formats. Pinnacle's jukebox software has built-in AppleShare support for Macintosh computers.

Pro-CD Library from JVC is a CD-ROM network-based solution. Pro-CD Library consists of a 100-disc CD-ROM capacity jukebox, double-speed CD-ROM drive, and intelligent archival storage management software. The management software binds individual CD-ROMs mounted in the jukebox into a single volume to provide access to data on any CD-ROM disc in the jukebox. Pro CD Library is priced at $8,995.

ROMBox 300 jukebox from Logical Engineering contains 300 discs with only 2 CD-ROM readers. The D1260 CD-ROM Library jukebox from Document Imaging Systems Corporation (DISC) contains 1,478 discs with 32 readers. TODD Jukebox contains 203 CD-ROM discs with 7 CD-ROM readers with an average loading time of six seconds. These jukeboxes have robotic mechanisms, administered by their own CPU file server.

Minichangers are usually jukebox enclosures with multiple-disc caddies and one CD-ROM reader. Multichangers, on the other hand, are jukeboxes with multiple-disc caddies and multiple readers. Minichangers are available from companies such as Pioneer and Kubik Technologies. Generally, changers are standard drives with a SCSI computer interface. The controller hardware and software keep track of which discs are in which caddy, so it can quickly pop the appropriate one into the drive to retrieve requested information. Table 2–2 describes some of the changers and jukeboxes on the market.

CD-ROM Towers and Server-Arrays

The problem with jukeboxes is the wait time from 5 to 30 seconds for the robotic arm to find, extract, move, and insert each disc. Instead of providing one reader to serve more than one disc, CD-ROM towers assign every disc its own reader in an array of linked drives. For this reason, arrays are much faster, but they are more expensive per megabyte than jukeboxes.

Many vendors are offering CD-ROM drives in towers, minitowers, or twin towers (fig. 2–1). The drives are already daisy-chained and enclosed in a case, and there is only one cable that the user should attach to the CD-ROM interface card in the computer. Some of these towers are enclosed in cabinets.

Table 2–2. A list of some changers and jukeboxes

Product	Company	Maximum discs/readers	Reader	Price
D1260 CD-ROM Library	DISC	1,478/32	Hitachi 2X, Sony 2X, Toshiba 2X	$135,000
D600 CD-ROM Library	DISC	722/24	Hitachi 2X, Sony 2X, Toshiba 2X, Yamaha 4X	$90,000
ROMBox 300	Logical Engineering	300/2	Toshiba 2X	$28,000
DRM-5004X	Pioneer	500/4	Pioneer 4X	$21,995
DRM-1804X	Pioneer	18/1	Pioneer 4X	$2,495
DRM-604X Minichanger	Pioneer	6/1	Pioneer 4X	$1,495
602X Minichanger	Pioneer	6/1	Pioneer 2X	$1,095
TAJ-2000	Todd Enterprises	174/14	Hitachi 2X	$33,490

Vendors usually refer to these cabinet-style arrays as towers. Drive arrays include more drives than towers.

Tower systems are produced by many companies, including CD Systems, Dynatek Automation Systems, Legacy Storage Systems, Micro Design, Micronet Technology, Morton Management, Online Computer Systems, Optical Access International, Plextor, ProTege Corporation, TAC Corporation, and Todd Enterprises.

TAC Systems' HotSwap SCSI TowerDrive arrays can be configured with 1 to 32 half-height SCSI drives. These arrays can accommodate CD-ROM drives as well as other options, such as hard disk drives, 4mm and 8mm tape drives, and multifunction optical disk drives. TAC also makes RackDrives for standard 19-inch racks (fig. 2–2).

Total Access tower from TODD Enterprises is equipped with 56 SCSI drive bays, while GigaRack from Morton Management can hold 98 drives. You do not have to purchase a full system. You can buy the cabinet separate then add as many CD-ROM drives as needed. These units occupy about five square feet of floor space.

Online Computer Systems' Optical Storage Units (OSUs) are available in SCSI or non-SCSI versions. OSUs can work with a minimum of two drives. The SCSI version supports up to seven drives off a controller installed in a CD server. You can use other CD-ROM brands on the OSU besides the one made by Online Computer Systems.

Optical Access International's (OAI) tower case, CD/Quartet, integrates four SCSI-2, 180- or 240-ms drives (depending on the model). It includes OAI's SuperCache software, which installs on your CD server to speed throughput.

Figure 2–1.   *TAC CD-ROM TowerDrives. Used with permission*

Figure 2–2.   *TAC CD-ROM RackDrive. Used with permission*

Networks can include Apple's AppleShare, Apple's System 7 with its built-in file-sharing facility, and Novell's NetWare.

CD/Maxtet tower, also from OAI, supports 7 drives using a single SCSI ID. You can add up to five more CD/Maxtets for a total of 42 drives to one server. It includes SuperCache software.

Legacy Storage Systems' M.A.S.S. SL CD-ROM is an eight-drive subsystem. Included with the tower is a utility that lets network administrators test

Table 2–3. *Some tower systems*

Product	Company	Maximum discs/readers	Reader	Price
CD Net 100	Meridian Data	8/8	Toshiba 2X, Sony 2X	$8,845
CD Net 314/M	Meridian Data	14/14	Toshiba 2X, Sony 2X	$18,245
CD Net 428/M	Meridian Data	28/28	Toshiba 2X, Sony 2X	$36,245
CD/Quartet	Optical Access International	4/4	Toshiba 2X	$2,595 (Mac) $3,399 (PC)
CD Maxtet	Optical Access International	7/7	Toshiba 2X	$6,595 (Mac) $7,195 (PC)
CD Tower-7	Procom Technology	7/7	Toshiba 2X, NEC 3X, Pioneer 4X	$5,945 (NEC 3X)
CD Tower-21	Procom Technology	21/21	Toshiba 2X, NEC 3X, Pioneer 4X	$23,999 (NEC 3X)
TA-56	Todd Enterprises	56/56	Hitachi 2X	$50,000
Twin Tower	TAC Systems	32/32	Sony 2X	$13,450

the drives, the interface card, and the cable connection. Table 2–3 lists some tower systems.

A few vendors, including Meridian Data, CBIS, and Micro Design, sell hardware/software combinations as turnkey systems, as well as the software component alone that can be used with any network hardware you might already have. These vendors integrate the server into the towers to create CD-ROM server-arrays, such as the following products.

The CBIS CD Server 2000 series

The CBIS CD Server 2000 series of dedicated CD-ROM servers run CBIS CD Connection software. This series includes CBIS CD Server 2014 file server, CBIS CD Server 2014/PC Conversion Tower, and CBIS CD Server 2007/PC Conversion Tower. The configurations in this series come bundled with Hitachi America CD-ROM drives and 16-bit SCSI adapters for fast access. The CBIS CD Server 2014 is a dedicated CD-ROM server that enables up to 250 users to have simultaneous access to as many as 28 CD-ROM drives. The CD Server works in conjunction with CBIS' CD Connection Software to provide the CD-ROM sharing. It is compatible with NetWare, CBIS Network-OS Plus, Banyan's VINES, and most NetBIOS-compatible LANs.

The CD Connection Server is a self-contained processor unit that includes a 486/66 MHz (megahertz) processor, 16 Mb RAM, SCSI host adapters, double-speed half-height internal drives, and 100 CD-user CD Connection software.

14-bay capacity with 7 drives is listed for $15,400

14-bay capacity with 14 drives is listed for $20,200

28-bay capacity with 28 drives is listed for $34,100

CD Connection software for 5 users on Novell, Banyan, or NetBIOS is listed for $395

CD Connection software for 50 users on Novell, Banyan, or NetBIOS is listed for $995

CD Connection software for 100 users on Novell, Banyan, or NetBIOS is listed for $1,395

CD Connection software for 250 users on NetBIOS is listed for $1,695.

You can also share CD-ROM drives on your existing LAN using CD Connection software. CD Connection runs CDs without MSCDEX. Each workstation requires about 22K of base memory. CD Connection software allows users to access multiple CD-ROM drives simultaneously over a LAN. With CD Connection, a CD-ROM disc is as accessible as a regular disk drive to all networked stations. When using CD Connection in conjunction with the CBIS CD Server, users have simultaneous access to as many as 28 CD-ROM drives. CD Connection is compatible with NetWare, CBIS Network-OS Plus, Banyan's VINES, MS-Net, PC LAN, 3+Share, and other NetBIOS-compatible LANs.

CD Connection CD-ROM sharing for Banyan's VINES uses the StreetTalk Protocol instead of NetBIOS. CD Connection is removable from workstation memory without rebooting when not in use.

InfoServer from Digital Equipment Corporation

Digital Equipment Corporation (DEC) produces a long list of servers, including InfoServer Local Area CD, InfoServer Librarian for Open VMS systems, and InfoServer Publishers for CD-Recordable (CD-R) discs. InfoServer supports different platforms, including MS-DOS (including DEC's PathWorks and Novell NetWare), Windows, Macintosh, Ultrix/RISC and /VAX, Open VMS, and UNIX.

At the high end of SCSI servers is Digital Equipment Corporation's InfoServer 1000, which is impressive for its scalability (the ability of the system to accommodate growth). Components available in the InfoServer 1000 line include

InfoServer Local Area CD (LA CD) This is the InfoServer 1000 base unit—a single tabletop CD-ROM drive that you can combine with other drives.

InfoServer Librarian This is a four- or seven-drive cabinet housed with the base unit; it can accommodate any 5.25-inch SCSI device.

InfoServer Publisher This lets you write to CD-R discs.

CD Net from Meridian

Meridian Data's CD Net Model 100NC is a 7-, 14-, or 28-drive tower that includes a 486 processor, a 3.5-inch floppy drive, and 4 Mb RAM. CD Net software is included, and the server supports NetBIOS or Novell NetWare LANs.

CD-ROM server from Procom

The system combines NetWare-compatible SCSI host adapter and peripheral tower with Meridian Data's CD-NET-server software and NEC Technologies' CD-ROM drives. A full system—seven triple-speed (450 Kbytes/sec) NEC CD-ROM drives in the Procom tower, SCSI-1/SCSI-2 host card, and 10-user CD NET license—lists for $6,640. For 100-user CD NET license, the same system costs $7,230. The system works with Novell's NetWare 3.1x or 4.0 networks.

CD-ROM Towers for NetWare from The Global Solution

This is a fully compatible NetWare Loadable Module (NLM) with Novell NetWare. It provides multiuser access and as many as 128 CD-ROM drives, and automatically configures up to 16 Mb of server memory cache. It supports an unlimited number of workstations and provides an icon-based application interface for Windows users. The memory of the server is dynamically allocated and freed up as needed.

EZ-NET from EZ-Systems

EZ-NET is a dedicated turnkey CD-ROM network. It is a complete plug-and-play CD-ROM system. Its capacity is from 6 to 500 CD-ROMs, with support for up to 255 CDstations. Easy to install and operate, it features a simple, user-friendly menu system; security; and CD-ROM/CDstation usage reports. Pricing for EZ-Net starts at around $15,000 for a six-disc jukebox and two CDstations.

EZ-CDserver from EZ-Systems

EZ-CDserver can be added to an existing network. It supports Novell, UNIX, Macintosh S-7, OS/2, Windows NT, and peer-to-peer LANs as well as jukeboxes and towers. Each server supports over 2,500 CD-ROMs. It can handle multimedia and CD-R discs. It includes applications metering and caching.

CDworks 1000 from Virtual Microsystems

The CDworks 1000 can act as an application server for PCs, Macintoshes, DEC VAX clients, and VT terminals on Ethernet networks. Up to seven processors can combine with up to 49 CD-ROM drives. Systems start with 14 or 21 drives and 8 Mb RAM.

SIRS CD-ROM LAN III Plus from Social Issues Resources Series, Inc.

This is a turnkey network with three Windows-ready workstations featuring 8 Mb RAM, 400 Mb hard drive, and mouse—priced at $14,700. It runs DOS and Windows applications. Three CD-ROM drives are attached to the file server. All necessary operating software is included and loaded onto the file server computer. The network runs under Novell NetWare 3.12 with five-user license, DOS 6.x, and Windows 3.11.

The SIRS LAN may be customized to suit specific requirements by adding workstations, CD-ROM drives, memory, or storage capacity. Each additional LAN Plus workstation costs $2,100.

Criteria for Selecting CD-ROM Drives

In order to be able to play CD Audio, CD-ROM, CD-R, and CD-ROM XA discs, a CD-ROM drive should support the following standards: Red Book for CD Audio; Orange Book for CD-R; and Yellow Book for ISO 9660, High Sierra, Rock Ridge, and CD-ROM XA (Mode 2, Form 1 and Form 2). When buying CD-ROM drives, you should consider the following criteria, which apply to almost all types of CD-ROM drives: standalone, drives in jukeboxes, towers, and server-array towers.

> Transfer rate or throughput
>
> Average access time
>
> Size of the drive's buffer
>
> Type of interface board, SCSI or proprietary
>
> Single Session and Multisession Photo CD (PCD)
>
> Playing music CDs on the CD-ROM drive
>
> Dust-free drives
>
> Multimedia PC (MPC) guidelines
>
> Loading mechanism
>
> Load/eject mechanism
>
> MTBF (Mean Time Between Failure)
>
> XA compatibility
>
> Customer technical support

The choice of which CD-ROM drive is installed in the LAN has an impact on the performance of the CD-ROM service provided. Most CD-ROM drives installed before 1992 are limited in speed, both in terms of data-transfer rate and average access time. The purchase of a CD-ROM drive is not like buying a floppy disk drive. Single vendors offer entire lines of drive models that vary in performance specifications, format-reading capabilities, and the types of adapters they can use to connect to PCs. According to these differences, prices vary widely.

Another matter: while most CD-ROM applications in academic libraries are textual in form, with some graphics, almost all CD-ROM drives are manufactured today with multimedia capabilities. Although there is little immediate use for multimedia capability in many organizations, it is better that a CD-ROM drive be ready to utilize a new technology rather than being replaced or subjected to a costly upgrade.

Another issue is that CD-ROM manufacturers are applying different techniques for expanding the capabilities of the laser technology. In entering these frontiers, you might encounter some nonstandard formats.

Before purchasing any drive, you need to familiarize yourself with the following issues so that you purchase only the CD-ROM discs that the drives are capable of reading.

Transfer Rate or Throughput

Data-transfer rate is simply the rate by which a CD-ROM drive reads and transfers a large sequential segment of data off the CD-ROM disc to the host computer after it reaches its maximum speed. The transfer rate is measured in kilobytes per second, or Kbytes/sec. The original standard was 153.6 Kbytes/sec, which is rounded to 150 Kbytes/sec. This standard was known as the "single speed." Before 1992, single-speed drives, which had continued for more than seven years, were considered the base line for CD-ROM drives. Double-speed drives, which were introduced in 1992, boosted the original speed to 307.2 Kbytes/sec (rounded to 300 Kbytes/sec). The double-speed technology was pioneered by NEC in its CDR-74 (external) and CDR-84 (internal) models. In 1993, this number was tripled to reach 460.8 Kbytes/sec. In 1994, that number was quadrupled to reach 614.4 Kbytes/sec. Manufacturers sometimes refer to single-, double-, triple-, and quad-speed CD drives as 1X, 2X, 3X, and 4X, respectively. As single-speed drives are becoming obsolete, the double-speed has become the base line for today's CD-ROM drives. Increasing the throughput was achieved by increasing the spinning speed of the drive's motor. Increasing the spinning speed simply means that the data are displayed faster on the screen, and the graphics and video images should look much smoother. First-generation CD-ROM drives could read both text and audio data at 150 Kbytes/sec. Today, although the computer data-transfer rate of double-speed CD-ROM drives has reached 300 Kbytes/sec, audio data are still read at 150 Kbytes/sec. As a result, the drive has to slow down to 150 Kbytes/sec when an audio track is encountered to be able to transfer the audio signal correctly. Hence, in addition to multispin technology, all double-speed drives must use "dual-speed" technology because they must read data at both 150 and 300 Kbytes/sec.

High data-transfer rates are particularly essential for multimedia applications. Pioneer, NEC, TEAC, and Plextor are considered the leaders in developing the quad-speed drives. Because discs recorded in Mode 2 do not include error checking and error correcting code (ECC), the transfer rate for these drives will be higher than Mode 1, which includes the ECC code. The end user should be aware that some manufacturers list the data-transfer rate for Mode 2, which is usually higher than that of Mode 1. Table 2–4 lists the transfer rates of Mode 1 and Mode 2, as well as access times.

Access Time

Access time is a critical factor when selecting CD-ROM drives for networking, provided that it is associated with the data-transfer rate. Access time is usually measured in milliseconds (ms = thousandths of a second). The lower the num-

Drive Type	Transfer Rate		Access Time
	Mode 1	Mode 2	
Single speed 1X	150 Kbytes/sec	175 Kbytes/sec	400–600 ms
Double speed 2X	300 Kbytes/sec	350 Kbytes/sec	200–360 ms
Triple speed 3X	450 Kbytes/sec	475 Kbytes/sec	195–250 ms
Quad speed 4X	600 Kbytes/sec	660 Kbytes/sec	140–200 ms

Table 2–4. *Transfer rates of Mode 1 and Mode 2*

ber, the better the performance—e.g., an access time of 180 milliseconds (0.18) is faster than that of 500 milliseconds (0.5 seconds). Quick average access times (300 ms or less) are especially important for text-based databases, reference titles, and electronic publications, such as electronic encyclopedias or telephone directories, which involve frequent random information searches.

When considering a CD-ROM drive performance, you should be concerned about three other important factors, along with access time: seek time, latency, and rotation speed.

Seek Time

This is the time it takes a drive to check the current position of the laser read head mechanism and to move the head across the platter to the target track to read data. During this operation, the drive has to control revolution speed of the platter: accelerate/decelerate to reach the target track. While doing this, it might do a rough search or an accurate search. Once it reaches the right track, it waits for the velocity of the disk to stabilize before data can be read; then the latency time starts.

Latency

Latency is the time it takes for a drive to vertically position the laser head over the track to begin data transmission. Latency is usually given by two numbers: the average latency for the inner tracks and the average latency for the outer tracks.

Rotation Speed

This is the number of disc revolutions per minute (rpm). Data will be displayed faster if the revolutions are higher.

First-generation CD-ROM drives had access time (sum of seek time and average latency) greater than 600 milliseconds (0.6 seconds), compared to many of today's CD drives, which have access time of less than 250 ms (0.25 seconds); some drives have access time of 180 ms. Frequent text searching and the retrieving of a great body of text both need a CD-ROM drive with a fast data-transfer rate and higher access time. These two figures should be read together. If the drive will handle multimedia applications with sound, graphics, full-motion video, and animation, the data-transfer rate will be much more important than the access speed.

Unless it is mentioned in the manual, you should ask the vendor whether or not the average access time means the typical access time of *1/3 stroke access* or *track-to-track access*. Some vendors measure the seek time from track to track, an inaccurate method since the distance the laser has to cover is very small. A more accurate method is the one-third stroke that searches across one-third of the disc. Most of the time, access rates advertised are an average taken by calculating a series of random reads from a disc.

The throughput, however, of a CD drive is controlled by three factors: transfer rate, access time, and the computer processor speed. The last component is governed by the speed of the microprocessor (or the Central Processing Unit) of the microcomputer in terms of megahertz (MHz); the higher the MHz, the less time it takes data to be displayed on the screen. So, a 486/50 MHz computer will display data faster than a 486/25 MHz computer will. Also, a CD drive equipped with a cache buffer and a computer that has a good cache memory will both boost the performance of any CD-ROM LAN.

Cache, or Buffer Size

A cache is basically a buffer, which is a temporary memory storage area that holds information briefly, then releases it in high-speed bursts as the buffer fills up. These buffers can be used to boost the performance of the drive as it buffers the recently retrieved information from the disc, anticipating that the user may want to read it over again. Buffers are actual memory chips installed on the CD drive's board that allow data to be stored in larger segments before being sent to the PC. Some types of caches have a read-ahead buffer. Such buffers automatically look ahead to the next block of data on the disc. Read-ahead caches might seem most useful for multimedia playback, where sequential reading is needed, but they are equally useful for paging through a database or electronic publication.

The cache buffer works like this: when the system CPU requests information from the CD-ROM drive, the drive buffer can have the data ready to go, which means faster access as the information is read directly from the memory, not from the CD-ROM disc. CD-ROM drive buffers are generally 32K to 256K, with the latter able to hold more data. Some disc-caching software, such as DOS (version 6.2) SmartDrive, Norton Speed Drive, OPTI-CDcache from Online Computer Systems, Lightning CD from Lucid, or Super PC-Kwik, can supplement a small hardware buffer by caching the CD-ROM drive as well as the other local drives. Although cache size is not considered a measure for speed, it has a substantial impact on perceived performance as it is essential for the speedy transfer of multimedia files in contrast to text files.

Interface Boards: SCSI vs. Proprietary

In order to establish a link between the CD-ROM drive and the computer, an interface card and a compatible cable are needed. The interface board is installed in the computer, then the board is attached to the CD-ROM drive via the cable. In some cases, the addresses on the board might need some adjustment and the user is usually referred to the manual that accompanies the interface board to do the needed adjustment.

The interface board acts as a physical connection between the CD drive and the computer. It is the interface board that is responsible for streaming the data signals between the drive and the PC. Most vendors offer two types of CD-ROM interface cables and cards: *proprietary* and *SCSI interface.* The SCSI interface is faster and its price is a little higher than the price of any proprietary card. However, SCSI adapters provide extra expandability by allowing you to daisy-chain several devices to one adapter card using extender cables. Proprietary cards are developed by an individual vendor, and they are used only with the CD-ROM drives offered by that vendor, while the SCSI interface is universal and can be used with any type of SCSI CD-ROM drives, and any other SCSI device.

Proprietary interface boards and cables

These are supplied by the manufacturer of the CD-ROM drive to work only with that drive. The problem with proprietary interface systems is that in case of upgrade and support, one must rely upon the manufacturer of the board. Sometimes, the only way to upgrade a proprietary interface is to buy a new CD-ROM drive and interface board. Also every peripheral device you attach will need an empty expansion slot inside the computer. If the user keeps adding more peripherals, the computer will run out of expansion slots.

SCSI

SCSI controllers, on the other hand, are built by several companies (e.g., Adaptec, Trantor, Future Domain, and Rancho Technology). A single SCSI interface board can be used to control up to seven SCSI peripherals in a daisy-chain configuration, thus saving the expansion slots in the computer. When adding a new peripheral to the SCSI chain, the software device driver should be updated in order for the computer to recognize the new peripheral. The SCSI interface board manufacturer should be able to provide the device driver software needed for that peripheral. However, CorelSCSI software offered by Corel Corporation provides device drivers for almost every SCSI peripheral on the market and works with DOS and OS/2 operating systems and Microsoft Windows.

In a small LAN with one or two SCSI CD-ROM drives and less than five workstations, an 8-bit SCSI board will deliver data with a good speed. If, however, more SCSI CD-ROM drives are used, then a 16-bit board should be used because using an 8-bit board will slow data delivery of the whole system. In contrast to PCs, Macintosh computers come equipped with SCSI ports, so a SCSI CD-ROM drive can just be plugged into it. Proprietary controllers, however, cannot be used with Mac computers.

Each SCSI device connected to a SCSI controller card is assigned an ID number, usually through a switch on the back of the drive. Also, the last drive is terminated with either a plug or a built-in terminator.

The standard SCSI software interface device driver to the host adapter hardware is the Advanced SCSI Programming Interface (ASPI). ASPI has been designed by Adaptec, a manufacturer of SCSI host adapters. Any SCSI device manufacturer can write an ASPI-compatible device driver to work with any ASPI-compatible host adapter or interface card made by Adaptec or another manufacturer. The function of an ASPI device driver is to translate the specifics of a particular manufacturer's hardware into the standard ASPI interface. It has to be noted that not every SCSI interface on the market is true SCSI. There are many types of SCSI interfaces that are not compatible with the ASPI specifications. SCSI standards include the following:

SCSI-1 was based on the original American National Standards Institute (ANSI) standard. It has a bus width of 8 bits and a maximum transfer rate of between 1.5 and 5 Mbytes/sec, and it supports seven peripherals. Because SCSI-1 does not support all peripherals, SCSI-2 has been developed.

SCSI-2 was originally defined in 1991. SCSI-2 drives are much faster and offer command queuing, and they can accommodate a 16-bit or 32-bit bus and have transfer rates of 10 Mbytes/sec for the 16-bit bus and up to 40 Mbytes/sec for the 32-bit bus. SCSI-2, which can handle simultaneous requests, is manufactured in two types:

Fast SCSI is a convention within the SCSI-2 draft specification and has a maximum throughput of 10 Mbytes/sec.

Wide SCSI-2 uses a 68-pin cable that expands the data path from 8 bits to 16 bits or 32 bits. Wide SCSI-2 provides 20 Mbytes/sec transfer rates. When combined with Fast SCSI-2, this "fast and wide SCSI" can provide 40 Mbytes/sec transfer rates over a 32-bit path.

For high performance, capacity, and flexibility in a high-traffic LAN environment, you should select CD-ROM drives with SCSI-2 technology.

CD-ROM drives of the future will have a different interface: the same familiar Integrated Device Electronics (IDE) interface found on many hard disks. The AT Attachment Packet Interface (ATAPI) extension to the IDE specification lets CD-ROM drives connect directly to compatible motherboards on newer computers.

Another advantage of SCSI interfaces is that you will not need to purchase different drivers every time you purchase a new device or change operating environments. Because SCSI controllers ensure interoperability among most hardware platforms, you can connect a variety of devices to a SCSI controller—as many as seven, including SCSI hard drives, CD-ROM drives, CD-ROM recordables, erasable drives, WORM drives, multifunction drives, printers (SCSI-2), scanners, removable drives, PC notebooks, DAT drives, QIC tape drives, and 8 mm tape drives. Also, if you add more CD-ROM cabinets, you will attach them to the same SCSI controller card.

Single-Session and Multisession Photo CD (PCD)

Photo CD (PCD) multisession capability ensures that the drive can read Photo CD digitized image files. Recording a group of photos on a new CD-R disc in one session produces a single-session Photo CD. However, adding another group of photos in a subsequent session at a later time will produce a multisession Photo CD, a process that requires the restructuring of the photo locations in the directory.

PCDs are discs containing scanned photographs at different resolutions that can be viewed and manipulated on almost any computer platform or a television set. One Photo CD can hold approximately 100 photos. Many CD-R drives can write PCDs using the write-once technology. These discs can be read on many drives such as CD-ROM XA (CD-ROM Extended Architecture) and CD-I (Compact Disc Interactive) drives. Virtually every double-speed CD-ROM drive sold today reads single- as well as multisession PCD. This capability is useful if the user periodically adds PCD images to a disc or if the disc is used for archiving data that are recorded in multiple sessions at different times.

After recording data on a CD, a full Volume Table of Contents (VTOC) is created for that disc. In the past, if data were needed to be updated or more data were needed to be added to the same disc, a new disc would be created all over again with a new VTOC (a single-session recording).

However, the Photo CD format, along with the CD-ROM XA and CD-I formats, allows for recording multiple sessions that can be read back on a fully Photo CD-capable CD-ROM drive. This capability will allow a CD-ROM drive to find the multiple VTOCs associated with the appended sessions.

The software for the drives that can read multisession PCDs usually continues to look for multiple lead-in commands on the disc after it encounters a lead-out command. Drives that do not have this capability will read only the first session of a multisession Photo CD.

In order to utilize the PCDs, single or multisession, the interface board and software device driver must support multisession Photo CD. There are many programs that enable the user to view and manipulate the photos stored on a Photo CD. They include Tempra Access, Magic Lantern, and Kodak's PhotoEdge.

Playing Music CDs on the CD-ROM Drive

The standards for the CD-ROM drives are based on the standards for the CD Audio (digital audio) players. Most CD-ROM drives on the market today have the capability to read computer data from CD-ROM discs as well as play music from audio CDs. When installed in a computer, a software audio utility and a sound card will be able to play CD Audio on a CD-ROM drive. Microsoft Windows uses the Media Player found in the Accessories Group. Many SCSI interface board manufacturers include an audio utility with their device drivers (e.g., Trantor includes Music Box, Future Domain includes Animotion's MCS CDMaster). You can use headphones, or you can connect an amplifier to the sound card. Some external drives include left/right audio plugs, which can be plugged into any external amplifier.

Dust-Free Drives

Dust and smoke are the number one enemy of a CD-ROM laser read head. The first thing to check when receiving frequent error messages is the laser read head. To prevent dust from entering the CD-ROM drive compartment, manufacturers use many techniques. These techniques include the covering of the drives with plastic film to seal all the holes in the drive's chassis where dust can enter the drive.

Extending connectors

Some extend all connectors (e.g., SCSI connector, audio connector) outside the main case of the drive, rather than mount them on holes cut through the chassis.

External doors

Selecting a drive with double doors and a caddy-loading mechanism will help in protecting the discs against dust and keeping the interior of the drive clean. It is important that drives have an external door that closes after a disc is inserted. This is especially important for drives mounted inside a computer because while computer fans suck hot air out of a computer, the fans might also suck in dirt and dust. An external door on the CD-ROM drive will seal the opening where the disc is inserted and help prevent dust from entering the interior of the drive.

Automatic lens cleaning

Some CD-ROM drives have an automatic lens-cleaning mechanism. The cleaning process is accomplished by sweeping the laser read head with a small brush each time a disc is inserted into or ejected from the drive.

MPC Guidelines

Under the umbrella of the Multimedia Marketing Council, a consortium of hardware and software manufacturers led by Microsoft and several other multimedia and upgrade kit developers established a set of guidelines called Multimedia PC (MPC) specifications, which outline the minimum requirements a PC-based multimedia system must meet in order to become MPC-compliant. The formation of the MPC Marketing Council originally was announced at Fall COMDEX in 1991 as a means of promoting multimedia computing. The MPC now is an independent body that promotes the use of the MPC trademark logo. The council does not test or certify products of any vendor; the goal of the MPC is to ensure that any product following the MPC guidelines will work when used with other MPC-approved products. There are two MPC levels:

MPC Level 1, the original MPC guideline, was established in 1991. MPC Level 2 guidelines, set in 1993, take a much more realistic view of the computational power needed for multimedia.

Level 1 sets the following minimum requirements:

A 286 processor (later upgraded to 386/25)

Minimum 2 Mb RAM

3.5-inch, 1.44 Mb floppy drive

Minimum 30 Mb hard disk

An 8-bit sound card with music synthesis capability

Microsoft Windows 3.1/MS-DOS operating system

VGA, or better, display (640 x 480), 256 colors

Two-button mouse

Serial, parallel, MIDI (Musical Instrument Digital Interface standard used for the exchange of musical information between computers and musical instruments or music synthesizers), and joystick ports

The CD-ROM drive should have at least 500 milliseconds' (0.5 second) average access time, 150 Kbytes/sec data-transfer rate (single-speed drive), and no more than 40 percent CPU utilization while the drive performs data transfers.

The MPC Level 2 sets the following minimum requirements:

A 486SX/25 processor (25 MHz clock speed)

Minimum 4 Mb RAM (8 Mb is recommended)

3.5-inch, 1.44 Mb floppy drive

Minimum 160 Mb hard disk

VGA or better display (640 x 480), 65,536 colors

Sound board with a 16-bit audio available, 8-note synthesizer and MIDI playback, a pair of external speakers or headphones, and joystick ports

Two-button mouse

Microsoft Windows 3.1/MS-DOS operating system

The standards for CD-ROM drives were raised to 400 milliseconds' or faster average access speed, 300 Kbytes/sec data-transfer rate (double-speed drive), no more than 60 percent CPU utilization, volume control, XA-ready drive with multisession capability, 64 Kbytes read-ahead buffer is recommended. The high-speed requirement is intended to incorporate full-motion video into multimedia systems.

Load/Eject Mechanism

There are two basic CD-ROM drive designs: those that use a standard Sony-style CD-ROM caddy case for discs and those that use a traditional tray or drawer like audio CD players. A caddy is a small plastic case used to insert a disc into a drive. After the caddy is inserted into the drive, a small metal window on its bottom swings open, allowing the laser read head beneath it to read data from the disc as it spins within the caddy—much like the metal window on the familiar 3.5-inch floppy diskette. Today, an increasing number of manufacturers have introduced tray loading drives. In addition to a slightly higher price, caddies do require more work of the user than a tray. Caddies usually help to protect CD-ROM discs against dust and scratches.

Another advantage of a caddy system is that it is less likely to break than a tray loading system. This is because fewer mechanical parts are involved. A tray has its own particular weakness. It is easy to damage a tray when it is extended from the drive. If the loading tray is bent or broken, the entire drive might be rendered useless. CD-ROM caddies can be purchased from such companies as QD Products and Walnut Creek CD-ROM. They cost about $12 each. In order to use a caddy, the CD-ROM drive should be designed to accept caddies.

Most drive failures are due to the load/eject mechanism, which is probably the most vulnerable part of the drive. Many drives are designed with a completely automatic load/eject caddy mechanism. When a caddy is pushed inside the drive, the automatic loading mechanism pulls the caddy in completely, in much the same manner that a VCR operates. The caddy will eject from the drive if the eject button is pressed or a software eject command is issued. Although this feature is very convenient, the most common cause of drive failure is a caddy that becomes jammed inside a drive. Some users force the caddy inside the drive even when they encounter resistance. If the mechanical parts are broken, it is very hard to pull the caddy out and the drive should be sent for repair. During the repair period, the CD-ROM application that is trapped inside the caddy will not be available to the LAN users until the drive is repaired or it is pulled out. You should realize that excessive force might result in the breaking of other parts, which usually voids the drive warranty.

To produce fewer chances for mechanical failures during loading of the caddy, some CD-ROM drives contain manual loading and eject mechanisms. A manual loading mechanism requires the user to push the caddy all the way into the drive until it settles inside the drive. An automatic eject mechanism offers fewer chances for misuse. The mechanism is usually backed up with an emergency manual eject mechanism, which the user can utilize to retrieve the disc stuck inside without having to take the drive apart. It is easy to spot the emergency eject mechanism by looking for a very small hole—not to be confused with the audio jack—on the front panel of the CD-ROM drive.

Drive's Durability

The life expectancy of the drives is expressed as MTBF, which stands for Mean Time Between Failure. Simply, it refers to the length of time the drive is expected to work, under normal operating conditions, before a failure that requires a repair occurs. In a library situation that requires long hours of operation and heavy use and misuse, a more durable drive would present less downtime. Academic libraries should expect the CD-ROM drives to work all semester long, 24 hours a day, without interruption. With reasonable care, the drives are generally immune to failure. However, the drive parts that are usually susceptible to failure include: the tractor mechanism that moves the lens, the loading mechanism, the ejecting mechanism, the cooling fan, and the lens (usually dirt).

Unlike a computer crash, a disc crash can never occur because there are few moving parts, which makes the drives highly dependable. Also, only a beam of light scans the disc's surface, and no magnetic field exists to become accidentally contaminated. The less-susceptible components to failure include the laser diode, the servo motor, the lenses and the beam splitter, and the photodetector.

The figures associated with an advertised MTBF are not exact figures because manufacturers usually calculate these figures based upon the MTBF of the primary components contained in the drive. Although these figures have been exaggerated, they give an idea about the quality of the product. Manufacturers do not tell which component will fail first; plastic gears or metal motors, or the points of contact between a user and a drive. At any rate, MTBF typically applies to motor life, but drives may fail because of bad power supplies or faulty lens assemblies.

XA Compatibility

XA stands for extended architecture. XA standard is designed to extend the capability of ISO 9660/High Sierra discs through the interleaving of audio data on the same track with computer text, graphics, and images for synchronized playback. Most current multimedia discs use separate audio and video tracks. To make it appear that someone is speaking in a video, they play a bit of the audio track, then a bit of the video track, alternatively. The drive buffers the information in memory, then sends it to the PC for synchronization. By making use of the CD-ROM drive's buffer, the software companies can usually come close to making the audio and video run in synchronization. Thus, the data is read off the disc in alternating pieces, and then synchronized at playback. However, on a drive with a slow data-transfer rate or poor buffering capabilities, the audio and video will not be in synch.

To play an XA title, you need an XA decoder board in addition to an XA-ready CD-ROM drive. Currently, only a few companies make these boards, and they are available only at a relatively high price. There are some companies working on developing a software-only XA solution that might replace expensive decoder boards, but their efforts thus far have been limited. Although most networks may probably have little immediate use for XA, buying a drive that is XA-ready probably is a good idea just in case the XA format does become popular in networks.

Multimedia

Since most networks lack the bandwidth necessary to process high-volume data requests, they can't handle video and sound playback to a workstation. However, on a low-volume network it is possible to play sound if you add the MSCDEX.EXE on each client's PC. You will also need at least dual speed CD-ROM drives. Better yet, consider four-speed CD-ROM drives with 600 Kbytes/sec transfer rate, which can make playback of long video clips much less painful. Fast networks, such as ATM or full-duplex Ethernet, will eventually accommodate multimedia on networks.

Because full-motion video with sound requires more bandwidth than most networks can provide, the audio breaks up and looses synchronization with the video. Novell has tried to overcome this problem by developing technology that monitors and scales the network traffic of each video/audio session. If network bandwidth becomes a limitation, the frame rate of the video sequence is reduced while the audio synchronization and quality are maintained.

Some solutions use FDDI cabling or other techniques such as segmenting the LAN to reduce the number of users on each LAN segment. By using segment-switching hubs, nodes can switch from one segment to another. This will eventually result in a network bandwidth that is equal to the cabling bandwidth multiplied by the number of segments.

Customer Technical Support

You will need technical support during installation and beyond. A toll-free number provided by the vendor is not enough without a knowledgeable technical staff. The best technical support services provide you with options; either you get direct access to a technical support staff member, or you can leave your name, telephone number, a brief description of your problem, and a time at which you want to be called back. You might also be able to fax in this information or post it on a computer bulletin board.

It is worthwhile to call the technical support department of the companies whose drives you are considering for purchase before ordering the drives. Describe the future LAN setup and ask about any problems likely to be encountered when installing CD-ROM drives. The speed and helpfulness of the responses should be a factor in deciding which CD-ROM drive to buy. Sometimes, a cheap CD-ROM drive means no technical support on the part of the vendor.

Conclusion

When buying CD-ROM drives for networks, always consider drives with the following specifications:

CD-ROM drives that use SCSI-2 interface

Data-transfer rate of 300 Kbytes/sec and up

Access time of 300 ms minimum; 240 ms recommended

Drives with cache buffer of 64K and above; 256K recommended

CD-ROM drives that are extended-architecture (XA)-compliant

Drives with internal disc-cleaning mechanism and outer dust-protection systems

Drives with sealed casing

Drives with manual eject mechanism

Single-session and multisession photo CD (PCD) capability

Playing music CDs on the CD-ROM drive

MPC Level 2 guideline supported

Loading mechanism with a caddy system

MTBF (Mean Time Between Failure) of at least 50,000 hours (5.7 years)

Quality technical support

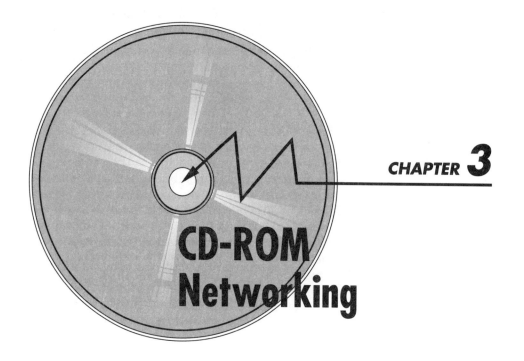

CHAPTER **3**

CD-ROM Networking

Standalone CD-ROM workstations have been used since 1985. However, as the popularity of CD-ROM has increased, so has the demand for sharing these sources of information. Basically, in any network, there is always a place for CD-ROM hardware and software. Providing network access to both commercial and in-house databases on CD-ROM in your organization has the potential to empower users with an enormous amount of information.

Essentially, all workstations in a CD-ROM LAN should have the ability to equally access and obtain information from any CD-ROM database on the network. This system, which allows CD-ROM drives to be eventually shared across a network, can be attained via many networking solutions and techniques. Whether you are building a CD-ROM network from the ground up or adding CD-ROM capability to an existing network, selecting one technique or the other is not easy because networking CD-ROM is complex and very challenging. All solutions to establish multiuser access to CD-ROM drives have unique features and options that differ greatly in cost and in their approach to CD-ROM networking.

Typically, CD-ROM networking solutions take either a standard Novell NetWare NLM (NetWare Loadable Module) approach or an MS-DOS redirector approach.[1] In the NLM approach, the CD-ROM NLM software is loaded only in the file server that runs Novell's NetWare network operating system. This NLM module allows the network server to see the CD-ROM drives as read-only NetWare volumes—i.e., server directories and files. The NetWare server is usually configured as a dedicated server. In the MS-DOS approach, the server runs under MS-DOS or Windows. The server can be dedicated or it can function as a server and workstation at the same time.

Advantages of CD-ROM Networking

CD-ROM networks are ideal for organizations where there is a wide user base with many users sharing CD-ROM discs and applications across the network. The cost of the LAN is usually justified by the number of uses. In situations where several people within an organization access the same information at different times using an online service, no matter who pays for this service, it is not practical to pay for that same information more than once. Networking CD-ROMs will help to eliminate this situation.

CD-ROM networks add more security to CD-ROM discs and drives as they eliminate the need for users to handle the CD-ROM discs. These devices are usually locked away from the public in a secured room. Another advantage is that a CD LAN user can access many databases and computer applications as well as other services provided by the organization, such as online public access catalogs (OPACs) from a single workstation. Eventually, a network will connect the users to wide area network (WAN) services, such as the Internet. Connecting users to the Internet will allow them to access other information resources and professional user groups.

A CD network is cost-effective as it eliminates the need to have a CD-ROM drive at every workstation. In addition, a CD-ROM server will eliminate the need to purchase and install CD-ROM applications in every workstation in the organization as CD-ROM applications will be installed on the network in one computer, the file server.

In libraries where space is scarce, CDs are attractive alternatives to some bound volumes. Also, bibliographic instruction labs can access the CD-ROM LAN to provide training on how to use the network. The lab, which is equipped with computer workstations, allows librarians to combine all aspects of bibliographic instruction and, through the LAN, to incorporate computer indexes, databases, and search techniques appropriate to the needs of each specific discipline.

CD-ROM Networking Problems

Although there are advantages to CD-ROM networking, there are many problems associated with CD-ROM technology. When establishing a CD-ROM network or adding a CD-ROM service to an existing network, you will encounter different types of obstacles. You will discover that not every step during installation proceeds smoothly according to the manuals. Almost every CD-ROM product needs special treatment. However, the real challenge is in assuring that all CD-ROM applications and other computing software work together in harmony and that users can run the programs they need, depending, of course, on access limitations. In some situations, you will find some anomalies. There are many areas where installing and running a CD-ROM application can be a painful experience. The following will give you an idea about the common problems associated with CD-ROM networking.

Software Sensitivity to Networks

Most CD-ROM software programs are designed to work on standalone workstations. When used in networks, they develop problems. These problems are due to the fact that developing CD-ROM application programs that will run in a network represents a new territory for programmers who have previously been writing only standalone CD-ROM programs.

Installation

During installation, some CD-ROM applications install themselves on drive C:, the hard drive of the workstation. In a network, drive C: is not used as a network drive. While this does not constitute a major problem on a standalone computer, most LAN operating systems designate drives higher than F as network drives and consider drive C: a local drive that may be accessed by LAN users. The LAN installer has to find ways to copy the software from drive C: to a LAN drive and create the necessary batch files to force the software to work from a LAN drive.

Other CD-ROM applications will abort installation if they are not installed in the root directory. On the contrary, a well-designed CD-ROM installation program allows users to choose and designate a network drive rather than forcing the installation on a preselected drive.

Temporary Files

Most CD-ROM applications require a temporary subdirectory to store overflow and temporary files. Some will not work if a temporary subdirectory on the hard drive is not found. Others perform well if they have at least 20 Mb of hard disk space. These files are erased upon exiting the application. Some installation programs force temporary files to be located in a preselected directory, which might not be suitable to a network situation. Others might just select the directory where the software programs for that application reside. The problem with this approach is that creating temporary files on the same subdirectory as the executables will create a network security problem, since deleting those files will require granting the workstations the right to write and delete files on the network file server itself.

Another problem is that there will be a file-sharing violation when you try to share a temporary file that has been created by another user in the same subdirectory.

A well-designed CD-ROM installation program allows users to specify a drive and subdirectory for temporary files and residual programs, rather than forcing the temporary files to be created in the same subdirectory where the executable files are installed.

There are two ways to overcome this situation:

First, designate a temporary area (scratch area) in every user's subdirectory on the file server to catch the temporary files created by any CD-ROM application on the network. This solution is only good if the workstation is using a diskless computer (a computer that has no local disk storage capability). However, in a busy network, this approach might overload the file server with unnecessary tasks.

Second, if the workstation has a hard disk drive, a subdirectory on the hard disk of the workstation could be created to collect these temporary files. These files will be erased upon exiting the application, or you can create a batch file to erase these temporary files during booting of the workstation. When the workstation boots, the batch file checks for the existence of a temporary directory and creates one if it does not exist. Batch files for each CD-ROM application should include the right code to recognize a temporary subdirectory to save its temporary files.

Sensitivity to Monitor Type

Some CD-ROM applications cannot recognize the monitor type and assume that every body has the same monitor type. A well-designed CD-ROM installation program should be able to sense the monitor type (mono, VGA, EGA, etc.) of every workstation and adjust itself accordingly.

RAM CRAM

Although anyone who installs CD-ROM applications on a network might rightfully complain about the small computer memory size left after loading the necessary network programs into the RAM of a workstation, some CD-ROM developers nevertheless still produce CD-ROM applications software of huge sizes that barely fit in the memory of a workstation. Programmers should take into consideration the limited size of a computer's conventional memory. They should also take advantage of the extended and expanded computer memory. Even if the computer has an 8-Mb memory, almost all CD-ROM application programs run in the first 640K of the memory of the computer, known as the conventional memory. (Because this problem is difficult to solve, chapter 9 of this book is devoted to explaining how to use the memory of the computer efficiently.)

Mounting CD-ROMs

Once a CD-ROM is mounted onto the file server and it runs correctly, there should be no problems. However, if discs need to be changed frequently, then problems arise because it takes time to mount and change the names of the CD-ROM application programs. Some network CD-ROM software managers allow you to mount and dismount CD-ROM discs only when the CD-ROM server is taken off the network.

Mapping

Many programs load search software onto the hard disk, then expect to find the CD-ROM data at a specific drive letter. If the data are mapped to a different logical drive, the application reports an error. There are two types of mappings: drive mapping and search drive mapping. A drive mapping is a shortcut reference to a long directory name, and a search drive mapping is a search path to a directory that contains executable program files. For example, if drive K: is mapped to the directory **SYS:CDROM/APPS**, users can access that directory each time they change to drive K:.

Licensing

Many CD-ROM publishers have not formulated solid policies in licensing their products to run in a network environment. Some publishers who have adopted licensing policies charge high prices. Many do not allow their CD-ROM products to serve remote users. Their definition of remote users is sometimes confusing.

Software Activation

Strangely enough, some vendors ask you to call them to provide you with a key code in order to activate the CD-ROM software. Some products require that you delete specific configuration files manually when you receive an updated disc, then copy new configuration files from the CD-ROM disk to the network.

Frequent Software Updating

Some products are issued monthly, and with every monthly disc, you have to update the software—a waste of time and effort. Sometimes after you update the software, the new disc won't work and you have to call the technical services for assistance.

Effective Search Strategy

It is not an easy task for patrons to formulate an effective search strategy to search CD-ROM databases. It could be difficult for users to effectively perform a good search. Because experience in bibliographic search is gained through training and experience, it could be difficult for users to perform effective searches.

Personalized Configurations

Some products require that each user's subdirectory include a configuration file. This will pose many problems if you have a large number of users and you have to change their configuration files with every reinstallation of the software, or you have to add additional CD drives to each user's configuration file.

Nonconformity of User Interfaces

The variety and nonconformity of user interfaces associated with CD-ROM products and the proprietary search software could certainly contribute to the confusion of users. The nonconformity among CD-ROM products requires the user to learn different formulations for search syntax, different meanings for function keys, and different protocols for printing and downloading data as the user switches from one database to another. This is in contrast to Windows-based applications that have some type of conformity.

Disk Operating Systems

A high percentage of all CD-ROM applications are written to a DOS operating system that operates on IBM computers and IBM compatibles. Very few are geared toward Macintosh, UNIX, VAX, or other types of computers. If you have other computer systems and you like to provide access to every operating system in your corporation, you will run into interoperability problems. In the meantime, many CD-ROM network solutions limit access only to those users working on DOS machines and running the same operating system that the library uses. Many libraries are frustrated because they cannot offer all patrons on all computer platforms an equal opportunity to access their information.

Sluggishness

Even if you purchase a network license for an unlimited number of concurrent users, some CD-ROM applications will slow down in response time if the number of concurrent users exceeds a specific limit. You have to experiment to find out the maximum number of users, after which the CD application will become sluggish. You have to limit the number of concurrent users when an application encounters this problem.

Network Growth Rate

While the capacity of CD-ROM discs is high (over 600 Mb/disc), many CD-ROM applications are published on multiple CD-ROM volumes (discs). If you are going to provide access to all discs on the network, you will soon find that the small network you have designed has grown very fast into a complicated system. This situation, in addition to posing some of the problems mentioned above, deterred some users from networking CD-ROM applications. Instead, if the same information were published on magnetic tapes, it would be accessible through mounting on minicomputers or mainframes. But, again, we have to think about the capacity of the equipment that would be used, the time needed to download the tapes, and the cost involved. The cost of the databases on tapes is usually higher than the cost of their counterpart published on CD-ROM.

Do You Really Need a CD-ROM Network?

Because of the costs involved, your decision to network CD-ROMs should be made according to the needs of the users and the quality of the present service. Besides the cost of hardware and software, you have to consider the recurrent costs such as annual network licenses for CD-ROM applications, network maintenance, and training of users. In order to decide if you need a CD-ROM network, you must collect statistics on the number of uses and observe the usage of the existing CD-ROM service—if it is provided in your organization. This way you will be able to predict how the network will affect the current service. Remember, CD-ROM networks are not for everyone. Depending on the number of users and the number of CD applications, you will be able to provide a reasonable service to your users. In general, your situation could be one of the following:

Few Applications/Few Users

In an environment where a limited number of CD-ROM products are used and the number of users is very small, you do not need a CD-ROM network. Rather, you should consider allowing users to access the CD-ROMs through a dedicated standalone CD-ROM workstation.

Few Applications/Many Users

Unless the CD-ROM application is used most of the time, the computer will be idle most of the time. If the CD-ROM application gets heavy use, you should consider adding an extra copy of the application and an extra PC and CD-ROM drive. This demands consideration in comparing the cost of this configuration with the cost of establishing a small CD-ROM network. You should take into account the rate by which the CD-ROM service is expanding. Also, you have to consider the cost of CD-ROM application network licensing.

Many Applications/Few Users

If you have many CD applications that are published on many CD-ROM discs, but you have a small number of users, you can daisy-chain the CD-ROM drives and access them through one PC. Daisy-chaining will eliminate the swapping of discs and will allow users to use the same search statements to search other volumes of the same CD application without rekeying these statements. You may also consider using a jukebox system in the form of a minichanger or multichanger.

Many Applications/Many Users

If you have many CD applications that are used by many users, you should start thinking about CD-ROM networking. In many organizations, one CD drive for many users is not enough—more drives are needed to handle many databases. Rather than duplicate purchases of often-costly CD-ROM discs, organizations usually look for ways to share them across networks. These organizations might have a network that can encompass a CD-ROM service, or they may have to establish new networks.

Approaches to Building CD-ROM Networks

The approach to establishing CD-ROM access on a network ranges from attaching a CD-ROM drive to a workstation to building a dedicated CD-ROM-based network. However, there are three ways to establish a CD-ROM LAN.

First, build a CD-ROM network from the ground up. This requires familiarity with networking techniques and greater in-house expertise. In this approach, you buy the hardware and software: the network operating system, the server, the workstations, the cabling, and the CD-ROM drives. Although you can save some money, you will always need someone who has the networking expertise, or you may hire a consultant or seek help from the computer services department in your organization, if one exists. When you buy the network components, you have to make sure that these components will work together in harmony. This approach will pay off in a large network.

Second, buy a CD-ROM server package that incorporates the network operating system, the server, and the CD-ROM drives in a tower array; then you provide the workstations and the cabling. Although this approach requires less effort, as you do not need to configure the server and set up the software, the cost will be higher than that of the first approach. But you will gain full technical support from the vendor on the software, the server, and the tower system.

Third, buy a complete package that includes the network operating system, the server, the CD-ROM drives, the workstations, and the cabling. Although the cost will be higher than those of the first two approaches, the vendor will construct the network for you and provide training and the technical assistance you need to operate the network. This approach is good for small CD-ROM networks.

Dedicated and Nondedicated CD-ROM Servers

For medium-size and larger network workgroups with multiple servers and more client workstations and shared resources, you should set up a separate CD-ROM server beside the file server to take the load off the file server and increase the network throughput. For small workgroups, hooking the CD-ROM drives directly to the existing network server that also acts as a workstation is an economical approach.

Depending on its network functionality and the size of the network, a CD-ROM server can take one of two configurations: dedicated or nondedicated CD server.

Dedicated CD-ROM Server

In this configuration, CD-ROM drives are attached to one or more central PCs, called CD-ROM servers. This central PC server does not provide any network services except CD-ROM services. Users cannot run applications on it. In this case, the CD-ROM dedicated server is no more than a PC that performs no client tasks; it only serves other clients. Although this will require an extra PC to dedicate as a CD-ROM server, the main benefit of a dedicated server is speed.

In addition to better network performance and tighter control, dedicated CD-ROM servers provide better equipment security, but without more ongoing management. They can be used on centric-server networks such as Novell NetWare as well as peer-to-peer networks such as LANtastic and other networks such as VINES. Dedicated CD-ROM servers direct queries to appropriate CD-ROM drives. And that is all these computers do.

A LAN may have more than one dedicated CD-ROM server. The number of CD-ROM servers and the CD-ROM drives installed on any network is governed by the network operating system and/or the selected CD-ROM network operating system. If more RAM is needed to increase the cache memory for better performance, it is better to consult the developer of the CD-ROM network management software you are using because some CD-ROM redirectors do not support RAM over 16 Mb.

There are some disadvantages to such servers, however, including high initial cost of dedicated equipment. The reason: you need to set aside a PC whose only purpose is to sit on a desk and allow access to CD-ROMs, and LAN users cannot use it to log in to the network. In some situations, the disadvantage is the cost of adding a third-party CD-ROM network operating system with an average price of $1,000 or more. In addition, if the CD-ROM server is down, all CD-ROM products will be down. In any case, if you are concerned about performance, it is better to establish a dedicated CD-ROM server in all situations.

Nondedicated CD Server

In peer-based LANs, any PC that answers requests for CD-ROM services from other PCs (excluding itself) on the network is known as a dedicated CD-ROM server. This is in contrast to a nondedicated CD-ROM server, which answers CD-ROM requests from all PCs (including itself). This machine provides other network services and lets users run applications on it. The CD-ROM drives are "published," or made available for use by other users in the same way as any other drive.

In this configuration, the CD-ROM drives are attached to a PC server that also acts as a workstation. This workstation-based, peer-to-peer implementation does provide other services than the CD-ROM services, and users can run other applications on the same machine. Here the server acts as a client and a server at the same time.

Basically, a peer-based LAN is an architecture in which two or more nodes can communicate with each other directly. In this configuration, CD-ROM drives will be attached to one or more nodes. This client and server node will be loaded with the necessary device driver software and Microsoft CD Extensions (MSCDEX). Through the network redirector software, the CD-ROM drives will become a network resource that can be shared among all nodes on the network, along with other network resources, such as hard disks, files, and printers. Because a node can be configured to be a client/server, there will be no need for a dedicated file server. Meanwhile, each PC can still run local applications. Peer-to-peer network operating systems include their own system management, system backup, and security. Popular peer-to-peer network operating systems include Microsoft Windows for Workgroups, Novell's Personal NetWare, and Artisoft's LANtastic.

Peer-to-peer LANs often offer the perfect solution for small workgroups (10 to 20 nodes). On an existing client/server installation, small workgroups can create their own peer-to-peer networks and connect these networks with the main corporate LAN. Some peer network operating systems include not only the capabilities that are found in larger LANs (e.g., Novell NetWare, Microsoft LAN Manager, and IBM LAN Server), but also functions such as electronic mail and chat and, in some cases, group scheduling. They offer control over printing, internetworking support, and memory configuration.

An advantage of peer LANs is their ease of installation. In most cases, adding nodes does not require purchasing a license for each individual client. The majority of peer LANs have built-in CD-ROM sharing. Some offer users links to Macintosh computers, as well as to dedicated servers running NetWare or LAN Manager.

Known also as nondedicated CD-ROM server solutions, peer-to-peer LANs include DOS-based as well as Windows-based LANs. However, some, such as Windows for Workgroups, support only the Windows environment. Most peer-to-peer LANs use Ethernet or Token Ring standards to share disk drives, printers, and CD-ROMs. Because virtually every peer-to-peer LAN operating system uses standard DOS as the underlying file system, such systems are also known as DOS-based networks. Others such as LANtastic and PowerLan can work under DOS or Windows, so it is easy to upgrade from DOS to Windows. This is very important because the number of CD-ROM titles migrating to Windows is increasing. At present, many CD-ROM applications are capable of running in DOS and Windows environments. You can install a 10-workstation LAN with a per-node cost of less than $200 on average.

Approaches to Configuring CD-ROM Networks

CD-ROM networking solutions can prepare a computer to function as a dedicated or nondedicated CD-ROM server. However, there are at least four approaches for sharing CD-ROM drives with users on a network.

> CD-ROM drives attached to workstations
> CD-ROM drives attached to file servers using an NLM solution
> CD-ROM drives attached to dedicated CD-ROM servers using an NLM solution
> CD-ROM drives attached to dedicated CD-ROM servers using a DOS-based solution

CD-ROM Drives Attached to Workstations

The CD-ROM server in a peer-to-peer environment is usually a DOS- or Windows-based server running under a peer-to-peer network operating system, such as LANtastic or Windows for Workgroups (fig. 3–1). A dedicated CD-ROM server used in this situation would enhance the network's ability to maintain a relatively uniform response time by using its caching abilities without disruption. In this configuration, the MSCDEX or an equivalent redirector is needed only on the machine that acts as a server. The client segment of the network operating system runs on the workstation. The CD-ROM applications software is installed on the server machine.

The CD-ROM networking solutions that fall into this category include the majority of peer-to-peer network operating systems that have built-in support for MSCDEX, such as:

> Desk to Desk from CBIS
> InvisibleLAN from Invisible Software

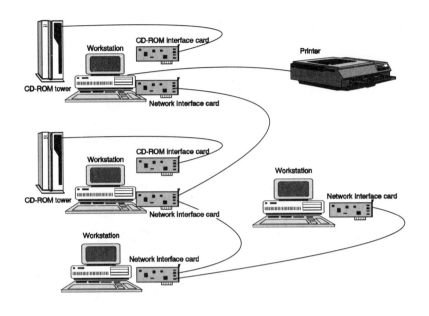

Figure 3-1. *In a peer-to-peer network, any workstation can be used as a file server. This workstation can also be used as a CD-ROM server.*

LANstep from Hays Microcomputer Products

LANtastic Network Operating System from Artisoft

Microsoft Windows for Workgroups 3.1 from Microsoft

Personal NetWare from Novell

PowerLan from Performance Technology

SilverNET from Net-Source

Simply LANtastic from Artisoft

Some peer-based LANs (e.g., 10NET from Tiara) require third-party software to be able to establish CD-ROM sharing.

CD-ROM Drives Attached to File Servers Using an NLM Solution

This method is used in Novell NetWare networks. In this approach, CD-ROM drives are installed in file servers, then appropriate software that makes CD-ROM drives available to users is also installed in the same machine, along with CD-ROM applications software (fig. 3–2).

In this environment, CD-ROM drives are attached directly to a centralized file server that manages the network and runs a CD-ROM NetWare Loadable Module (NLM) to serve all workstations in the network.

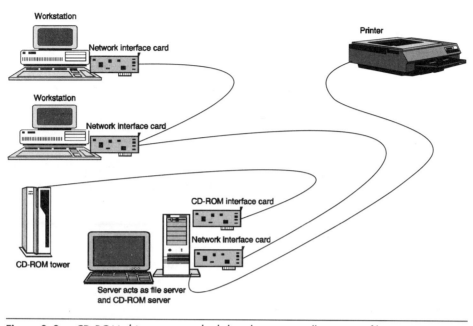

Figure 3–2. *CD-ROM drives are attached directly to a Novell NetWare file server.*

All NLM programs run on Novell NetWare networks version 3.0 and above. NetWare versions before 3.0 use some products known as VAP (value-added products), such as OPTI-NET for NetWare 2.x, and SCSI Express for NetWare 2.x.

The NLM software provides the support for mounting CD-ROM drives as NetWare volumes for users to access. This approach is used in smaller or less active networks. The NetWare server will handle the network file management and provide other network services, including CD-ROM access. These NLMs are needed only on the network file-CD-ROM server machine. Because this machine provides other network services, the performance might be affected in medium- to large-size networks. If you have the financial means to dedicate a server to provide CD-ROM service only, the third solution will be your best choice. The following products can be used to build this configuration:

> CD Net for NetWare from Novell
>
> CD Connection from CBIS
>
> CorelSCSI NLM
>
> DiscPort from Microtest
>
> LanCD from Logicraft
>
> OPTI-NET NLM from Online Computer Systems
>
> SCSI Express from Micro Design International

This approach requires no workstation terminate-and-stay residents (TSRs), but it comes at a price. It is recommended that you allocate 1.2 Mb of RAM (cache) for each 650K CD you want to mount. So, if you have 56 CD-ROM drives attached to the file server, you should allocate at least 67 Mb RAM in the server in order to provide a smooth CD-ROM service. Also, if you have many CD drives, there will be added I/O volume on the server that may affect your server performance. Many file servers have as much hardware attached to them as they can handle or are underpowered and can't afford one more CPU cycle for any more CD-ROM drives.

CD-ROM Drives Attached to Dedicated CD-ROM Servers Using an NLM Solution

This method is used in Novell NetWare networks. In this method, CD-ROM drives will be attached to a dedicated CD-ROM server, then appropriate driver software that makes CD-ROM drives available to users is installed in the same machine.

In this centralized environment, a CD-ROM server runs a CD-ROM NLM on a Novell NetWare network, similar to the second method, but the network has two servers instead of one: a file server that manages network operations and a separate CD-ROM server that provides access to CD-ROM drives. This approach is used in active networks to increase the throughput of the CD-ROM services. The CD-ROM drives and the CD-ROM NLM are installed in the CD-ROM server machine, while the CD-ROM application software is installed in the file server.

The problem with this approach, in addition to one's having to install two servers on the network, is that one needs two copies of Novell's NetWare—one for the network file server and another for the CD-ROM server. Of course, providing CD-ROM services through a dedicated machine and other network services through a separate machine will add to the cost; but your users will appreciate the speed.

While small groups accessing a CD-ROM won't slow down a CD-ROM server by much, the load from several servers at once will affect the whole network because of heavy traffic. The products that can be used in this situation are those mentioned in the second approach, above.

CD-ROM Drives Attached to Dedicated CD-ROM Servers Using a DOS-Based Solution

This approach is used in many network environments. For example, in a Novell NetWare network, a DOS-based CD-ROM server can be attached to the network. This CD-ROM server will run under a third-party solution software redirector, such as OPTI-NET for DOS, SCSI Express for DOS, and CD Net for DOS. The CD-ROM device driver, the MSCDEX, and the workstation part of the solution software redirector are needed on every workstation. Meanwhile, the CD-ROM server runs the CD-ROM device driver and the server part of the solution software redirector, which makes the CD-ROM drives sharable among Novell workstations. In this configuration, the retrieval software for each CD-ROM product is installed on the Novell NetWare file server, not on the CD-ROM server. The layout of this approach is the same as with an NLM solution (see fig. 3–3).

The problem with this approach is that the conventional as well as the upper memory of the workstation will be so overloaded with all types of terminate-and-stay residents (TSRs) in addition to the network drivers (at least IPX and NETX) that there will hardly be any room left in the conventional memory of the workstation to run CD-ROM applications software. You might employ a loader such as Intel's LANSelect to swap out the PC's RAM contents to disc, load the CD access drivers and CD application, and then unload the lot when finished. Even this solution might lock up the computer as potentially conflicting drivers compete for control over interrupt vectors and memory space. You might use Multimedia Cloaking from Helix, which runs a replacement for MSCDEX in the extended memory. You have to experiment or just switch to an NLM solution.

CBIS's CD Connection provides a partial solution that loads its own redirector in the memory of the workstation. It uses 28K of the conventional memory and can be taken off the memory when not needed. Another problem with this approach is that when running MSCDEX on the workstation, MSCDEX reserves letters for every virtual CD-ROM drive. This can result in some problems if you wish to add a virtual memory or RAM discs to workstations. Products in this category, such as OPTI-NET for DOS, can run on other NetBIOS network operating systems (Microsoft's LAN Manager, IBM's LAN Server, Torus Systems' Tapestry, and Banyan's VINES).

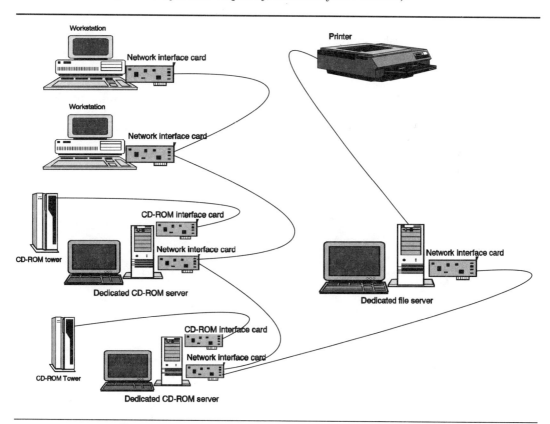

Figure 3–3. *In Novell NetWare networks, CD-ROM drives can be attached to a dedicated CD-ROM server.*

CD Connection from CBIS runs on Novell's NetWare, NetBIOS, and Banyan's VINES networks.

Meridian's CD NET software is available in a NetBIOS version for NetWare (not running IPX), 3Com 3+Open, Microsoft's LAN Manager, Ungermann-Bass, AT&T's StarLAN, and IBM's LAN Server.

Lanshark's CD Direct for VINES, Meridian's CD NET VINES upgrade, Trellis Optical Redirector for VINES, and LanCD from Logicraft, which supports UNIX, are all examples of CD-ROM access solutions.

Note

1. Network requester software allows a computer to access network peripherals, such as disks and printers. The word *redirector*, sometimes used interchangeably with *requester*, pertains only to MS-DOS and has a broader meaning. It refers to a program that redirects DOS function calls to either a non-DOS CD-ROM file format or a networked peripheral (see also appendix D).

   For CD-ROMs, the best-known redirector is Microsoft's MSCDEX. Even though data are stored on a CD-ROM disc in High Sierra or ISO-9660 format, MSCDEX allows it to appear as a DOS file system to your application program. Both LANtastic's REDIR program, which provides access to a LANtastic network, and Microsoft's CD-ROM Extensions (MSCDEX), which provides access to the non-DOS file format of a CD-ROM, are redirectors.

   TRELLIS/Optical Disk Redirector is another example of redirector software that allows the connection of laser optical discs to Banyan's VINES networks and makes them available to users on the LAN/WAN. Trellis/ODR supports CD-ROM, WORM, and erasable media. The MSCDEX extensions are supported, as are Windows and OS/2 workstations.

   CDREDIR is another terminate-and-stay resident (TSR) redirector that simulates MSCDEX. It is used on Banyan's VINES networks. Novell NetWare, on the other hand, requires a different type of redirector in the form of a NetWare Loadable Module (NLM). NLM is a LAN driver that runs under Novell's NetWare network operating system.

CHAPTER 4

Sharing CD-ROM Drives on Peer-to-Peer LANs

Most peer-to-peer LANs use either Ethernet or token ring adapter cards and coaxial or twisted-pair cabling, while some support ARCNET networks. Peer-to-peer LANs allow CD-ROM drives to be attached to one or more computers as these LANs have a built-in capability to connect a CD-ROM drive to any workstation and provide access to it without resorting to third-party software. In general, if your LAN supports peer-to-peer resource sharing, there is a great possibility that it allows access to CD-ROM drives. However, not every peer-to-peer LAN operating system provides support to CD-ROM drives; you have to check with the LAN developer.

To access CD-ROM drives in a peer-to-peer LAN, you have to install the CD-ROM device driver and the MSCDEX on the workstation connected to the CD-ROM drives only (fig. 4.1). The majority of peer-to-peer LANs use MSCDEX for accessing the CD-ROM drives. Through MSCDEX you can assign a drive letter to any CD-ROM drive attached to the server-workstation PC. This way all computers on the network can access the CD-ROM drive in the same way they access a hard disk. Also, providing CD-ROM service from a dedicated PC, which does not run other applications except CD-ROMs, ensures better performance.

Peer-to-peer LANs work just as well as client-server environments when users only need to share files. Any microcomputer in this configuration is allowed to function as a file server, while printers, modems, CD-ROMs, the hard drives of any computer, and other peripherals are shared among stations.

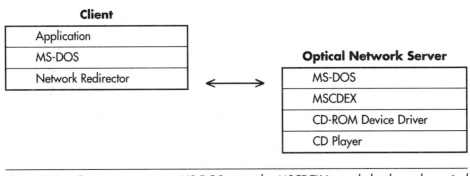

Figure 4–1. *On true peer-to-peer MS-DOS networks, MSCDEX is needed only on the optical server. On the workstation, the network operating system installs the network redirector.*

Advantages and Disadvantages of Peer-to-Peer LANs

Peer-to-peer networks are powerful and reliable for small CD-ROM LANs. However, in a medium-size LAN, sharing CD-ROMs and other resources might require a dedicated server to increase performance. As the peer network grows, it is imperative that you implement the client/server model for specific services by just dedicating a computer to that service—e.g., a dedicated CD-ROM server in a peer-to-peer LAN that will no longer function as a user workstation.

Although peer-to-peer CD-ROM LAN seems to be an economical solution because any computer can act as a server and workstation at the same time, the access rate can be affected as the microprocessor of the server-station is always interrupted by users trying to run other local software applications in the same machine. So, the microprocessor has to divide the processing activities among other computer applications and CD-ROM services.

Peer-to-peer solutions are ideal, simple network situations. In terms of security, however, these networks provide minimum security to the hardware because the CD-ROMs are usually visible. There will always be security problems if the machines are located in a public area since users can eject the CD-ROM discs if they are not locked, or turn the drives or the workstation off. If the workstation is turned off, all searches by other network users in this station will be terminated. Also, this configuration has less reliability—if a local application crashes, then the optical server crashes. However, if the workstation that also functions as a server goes down, other CD-ROM drives attached to other server-stations on the network will still be unaffected.

In terms of cost, peer-to-peer LANs are better buys than expensive client-server systems. They cost from $800 for a starter kit to about $2,800 for a fully operational, eight-station LAN (including LAN operating system, cables, and network interface cards). Peer-to-peer LANs are easy to use and maintain, while they have performance, security, and management options. Some can serve from 50 to 100 users without a problem.

Although most of these peer-to-peer network operating systems are useful in small- to medium-size sites running a reasonable number of CD-ROM drives, they can complement server-centric operating systems in larger sites. These systems provide an inexpensive way for networking as they let LAN users share disc drives, printers, and CD-ROMs. Peer networking capabilities are being used in many corporations as part of their desktop operating systems. Apple Computer, for example, added peer networking capabilities to its System 7 desktop operating system for the Macintosh computers. Microsoft has included peer services in Windows NT, and similar services are also included in Windows 95. However, peer-to-peer LANs might not meet the needs of large CD-ROM networks as the performance of the network might suffer when running intensive CD-ROM applications.

Most of the products in this chapter can create dedicated as well as non-dedicated file servers. Some LANs take advantage of the cache memory to optimize their performance such as LANtastic, PowerLan, and SilverNET. Most of the hardware used with these LANs will work on other expensive LANs such as NetWare 3.11. So, if you decide to move to a powerful and expensive system, you can always use the same hardware. However, some of the LANs discussed in this chapter provide their own adapters and cabling, which would make the user dependent on a particular LAN vendor.

Selecting a Peer Network

The main issue when selecting a peer network is compatibility and capability. Many peer-based LANs provide modules for linking peer networks to larger client/server networks and to WANs. If you are adding a peer LAN to another LAN such as NetWare, make sure the peer LAN is compatible with NetWare and the existing hardware. Always look for standard protocol support in the drivers of the interface cards; these can include support for the Server Message Block (SMB) protocol for interoperability with LAN Manager and UNIX servers, the UNIX-based Network File System (NFS), NetWare Core Protocol (NCP), or Novell's IPX transport protocol for interoperability with NetWare systems.[1] Some peer network products will work over any LAN adapter that runs with a compatible implementation of NetBIOS or any adapters shipped with the Network Driver Interface Specification (NDIS) developed by Microsoft and 3Com.

Look at the features and performance in relation to file and application sharing as well as the network's ability to redirect print jobs to a network printer, to queue and spool print jobs from servers, and to view the status of the print jobs.

Security

Probably the main concern is to protect the directories and the files on the server-station, where the CD-ROM applications software resides; most peer LAN products can provide this protection adequately. Many peer-based products provide good management tools that can detect disconnected adapters, warn of bad frames or packets, log errors, and track users.

Connecting to Other LAN Operating Systems

The ability to connect to other network operating systems is important. Some peer-based LANs use a separate gateway computer (not necessarily a dedicated machine) without the need for extra hardware or software on the client PCs. LANtastic and PowerLan, for example, provide an optional gateway to link to Macintosh computers running AppleTalk. LANtastic, PowerLan, Windows for Workgroups, and Personal NetWare have protocols to connect to Novell's NetWare servers.

Connecting to other network operating systems is achieved through a suite of protocols that are compatible with other products. For example, Windows for Workgroups, SilverNET-OS, and PowerLan use the SMB (Server Message Block) protocols over a NetBEUI (NetBIOS Extended User Interface)-based device driver to interact with IBM's LAN Server and Microsoft's LAN Manager.

Management Tools

Although management tools in most of the peer LANs are not sophisticated enough, compared to large and expensive network operating systems, some products such as LANtastic can produce reports showing such activities as which files users have opened, the number of files they have opened, the password to the directory and subdirectories of a hard disk, the amount of disk space they are using, and how users are organized into groups and then assigned specific rights to those groups. However, all of the peer-to-peer systems allow anyone sitting at the keyboard of a particular computer to have full access to all the files stored on that PC, regardless of the extent of that user's network rights. In a CD-ROM network, limiting physical access to the server-station is a sure solution for this problem.

Memory Management

The majority of the peer-based LANs allow the user to use third-party memory managers. However, InvisbleLAN and Windows for Workgroups have their own memory manager. The consumption of the conventional memory depends on the configuration of the PC, the MSCDEX, and the drivers for the network interface card.

Windows-Based Peer-to-Peer Network Operating Systems

Most of the DOS-based LANs have a Windows interface. Using Windows functionality in LANs is appealing because it allows access to network services through the easy-to-use graphical user interface (GUI) of Windows and menus. However, adding Windows functionality means adding Windows to each workstation or buying a network version with special site licensing, which can be expensive. Even so, most organizations will agree that the ease of use and flexibility of the Windows GUI more than compensates for the extra cost of adding Windows.

Windows makes networking an almost invisible, back-end function. For example, network administration, adapter configuration, user and resource setup, and access to network services all operate as Windows applications through extensions of such familiar Windows desktop metaphors as File Manager, Print Manager, and Control Panel. In all current releases of peer-to-peer network operating systems with Windows support, programs can still run as DOS guest applications through Windows, but they will not benefit from the services provided by Windows, such as cut and paste.

Most of the peer LAN products provide network setup programs written for Windows. The most powerful in this area is Microsoft Windows for Workgroups. A major advantage of using Windows is the capabilities of Dynamic Data Exchange (DDE), which comes with Windows and offers a powerful means of sharing information between applications. With this DDE capability, you can create a link between data objects that you can cut, copy, and paste inside Windows applications, no matter where those applications exist on the network. This is most appealing because it allows you to run two or more applications at the same time. For example, you can use a word-processing program to work on a document, search a CD-ROM database, highlight selected information, and download the highlighted information from the CD-ROM database directly to the document, using the cut, copy, and paste capabilities of Windows. With another click of a button, the document can be sent to the printer after editing or saved as a file. Windows-based peer-to-peer network operating systems (NOS) include the following:

> InvisibleLAN from Invisible Software
>
> LANtastic Network Operating System from Artisoft
>
> Personal NetWare from Novell
>
> SilverNET from Net-Source
>
> Windows for Workgroups from Microsoft

Requirements

To set up a peer-to-peer NOS, you need network adapters, connecting cables, sufficient memory, and possibly other peripheral devices such as printers. It is a good idea to buy the network hardware and NOS software from the same LAN vendor, if applicable. This will make installation easier and hardware compatibility less of a problem. Also, the device drivers will be compatible with the associated hardware. Another advantage is that the technical support will be easier. It is also recommended that you use a NOS that uses standard controller cards and cables rather than using proprietary hardware. Most of the vendors offer starter kits which include network controller cards and cables, enough for two machines, and the network operating system software. Some of the LANs in this group do not support remote booting ROM, which allows a workstation to boot remotely from a server machine. Below are important considerations for DOS-based peer LANs.

Minimum computer memory

For DOS-based peer LANs, PC computers with a minimum of 4 Mb of memory on workstations and 8 Mb on servers are recommended. For Windows-based peer LANs, PC computers with a minimum of 8 Mb of memory on workstations and 12 Mb on servers are recommended. Effective management and use of system memory is crucial in running networking software. If you are going to use a Windows operating environment, then managing and using the memory is more crucial.

Network adapter

Each LAN server and client workstation must be physically connected to the network. Use industry standard Ethernet adapter cards such as the Novell/Eagle Technology NE2000 and the Standard Microsystems/Western Digital WD8003/8013. Most likely, these cards will work without their default settings being changed. Always buy self-configured adapter cards rather than manual-configured cards.

CD-ROM controllers

Use SCSI-2 CD-ROM drives and a SCSI-2 controller interface.

Hard disk drives

In CD-ROM networks, it is highly recommended that you use a hard disk in all computers to accommodate the temporary files generated by most CD-ROM applications.

Other peripheral devices

Other devices are needed, such as a printer and a tape backup system, modems, and faxes. Uninterruptible power supply (UPS) is highly recommended. Most of the peer network operating systems support printing to local as well as remote printers. A printer is considered local if it is attached directly to a workstation, or remote if it is attached to a server or not directly attached to a workstation.

LAN administration

Every LAN requires installation, configuration, and occasional maintenance. Hard disk backup and archiving of all the installed software are important issues for network system administration.

Peer-to-Peer LAN Operating Systems

The following are some peer-to-peer LAN operating systems that support CD-ROM networking.

Complete Network/2-Node Package from Buffalo Products

Maximum number of nodes	255 nodes
Network interface cards	Standard NICs are used. Supports NE2000/WD8003/3Com Etherlink III controller cards.
Networks supported	ARCNET, Ethernet, Token Ring
Cable type	Twisted-pair or coaxial
Program interface	DOS 3.1 or later, Microsoft Windows 3.1
Network management interface	DOS 3.1 or later, Microsoft Windows 3.1
Number of shared printers	Unlimited
Pricing	$495 starter kit (two users)

Complete Network is easy to install and uses a peer-to-peer network. It includes all necessary hardware and software to network IBM-compatible PCs, and is expandable to 255 nodes. Complete Network includes the latest version of WEB network operating system software from WEBCORP. The WEB NOS features full DOS and Windows networking: DOS-to-DOS, Windows-to-Windows, and DOS-to-Windows. WEB is also NetWare-compatible and offers full IPX/SPX and application programming interface (API) support. WEB NOS can fully reside in high memory, thus maximizing system memory. Security options include hide, read only, and password protection, down to the file level. It provides complete file and device sharing. WEB supports CD-ROMs, uninterruptible power supplies (UPS), and tape backup units. Complete Network supports Intel EtherExpress 16 network interface cards. These industry-standard cards have no jumpers or dip switches. All additional hardware is included with Complete Network: thin Ethernet cable, connectors, terminators, and cable stripper (with five or more nodes). It includes e-mail and Windows interface. It provides unlimited, toll-free technical support.

Desk to Desk from CBIS

Maximum number of nodes	255 nodes
Network interface cards	Standard NICs are used. Supports NE2000/WD8003/3Com Etherlink III controller cards.
Networks supported	ARCNET, Ethernet, Token Ring
Cable type	Flat telephone wire, unshielded twisted-pair, or coaxial
Software requirements	23K RAM (client), 50K RAM (server, client/server), and 2 Mb hard disk space.
Program interface	DOS 3.1 or later, Microsoft Windows 3.1

Network management interface	DOS
Protocol stacks supported	ODI
Number of shared printers	Unlimited
Pricing	$129 for up to 255 users

Desk to Desk from CBIS supports CD-ROM sharing. It operates with standard networking hardware, so any hardware investment should be totally transferable. Like traditional peer-to-peer products, the software loads on each DOS or Windows PC participating in the network. With password-driven security, users can set up the network for all files to be shared, and limit access to sensitive files. The product also features authority levels for print management. Users with priority jobs can suspend others. Desk to Desk also can be used in bridged networks. To do this, users set up designated PCs as bridged servers. These machines need not be dedicated.

Users can set up Desk to Desk to allow or deny sharing between any or all of the connected PCs. For example, if users do not wish to share specific devices, they can set up the software to have these PCs function in Workstation mode. In this mode, the PCs can still use other drives, printers, and CD-ROMs. Users also can set up an unlimited number of passwords to protect information. Desk to Desk uses Microsoft's SMB, so you can connect to Microsoft Windows for Workgroups or Windows NT server from any client. It supports NetBIOS and IPXODI.[2]

InvisibleLAN from Invisible Software

Maximum number of nodes	255 nodes
Network interface cards	Standard or proprietary NICs are used. Supports NE2000/WD8003/3Com Etherlink III controller cards.
Networks supported	ARCNET, Ethernet, Token Ring
Cable type	Unshielded twisted-pair or coaxial
Software requirements	Software can load in expanded or extended memory. The software requires 45K to 90K RAM (server), 55K to 90K RAM (client), 65K to 110K RAM (client/ server), and 2.5 Mb hard disk space.
Network management interface	DOS 3.1 or later, Microsoft Windows 3.1
Protocol stacks supported	NDIS
Number of shared printers	Unlimited
Pricing	$499 starter kit (two users); $579 software only (five users); $399 ULTRA Server, dedicated server software

InvisbleLAN provides good performance as well as security in both DOS and Windows environments. Features include disk caching, hard disk sharing, CD-ROM sharing, printer sharing, and spooling. Other features include memory manager, security, audit trails, uninterruptible power supply (UPS) monitoring, and e-mail.

InvisibleLAN software is included when purchased in the InvisibleLAN Starter Kit. InvisibleLAN A1, adapter independent software, is $149 per node or $1,999 per network. InvisibleLAN A1 is compatible with NE1000, NE2000, NE/2, WD8003, WD8013, or compatibles plus any card with a network driver interface specification (NDIS) driver. InvisibleLAN supports NetBIOS network protocol and also provides NDIS drivers, so you can load the software needed to connect to other networks such as NetWare.

InvisibleLAN is designed for use over industry-standard coaxial cable and 10Base-T. It runs in nondedicated or dedicated modes with multiple servers. It includes menu-driven or command-line installation and initialization and online help, and it operates from both DOS and Windows.

Invisible Software also sells ULTRA Server, a 32-bit software that runs in protected mode for its InvisibleLAN peer-to-peer network. Users maintain peer access with each other's station resources but can share applications and storage faster if a 386 or 486 is dedicated as an ULTRA server. ULTRA is used in conjunction with InvisibleLAN's peer-to-peer software, providing the performance of a dedicated server with the printer and hard drive sharing of a peer-to-peer LAN. ULTRA supports up to 24 CD-ROM drives with no additional software required and a multitasking disk cache that allows users to access data simultaneously.

LANsmart Network Operating System/LS-300 from D-Link Systems

D-Link's LANsmart Network Operating System is a powerful peer-to-peer NOS that allows users to share printers, plotters, discs, files, and CD-ROMs. Local resources can be shared across the entire network. Hard disk drives and printers can be utilized from any workstation in a nondedicated mode. Furthermore, LANsmart NOS is NetBIOS-compatible with easy-to-use menu screens, virus detection, and file/password security. It is compatible with Windows and has online communication features, while supporting multiuser application software that requires the DOS 3.1 file/record locking system.

LANsmart supports ARCNET, Ethernet, Token Ring, and proprietary hardware. It uses IPX/SPX and NetBIOS. It supports 1,024 DOS or Windows users and a 1 Mb minimum of disk space. File, print, and messaging services are provided, and network-management software is available. LANsmart NOS can run concurrently with NetWare and other TCP/IP-based systems. LANsmart uses as little as 2K per workstation and 40K per server. The price is $395.

LANsmart for Novell/NV-100 from D-Link Systems

LANsmart for Novell is a peer-to-peer NetWare Enhancement Utility that allows users to share printers, disks, files, and CD-ROMs. Hard disk drives and printers can be utilized from any workstation. LANsmart for Novell enhances the NetWare network with easy-to-use menu screens and online communications features. It can run on as little as 2K of RAM. The price is $395.

LANstep from Hays Microcomputer Products

Maximum number of nodes	255 nodes
Network interface cards	Standard NICs are used. Supports NE2000/WD8003/3Com Etherlink III controller cards.
Networks supported	ARCNET, Ethernet, Token Ring
Cable type	Unshielded twisted-pair or coaxial
Software requirements	Software can load in extended memory. The software requires 50K conventional memory and 1.5 Mb extended memory (server, peer), 9K to 120K RAM (client), and 1 Mb hard disk space (server, peer), 20 Mb hard disk space (primary file server), 250K hard disk space (client).
Network management interface	DOS 3.3 or later, Microsoft Windows 3.1
Protocol stacks supported	NDIS
Number of shared printers	Unlimited
Pricing	$595—up to five concurrent users

Hays LANstep, one of the fastest file-transfer packages, has good security and management features. However, it requires large base memory to operate and 1.5 Mb of extended memory. While installing, you have to decide how much of the extended memory goes either to LANstep or Windows. User accounts and access rights are managed at a single location instead of from server to server. To users, access to networked resources is transparent. To allow access through Windows, you have to edit configuration files after the installation procedure. LANstep supports up to 255 simultaneously active users and 255 workstations and is architectured to support both peer-to-peer and dedicated server operations.

The software does protect network files stored on a node from users. It does not include Windows-based administration features, which requires users to go back to the DOS interface. Because it requires about 1.5 Mb of extended memory, incompatibility might occur when Windows is run in the enhanced mode, especially when the machine has only 4 Mb of memory.

LANtastic from Artisoft

Maximum number of nodes	Licensing can be up to 500 nodes
Network interface cards	Standard NICs or proprietary can be used. Supports NE2000/WD8003/3Com Etherlink III controller cards.

Networks supported	ARCNET, Ethernet, Token Ring
Cable type	Unshielded twisted-pair or coaxial
Software requirements	640K conventional memory and 3 Mb hard disk space (server, peer), 2 Mb hard disk space (client)
Network management interface	DOS 3.3 or later, Microsoft Windows 3.1
Protocol stacks supported	ODI, NDIS
Number of shared printers	Unlimited
Pricing	Six-user, DOS-only starter kit ($659), or DOS/Windows Ethernet starter kit: includes software, two NodeRunner Ethernet adapters, and cable ($759); $119 each additional node (software only)

LANtastic provides good security and easy-to-use DOS and Windows interfaces. It is ideal for medium-size and large organizations. LANtastic system can operate as a peer-to-peer or a dedicated server. It uses NetBIOS and supports DOS or Windows users. Through add-in drivers, it provides support for NetWare, TCP/IP networks, and Macintosh computers. File, print spooling, security tasks, e-mail, chat and messaging, group scheduling, and communications are provided. It supports the sharing of CD-ROM and WORM drives. Routing and backup services are available. Network management software is available for creating accounts, passwords, groups, and access-control lists. These lists help in assigning and changing access rights for individuals, groups, files, or subdirectories. It provides duration and time-of-day log-ins limitations and keeps track of network users or groups.

Enhanced administration features include remote accounts, global resources, and remote server management. LANtastic also offers hyperprinting, which streams print jobs to the printer before the application has finished building the entire job—a helpful feature for large printing jobs. The software includes disk-caching of multiple drives and resource-caching. Network management can be done from DOS as well as from Windows. It displays all active users on the network but does not detect disconnected adapters. LANtastic can reliably bring DOS, Macintosh, Microsoft LAN Manager, Microsoft Windows, and Novell's NetWare systems into the interoperability fold.

LAN Products from Artisoft include:

LANtastic A2Mbps starter kit

This starter kit provides the LANtastic 5.0 Network Operating System license, two A2Mbps proprietary adapters, a 15-foot cable, and manuals. It is designed to bring networking capabilities to small businesses and home offices such as printing, CD-ROMs, and program and file sharing. Prices start at $499.

Artisoft produces other versions of LANtastic that support Macintosh, Novell's NetWare, UNIX, and Microsoft Windows.

LANtastic for Macintosh

This product establishes a dedicated gateway PC between LANtastic and AppleTalk networks. Macintosh users can view PC servers through the logical drives from the gateway PC. The price is $599.

LANtastic for Windows 5.0

This LANtastic version for Windows lets users run LANtastic's NET and NET MANAGER programs (4.0 or higher) from within Microsoft Windows (3.0 or higher), using pull-down menus, icons, and online help. This utility supports Dynamic Data Exchange (DDE) so that Windows applications can use LANtastic e-mail to exchange messages and transfer data. LANtastic for Windows also has the capability of using Voice Chat, LAN Radio, and voice error messaging features (requires Artisoft Sounding Board). The network scrapbook feature allows users to share text, graphics, and sound items across the network. This feature can be used locally or shared with other LANtastic users. It is available as an upgrade to LANtastic DOS networks for $50.

LANtastic for NetWare 5.0

This product is installed on top of Novell NetWare version 2.2 or 3.11 networks and provides up to 500 users with peer-to-peer functionality while still maintaining their connection to the NetWare server. In addition to peripheral sharing, LANtastic for NetWare allows NetWare users to expand their network without purchasing expensive upgrades. It also acts as a valuable backup network that keeps operating when the NetWare server or network is down. LANtastic for NetWare runs on top of Novell's NetBIOS emulation and requires Novell's NetBIOS to operate. Its features include file and printer sharing (up to five printers per LANtastic server), CD-ROM networking, uninterruptible power supply (UPS) support, disk caching, full security (by user name, password, and access control lists), and audit trails.

This version supports ARCNET, Ethernet, and Token Ring and uses IPX and NetBIOS. The client workstation requires 13K of RAM plus Novell's NetBIOS. To operate as a server on a peer-to-peer LAN, a workstation needs 40K of RAM plus NetBIOS. The price is $499.

LANtastic Z 5.0

LANtastic Z is a two-station network that does not require PC slots for network adapters. Instead, the network is established through parallel or serial ports, or remotely with a modem. The kit includes an 18-foot parallel cable, a 25-foot serial cable, and a software license for both computers. LANtastic Z offers full network capabilities, including file and printer sharing, CD-ROM networking, e-mail, security (user name, password, access control lists, file-level security), and uninterruptible power supply (UPS) support. The network includes the LANcache disk-caching program and supports DOS file and record locking. The price is $125.

NDIS support kit for LANtastic

The NDIS support kit for LANtastic provides LANtastic users with interconnectivity to other operating systems by providing a network driver interface specification (NDIS) interface to the LANtastic NetBIOS. This utility allows LANtastic users to load or stack multiple protocols such as UNIX via Network File System (NFS), NetWare (using a separate IPX NDIS driver), and IBM mainframe environments. The support kit also allows adapters that come with NDIS drivers to be compatible with LANtastic/AI, the adapter independent version of the LANtastic Network Operating System. The price is $199.

Microsoft Windows for Workgroups, Version 3.11 from Microsoft

Maximum number of nodes	Unlimited
Network interface cards	Standard NICs are used. Supports NE2000/WD8003/3Com Etherlink III controller cards.
Networks supported	ARCNET, Ethernet, Token Ring
Cable type	Flat telephone wire, twisted-pair, coaxial
Software requirements	Software can load in extended memory. The software requires 3 Mb RAM (server, peer), 2 Mb RAM (client), 7 Mb hard disk space.
Network management interface	DOS 3.3 or later, Microsoft Windows 3.1
Protocol stacks supported	ODI, NDIS
Number of shared printers	Unlimited
Pricing	$219.95 complete package; $69 add-on for Microsoft Windows per node; $49.95 add-on for DOS

Microsoft Windows for Workgroups offers good performance, e-mail, a scheduling package, CD-ROM support, fax, and remote access. It has toll-free technical support and uses 386-based PCs or higher. Windows for Workgroups peer-to-peer NOS supports ARCNET, Ethernet, and Token Ring. It uses TCP/IP, DECnet, Named Pipes, NetBIOS, and NetBEUI. It supports DOS, Windows, Windows NT operating system, Windows NT Advanced Server, Microsoft LAN Manager, Novell NetWare, 3Com 3+Open, DEC Pathworks, and IBM LAN Server. File, print, messaging, communications, directory, imaging, and database services are provided, and network management software is available. It costs $99.95 as an upgrade from Windows 3.1, or $249.95 as an upgrade from MS-DOS.

Windows for Workgroups holds a potential connectivity advantage with LAN Manager and Microsoft Windows NT.

True Windows peer-to-peer networking software, such as Windows for Workgroups 3.1 and other fully Windows-compliant products, provides networking services through a graphical user interface (GUI). Through the GUI, network administration, adapter configuration, user and resource setup, and access to network services all operate as Windows applications through extensions of such familiar Windows desktop metaphors as File Manager, Print Manager, and Control Panel.

In Windows for Workgroups 3.1, for example, the Control Panel lets you specify and change configuration and setup for such functions as selection and configuration of network adapters, network types, and printers. You can also organize files and directories and access network drives through File Manager. Print Manager lets you execute network printing services, such as selecting printers and queues, and connecting to and disconnecting from printers. Other network services and applications, including e-mail and network management, are explicitly implemented as Windows applications by each peer-to-peer network vendor.

Network-OS/Plus from CBIS

Network-OS/Plus is a peer-to-peer LAN that supports up to 255 users. Network-OS/Plus is hardware-independent, supporting more than 50 network interface cards, including Micro Channel, ARCNET, Ethernet, token ring, bus, and interface adapters for portable computers. No dedicated file server is required. Features include CD-ROM sharing, Windows 3.1 support, Open Datalink Interface (ODI) support, modem sharing, PCcache hard disk cacher, Network Print Control, Data Security, E-mail Intercom, Advanced Network Monitoring, and Instructional Interactive Monitoring. The company offers a six-month limited warranty and free technical support via phone or an online bulletin board system. Prices are from $190 to $2,587.

PC/NOS Plus from Actrix Systems

PC/NOS Plus is a DOS-based peer-to-peer network that supports up to 64 DOS or Windows users. No dedicated server is necessary. Features include e-mail, messaging, CD-ROM networking, print spooling, and an automatic default setup that configures workstations to share a hard disk and printer (or user can customize configuration). The security supports resource level, user level, and file encryption. E-mail supports individual, group, and broadcast destinations. The installation program can run in English, Italian, Spanish, French, or German. The price is $195+.

Personal NetWare from Novell

Maximum number of nodes	240
Network interface cards	Standard NICs are used. Supports NE2000/WD8003/3Com Etherlink III controller cards.

Networks supported	ARCNET, Ethernet, Token Ring
Cable type	Flat telephone wire, twisted-pair, coaxial
Software requirements	Software can load in extended memory. The software requires 45K RAM (server), 137K RAM (peer), 92K RAM (client), 4.3 Mb hard disk space (server), 7.4 Mb hard disk space (peer, client).
Network management interface	DOS 3.3 or later, Microsoft Windows 3.1
Protocol stacks supported	ODI
Number of shared printers	Unlimited
Pricing	One user $99; five users $395; upgrade from Novell Lite $39.95 per user; upgrade from DR-DOS 6 to Novell DOS 7, $39.95 per user; Novell DOS 7 includes Personal NetWare

Personal NetWare, a replacement for Novell's NetWare Lite, makes it easy to add peer-to-peer capabilities to the server-based NetWare 2.x, 3.x, or 4.x network. During installation the software detects the presence of NetWare. Because it uses ODI, the software works with almost any Ethernet card. It can connect client PCs to any Personal NetWare or regular NetWare server. Network management is done through DOS or Windows from any workstation on the network. Personal NetWare also offers better support for laptops and other portables.

Print queues can be displayed and prioritized. Personal NetWare allows the administrator to gather information about user activities on the network. The software has disk-caching capability. However, it lacks e-mail and workgroup scheduling. It has toll-free technical support.

PowerLan from Performance Technology

Maximum number of nodes	255
Network interface cards	Standard NICs are used. Supports NE2000/WD8003/3Com Etherlink III controller cards.
Networks supported	ARCNET, Ethernet, Token Ring
Cable type	Flat telephone wire, twisted-pair, coaxial
Software requirements	640K RAM (server), 25K RAM (peer), 13K RAM (client), 2.2 Mb hard disk space (DOS server, DOS peer), 4.8 Mb hard disk space (Windows server, Windows peer), 1.7 Mb hard disk space (DOS client), 4.1 Mb hard disk space (Windows client)

Network management interface	DOS 3.1 or later, Microsoft Windows 3.1
Protocol stacks supported	ODI, NDIS
Number of shared printers	Unlimited
Pricing	$198 (two-user starter pack); $99 (single-user add-on); $395 (five-user pack); $750 (10-user add-on); $1,399 (20-user add-on)

PowerLan is ideal for medium-size and large organizations It fits in peer-to-peer and server-based networks. It includes PowerServe, a server program that makes it a client-server product. It supports 386-based PCs or better, and it is easy to install and use. It can connect DOS and Windows clients and has excellent integration with Windows NT. It has a good printer management and performance. An administrator can assign file-protection rights, set log-on time restrictions, and set account expiration dates. It has an e-mail package and toll-free technical support.

PowerLan supports ARCNET, Ethernet, Token Ring, and FDDI and uses NetBIOS and NetBEUI. It supports up to 255 DOS or Windows users, an unlimited number of files, and 4 Gb of disk space. File, print, and directory services are provided, and network-management software is available.

The PowerLan Windows interface provides users with implementation of graphical user interfaces for system operations. A system administrator's screen depicts users on the network graphically, which allows administrators to update member groups by dragging and dropping icons. The software allows a print queue to be linked to multiple printers and will print when any printer becomes available. The operating system displays a graphical map of the office to show users which printer the queue printed out on.

The Windows interface makes connecting to shared resources easy. PowerLan supports a broad variety of third-party hardware as well as boasting SMB (Server Message Block) compliance for interoperability with Windows for Workgroups and other products.

The package ships with NetBIOS drivers for many network cards, so hardware compatibility shouldn't be a problem. PowerLan's SMB compliance and use of NetBIOS should provide significant interoperability with Microsoft's networking offerings and IBM's LAN Server. It has the ability to share files between a DOS machine running PowerLan and a Windows for Workgroups machine.

The metaphor for attaching to shared resources is called "powerplugs." By dragging a plug icon from a drive letter or printer port to a network volume or print queue, users will be able to map drives and printers. This is much easier than any sort of command line-based drive mapping, as well as noticeably more convenient.

A similar graphical interface expedites administration. A screen shows which groups a user is in; dragging a group from the nonmember side of the display to the member side makes the user a member of that group.

With PowerLan, security can be regulated at the share level as well as by user. This allows for interoperability with Windows for Workgroups while providing solid security.

Multiple print queues can access the same printer in different modes—for example, one queue for legal and one for letter—eliminating the need for users to know how to choose a paper tray in software, or the need for one queue for CD-ROM databases and one for word processing and spreadsheets. Also, a queue can be connected to multiple printers, and a job will print to whichever printer is available first.

SilverNET-OS from Net-Source

Maximum number of nodes	254
Network interface cards	Standard NICs are used. Supports NE2000/WD8003/3Com Etherlink III controller cards.
Networks supported	ARCNET, Ethernet, Token Ring, LocalTalk
Cable type	Twisted-pair or coaxial
Software requirements	38K RAM (server, peer), 20K RAM (client), 200K hard disk space
Network management interface	DOS 3.3 or later, Microsoft Windows 3.1
Number of shared printers	Unlimited
Pricing	$99 single-user; $1,999 up to 254 users

SilverNET-OS is a DOS-based peer-to-peer networking system that features disk caching, e-mail, messaging, interactive chat, audit trailing, configuration of all network resources, simultaneous access to 16 network printers per workstation, and remote browsing to view all network resources. Servers can optionally be installed in dedicated mode, which boosts LAN throughput. Connecting to a shareable device is easier, because available servers appear in a list, along with their shareable drives and printers. When a server that has gone down comes back online, SilverNET reestablishes connections with that server.

SilverNET is easy to install and use. Its print spool works smoothly. It has toll-free technical support. It supports 254 DOS, Windows, or Windows NT users. It has file, print, messaging, communications, and directory services. It also supports 3Com 3C503, Intel, and Zircom pocket adapters. SilverNET-OS is a full-featured peer-to-peer NOS that utilizes the interoperable IBM SMB protocol. It is compatible with UNIX, XENIX, IBM PC LAN, OS/2 Manager, Novell/386 3.11, Windows for Workgroups, and many mainframes.

Simply LANtastic from Artisoft

Maximum number of nodes	30 per server
Network interface cards	Standard NICs or proprietary can be used. Supports NE2000/WD8003/3Com Etherlink III controller cards.

Networks supported	ARCNET, Ethernet, Token Ring
Cable type	Twisted-pair, coaxial
Software requirements	640K RAM, 3 Mb hard disk space
Network management interface	DOS 3.1 or later, Microsoft Windows 3.1
Protocol stacks supported	NDIS
Number of shared printers	Unlimited
Pricing	$299 starter kit (for two nodes); $79 each additional node

Simply LANtastic is a scaled-down version of LANtastic and is designed for small offices as an entry-level operating system, or for those who want to build a small LAN, then grow in the future through the use of the LANtastic network operating system from the same company. Installation is very easy. It features e-mail and DOS and Windows menus. In addition, it allows the sharing of hard disks, CD-ROM drives, and printers. Its proprietary NICs are compatible with both standard Artisoft NodeRunner cards and Ethernet cable. Its security is limited to password protection and full, read-only, or no-access privileges to resources. Because Simply LANtastic uses the NetBIOS protocol, you can access volumes and drives on a NetWare network simply by going through a LANtastic server.

Notes

1. The Server Message Block (SMB) is a distributed file system network protocol, developed by Microsoft and adopted by many other vendors, that allows a computer to use the files and other resources of another computer as though they were local. For network transfers, SMBs are encapsulated within the NetBIOS network control block packet. The Server Message Block is a formatted message used to request and reply to requests for file and print services in network systems.

   NCP (NetWare Core Protocol) is NetWare's format for requesting and replying to requests for file and print services.

2. IPXODI (Internetwork Packet eXchange Open Datalink Interface). In recent versions of Novell NetWare, the requirement to generate a unique DOS client protocol file (IPX.COM) for each workstation has been replaced by three new components: the link-support layer (LSL), the multiple-layer interface driver (MLID) or network interface card device driver, and the Open Datalink Interface (ODI) version of the IPX (Internetwork Packet eXchange).

   This approach has two major benefits: the ability to bind two different protocols to a single network interface card, and the ability to load and unload individual drivers as required. In earlier NetWare versions, the only way to remove the IPX driver was to reboot the workstation.

CHAPTER 5

Sharing CD-ROM Drives on Novell NetWare Networks

Since Novell NetWare is the most widely used network operating system, CD-ROM network developers have introduced two important approaches to sharing CD-ROM drives in Novell NetWare Networks: the NetWare Loadable Module (NLM) solution and the DOS-based solutions. If you are running NetWare with a version less than 4.x, you could upgrade your file server to NetWare 4.x, which has CD-ROM support. If you prefer to stay with the version you are using, and you're running NetWare 3.11 or earlier, these versions don't have built-in support for CD-ROMs, but you can add third-party hardware/software combinations to your server to share CD-ROMs.

Novell NetWare 2.x, 3.x, and 4.x

There are many versions of NetWare including NetWare 2.x, 3.x, and 4.x ("x" stands for any version). Major companies that provide CD-ROM–sharing operating systems include Meridian, Corel Systems, CBIS, Micro Design International, and Online Computer Systems. They designed their products to work in the NetWare 3.x platform. Novell added CD-ROM–sharing capabilities to NetWare as of NetWare 3.12.

NetWare 2.x network series of operating systems all use a technique called the value-added process (VAP) to add services such as CD-ROM sharing to a NetWare 2.x file server. For example, CBIS does market a CD-ROM VAP through IBM, but it is limited to use with Micro Channel computers. You can set up a separate CD-ROM server using the CBIS CD Connection software, which supports 100 users—suggested retail price is $1,395. CD-View from Ornetix Network Products supports NetWare 2.x, SCSI Express for Novell NetWare 286, and Ornetix Technologies' SerView; all support Novell's NetWare 2.x.

Building a CD-ROM network using NetWare 2.x is not recommended since most CD-ROM vendors are supporting NetWare 3.x series and above. If additional power, capacity, and support are required, or if a server needs to support more than 20 users, it is highly recommended that you consider upgrading to the NetWare 3.11 platform in order to be able to use more products from these vendors.

NetWare 3.x server-based NOS supports ARCNET, Ethernet, Token Ring, FDDI, and LocalTalk, and uses TCP/IP, IPX/SPX, NetBIOS, AFP (AppleTalk Filing Application), and OSI. It supports 1,000 DOS, OS/2, Windows, Macintosh, or UNIX users. Print, messaging, communications, database, routing, and backup services are provided, and network-management software is available.

NetWare 3.11 is a full-featured, 32-bit NOS that supports all key desktop operating systems—DOS, Microsoft Windows, OS/2, UNIX, and Macintosh—as well as the IBM Systems Application Architecture (SAA) environment. NetWare 3.11 provides a high-performance integration platform for businesses that need a sophisticated, enterprise-wide network computing solution in a multivendor environment. It offers centralized network management and is available in various user configurations, enabling you to standardize on a high-performance networking solution regardless of the size of your organization.

NetWare 4.0 is Novell's most advanced NOS. This server-based network operating system has revolutionized network computing by turning a multi-server network environment into a single integrated system. It supports ARCNET, Ethernet, Token Ring, FDDI, and LocalTalk, and uses TCP/IP, IPX/SPX, NetBIOS, AFP, and OSI. It supports 1,000 DOS, OS/2, Windows, Macintosh, or UNIX users. File, print, messaging, communications, directory, imaging, database, routing, backup services, and network-management software are provided.

NetWare Loadable Module (NLM) Solutions

NetWare Loadable Module (NLM) solutions allow CD-ROM drives to run on Novell NetWare networks without the need to run the Microsoft DOS Extensions (MSCDEX). The NLM allows CD-ROM drives to be attached directly to a dedicated file server (the machine becomes a file server and CD-ROM server) or a dedicated CD-ROM server (the machine will handle CD-ROM services only).

NLMs are programs that can be added or subtracted from the Novell NetWare, operating without downing the file server. NetWare 386 (which works on 386 computers and higher) has an expandable architecture that allows additional software modules to be added to the network, even while the network server is running. In general, NetWare NLMs come in four fundamental varieties, and, consequently, four different file extensions: disk drivers (.DSK), network drivers (.LAN), name space modifiers (.NAM), and management utilities (.NLM). NetWare stores these modules in the SYS:\SYSTEM directory of the server. Third-party products which supply additional NLMs for special purposes are allowed on Novell's NetWare networks. This allows such applications as CD-ROM drivers and utilities to become a part of the network operating system. Even Novell has added its own CD-ROM NLM to its NetWare, starting with version 3.12. Novell netware includes a loadable module, CDROM.NLM, which lets you load CD-ROM drives as network disc volumes without any need for workstations to load terminate-and-stay residents (TSRs) or MSCDEX. The NLM lets you list available CD-ROM devices (in groups of 10 at a time) by device and drive numbers, mount drives by device number and volume name, change the disc within a mounted drive, and view the contents of the volume's root directory. Novell recommends you devote 1.2 Mb of cache for each drive you intend to network. The file-server software makes a CD-ROM drive appear as another hard drive to the user. The network administrator usually keeps the drive letters in sequence. The drive letters can be any letters from D to Z.

Because the NLM's modules are mounted on the file server and the CD-ROM drives are installed on the same file server, the cost seems to be lower. Also, the response time is faster than that of peer-to-peer networks. If other applications are handled by the file server, the network response time may be affected because the file server must handle the CD-ROM drives as well as other volumes on the file server. This situation might be solved by having two NetWare servers: a file server and a CD-ROM server. The NetWare CD-ROM NLM is an appropriate solution only if the number of concurrent users is low. If you expect many users to access the Novell-mounted CD-ROM drives simultaneously, you may find the I/O traffic deteriorates your server performance— or, worse, hang the server. The products that can be used to create CD-ROM servers on Novell NetWare networks include Meridian Data's CD Net and CBIS' CD Connection. Lotus Development's Lotus CD/Networker (a software solution for NetBIOS, Banyan's VINES, or NetWare IPX/SPX) will install only on a dedicated CD-ROM server. In addition to improving the throughput, these solutions have full integration with NetWare security features and have extensive means of configuring and accessing CD-ROM resources on a network.

CD-ROM NLM Products

There are many CD-ROM NLM products that allow CD-ROM drives to be shared across a Novell NetWare network. During installation, most CD-ROM NLM products ask for a network volume name to assign a CD-ROM drive. The program usually has a special metering utility that controls access to the CD-ROM. Also, the number of simultaneous users can be limited during installation. After installation, use NetWare's SYSCON to create a shared account name such as CDUSER and grant explicit rights to the CD directory.

CD-ROM application programs are installed on the file server. The following screen is an example of a batch file (SPIRS.BAT) that you can use to log in to the CD-ROM server (CDSERVER) and run a program called SPIRS.EXE.

```
REM FILENAME: SPIRS.BAT
@ECHO OFF
CLS
REM Start by attaching to the server and the account
ATTACH CDSERVER\CDUSER
REM the following line will map drive R: to volume CDVOL
REM on a server named CDSERVER. Always use a temporary
REM drive map to avoid conflicts with other batch files
REM that may have to use the same drive letter
MAP R:=CDSERVER:CDVOL:
REM Locate an application named SPIRS.EXE on volume R:
REM and launch the program
R:
R:CD\
R:SPIRS.EXE
REM Don't forget to Logoff upon termination of the
REM CD-ROM SPIRS.EXE application
LOGOUT CDSERVER
```

Remember, you don't need to copy the file to everyone's local hard disk. However, the SPIRS.BAT file will be located in the Sys:Public directory. Because this directory is mapped as a search drive by default, you can launch the batch file from any workstation.

Programs running under Windows require a different approach. First, you have to grant access to the CD-ROM in the users' log-in scripts. Create a group name from SYSCON and add the appropriate members to the group. Grant them Read and File Scan rights. Then, from SYSCON, select Supervisor Options and Login Script, then add the following line, which will allow users to access the CD-ROM drives through drive R: each time they log in: IF MEMBER OF "CD-ACCESS" MAP R:=CDSERVER\CDVOL:

Unless you have created a system to perform network-wide updates, you must do the following in every workstation in the network. At each workstation, run Windows and create a program group (if it has not been already created) in order to add the new CD-ROM application as follows: Select File, New, Browse. From the Drive, select R: (the directory mapping you added in the log-in script), and switch to the directory where the Windows application is located. Select the program's filename, click on OK, enter a title for the program icon, and click on OK again. That workstation now has access to the Windows application.

CD Net for NetWare 4.4 from Meridian Data

Workstation O/S supported	DOS, Windows, OS/2, Macintosh System 7
Number of CD-ROM drives supported	128 CD-ROM drives

Number of simultaneous users supported	150 simultaneous users
Number of CD servers supported	29 CD servers per network
Dedicated server	Yes
Workstation software type	Proprietary CD extensions, 12K
Minimum workstation RAM	28K
Software unloadable from memory if not needed	Yes
Caching	Provides CD server and workstation caching
Security	Provides internal security, in addition to the native network operating system security
CD drives supported	Hitachi, LMSI, Panasonic, Sony, Toshiba
Jukeboxes and changers supported	Pioneer
Warranty	one-year guarantee
Technical support	one-year free technical support
Pricing	$3,595 (single-drive system, up to 28 drives available)

CD Net can multitask several DOS or Windows CD-ROM applications, each using the same drive letter for the CD-ROM. This allows you to conserve drive letters and maintain consistent drive mappings, in contrast to MSCDEX. CD Net 4.4 for NetWare, from Meridian Data, is an NLM for NetWare 3.x and 4.x servers that lets you configure up to 28 CD-ROM drives per server as either DOS drives or NetWare volumes. Workstations can use any of the networked discs to which the network administrator has permitted access.

CD Net products do not require users to load MSCDEX on their workstations; Meridian provides its own redirector. CD Net for NetWare CD-ROM drives are password-protected. The ability to unlock the drives requires administrator-level access to the NetWare file-server console. All CD Net products for DOS and NetWare can limit user access through a standard concurrent-use licensing scheme.

CD Net allows CD-ROM-based information to be shared across a multiuser environment by integrating CD-ROM drives into a standard LAN. It caches frequently used data and transfers information out of RAM to lower retrieval times. Data caching is extendable to 16 Mb.

In addition to the NLM version, Meridian's software is available in a NetBIOS version for NetWare (not running IPX), 3Com 3+Open, Microsoft's LAN Manager, Ungermann-Bass, AT&T's StarLAN, Banyan's VINES, and IBM's LAN Server. Network topologies can be Ethernet, Token Ring, or ARCNET; drives may be run from a separate CD-ROM server using Meridian CD Net towers.

Meridian has also produced CD Net for Windows. It requires 256K RAM and 1 Mb hard disk space. Its price is $495. If you are running CD Net from Windows, one feature worth mentioning is the software's ability to transparently map several CD-ROM applications, one at a time, to a single local drive letter and make the change as you go from window to window.

Visual CD is a support product from Meridian that helps users install, manage, and use CD-ROMs. Visual CD automatically scans a CD-ROM inserted into the PC and prompts the user on how to install the CD-ROM. The software also automatically adds new CD-ROM titles to a library and provides the tools for examining each CD-ROM's contents, such as audio, video, or graphics files. The price is $69.95.

CD/Networker from Lotus Development

Network O/S supported	NetWare, Banyan's VINES, Microsoft's LAN Manager, and IBM's LAN Server
Pricing	$995 per server

CD/Networker enables users to set up CD-ROM servers. It is easy to install and offers support for a number of network operating systems. Among the network operating systems that CD/Networker runs on arc NetWare, Banyan's VINES, Microsoft's LAN Manager, and IBM's LAN Server. CD/Networker can support up to 28 drives, and a network can have an unlimited number of CD/Networker servers. The licensing utility accompanying the program can be used to alter the number of simultaneous users permitted to access each CD-ROM disc as decided by the license of each CD-ROM publisher.

At each CD/Networker server you can use the management console to view the CD-ROMs installed on the drives attached to the server. You can assign each CD-ROM disc an alias name that network users use to attach to the disc. At each user workstation you can run a Lotus terminate-and-stay-resident program to enable users to use either DOS or Windows as a front end for attaching to the CD/Networker servers on the network.

CD Connection from CBIS

Network O/S supported	NetWare, CBIS' own Network-OS Plus, and most NetBIOS LANs, LAN Manager, LAN Server, NT Advanced Server, Windows for Workgroups, VINES, LANtastic, Desk to Desk
Workstation O/S supported	DOS, Windows, Windows NT, OS/2
Number of CD-ROM drives supported	21 CD-ROM drives per server
Number of simultaneous users supported	Supports up to 250 simultaneous users
Dedicated server	Yes

Workstation software type	Redirector (22K) can run in high memory
Software unloadable from memory if not needed	Yes
Caching	Provides CD server cache; workstation software provides caching
Security	Provides internal security, in addition to the native network operating system security
CD drives supported	Any SCSI CD-ROM drive
Jukeboxes and changers supported	Pioneer
Warranty	Six-month limited warranty
Technical support	Unlimited technical support
Pricing	For 5 users on Novell, Banyan, or NetBIOS is listed for $395. For 50 users on Novell, Banyan, or NetBIOS is listed for $995. For 100 users on Novell, Banyan, or NetBIOS is listed for $1,395. For 250 users on NetBIOS is listed for $1,695.

CD Connection works as a redirector and supports most networks, including NetWare, CBIS' Network-OS Plus, Banyan's VINES, MS-Net, PC LAN, and other NetBIOS-compatible LANs. It can be used in conjunction with existing hardware, or with CBIS' line of CD servers and add-on PC Conversion Towers. CD Connection takes advantage of cooperative multitasking, advanced caching algorithms, and other technologies. CD Connection software allows users to access multiple CD-ROM drives simultaneously over a LAN. With CD Connection, a CD-ROM disc is as accessible as a regular disk drive to all networked stations. When used in conjunction with the CBIS CD Server, CD Connection offers users simultaneous access to as many as 28 CD-ROM drives. It does not require MSCDEX unless an application does not work without it.

It is installed on top of the existing LAN. It requires a dedicated server with a minimum configuration of 80286, 2 Mb memory. It can support up to 240 dedicated servers and 250 users depending on network layer user support. It supports High Sierra and ISO 9660 formatted CD-ROMs.

It includes an automatic CD-ROM configuration program, a CD data accelerator program that allows caching in extended or expanded memory, and a SCSI host adapter driver. These three components are installed on the dedicated CD-ROM server. It makes each CD-ROM drive appear as a logical drive on the network. This drive does not need to be mapped into the network; instead, each drive is controlled through the same MS-DOS commands that typically access a LAN peripheral.

CD Connection uses its own redirector instead of MSCDEX. CD Connection and drive-mounting utilities load from the workstation. These utilities take up about 22K of RAM per workstation on NetWare networks. The configuration is done through a menu that prompts the administrator to input the number of users, assign letters to CD-ROM drives, and access expanded or extended memory. A minimum of 2 Mb of RAM on the file server is recommended for caching. The CD-ROM network system status can be checked from the server. The system relies on the network security features.

CD Connection can be used with any file server or with CBIS' CD Server. It needs cabling, interface cards, and CD-ROM drives. The company offers on-site installation and training classes. CBIS sells also a version of its CD Connection networking software that uses Banyan's VINES ($695 for 10 users). As many as 99 users on a VINES network can have simultaneous access to up to 28 CD-ROM drives in a single CD server system.

CorelSCSI! Network Manager 1.2 and SCSI Pro! from Corel Systems

Network O/S supported	Novell's NetWare
Workstation O/S supported	DOS, Windows, Macintosh
Number of CD-ROM drives supported	Supports 32 drives per server
Number of simultaneous users supported	Depends on Novell license
Number of CD servers supported	Unlimited
Server software	Loads its own NLM on a NetWare Server. The NLM is used to mount and unmount the volumes, set the amount of dedicated CD-ROM cache, and determine the size of the workspace buffer.
Server RAM required for drivers and/or NLM	Requires 91K (150K for each mounted CD)
Dedicated server	No dedicated server required
Workstation software type	A redirector (12K) can be loaded in EMS. A proprietary CD extensions CorelCDX (3K with EMS or 37K without EMS). Microsoft CD-ROM Extensions (MSCDEX) (32K) can run in high memory.
Minimum workstation RAM	1 Mb
Software unloadable from memory if not needed	Yes
Caching	Provides CD server cache. Workstation software provides caching.
Security	Provides internal security

CD drives supported	CMD Technology, Chinon, Hitachi, IBM, JVC, LMSI, NEC, Panasonic, Pioneer, Smart & Friendly, Sony, Texel, Toshiba
Jukeboxes and changers supported	DEC, HP, ISI, K&S, Kodak, LMSI, Magstore, MaxOptix, Panasonic, Pioneer, Plasmon, Reflection Systems, Ricoh, Sony
Warranty	30-day money-back guarantee
Technical support	Unlimited technical support
Pricing	$99, CorelSCSI Pro! $495, registered users of CorelSCSI! 1.1 can upgrade to CorelSCSI Pro! for $199

CorelSCSI! is a comprehensive DOS, OS/2, Windows, and Novell NetWare driver package. CorelSCSI Pro! has all the functionality of CorelSCSI!, plus the ability to use CD-Rs and scanners. CorelSCSI! Network Manager can connect CD-ROM and jukebox drives, as well as WORM, and rewritable drives to a NetWare file server. CorelSCSI! 1.2 supports LAN Manager, LAN Server, and NetWare 3.x and 4.x. The SCSI network-management software is equipped with Corel's CD-ROM server software, which allows users to create an index file for each CD-ROM and define a portion of the NetWare Loadable Module for caching (from no cache to full CD-ROM capacity), which can significantly reduce the access time of the CD-ROM drive.

CorelSCSI Pro!, on the other hand, connects SCSI devices to microcomputers and servers. The setup routine identifies devices and provides for drivers for host adapters and CD-ROM readers.

CorelSCSI Pro! provides sophisticated drivers and system management tools for connecting almost any type of SCSI device to both standalone PCs and network servers. It works with ASPI (Advanced SCSI Programming Interface)–based host adapters and can be used with DOS, Windows, OS/2, and NetWare.

CorelSCSI Pro! comes in two parts: a NetWare Loadable Module (NLM) part installs on a server, and a Terminate and Stay Resident (TSR) part installs on DOS or Windows workstations. CorelSCSI Pro! mounts CD-ROMs as drives, not volumes. It creates its own device type, called a database, which represents one or more CD-ROMs on the file server.

The NLM installation copies files into the System directory on the file server and modifies the AUTOEXEC.NCF file. You then must load these NLMs: Btrieve, Nut, Clib, and Streams. You must also load CorelSCSI Pro!'s own device driver, UNIV. Then, you need to load CDSVR NLM, the CD-ROM utility. CDSVR NLM manages the CD-ROMs connected to the file server, creates and uses the databases, utilizes the caches for better performance, and scans your system for SCSI devices.

CorelSCSI Pro! also makes management easy by providing some useful functions. For example, by using the utility that manages the database information, you can attach a workstation to a CD-ROM device and mount or dismount the CD. This utility also lets you access user information and scan the SCSI bus to check for any potential problems.

Another CorelSCSI Pro! utility, CDCON implements security by letting you assign access rights to the server by user or by group. The software obtains a list of names from users currently registered on the network. CorelSCSI Pro! also has a utility that locks the drive in place to keep someone from ejecting a CD that someone else is still using.

On the workstation side, these utilities provide options that let you load device drivers into Expanded Memory Specification (EMS), enter the number of cache buffers, and map the database.

DiscPort from Microtest

Network O/S supported	NetWare
Workstation O/S supported	DOS, Windows, OS/2, Macintosh System 7
Number of CD-ROM drives supported	Unlimited
Number of simultaneous users supported	Unlimited
Server RAM required for drivers and/or NLM	300K
Dedicated server	No
Workstation software type	Redirector (20K) can be loaded in high memory
Minimum workstation RAM	4 Mb
Software unloadable from memory if not needed	Yes
Caching	Provides CD server cache
Security	Provides internal security, in addition to the native network operating system security
Jukeboxes and changers supported	Pioneer
CD drives supported	Apple, DEC, MDI, Panasonic, Plextor, Texel. (Ask vendor about incompatibility problems for the following models: Chinon, Hitachi, NEC, Sony, Todd Enterprises, and Toshiba, as they are not compatible)
Warranty	Three months with 30-day money-back guarantee
Technical support	Unlimited free technical support
Pricing	$795 for Ethernet; $995 for Token Ring

Microtest's DiscPort is a combination of DOS and Windows software and a small black box that you plug directly into your LAN at any point in your network. DiscPort is a good, easy-to-use, and secure product. It is a network SCSI port device that supports up to seven daisy-chained SCSI-2 CD-ROM drives. For NetWare 3.x and 4.x users, DiscPort accesses CD-ROM drives as if they were hard drives on a NetWare file server. DiscPort is a device (4″ × 7½″ × 1⅛″) with 10BaseT and thin Ethernet connections and a SCSI port for linking CD-ROM drives. For more drives, you can connect multiple DiscPorts to the LAN. DiscPort has a SCSI connector on one end and Ethernet BNC and RJ-45 connectors on the other.

All NetWare features are available through DiscPort, including caching, drive mapping, and security. The security feature allows departments or workgroups to control access to their particular titles.

Included with DiscPort is a Windows-based software application called DiscView that lets the LAN administrator mount or unmount drives and perform other administrative tasks. Users can drag and drop icons to map network drives to CD-ROM volumes, and Discview will retain information on an individual user's last session. Because of DiscPort's integration with NetWare, this solution needs no redirector or TSR loaded on the workstation.

Up to 10 DiscPort units can be attached to any one file server running Novell NetWare 3.11 and higher. Access to CD-ROM drives is accomplished by loading an NLM module on the file server. The size of the NLM is about 150K. DiscView is the software that handles the installation of the NLM module and the management of the CD-ROM drives. DiscView can run in DOS as well as in the Windows environment. Thin Ethernet or 10Base-T cable can be attached to one side of the DiscPort. On the other side of the DiscPort, there is a standard SCSI port connector that is attached to the CD-ROM drives through a SCSI cable.

DiscPort offers a graphical interface, good documentation, and an installation utility. The installation utility walks you through the task of adding DiscPort to your LAN, including loading DiscPort's NLM without having to down your server.

Users see an icon for each CD in the library, and DiscPort keeps track of all CDs that have been mounted on the drives. To select a volume, the CD manager simply drags its icon to an unmapped drive at the top of the window. The manager can also set up an optional batch file so that an application automatically runs when users select a particular CD.

DiscServ and DiscShare from Microtest

Both DiscView and DiscShare enable administrators to configure server-attached and workstation-attached CD-ROM drives, respectively, as NetWare volumes. This gives the administrator the tools to make any CD-ROM drive on the network available to network users.

DiscShare is composed of an NLM and a terminate-and-stay resident (TSR) program that makes internal workstation CD-ROM drives available to the network as NetWare volumes. It supports up to 28 CD-ROM drives per server.

Three products—DiscServ, DiscShare, and DiscPort—ship with an administrative utility called DiscView, which is a Windows-based utility that provides a graphical presentation of CD-ROM drives and servers. DiscView is priced at $795, and DiscShare is priced at $495.

OPTI-NET NLM from Online Computer Systems

Network O/S supported	NetWare
Workstation O/S supported	DOS, Windows
Number of CD-ROM drives supported	Supports 255 drives
Number of simultaneous users supported	100
Number of CD servers supported	One at a time
Server RAM required for drivers and/or NLM	1 Mb
Dedicated server	No
Workstation software type	MSCDEX (25K), loadable in high memory
Minimum workstation RAM	7K
Software unloadable from memory if not needed	Yes
Caching	Provides CD server caching, and the client software provides workstation caching
Security	Provides internal security, in addition to the native network operating system security
CD drives supported	All SCSI CD drives
Jukeboxes and changers supported	NSM, Pioneer
Warranty	30-day money-back guarantee
Technical support	One-year technical support
Pricing	$795 (8-workstation license), $1,495 (100-workstation license)

Online Computer Systems' family of CD-ROM networking software includes products that will work with Novell and NetBIOS compatible networks to make CD-ROM drives simultaneously accessible to multiple users.

While OPTI-NET NLM allows you to add CD-ROM drives directly onto NetWare 3.x and 4.x file servers and run OPTI-NET as an NLM, OPTI-NET VAP (value added product) works with NetWare 2.x servers. Features include extended memory (XMS) caching at the user workstation and the CD-ROM server. The 100-user license for the NLM version costs $1,495, while a 100-user VAP version costs $1,795.

A nice feature of OPTI-NET is that although it requires you to load device drivers and MSCDEX onto each client workstation, users can remove them from memory when they are no longer needed without rebooting the system.

Because OPTI-NET can address CD-ROM drives by Logical Unit Numbers (LUNs), each of seven SCSI devices connected to the board can in turn support seven additional drives. In other words, a server hosting one CD-ROM SCSI adapter under the LUN system could accommodate a maximum of 56 CD-ROM drives per adapter.

OPTI-NET NLM requires no extra hardware for installation and once in place enables users to access a networked CD-ROM drive as easily as they would access local drives. OPTI-NET NLM includes several features designed to improve overall performance, such as XMS caching of CD-ROM data at the client server to increase speed and decrease network traffic.

SCSI Express from Micro Design International

Network O/S supported	NetWare, LAN Manager, LAN Server, Windows for Workgroups, LANtastic
Workstation O/S supported	DOS, Windows, OS/2, SCO UNIX
Number of CD-ROM drives supported	Supports 63 drives per server
Number of simultaneous users supported	Unlimited
Number of CD servers supported	Unlimited
Server RAM required for drivers and/or NLM	800K
Dedicated server	No
Caching	Caching available through NetWare OS for the server
Security	Security available through the native network operating system
CD drives supported	Micro Design, Toshiba, Hitachi, LMSL, NEC, Panasonic, Pioneer, Sony
Jukeboxes and changers supported	Pioneer
Warranty	One year with 30-day money-back guarantee
Technical support	One-year technical support
Pricing	$795 with one MIDI laserBank drive $1,295 with other vendors' hardware $1,295 for a 20-user license $1,895 for a 250-user license

SCSI express software is a package of device drivers that supports many network systems including MS-DOS, Macintosh, AT&T's UNIX, DOS, Interactive's UNIX, Novell 286 and 386, OS/2, SCO's XENIX, and SCO's UNIX systems. For each operating environment, the software can support eight device types. These are CD-ROMs, WORMs (Write Once, Read Many), rewritable optical drives, multifunction drives, jukeboxes, hard disks, removable hard disks, and DAT (Digital Audio Tape) backups. The distribution disc of SCSI Express includes the software required to support all eight device types. A unique feature of Micro Design software is that all supported devices can coexist on the same SCSI host adapter—i.e., only one host adapter is required for multiple devices and device types. Because SCSI Express is mounted on Novell NetWare 386's file server, it uses NetWare 3.x's caching and offers fast access to data. It eliminates the use of a redirector to access CD-ROM drives. Each CD-ROM drive connected to a NetWare file server becomes a mounted volume like any other disk drive on the network. This approach increases access speeds, especially when a group of users are using the same volume at the same time.

SCSI Express for Novell NetWare 386 provides transparent support for CD-ROM. The software is loaded directly onto Novell's NetWare file server. None of the workstations need to run any software locally. The CD-ROM drive will appear to Novell as a NetWare volume. This volume can do anything that can be done with a regular hard disk, except write to it. It can handle many types of CD-ROM application software without using MSCDEX. It also enables the Macintosh, PCs, and dumb terminals to access the CD-ROM stack.

SCSI Express is installed with NLMs. You load the NLMs you need based on your particular system and devices. CD-ROM drives are connected directly to the file server. With direct connection to the file server, workstations no longer need a special CD-ROM redirector or TSR software to access a CD, thus saving valuable RAM. SCSI Express also eliminates the need for additional programs loaded at the workstation. Performance can be improved by adding more caching capabilities. The 16K read-ahead buffer size of SCSI Express also contributes to its fast access.

Other SCSI products from Micro Design include SCSI Express for UNIX; SCSI Express for DOS: DOS CD-ROM Interface; and SCSI Express OS/2 CD-ROM Interface.

SCSI Express for Novell NetWare 286 is another product that installs as a regular Value-Added Device Driver (VADD), using NetWare 2.x. The VADD links with the NetWare operating system during the generation process.

NetWare Peer-to-Peer Access

Even if you have a massive NetWare network, there are times when you might like to provide access to a peer-based CD-ROM network. Bridging the gap between NetWare and peer LANs and bringing peer-to-peer file services, including CD-ROM services, to the NetWare environment can be done through many products, such as AHAccelerator CD/NLM, CD-View, Map Assist, and SerView. Windows for Workgroups, LANsmart, and LANtastic, which were discussed in the previous chapter, can be used with NetWare, but these solutions really end up creating two logical networks that share the same workstations and cabling system, and each need different administration tools.

AHAccelerator CD/NLM from Procomp USA

Pricing	$399 (license per file server, unlimited users)
Requirements	Nondedicated 386 or better, NetWare 3.1x or 4.x file server, SCSI adapter with its own ASPI Manager software

AHAccelerator adds up to seven CD-ROM drives to a NetWare 3.1x or 4.x file server. It requires an ASPI-compatible SCSI host adapter in the file server. This NLM lets you attach, define, mount, and dismount CD-ROM discs. You can define unlimited CD-ROM volumes with virtually no server or client overhead, and the volumes stay defined even if the server is turned off.

CD-View from Ornetix Network Products

Network O/S supported	NetWare
Workstation O/S supported	DOS 3.3+, Windows, Windows NT, OS/2, Macintosh System 7 with SoftPC
Number of CD-ROM drives supported	Supports 24 drives per server
Number of simultaneous users supported	Supports 100 simultaneous users
Number of CD servers supported from the workstation	Supports an unlimited number of CD servers
Server software	Any PC in a Novell NetWare network can act as a CD server. The CD server loads CD-View and Microsoft CD-ROM Extensions (MSCDEX).
Server RAM required for drivers and/or NLM	45K
Dedicated server	Optional
Caching	Provides CD server cache
Security	Dependent on native network operating system security
Jukeboxes and changers supported	DOS-compliant jukeboxes and changers
CD drives supported	DOS-compliant CD-ROM drives

Warranty	Three months with 30-day money-back guarantee
Technical support	One-year free technical support
Pricing	$295 single-server license $395 (5 users), $595 (10 users), $695 (25 users) $795 (50 users), $895 (100 users)

CD-View installs on any PC with attached CD-ROM drives. The PC loaded with CD-View looks like a NetWare server to other clients, with CD-ROM drives appearing as NetWare volumes. So, there is no need for additional software on client stations, which means those stations can access CD-ROM information with standard NetWare utilities, and use existing DOS and Windows commands and menus. It works with the NetWare 2.x, 3.x, or 4.x series of network operating systems.

Map Assist from Microtest

Map Assist is software that supports NetBIOS and NetWare 3.x, and allows authorized network users to access hard disk drives, floppy disk drives, CD-ROM drives, and other drives that are attached to computers on the network. While it lets users access CD-ROM drives as well as other users' local hard drives, it requires a TSR on both the workstation sharing the disk and the workstation accessing the shared disk. Map Assist also maintains security while making local resources available. The host controls which clients have access and what kind of access they have. This access may include an entire drive, a group of subdirectories, or a single subdirectory. The host user can set up multiple rights possibilities for different clients. The price is $595.

SerView from Ornetix Technologies

Pricing	A 1-server version is $295; a 94-user license 10-server version is $995.
Requirements	A NetWare shell and IPX. NetWare 2.x or higher is needed for the utility programs. The peer server needs 40K of memory to load SerView. It can be loaded into high memory. It requires at least 286-based PC and NetWare 2.x or higher.

Ornetix Technologies' SerView provides another way to share hard disk drives, CD-ROM drives, and WORM drives. SerView can ease network overload while saving most of the cost of adding another copy of Novell NetWare and another NetWare server to your network. But since it runs on DOS rather than on NetWare's optimized system, SerView is slower than NetWare.

After its installation on DOS-based workstations and after running the NetWare Services suite, SerView emulates NetWare, so the workstation behaves almost like a NetWare file server. SerView can run in dedicated or non-dedicated mode. It creates Login, Mail, Public, and System directories, but unlike NetWare, it creates none of the accompanying files. You will need to map a drive to the new SerView server and copy the NetWare server's public files after installation. You must also generate an IPX driver for the adapter installed in the workstation. Afterwards, you'll need to execute SHARE.EXE and then SerView's SERVU.EXE.

Ornetix's SerView brings peer-level file services to clients on NetWare LANs. Workstations running SerView become NetWare Core Protocol file servers and can be managed with usual NetWare management utilities, including SYSCON. You can use most of the NetWare commands on the SerView server, including Map, SYSCON, and VOLINFO, and you can create users, groups, and log-in scripts. Up to 16 different DOS directories or devices may be shared as volumes with names you choose, although, like NetWare, SerView requires that one volume be labeled SYS:.

SerView can relieve a NetWare server by load balancing; that is, if CD-ROM or e-mail traffic is causing undue stress to the server, SerView will relieve the strain cheaply and transparently. SerView also offers interesting configuration options for managers concerned with network security. For example, it lets you offer access to network-based files to someone outside your company. One workstation on the Novell network can be configured with SerView, a modem, and a remote dial-in program such as Triton Technologies' Co/Session. By offering Novell users SerView-based access to the workstation's hard disk and the attached CD-ROM drives, and by allowing outside dial-in access, the administrator can permit both in-house and outside access to the same resources without opening a potentially dangerous route into the Novell network itself.

SerView can be loaded onto bulletin board systems (BBS) to read data from the local drive, so NETX, the driver, doesn't have to be loaded and a BBS dial-in user can never gain access to the other file servers on the network. With SerView, other LAN users can access BBS data without the security problem that could be caused by having the BBS logged into a file server.

CD-ROM DOS-Based Products

This category includes such products as OPTI-NET for DOS, SCSI Express DOS, and CD-NET DOS. These solutions require MSCDEX to be loaded on the workstation in addition to a user suite and other network drivers. Any fully functional workstation on the network can be turned into a CD-ROM server by attaching CD-ROM drives to it via cables and controller cards. The server part of the software is installed on the CD server. This server should be a powerful machine in order to be able to handle multiple access to the CD-ROM drives. The cache size in this machine is controlled by the CD-ROM DOS-based product. For example OPTI-NET for DOS, version 2, supports up to 8 Mb of cache.

If you are considering a Novell NetWare network or already have a Novell NetWare network, you will be able to provide a CD-ROM service to your users using either an NLM or DOS-based technique.

OPTI-NET for DOS from Online Computer Systems

Network O/S supported	NetWare, LAN Manager, LAN Server, LANtastic, NT Advanced Server, Windows for Workgroups, Torus Systems Tapestry, VINES
Workstation O/S supported	DOS, Windows
Number of CD-ROM drives supported	Supports 255 drives
Number of simultaneous users supported	100
Number of CD servers supported	One at a time
Server RAM required for drivers and/or NLM	190K
Dedicated server	Optional
Workstation software type	MSCDEX (25K), loadable in high memory
Minimum workstation RAM	7K
Software unloadable from memory if not needed	Yes
Caching	Provides CD server caching, and the client software provides workstation caching
Security	Provides internal security, in addition to the native network operating system security
CD drives supported	All SCSI CD drives, including Online's multidrive optical storage units, Amdek, Hitachi, NEC, Philips, Sony, and Toshiba
Jukeboxes and changers supported	Pioneer
Warranty	30-day money-back guarantee
Technical support	One-year technical support
Pricing	$1,495 (100-user license)

OPTI-NET for MS-DOS is an optical-storage LAN management program. It is software that is installed on top of an operational network that fully supports NetBIOS or the Novell IPX/SPX protocol. It works with NetWare 3.x and 4.0.

OPTI-NET lets users share databases on CD-ROM discs over a network just as they share files on hard disks on that network. The CD-ROM drives are usually attached to the CD-ROM server that runs OPTI-NET; that server may or may not be the same as the network file server. Users can access the CD-ROM drives through MS-DOS using MSCDEX or through physical reads from the networked CD-ROM device drivers. The problem with using OPTI-NET Version 2.0 for DOS is that administration of the server cannot be done while users are accessing the CD-ROMs. All users must be off the system to mount or dismount databases. The 100-user license for the MS-DOS costs $1,495.

SCSI Express for DOS: DOS CD-ROM Interface from Micro Design International

This non-networkable SCSI Express CD-ROM interface for DOS supports most as well as multiple Industry Standard Architecture (ISA), Extended Industry Standard Architecture (EISA), and Micro Channel Architecture (MCA) host adapters. It supports booting DOS from a SCSI Express–controlled device, high-loading drivers, Windows, and memory managers for the DOS system such as QEMM386 and 386MAX. It emulates a standard read-only DOS volume. It supports High Sierra Group–formatted CD-ROMs as well as ISO-9660–formatted CD-ROMs. It also supports multiple CD-ROM drives simultaneously.

In order to provide access to CD-ROM drives, MSCDEX must be installed. Once installed, MSCDEX and the SCSI Express CD-ROM interface provide DOS users with access to CD-ROM databases. Users can access data using DOS commands or other applications that use DOS calls for information retrieval.

SCSI Shuttle from TAC Systems

Network O/S supported	NetWare
Workstation O/S supported	DOS, Windows, OS/2, UNIX
Number of CD-ROM drives supported	New SCSI Shuttle version 4.0 supports an unlimited number of drives. Old SCSI Shuttle version supports 64 drives per server.
Number of simultaneous users supported	Unlimited—depends on the amount of RAM for caching
Number of CD servers supported	Unlimited
Server RAM required for drivers and/or NLM	256K
Dedicated server	No
Caching	Caching available through NetWare OS for the server

Security	Security available through the native network operating system
CD drives supported	Any SCSI drive
Jukeboxes and changers supported	None
Warranty	One year with 30-day money-back guarantee. Includes unlimited updates.
Technical support	One-year technical support
Pricing	$1,295 full system with unlimited number of drives $695 SCSI Shuttle light supports seven drives

SCSI Shuttle is an NLM that enhances the ability of the file server to manage and share CD-ROM resources. It is fully compatible with NetWare versions 3.1x and 4.x. With SCSI Shuttle, a NetWare server can provide access to up to 64 CD-ROM drives. The client computer can use DOS, Windows, and NetWare commands. Because SCSI Shuttle is a NetWare NLM, no terminate-and-stay-resident (TSR) additional software is needed on the client PCs.

Table 5–1 summarizes the features of five Novell NetWare networks.

Table 5–1. *Summary of product features*

	CD-View	OPTI-NET/DOS OPTI-NET/NLM	DiscPort	CD-Net/DOS CD-Net/NLM	SCSI Express
Server software type	DOS	DOS/NLM	NLM	DOS/NLM	NLM
Client software required	No	Yes/Yes	No	Yes/Yes	No
Uses NetWare utilities	Yes	No/No	Yes	No/No	Yes
Adds load to NetWare server	No	No/Yes	Yes	Yes/No	Yes
Nondedicated operation	Yes	Yes/NA	NA	No/NA	NA
Doubles network traffic	No	No/No	Yes	No/No	No
Doubles server overhead	No	No/No	Yes	No/No	No
Independent server	Yes	Yes/No	No	Yes/No	No
Provides hard disk sharing	Yes	No/NA	NA	No/NA	NA

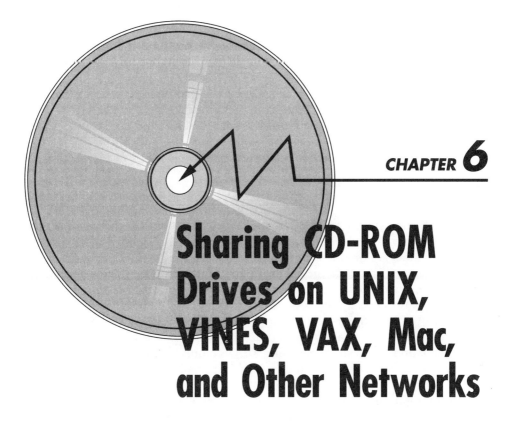

CHAPTER 6

Sharing CD-ROM Drives on UNIX, VINES, VAX, Mac, and Other Networks

Any computer operating system is responsible for allocating system resources, such as memory, disk space, processor time, and peripheral devices (printers, modems, monitors, etc.). It is the operating system that stands between the application programs and these resources. The operating system is the first to load into the computer as it boots, and it remains in the memory throughout the session. When you issue a command at the prompt, you interact with just one part of the operating system—the command shell.

A single operating system such as MS-DOS, however, cannot run more than one application at a time. Although Windows can run multiple applications simultaneously, Windows is not an operating system. But because Windows is a very smart shell, it runs on top of MS-DOS and creates a Windows environment for all applications that run under it. Still, it is MS-DOS that controls the interactivity with computer resources. This is why many MS-DOS applications are still limited by the 640K of conventional memory, even when they run under Windows.

Other operating systems such as UNIX can utilize all the memory provided by the computer. Applications can take as much memory as the system permits (the 640K does not apply in UNIX). UNIX is an example of a multitasking operating system. MS-DOS applications, including CD-ROM applications software, can run under UNIX using MS-DOS emulators. This approach is very popular. Emulation programs such as VP/ix and SoftPC enable MS-DOS to run on systems as varied as SCO UNIX, UNIXWare, NeXTStep, and the Macintosh System 7. When a program issues a BIOS or DOS request, the emulator intercepts the request and translates it into a UNIX equivalent. The request is then passed to the right computer resource. Because of the processing overhead, the performance of any operating system using an emulator is affected.

Table 6–1 lists some of the CD-ROM solutions and the network operating systems they support.

DOS Emulators

Since DOS and Windows CD-ROM applications account for the vast majority of all commercial CD-ROMs available, users on different platforms, including UNIX and Mac, are unable to run these products directly on their native computer platforms. In academic institutions and businesses, average users are more familiar with DOS applications. Today, in a world full of different operating and network systems, software developers are competing to reach the minority of users who are using non-DOS and non-Windows systems.

Emulating DOS means that you actually duplicate a DOS PC within the confines of another system. By using a DOS emulator in a Mac or UNIX machine, you can run DOS or Windows applications just as if you were running a PC. Everything is supposed to look the same—the screen layout, icons, mouse orientation, commands, menus, etc. However, because Windows is a GUI (graphical user interface) running on top of DOS, DOS emulators do not necessarily support Windows. Some emulators need large memory to run. Before purchase, find out from the vendor the size of RAM needed to run an emulator. If you do not have enough RAM, you may resort to creating a large disk swap space, but the performance will be much affected as the program reads from the disk rather than from the memory.

On most workstations, DOS emulators run at least as fast as a 286 machine. A fast workstation running as 486 CPU, combined with a large RAM, will increase the speed of an emulator to handle programs at the speed of a 386 machine. DOS emulators include the following:

Insignia Solutions SoftPC

This is emulation software that supports Macs and all UNIX platforms. Protocols supported include TCP/IP and NFS (Network File System). DOS software supported includes DOS 5.0 and Windows 3.1. It supports GUIs such as Motif and Open Windows.

Logicraft Multiuser Omni-Ware

This is a server PC with multiple 486 boards that runs on Sun, IBM, DEC, HP, System V, and SCO platforms. Protocols supported include TCP/IP and XNS (Xerox Network Services, a multilayer communications protocol). DOS software supported includes DOS 3.3, with OS/2 1.3 option, and Windows 3.1. It supports GUIs such as Motif, DEC, Open Windows, SunView, and HP.

Table 6–1. CD-ROM products and the network operating systems they support

CD-ROM Network Product	Company	NetWare	LAN Manager	LAN Server	NT Advanced Server	Windows for Workgroups	VINES	LANtastic	PathWorks for DOS	AppleTalk
CD Connection	CBIS	Yes	Yes	Yes	Yes	Yes	Yes	Yes	—	—
CD NET	Meridian	Yes	Yes	Yes	—	Yes	Yes	Yes	—	—
CD-Direct	LANshark	—	—	—	—	—	Yes	—	—	—
CD-View	Ornetix Network Products	Yes	—	—	—	—	—	—	—	—
CorelSCSI!	Corel	Yes	—	—	—	—	—	—	—	—
DiskPort	Microtest	Yes	—	—	—	—	—	—	—	—
InfoServer 1000	Digital	Yes	Yes	Yes	Yes	Yes	Yes	Yes	Yes	Yes
LanCD	Logicraft	Yes	Yes	Yes	—	—	Yes	Yes	Yes	—
OPTI-NET for DOS	Online Computer Systems	Yes	Yes	Yes	Yes	Yes	Yes	Yes	—	—

Puzzle Systems Synergy

This is emulation software with an accelerator that runs on the Sun platform. Protocols supported include TCP/IP and NFS. DOS software supported includes DR DOS 5.0 and Windows 3.1. It supports GUIs such as Open Windows and SunView.

Quarterdeck DESQview/X

This is server software that runs on all X workstations. Protocols supported include TCP/IP. It supports all DOS software and GUIs such as Open Windows and Motif.

SunSelect SunPC and Accelerator

This is emulation software with an accelerator that runs on Sun platforms. Protocols supported include TCP/IP, NFS, and NetWare. DOS software supported includes DOS 5.0 and Windows 3.1. It supports GUIs such as Open Windows and Motif.

SunSoft VP/ix

This is a virtual machine that runs on INTERACTIVE and Solaris platforms. DOS software supported includes DOS 3.3 and Windows 3.1. It supports GUIs such as Motif.

TERA Technologies Network PC Access

This is server software that runs on Sun, SCO, and INTERACTIVE platforms. Protocols supported include TCP/IP, NFS, NetBIOS, and NetWare. It supports all DOS software and GUIs such as Open Windows and Motif.

WABI (SunSelect's Windows Applications Binary Interface)

WABI can put Windows 3.1 on SPARCstations. In this approach, Windows calls are captured and translated into equivalent native UNIX and X Windows commands.

UNIX

Basically, in order to run DOS-based applications on UNIX, you must run any of the DOS emulators mentioned above. You can also use such products as Beame & Whiteside's BW-Server, Insignia's SoftPC X Windows or SoftWindows, or Micro Design International's SCSI Express for UNIX.

BW-Server Network Software from Beame & Whiteside Software

BW-Server software lets the PC act as an NFS server. The BW-NFS server-based NOS supports ARCNET, Ethernet, and Token Ring and uses TCP/IP. It supports an unlimited number of DOS or Windows users, files, and disk space. File, print, messaging, communications, directory, and backup services are provided.

BW-Server provides UNIX users with the means to use PC resources. It converts a PC into an NFS host, allowing users of UNIX systems to access data and other PC drives and resources, such as printers and CD-ROM drives on PCs. The software will act as a gateway to Novell NetWare local area networks. When combined with other Beame & Whiteside products that provide UNIX-like functions on DOS PCs, BW-Server makes a PC indistinguishable from a UNIX system to the network.

BW-Server can operate in three different modes: It can operate as a stand-alone DOS application, dedicating the host PC to NFS file and resource sharing. It can run as a terminate-and-stay-resident (TSR) program, so the workstation can act as a server in the background while also running other applications. Third, it can be used as a Microsoft Windows server, allowing other applications—either DOS or Windows—to run in the foreground.

BW-Server supports peer-to-peer resource sharing among workstations, making it well suited to the increasingly popular concept of workgroup computing. The software runs on any 80x86 PC with DOS 3.1 or later, and supports Windows 3.0 and 3.1. According to Beame & Whiteside, the software can be loaded into high memory, and consumes about 30K of base memory when expanded memory is used. The BW-Server and the TCP/IP lists for $245.

SoftPC 3.1 Insignia Solutions' X Window System

Insignia Solutions' SoftPC 3.1 X Window System (terminal emulation software) makes MS-DOS and Windows available on non-Intel systems (e.g., Sun Microsystems SPARCstation 1040). Although the user's guide indicates that the program emulates an 80286 computer, applications can run faster on a 486 machine. SoftPC lists for $549.

Insignia Solutions' SoftWindows Emulation Software

Insignia Solutions' SoftWindows is a version of its DOS/Windows emulation technology for UNIX. SoftWindows is based on Insignia emulation technology along with Microsoft Windows. With SoftWindows, UNIX users can run almost any MS-DOS or Windows source code.

SoftWindows supports utilities, screen savers, font managers, and other programs operating with Windows. Users can cut, copy, and paste between Windows applications and to and from host applications.

SoftWindows also provides access to all PC devices and systems, including COM and LPT ports, floppy drives, memory systems, video displays, networks, and PC CD-ROMs. The software also includes built-in support for NetWare, LAN Manager, and TCP/IP. SoftWindows costs $549 per user.

SCSI Express for UNIX from Micro Design International

SCSI Express is available for many UNIX systems, such as AT&T UNIX, Interactive UNIX 386/ix, and the Santa Cruz Operation SCO Xenix. It provides support to many device types, including CD-ROM, WORM, rewritables, and hard disks. Since UNIX is based on mountable file systems, SCSI Express allows devices to mount onto the root as an extension of that file system. The UNIX version translates the CD-ROM file format into a read-only mountable UNIX format. This means that the operating system thinks it is dealing with a read-only UNIX hard disk. The files on the CD-ROM can be accessed with standard UNIX commands. If the UNIX machine is on the campus network, any UNIX user that can access it can also access the CD-ROM files. It handles both the High Sierra and the ISO 9660 CD-ROM formats.

Under UNIX, the SCSI Express CD-ROM interface allows a CD to appear as a read-only file system. This utility allows the creation of a "file set" that contains translations between the CD-ROM file system and the native UNIX file system.

Banyan's VINES

Banyan Systems' VINES is a server-centric network. It does not have support for CD-ROM networking. However, it has some solutions for sharing a CD-ROM drive on a VINES network.

Basically, in order to share applications on VINES, applications must run from the server. One possible solution is to add peer-to-peer networking capabilities on the server-based network by running Microsoft's Windows for Workgroups on workstations. This approach will make any workstation access drives on any other workstation, including CD-ROMs.

Another approach is to set up a CD-ROM server on the network using CD-Direct software, a LANshark Systems product that lets you share CD-ROM drives with other network users. CD-Direct includes a TSR redirector, called CDREDIR, that simulates Microsoft's MS-DOS Extensions (MSCDEX). If you use VINES and have drives you want to share—including CD-ROMs—CD-Direct provides a solution.

CD-Direct from LANshark Systems

Pricing	$995 (10 users per server), $1,995 (unlimited number of users)
Network O/S supported	VINES
Workstation O/S supported	DOS, Windows, Windows for Workgroups, Windows NT, OS/2, SCO UNIX
Number of CD-ROM drives supported	7 per server
Number of simultaneous users supported	50 (upgradable to 100 users)

Dedicated server	Yes
Workstation software type	Proprietary client software (31K) not loadable in high memory. MSCDEX (48K) loadable in high memory. Redirector for PathWorks only.
Minimum workstation RAM	1 Mb (system), 4 Mb (extended)
Software unloadable from memory if not needed	Software can be unloaded from memory for PathWorks and Macintosh only
Caching	Provides CD server cache. A disk cache of at least 1 Mb is a must. You also need to run the DOS SHARE program.
Security	Provides internal security
Jukeboxes and changers supported	None
CD drives supported	DEC. Other SCSI-2 CD-ROM drives are compatible but not guaranteed by warranty and do not qualify for technical support.
Warranty	Three months with 30-day money-back guarantee
Technical support	Unlimited free technical support

CD-Direct from LANshark Systems allows sharing CD-ROM, WORM, and local hard disks across the network with no memory overhead in the workstation as there are no TSRs. You can access the drive as a standard file service, using VINES' SETDRIVE and SETARL programs. The software enables CD-ROM servers to be set up on Banyan Systems' VINES networks. CD-Direct enables VINES network users to share any DOS file service, not just CD-ROM drives, with no additional overhead on the workstation side. It can accommodate such removable media as optical drives as well as conventional hard disks. CD-Direct requires VINES 5.x and a dedicated PC for DOS operation.

Installation requires modification of a configuration file (a text file) on the server-workstation. The user making this change requires group-management capabilities. CD-Direct is transparent at the workstation end, once a connection is made. This connection is often established by the log-in profile, so users may not even know that a network drive is located on a workstation.

CD-Direct can also share any DOS file service with any VINES user anywhere on the enterprise network. It allows users of other networks—e.g., a NetWare network—to share those drives with VINES users. It can share up to 24 DOS devices with as many as 100 users. The connection is made through a VINES server, but data exchange occurs directly between the CD-Direct workstation and the client workstations. The clients can be any VINES workstations, including those running DOS, Windows, and OS/2. The PC that is operating as the CD-Direct server (the machine that's making files available to other network clients) can be running either DOS, Windows, or OS/2. When CD-Direct is running on DOS, it takes over the PC, becoming a dedicated server because DOS is not a multitasking operating system. Windows and OS/2 let you use the CD-Direct server to run other applications while CD-Direct runs in the background.

LanCD from Logicraft

Pricing	$695 (10 users), $1,995 (100 users)
Network O/S supported	VINES, NetWare, LAN Manager, LAN Server, LANtastic, PathWorks
Workstation O/S supported	DOS, Windows, OS/2, SCO UNIX
Number of CD-ROM drives supported	255 drives
Number of simultaneous users supported	100 simultaneous users
Dedicated server	Yes
Workstation software type	Proprietary CD extensions (16K to 24K) can be loaded in high memory
Minimum workstation RAM	33K
Software unloadable from memory if not needed	Yes
Caching	Provides CD-ROM server caching. Client software provides workstation caching.
Security	Provides internal security, in addition to the native network operating system security
CD drives supported	Any CD-ROM drive
Jukeboxes and changers supported	DISC, Kubic, Pioneer, NSM
Warranty	Three months with 30-day money-back guarantee
Technical support	Three months technical support

LanCD can support as many as four protocols simultaneously—one IPX/SPX and three NetBIOS. This means users on different networks (Novell NetWare, Banyan's VINES, Digital PathWorks) can be using the CD-ROM applications at the same time.

LanCD—CD-ROM networking software—allows network access to multiple CD-ROM drives. If used with Logicraft's PC network servers 486Ware and Omni-Ware, LanCD provides CD-ROM connectivity to UNIX and VMS systems. LanCD requires a dedicated microcomputer as a CD-ROM server. It has a text-based interface and a parallel-port copy-protection device that plugs into the dedicated computer. Logicraft's installation is fairly straightforward, provided you follow the manual carefully. It requires that you plug a LanCD server key into the parallel port of your dedicated PC.

With the administrator's utility, you can set the number of simultaneous users and control the CD-ROM drives from any workstation. From the client utility, users can see which CD-ROM drives are available and pick one. The utility then automatically maps the CD to a free drive letter. Logicraft includes Menuworks, a menuing application that lets users pick a CD from a list of application names.

LanCD CD-ROM Server/Software from Logicraft

Logicraft has also developed a dedicated CD-ROM server, based on an Intel 386 or 486 and MS/DOS. The software, LanCD, was designed to support several operating systems, LAN transport protocols, and access platforms, including PCs, Macintoshes, VT (Virtual Terminal), and Digital's X terminals. Virtual Terminal is an ISO protocol that provides remote terminal emulation similar to the Internet's Telnet protocol. (Users at remote terminals can run applications on remote computers as if they were sitting at that computer.)

Optical Disk Redirector from Trellis Software

Pricing	$995 (10-user license per CD server), $1,695 (unlimited license per CD server)
Network O/S supported	VINES
Workstation O/S supported	DOS, Windows, Windows NT, OS/2
Number of CD-ROM drives supported	Unlimited
Number of simultaneous users supported	100 per CD server
Server RAM required for drivers and/or NLM	640K
Dedicated server	Yes
Caching	Provides CD server cache
Security	Provides internal security, in addition to the native network operating system security
CD drives supported	Any DOS-compliant CD-ROM drive
Jukeboxes and changers supported	Pegasus, Todd Enterprises
Warranty	Three months guarantee
Technical support	No

Trellis Redirector is a redirector software that connects laser optical discs to VINES networks. It supports CD-ROM, WORM, and erasable media. Microsoft CD-ROM extensions, Windows, and OS/2 workstations are supported.

CD Net for VINES from Meridian Data

Meridian Data's CD Net Integrated Systems servers provide native CD-ROM access for Banyan Systems' VINES networks. The CD Net for VINES software includes a CD information manager for VINES 4.x and 5.x clients. When integrated as a normal VINES file service with device-level VINES security service, the CD Net software allows DOS, Windows, and OS/2 users to share as many as 24 CD-ROM drives over Ethernet or Token Ring LANs.

Prices for the CD Net for VINES server line, including the CD Net for VINES software, start at $4,890. The product family includes the CD Net 100/M, which supports as many as eight drives; the CD Net 314/M, which supports as many as 14 drives; and the CD Net 428/M, which supports as many as 28 drives. Users of CD Net 4.3 or higher can buy the VINES software upgrade for $1,995.

CD/Networker from Lotus Development

Pricing	$995 per server
Network O/S supported	NetWare, Banyan's VINES, Microsoft's LAN Manager, and IBM's LAN Server

Among the network operating systems that CD/Networker runs on are Net-Ware, Banyan's VINES, Microsoft's LAN Manager, and IBM's LAN Server. For more information, see chapter 5.

Clovis Intellistor (RAID Array System)

Clovis is using its Intellistor RAID storage subsystem to give VINES servers direct access to CD-ROM drives. This subsystem includes software that translates data from the High Sierra CD-ROM format to StreetTalk, Banyan Systems' global directory services. Because the VINES network operating system does not include support for CD-ROM, this device gives users of Banyan's VINES an option to access CD-ROM.

In addition, Clovis sells the subsystem with a RAID (Redundant Array of Independent Disks) controller. With Intel's i960 CPU on the RAID controller and up to 64 Mb of cache, Intellistor can support RAID systems. Intellistor starts at $9,995 for an eight-bay model featuring a 66 MHz IBM 486SLC2-based subsystem with a Fast SCSI interface and an 8-Mb cache, conversion software, and Banyan support software.

Banyan's ENS for NetWare 1.1

Banyan Systems' Enterprise Network Services (ENS) for NetWare 1.1 provides interoperability between Novell's NetWare 4.0 and Banyan's own VINES network operating system. At the center of ENS for NetWare 1.1 is StreetTalk III, which provides support for Apple Macintosh and IBM OS/2 and includes cross-platform file and print functions, enabling NetWare users to print to any VINES queue. It also supports mainframe communications features and global directories. Through StreetTalk, ENS narrows the connectivity gap between its VINES operating system and Novell's NetWare 4.0.

The ENS environment lets users run peripherals from any VINES server, connect CD-ROM drives to any server, and run Internet without having to purchase additional communication servers.

While ENS delivers interoperability between server-centric NetWare and network-centric VINES, it provides access to both VINES and NetWare networks through a single log-in.

CD Connection for VINES from CBIS

CBIS developed a version of its CD Connection networking software, which uses the StreetTalk protocol of Banyan's VINES. As many as 99 users on a VINES network can have simultaneous access to up to 28 CD-ROM drives in a single CD server system. The price is $695 for 10 users.

VAX

CD-Ware from Logicraft

Logicraft's CD-Ware is a multiuser network server that allows terminals, workstations, X terminals, PCs, and Macintoshes on a VMS or UNIX network to access CD-ROM applications. CD-Ware server has five 16-bit expansion slots.

The three models of CD-Ware available are CD-Ware, which supports up to 16 simultaneous users and 21 CD-ROM drives; CD-Ware 428, which consists of 386/486Ware and Meridian Data's CD Net (386/486Ware and CD Net communicate over the network using IPX or PathWorks); and CD-Ware 150, which consists of 386/486Ware and Digital Equipment Corporation's InfoServer (386/486Ware and the InfoServer communicate using PathWorks).

CD-Ware supports MSCDEX and any PC-compatible application program that accesses ISO 9660– or High Sierra–formatted CD-ROM discs. The MSCDEX.EXE program and the CD-ROM device driver are both installed on a logical disk. CD-Ware supports emulation for EGA, VGA, Hercules, and CGA resolution graphics.

CD-Ware supports XNS (Xerox Network Systems) and the TCP/IP protocols. While XNS is used in the VMS environment, TCP/IP is used in the UNIX or VMS environment to access the same server simultaneously. For VMS, Logicraft supports DEC's ULTRIX Connection software (Digital's version of UNIX) and TGV's Multinet.

CD-Ware supports up to four controllers allowing for a total of 21 CD-ROM drives. CD-Ware 150 supports up to 13 CD-ROM drives, and CD-Ware 428 supports up to 28 drives.

The components required include a VMS or UNIX system, Ethernet LAN, cable and connectors for attaching servers to the thin-wire network or a transceiver, and cable for attaching servers to thick-wire LAN.

The platforms supported by Logicraft's CD-Ware include DEC VAX systems (VMS or ULTRIX), DECstations, and DECsystems; SPARCstations and Sun 3 and Sun 4 workstations; HP 9000 series 700 and series 400 workstations; IBM RS/6000 workstations; and Intel 302 and 402 workstations.

CD-Ware allows users to access CD-ROM applications simultaneously. There can be an unlimited number of servers connected to the Ethernet giving users the capability of providing the entire VMS and UNIX community with access to CD-ROMs. In addition, CD-Ware 428 and CD-Ware 150 allow existing PC users to have peer-to-peer access to the CD-ROM servers.

CD-Ware supports up to six logical disks per CD-ROM session. Logicraft provides PCSA/PathWorks client support via DECnet (print, disk, and file services) and NFS client support. CD-Ware's software includes a file transfer utility enabling data transfer from CD-ROM disc to VMS or UNIX files. Users on X terminals or workstations can also copy and paste between windows.

There is a limit of 16 simultaneous users per Logicraft box. On a VAX network, a terminal can download information from a CD application on the disk space reserved for the CD-ROM on the VAX. If you are using a terminal or a PC emulator on the VAX, some control functions do not operate correctly.

CD 4000 Expansion Cabinet from Logicraft

Logicraft's CD 4000 is a CD expansion cabinet that contains up to 7 CD-ROM drives and is fully compatible with Logicraft's 486Ware product line. The CD 4000 is configured with CD-ROM SCSI drives and a SCSI interface card. It is available as a rackmount, a desktop unit, or a tower unit. As many as three CD 4000s can be attached to each 486Ware server, allowing up to 16 users simultaneous access to 21 CD drives. Two CD 4000s with up to 12 drives can be attached to DEC's InfoServer 150.

The CD 4000/486Ware configuration is accessible concurrently by all users on the network—PCs, Macintoshes, X terminals, VT terminals, and workstations. The CD 4000 is priced at $5,995 for a seven-drive unit.

InfoServer Solutions from Digital Equipment Corporation (DEC)

Digital's InfoServer products address specific customer needs such as CD-ROM database serving, tape backup, X terminal services, and CD-ROM mastering. You can start with an entry-level CD server package and add to the unit over time. The networked CDs that come with the DEC InfoServer can read a variety of CD formats, provided you install the appropriate client-side software drivers. The box runs over an Ethernet network and includes drivers for Mac, Windows, and DOS clients (called MSCDEX), and DEC-formatted CDs to attach to it. You can also add a Sun client driver.

The company's Local Area CD package combines an InfoServer 1000 and a single DEC CD-ROM drive. The $2,995 system can be upgraded with as many as six additional CD-ROM drives.

DEC is also offering the InfoServer with either four or seven DEC CD-ROM drives as part of its InfoServer Librarian systems. The four-drive model lists for $6,100, while the seven-drive model is $8,250.

DEC's InfoServer Publisher configuration lets users record their own CDs over the network. The system requires an InfoServer, a Mac version of DEC's

$1,000 CD-R Function Access software, a DEC hard drive, and Sony's CD-R recording device. DEC's 665-Mb drive in an expansion cabinet costs $2,845. Mac client software compatible with all of DEC's InfoServer systems is available separately for $785.

The following InfoServer application packages are available from Digital:

> Enhancements to InfoServer client software for Macintosh, ULTRIX, and DOS users, and new OpenVMS AXP client support.
>
> InfoServer Local Area CD, an entry-level package that provides CD-ROM services to multiple users in a LAN.
>
> InfoServer Librarian, a fully integrated package for users of networked CDs and large databases.
>
> InfoServer VXT, a modular system that provides LAN services to Digital's X terminal users.
>
> InfoServer Publisher has been tailored to users planning to master their own CD databases for software, data, and document distribution.
>
> The InfoServer System Manager offers system managers the ability to provide multiple InfoServer services to network users simultaneously, including CD-ROM, disc, and tape.

InfoServer 150 Network Storage Server/SEACx from DEC

The InfoServer 150 from DEC is a dedicated network storage server. Via two SCSI ports, it can provide 100 Ethernet LAN clients simultaneous access to 14 SCSI-compatible storage devices, including CD-ROM, magneto-optical drives, hard disk, and tape drives. To serve applications written in different file formats, such as ISO 9660, High Sierra, and OS/2, the InfoServer 150 transmits information in a file format–independent, block-level protocol. It works with thin and thick Ethernet and accommodates VMS, ULTRIX, PathWorks for DOS, and NetWare. InfoServer 150 prices start at $8,800.

The original InfoServer ISO has been used mostly to serve read-only data to multivendor networks from CD-ROMs. It uses Digital's LASTport high-performance local area transport (LAT) protocol, so special communications software must be loaded onto each client that accesses the InfoServer. The InfoServer is especially well suited to serving large databases and distributing software from CD-R.

DEC InfoServer 1000

Pricing	$5,750 (including seven CD-ROM tower and client licenses for 50 connections), $4,750 (for a CD-ROM tower version)
Network O/S supported	Novell's NetWare, LAN Manager, LAN Server, NT Advanced Server, Windows for Workgroups, VINES, LANtastic, PathWorks for DOS, AppleTalk

Workstation O/S supported	DOS, Windows, Macintosh
Number of CD-ROM drives supported	32 drives per server
Number of simultaneous users supported	Depends on Novell license
Number of CD servers supported	An unlimited number of CD servers
Server software	Loads its own NLM on a NetWare server. The NLM is used to mount and unmount the volumes, set the amount of dedicated CD-ROM cache, and determine the size of the workspace buffer.
Server RAM required for drivers	91K (150K for each mounted CD)
Dedicated server	None required
Workstation software type	A redirector (12K) can be loaded in EMS. A proprietary CD extensions CorelCDX (3K with EMS or 37K without EMS). Microsoft CD-ROM Extensions (MSCDEX) (32K) can run in high memory.
Minimum workstation RAM	1 Mb
Software unloadable from memory if not needed	Yes
Caching	Provides CD server cache. Workstation software provides caching.
Security	Provides internal security
CD drives supported	CMD Technology, Chinon, Hitachi, IBM, JVC, LMSI, NEC, Panasonic, Pioneer, Smart & Friendly, Sony, Texel, Toshiba
Jukeboxes and changers supported	DEC, HP, ISI, K&S, Kodak, LMSI, Magstore, MaxOptix, Panasonic, Pioneer, Plasmon, Reflection Systems, Ricoh, Sony
Warranty	Flexible
Technical support	No

DEC InfoServer 1000 Network Storage Server is an entry-level, modular storage server that enables users to simultaneously share volumes of data from remote SCSI devices (CD-ROM, tape, hard disk, and magneto-optical drives) on the LAN. Each InfoServer 1000 features one SCSI bus that supports up to 50 users simultaneously, including any combination of MS-DOS, Macintosh, PathWorks for DOS, ULTRIX, or Open VMS systems.

CDworks 1000 from Virtual Microsystems

Virtual Microsystems' CDworks 1000 family is based on Digital's InfoServer 1000 technology. The systems can combine up to 49 CD-ROMs and seven server processors with support for up to 350 simultaneous users on an Ethernet network. The CDworks 1000's Symmetrical Server Architecture allows multiple server processors to share the processing load and provide redundancy. These multiprocessor CD-ROM systems allow simultaneous access to large CD-ROM databases from networked VAXs, VT terminals, PCs, and Macintoshes on Ethernet networks.

The CDworks systems connect directly to an Ethernet network and allow users network access to multiple CDs. The server modules can automatically shift users to a different InfoServer to balance network traffic or if a drive or server fails.

Virtual Microsystems is offering two DEC InfoServer 1000's and 14 Toshiba CD-ROM drives as the $33,990 CDworks 1014, and three InfoServers and 21 drives in a rackmount configuration as the $46,990 CDworks 1021. Both models include DOS client software; Mac client support is $785 for 100 users. The price of the systems includes installation, as well as one year of support and software upgrades.

The CDworks 1014 supports 100 simultaneous users, while the CDworks 1021 supports 150 simultaneous users.

V-Server/Gateway from Virtual Microsystems

A companion to the CDworks system, the V-Server/Gateway allows non-PC users—such as VAX terminals, Macintoshes, workstations, and remote users—to simultaneously access PathWorks and Novell LANs. The V-Server/Gateway also allows users to run DOS-based CD-ROM databases. By using Digital's own network software to interface to DECnet, the V-Server/Gateway enables VAX users to directly access a PC-LAN application or service from any site on a wide area DECnet network.

Each V-Server/Gateway system provides the ability of up to four simultaneous VAX users to emulate PathWorks, Novell, or any other PC-LAN resident workstation. Each server contains four independent, MS-DOS client processors. Each client processor utilizes its own dedicated network interface card to optimize throughput to the PC-LAN. It also contains a master CPU to manage each of the four client processors' DECnet communications with the V-Server/Gateway software that is resident on the VAX.

V-Server/Gateway software enables any terminal, workstation, or Macintosh user logged on to the host VAX to request a V-Server/Gateway client processor. The V-Server software locates an available client processor, loads MS-DOS and the PC-LAN operating system onto the client processor, and establishes a logical link between the requester's desktop device and the allocated client processor. Once this link is made, all screen and keyboard I/O to and from the client processor is directed to the VAX user's desktop device allowing the user to perform the same operations as a user whose dedicated PC is physically connected to the PC-LAN. The cost of a V-Server/Gateway is $24,490.

CDworks 2000 from Virtual Microsystems

CDworks 2000 is a Windows NT-based CD information server that can provide access to CD-ROM applications. The CDworks 2000 server enables multiple users to concurrently access information databases mounted in the server's CD-ROM drives. CDs mounted in the CDworks 2000 servers are made available to workstations on the network as standard Windows NT file services. Windows for Workgroups and Macintosh users can access the CDworks' applications without having to modify their workstations' configuration, using the network drivers and protocols already loaded. Novell users running Windows or DOS can also natively access the CDworks' CD applications without having to modify their workstations' configuration, by installing and running an optional CDworks server-based software module. CDworks' AddOn for NetWare enables the CDworks 2000 servers to present the CD databases to users on the network as standard NetWare file services.

Each CDworks 2000 employs multiple processors for peak performance. It includes software that enables system administrators to catalog, mount/dismount, meter, and track usage of their CD-ROM applications. Meter and track allow the exact licensed number of users to use a specific CD-ROM application. They also capture statistics and generate simple reports that summarize the number of times each application has been accessed by user and duration.

CDworks 2000 supports Windows, DOS, and Macintosh users. It is compatible with a variety of network protocols, including TCP/IP, IPX/SPX, DECnet, NetBEUI, and AppleTalk.

The CDworks 2000 product family includes:

> CDworks 2114
> Single server, 14 CD-ROM drives with one CPU—$31,990
>
> CDworks 2228
> Dual server, 28 CD-ROM drives with two CPUs—$57,990
>
> CDworks 2342
> Tri Server, 42 CD-ROM drives with three CPUs—$79,990

Additional CDworks 2000 servers can be linked together.

CDaccess from Virtual Microsystems

CDaccess, an alternative to the V-Server, is a network gateway that provides universal access to DOS-based CD databases from any desktop device. When coupled with CDworks 2000 information servers, CDaccess provides a comprehensive solution to CD-ROM networking that supports multiple computing platforms. Terminal users or PC, Macintosh, or workstation users running terminal emulation can establish a network or modem connection to CDaccess. Once connected, the user can access CDworks Information Server.

Each CDaccess system contains five DOS processors, each with its own interface card. A single CDaccess system typically supports the needs of 35 or more users on a shared basis. Additional CDaccess units can be added to the network in a modular fashion to increase the number of simultaneous users. Terminal and modem users can connect through a LAT or Telnet terminal server. Network-resident PC, Macintosh, and workstation users can make a LAT or Telnet connection to a CDaccess processor. Terminals connected directly to a UNIX or VAX host can connect to CDaccess by making a simple menu selection on the terminal screen.

IBM's OS/2

IBM's OS/2 operating system is able to handle concurrent emulations of the MS-DOS operating system and Microsoft Windows efficiently. OS/2 accomplishes this because it is capable of multithreading in addition to multitasking. In multithreading, a number of processes with multiple control threads can share a single address space. Therefore, performance is improved because one thread can continue working while another waits for resources. Additionally, OS/2 includes actual Windows 3.1 source code, and as such it is the only operating system capable of running Windows in enhanced mode. Windows sessions under OS/2 have full access to such Windows features as TrueType and object linking and embedding.

To run DOS-based CD-ROM software, you need either an OS/2 version of the search software or a program to run DOS applications under OS/2. SCSI Express for OS/2 provides transparent support for CD-ROM and other optical devices. You may add one device or daisy-chain any combination of these devices to your system. Only one host adapter is required for multiple devices and device types. The OS/2 version lets users of a LAN Manager 2.0 network share a CD-ROM drive installed on the server.

Macintosh Computers

Macintosh computer networks can be established using the built-in networking protocol, AppleTalk or the AppleShare server. Networking with the Macintosh is extremely simple because networking functions are built directly into the Macintosh. On a Mac, if you enable file sharing through System 7, other Mac users on the network can view the information on a CD without having to worry about running a new protocol. This is in contrast to PC computers, which would need a peer-to-peer LAN, Windows for Workgroups, some LAN CD extensions, or Microsoft's LAN Manager and more integration time to make it all work.

Macintosh networks support Macintosh hard disk and floppy disk storage as well as CD-ROM, ISO 9660, and High Sierra formats. DEC offers Mac client software, which is compatible with all of DEC's InfoServer systems, for $785.

AppleTalk

AppleTalk is a built-in networking protocol used with Macintosh computers. The AppleTalk specifications describe how to connect Apple Macintosh computers, printers, and other resources or computers into a communications network. AppleTalk was designed to use the LocalTalk cabling system, but AppleTalk now supports Ethernet and token ring topologies. The LocalTalk cabling system consists of simple connectors that attach to Macintosh systems and provide plug attachments for LocalTalk Cable or telephone wire. Transmission rates are relatively slow at 230.4 Kbits/sec, but the total installation cost is low since network adapter cards and workstation software are not required.

Another approach for high speed is to install EtherTalk (Ethernet) or TokenTalk (token ring) network segments using special adapters (e.g., NuBus card) and cabling systems. In order to use both protocols in a single Mac network, a software or hardware router may be established in a file server to bridge both protocols and perform file sharing and/or print service. The CD-ROM drives will be connected to the file server.

AppleShare

AppleShare is a centralized file and print server software product developed by Apple Computer that uses system software 7.0 or higher. It runs on top of AppleTalk on a Macintosh system. It requires a dedicated Macintosh computer acting as a centralized server and includes both server and workstation software. AppleShare provides other services such as e-mail handling. Additional modules such as management systems are available. AppleShare uses the AppleTalk Filing Protocol. It can support 120 workstations running a mix of 6.05+ or 7.0 systems. A SCSI bus can support up to six external CD-ROM drives which can be shared via AppleShare. It can provide queue services for up to five network printers. Selective access may be established for each user or application.

AppleShare is built on the AppleTalk protocols and thus provides access to users over LocalTalk, EtherTalk, or TokenTalk network topologies. While AppleShare is Apple's centralized file server software, Macintosh System 7 provides peer-to-peer networking services. A user can share files with other users by designating which files to share, and access files on other systems that have been shared.

The built-in networking support is sufficient to serve 10 or fewer users accessing text files archived on CD-ROM or another SCSI device. Macintosh systems come equipped with at least twisted-pair LocalTalk connections for use with the AppleTalk protocol, and Ethernet or Token Ring is better for heavier traffic. But if CD-ROM activity is great, Apple recommends that you dedicate the system sharing the CD-ROM drives. Also, if you need to ease the network load, your best option is to run AppleShare on top of System 7 with a dedicated server for up to about 50 users. AppleShare Pro is intended for greater numbers of users.

Mac-PC Connection

Mac users have been running DOS and Windows on Macs for years, using either Insignia Solutions' inexpensive-but-slow SoftPC software or the quick-but-costly OrangePC card from Orange Micro.

A Mac computer cannot access a PC network, nor can a PC access a Mac network except through a gateway computer. This gateway solution applies only to simple operations such as e-mail and file transfer. When it comes to running an application, or accessing CD-ROM databases on a PC network, from a Mac machine, there should be some type of terminal emulation. This works only if the CD-ROM application is running on a PC network (e.g., Novell's NetWare) and the Mac computer is treated as if it were another PC on the network.

An Ethernet or Token Ring network can also be used to connect PCs to a NetWare file server, and in this case the protocol used is called IPX. The same Ethernet network can interconnect Macintosh computers and PCs, and the two protocols can coexist without interfering. SoftNode enables SoftPC to communicate with Ethernet or the Token Ring file server using IPX protocol. SoftNode programs run on a Macintosh and convert the AppleTalk protocol to IPX so that SoftNode can communicate with the file server on the network.

Macintosh computers on Ethernet networks can communicate with UNIX-based computers using TCP/IP protocols. SoftNode can then support PC packages for PC-to-UNIX communication, like Novell's LAN WorkPlace for DOS.

The following products allow you to add IBM compatibility to Macintosh systems.

OrangePC 2.01 from Orange Micro

The OrangePC remains the high-end choice. This PC-on-a-NuBus-card includes as much as 16 Mb of RAM and one of three types of 386 or 486 microprocessors: a 25-MHz Intel 80386SX, a 25-MHz 486SLC, or a 50-MHz IBM 486SLC 2/50 with an internal cache. You also get a PC AT bus slot for an add-in card, a VGA video chip, and parallel and serial ports. The OrangePC package comes with DOS 6; an 80387SX math coprocessor is optional. The OrangePC is implemented as a coprocessor, running DOS or Windows at the speed of a PC without slowing down your Mac applications.

Version 2.01 makes the OrangePC's software-based features look like Soft-PC's. Mac and DOS applications can now share Finder and AppleShare folders, CD-ROMs, and other mounted volumes. In addition, the OrangePC lets you print from DOS or Windows applications to PostScript printers over Apple-Talk. You can also copy and paste between DOS and Mac applications. The 25-MHz 80386SX lists for $599, the 25-MHz 486SLC lists for $1,599, and the 50-MHz 486SLC 2/50 lists for $1,974.

SoftPC 3.1 from Insignia Solutions

Insignia offers two versions of its software-only product: SoftPC Professional (DOS only) and SoftPC with Windows. Both emulate an Intel CPU in software, resulting in much slower response than what you get with the OrangePC. SoftPC costs about $500; the 486 versions of the OrangePC cost as much as some actual PCs. SoftPC Professional 3.1 costs $325. SoftPC with Windows 3.1 costs $499.

NetWare for Macintosh 4.01

For heterogeneous networks that include Macintoshes, NetWare 4.0's NetWare for Macintosh NLM makes NetWare look like an AppleShare server connected to Macintoshes. Connecting Macintoshes to a UNIX NFS server is another option for heterogeneous networks. And if your workgroup of Mac5 is small but you still need to hook up with a larger, non-Mac network, gateways and routers from vendors such as Cayman Systems or Shiva Corporation can provide the link between LocalTalk wiring and Ethernet.

Novell's $1,195 NetWare for Macintosh 4.0 includes support for Mac CD-ROM drives, a Finder that can address more than 2 Gb, improved NetWare utility programs, and better integration with NetWare print services. Under NetWare version 4.0, users can attach Macintosh Hierarchical File System CD-ROM drives to a NetWare server. This lets users access the drive through the Chooser, like any other server.

Macs can also access server-attached SCSI CD-ROM drives and volumes larger than 1 Gb. NetWare 4.01 includes free 5-user Macintosh support, which can be extended to support 1,000 users with NetWare for Macintosh 4.0, depending, of course, on the Novell NetWare license.

NetWare Tools allows print queues, users and groups, messaging, NetWare rights, and files to be managed from a Mac client. Assigning user rights has been simplified with some preset access rights choices for files and folders: User, Owner, View, Drop, Read, and Custom. These choices are familiar to Macintosh users and should eliminate some of the confusion associated with matching NetWare rights with AppleShare rights.

List prices are: NetWare for Macintosh, Version 4.01, $1,195 (1,000-user license); upgrade from 3.11, $400; upgrade from 3.12, $200; and NetWare for Macintosh Client, Version 1.0, $30.

Personal MacLAN Connect from Miramar Systems

Miramar's Personal MacLAN Connect is a software package that brings the benefits of System 7 file sharing directly to the PC desktop. Personal MacLAN Connect provides Microsoft Windows users with the ability to selectively share any local storage device with any Macintosh user. The PC's hard disks, floppy drives, CD-ROM, and removable media are within reach of the Macintosh desktop. Personal MacLAN also functions as a print server directing PC or Macintosh print jobs to shared PC printers. All PC files and printers are accessed using the standard Macintosh AppleShare Chooser interface. In addition, Mac users see PC files as standard Macintosh folders and application-specific icons. The price is $199.

Miramar Systems' Personal MacLAN Connect version 3.0 software package provides transparent connectivity on AppleTalk networks for Macintoshes and PCs running Microsoft Windows. The program lets Macintosh users access PC files, output files to a PC printer, and share a PC's hard disks, floppy drives, or CD-ROM. However, PC users cannot launch PC applications from, or access files on, a Macintosh; nor can they print to a Macintosh-connected output device. PCs must be equipped with a LocalTalk, EtherTalk, or TokenTalk network card; the Macintosh connects to the network card, and the program is installed under Windows. Several Macintoshes can access data at the same time and can open, move, copy, edit, or delete files on the server, but an open file cannot be used by more than one user at a time. The program complements various network environments in which Windows-based PCs and Macintoshes must work together; it costs $199 for a single-user license and $999 for a 10-user license.

Once both PC and Macintosh users on Ethernet, AppleTalk, or token ring networks can share files, mail, and printers through Personal MacLAN Connect, a peer-to-peer network operating system that's similar to Microsoft Windows for Workgroups is created. It can operate on top of NetWare and LANtastic networks, loading itself into 400K of high memory on every participating PC and tapping the built-in personal file-sharing services of Macintosh System 7 for directory synchronization across networks. It offers the usual read-only and read-and-write file- and directory-access privileges. The price is $199 per user.

SCSI Express from Micro Design International

SCSI Express allows Macintosh computers to access CD-ROM discs as NetWare volumes on a Novell NetWare network, provided that the NetWare server is able to support Macintosh computers through NetWare for Macintosh NLM.

V-Server/Gateway from Virtual Microsystems

Users can access CD-ROM databases from Macintosh computers through the V-Server/Gateway that allows non-PC users, such as VAX terminals, Macintoshes, workstations, and remote users, to simultaneously access PathWorks and Novell LANs. See section on VAX, above.

Other Networking Solutions

Accessing CD-ROM Networks via TCP/IP

If you are using a Novell network, you can telnet to a computer on the network to access CD-ROM databases. Products such as Everywhere Access establish a Telnet server for DOS computers. They support many TCP/IP packages on the market, including FTP, Clarkson University, and Beame & Whiteside. Everywhere Access allows any machine running VT-100 terminal emulator and mainframes to telnet into a DOS computer.

Connecting ASCII, or "Dumb," Terminals to CD-ROM Networks

ASCII, or "dumb," terminals, which support VT-100 terminal emulation, can access CD-ROM products. However, such terminals can display only text, not graphics and audio. Also, because CD-ROM products use some special function keys, this approach will not work well with all CD-ROM products. The most common approach is to use a Telnet-based link through a UNIX server, and from that server the VT-100 terminal can access the CD-ROM server. However, some library automation products from companies such as SIRSI and DRAnet have the capability of accessing CD-ROM networks and the Internet. Consequently, these open systems will help in the construction of integrated library systems. Such systems will allow users to access a multitude of library services, including cataloging, circulation, serials, acquisitions, OPACs, authorities, CD-ROM databases, and the Internet from high-end PC, VAX, or UNIX platforms.

Connecting a CD-ROM Network to an IBM Mainframe

If you are using a Novell network, you can use Novell's LAN Workplace for DOS or the Clarkson University TCP/IP program to establish a communication link between workstations and the mainframe. There are some drawbacks to this approach as the drivers software consumes the memory of the workstation.

Another approach is to maintain a gateway computer between your CD-ROM LAN and the mainframe. This can be done using products such as LinkUP 3270 from Chi, DI3270 from Data Interface Systems, pcPATH SNA-3270 from ICOT, or NetWare 3270 from Novell.

CD-ROM Network Access via a Modem

You can provide remote access to your CD-ROM network through the use of dial-up lines and remote communications software such as Carbon Copy from Microcom, Close-up from Norton-Lambert, Co/Session from Triton Technologies, pcANYWHERE from Symantec, or ReachOut from Ocean Isle. You need one or more host PCs, a license from the producer of the remote communications software package, a modem for each host PC, and a dedicated phone line for each modem.

Other solutions include LAN Central System-Asynchronous Communications Server from Cubix and Telebit, ChatterBox/Network Resource Server from J&L Information Systems, and CAPserver from Evergreen Systems. These systems use multiple CPUs that are mounted on separate cards. These cards are inserted in a special communications server tower. Each card in the tower has its own network adapter and modem. CPU cards appear to the network as individual diskless workstations.

A QL4222 Remote Access server board from Cubix is an example of a CPU card. For managed dial-up access to your LAN, this board is inserted into a NetWare server or router. QL4222 features two 486DX-2/50 remote control host processors for sites using ReachOut, pcANYWHERE, Carbon Copy, Close-up, or Co/Session. This board replaces two standalone PCs.

Novell's networks can utilize Novell Access Server. Novell uses the pcANYWHERE ATERM program and Quarterdeck's DESQview along with a multiplexed IPX, which is a unique version of NetWare's IPX. Novell also uses a communications board that allows multiple modems to be connected to the same PC.

Client-Server Alternative: The Electronic Reference Library (ERL) from SilverPlatter

The Electronic Reference Library is based on client/server architecture. This client/server retrieval technology enables users to provide wide area network access to database collections throughout an institution or across a consortium. Using ERL technology, databases mounted on one or more UNIX ERL servers are searchable using ERL retrieval clients for Windows, Macintosh, DOS, or UNIX platforms.

SilverPlatter designed ERL technology as a database networking solution for libraries, so it includes tools to manage database access, system security, user accounts, and usage statistics through a DOS-based administration program.

Because ERL is media independent, CD-ROM, hard disk, and Internet access are all supported. SilverPlatter currently offers retrieval clients for DOS, Windows, and Macintosh platforms. A UNIX character client that will support terminal access is in development. The first release of ERL supports the SCO UNIX server on an Intel platform. ERL server software for the Sun Solaris platform as well as other UNIX platforms such as IBM AIX, DEC OSF-1, and Hewlett Packard HP-UX will be available (see fig. 6–1 for a summary of server requirements and fig. 6–2 for a summary of client requirements).

ERL servers: Institutions that have the hardware and UNIX expertise available may choose to have their database collection locally mounted for institution- or consortium-wide access. In this case, a UNIX-based ERL server can be integrated into an existing TCP/IP network and accessed by all authorized users through their retrieval client of choice. As your database collection grows, additional ERL servers can be added to support additional databases or an increased user community.

	SCO Server	Solaris Server
	Minimum	Minimum
Computer	486DX/50 MHz IBM-compatible PC	Sun SPARCstation 10
Memory	36 Mb (1 to 15 users) Add 2 Mb per user over 15 users.	48 Mb (1 to 15 users) Add 2 Mb per user over 15 users.
Video	VGA color monitor	Standard color
Operating environment	SCO UMIX 3.2v4.x	Sun Solaris Version 2.3 or higher
Hard disk	400 Mb or greater	400 Mb or greater
CD-ROM drive	ISO 9660, 680 Mb	ISO 9660, 680 Mb
Floppy drive	One high-density	One high-density
Mouse	No	No
Other	Additional hard disk space required for loading databases to hard disk	Additional hard disk space required for loading databases to hard disk
Network Protocols	SCO TCP/IP Version 1.2 or higher SCO IPX/SPX (required for IPX client)	TCP/IP

Figure 6–1. *ERL technology server hardware requirements*

	WinSPIRS		PC-SPIRS		MacSPIRS		UNIX-SPIRS
	Minimum	Recommended	Minimum	Recommended	Minimum	Recommended	Minimum
Computer	80386sx IBM-compatible PC	80486 IBM-compatible PC	80286 IBM-compatible PC	80486 IBM-compatible PC	Macintosh SE or higher	68040 Macintosh	Sun SPARC-station 10
Memory	4 Mb	8 Mb	1 Mb (500K free conventional memory)	4 Mb	System 6.x-2 Mb System 7.x-4 Mb	8 Mb	16 Mb + 2 Mb per simultaneous user
Video	VGA mono	VGA color	Monochrome	VGA color	Standard	Color	Standard
Operating environment	MS Windows 3.1 or higher	MS Windows 3.1 or higher	MS-DOS or PC-DOS 3.1 or higher	MS-DOS or PC-DOS 5.0 or higher	System 6.0.7 or higher	System 7 or higher	Sun Solaris Version 2.3 or higher
Hard disk	7 Mb	7 Mb	4 Mb	6 Mb	7 Mb	7 Mb	3 Mb
CD-ROM drive	NA	NA	NA	NA	NA	NA	NA
Floppy drive	One high-density	One high-density	One low-density	One high-density	One low-density	One high-density	Not required
Mouse	Yes	Yes	No	No	Yes	Yes	No
Other	Parallel port for printer	Parallel port for printer	Parallel port for printer	Parallel port for printer, EMS Memory Manager	Printer port	Printer port	NA
Network Protocols	Windows-compatible TCP/IP software package that implements Winsock 1.1 or higher		Choose from Novell's LAN Workplace for DOS, Sun's PC-TCP, FTP's PC-TCP, Ethernet-compatible packet driver, or Novell IPX		MacTCP 2.02 or higher. (The network connection occurs either as an Ethernet connection on the Macintosh or as a gateway from LocalTalk to Ethernet. ERL servers will not support direct LocalTalk connections.)		TCP/IP

Figure 6-2. *ERL technology client hardware requirements*

ERL technology can integrate into a typical campus environment. The ERL retrieval client and server software communicate using TCP/IP. ERL server for SCO UNIX and PC clients also supports Novell NetWare's IPX protocol. It also supports serial connections and long-distance phone connections. In addition, it supports Token Ring, Ethernet, fiber optics, and any communications technology that supports TCP/IP or IPX.

SilverPlatter's databases can be loaded onto hard disk for high usage or into CD-ROM drives that are attached directly to the ERL server. An alternative is to access these databases through the Internet. You might consider mounting primary or most frequently used databases into CD-ROM drives, while secondary databases—those not so heavily used—can be offered via Internet subscription.

Based on client/server architecture, ERL has two main software components: the ERL retrieval clients (user interface) and the ERL server software (search engine). Databases mounted on one or more ERL servers are searchable using SilverPlatter WinSPIRS, MacSPIRS, UNIX-SPIRS, or PC-SPIRS retrieval software with the user's operating system of choice. SilverPlatter's Data eXchange Protocol (DXP) standardizes the communication between clients and servers. By using DXP, independent software developers can create database interfaces that are ERL-compliant. The following components of ERL technology are available:

ERL Server Software   available for Solaris and SCO-UNIX operating systems

ERL Retrieval Clients   WinSPIRS, MacSPIRS, PC-SPIRS, and UNIX-SPIRS. Each SPIRS ERL client offers users the same search functionality as that of the standalone versions without sacrificing the familiar SPIRS interface.

ERL Admin   A DOS-based system administration client enables you to manage user accounts and passwords, control database access privileges, maintain system security, and retrieve database and system usage statistics.

ERL-Compliant Databases   There are currently more than 250 ERL-compliant databases available from SilverPlatter.

If you plan to run the ERL Solaris server and UNIX-SPIRS on the same machine, use Sun SPARCstation 20 and ERL Solaris server minimum memory plus 2 Mb per simultaneous UNIX-SPIRS user.

Internet subscriptions enable institutions without the hardware and systems resources necessary for managing a local ERL server to take advantage of ERL technology to access databases via the Internet. Databases mounted on an ERL server at SilverPlatter can be accessed by workstations with a full Internet connection and an installed ERL retrieval client. This solution enables libraries to provide network access to their database collection without sacrificing search functionality. You may access SilverPlatter's Guest Account via the Internet.

A Guest Account has been established for public access to ERL services, including the ERL client software PC-SPIRS, MacSPIRS, and WinSPIRS. It provides access to subsets of MEDLINE, AIDSLINE, and ERIC.

To access SilverPlatter's Guest Account via the Internet (ERL-Remote), you will need to FTP an ERL client from the FTP server: ftp.silverplatter.com.

Once you retrieve the client, refer to the appropriate install-text file (for example, winstall.txt), located in the "spirstmp" directory, for client installation instructions.

To FTP the ERL-Remote client:

(1) Create a temporary directory (or folder) called spirstmp on your local hard drive:

```
C:\>md spirstmp<Enter>
```

(2) Open an FTP connection to SilverPlatter's FTP server:

```
C:\>FTP<Enter>
ftp>open ftp.silverplatter.com<Enter>
```

    or

```
ftp>open 192.80.71.12<Enter>
220 norwood2.silverplatter.com FTP server ready
Remote User Name: anonymous<Enter>
Remote Password: (type your Internet e-mail address)<Enter>
```

(3) Retrieve the ERL-Remote client software from one of the following directories, depending on your computer and software situation:

```
/software/erl-remote/pcspirs.323/lwp4dos (for LAN WorkPlace for DOS)
/software/erl-remote/pcspirs.323/pcnfs (for SUN PC-NFS)
/software/erl-remote/pcspirs.323/pctcp (for FTP PC-TCP)
/software/erl-remote/pcspirs.323/wattcp (for packet drivers)
/software/erl-remote/macspirs.22
/software/erl-remote/winspirs.10
```

Change to the directory of the ERL-Remote client you wish to FTP. For example:

```
ftp>cd/software/erl-remote/pcspirs.323/lwp4dos<Enter>
```

(4) Set file transfer type to binary:

```
ftp>TYPEI <Enter> or
ftp>BINARY <Enter>
```

(5) Change to the local directory where the ERL client will be installed:

```
ftp>lcd\spirstmp <Enter>
```

(6) Copy the files from the ERL-Remote client subdirectory to your local hard disk:

```
ftp>mget* <Enter>
```

(7) Exit out of FTP:

```
ftp>bye <Enter>
```

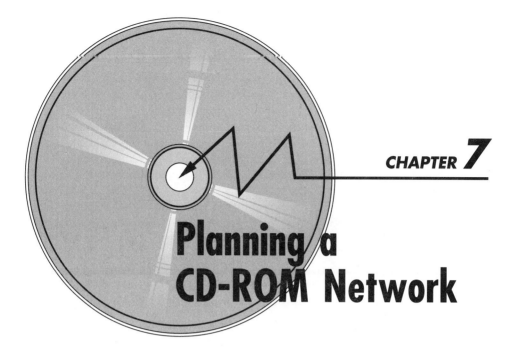

CHAPTER 7

Planning a CD-ROM Network

Basically, building a network is not a short-term project. Any network has to be built in an orderly fashion for the network to last and serve. In order to minimize design errors, one should visit network sites in similar corporations and observe how the networks in these sites are designed and managed.

The emphasis when planning a CD-ROM network is to appoint a project leader. The project leader gathers information about all aspects of the projected network. Self-education and attending orientations about networks in general and CD-ROMs in particular, as well as joining network training classes, will all help in developing a good CD-ROM network. During the period of planning, collecting articles on the topic and researching different network products and vendors have proved helpful because the more you know before you start, the less time and money you'll spend during implementation.

A network should meet the needs of the organization as economically as possible. A thorough analysis of the network site is required for planning, designing, and implementing a good network.

Networks experience addition, expansion, or growth over time. They evolve spontaneously with cables running across corridors, out of walls, and through ceilings. When networks grow, they become more complex in hardware and management. Some network operating systems might not be able to handle a growing network. In order to meet the network growth, you might have to replace it with a different network operating system.

Planning Considerations

Before you form a network planning committee and before this committee can formulate its objectives, you have to collect information about all the PCs and terminals in your organization, such as sources of data, number of CD-ROM workstations and number of databases available on CD-ROM, total hours a single workstation is used on a weekly basis, total hours each database is used, methods for scheduling users for these drives, and user satisfaction with the present system. This information can become the basis for setting the objectives of a network.

Always try to adopt the technology that gains universal support. Study your plan thoroughly and talk to people in other corporations. Conduct regular meetings and work closely with all parties in your department and other departments involved. Solicit the support of your superiors and gain their confidence. This will help you to acquire a good location and improve the network budget allocations. You should also include a financial justification for everything you recommend. Send staff out for training as early as possible.

Project Goals

In order to formulate your objectives, you should collect information about the following:

> number and type(s) of workstations desired
>
> types of software programs to be included in the network: statistical, word processing, spreadsheets, database programs, desktop publishing, presentation packages, and other local programs and services
>
> other networks in the corporation the user will be able to access
>
> telecommunications gateway to connect workstations to external computing systems both within and beyond the corporation premises to provide services such as online public access catalog of major university libraries, economic and medical databases, national academic networks, and government networks
>
> Internet services
>
> limitations of the present services and how the proposed network would overcome these limitations and save the user's time
>
> all software packages and CD-ROM databases that are expected to be on the network.

It is recommended you form a team to plan for the CD-ROM network. In an academic library, for instance, the team would include members from the systems office, reference services, department of academic computing services, acquisitions, and the computer studies faculty. Hiring a consultant will always prove helpful because of the complexities of selecting the appropriate hardware and software. You may also include representatives from the offices that will be most affected by the CD-ROM network.

During the first meeting, you should explain the purpose of forming the team, which is to establish a CD ROM network that will support the needs of your institution. You should also state why a CD-ROM network is needed and what the expectations of the new system will be. For example, the goals to establish a CD-ROM network could be to:

   provide computing facilities to meet instructional goals

   enhance the overall education of students

   increase access to and interactions among people (teachers, students, coworkers, local and remote peers, etc.), data (research, theories, etc.), and formats of knowledge (text, graphics, photos, etc.)

   increase students' and researchers' access to library resources

   overcome the problems associated with standalone CD-ROM workstations

   upgrade microcomputer capabilities for faculty and students

   facilitate research activities by allowing faculty and students to access other information resources not available within the library

   facilitate computer-aided instruction and research through the use of personal workstations

   participate in efforts that bring the educational institutions close together

   share computing facilities

   use both local area networks and wide area networks in order to enhance user access to computer applications and research services.

You have to realize that networks usually evolve. A small network will soon become part of the enterprise network (campus network). When this happens, other enterprise subnetworks will benefit from this connection. The internetwork will allow researchers at other subnetworks to take advantage of the proposed network. In the meantime, the internetwork will allow the proposed network to access other services beyond the premises of the parent corporation via a gateway through Internet or any other service.

Gaining Support

Not only will you want to win the support of the administration, but you will also need to receive support from many other sources in your organization, such as the telecommunications staff, mainframe system managers, computer support staff, and security personnel. These groups should be briefly presented with the project objectives. You will need the telecommunications department to lay out the cables for the network and connect your network to the backbone and the Internet; this department will help in deciding which network architecture to choose and the equipment you will be needing. The mainframe manager will be the one to address when you need your users to access the mainframe as well as online services and other sources. Computer support staff will be needed to help in selecting the network software and hardware. And the security office will help in securing the hardware and determining access to the network control room. During your first meeting, identify the contact persons in these departments. Make notes of new ideas and have someone record the meeting.

Selecting the Site

When selecting the site, you will be concerned about two important issues: topology and cabling. There are some factors, such as building constraints, that may influence the choice of a topology. In some buildings it may be prohibitively expensive to run cable or wire directly. When routing problems are a factor, bus topology is the least costly as it involves the least amount of cable. Ethernet uses bus topology (except for that specifically designed for star topology). Because the key to connectivity is standards, your topology should conform to well-known standards (e.g., Ethernet, Token Ring, etc.), as these standards offer the greatest interconnectivity potential.

Where cabling is concerned, a combination of fiber-optic (for the backbone) and unshielded twisted-pair (UTP) wiring (to connect the desktop) seems to be the preferred standard for today and tomorrow in terms of technology and cost.

UTP will support 10BaseT Ethernet, 16-Mb/sec Token Ring, and FDDI over copper. However, if you use UTP, you will need a hub. On the other hand, thin Ethernet can be used for small networks where you do not need a hub. In either case, there is a length limit imposed by the type of wiring selected.

A preliminary site location should be suggested. That site might have to accommodate the following: the public workstations area, a staff consultant area, a control room, and a room for the network coordinator. Make sure the area will allow future expansions without moving the workstations or the control room to a bigger place. In other corporations, where a public service area is not needed as the workstations are located in the offices, only a control room and a printer pooling area furnished with bins to collect printouts and a network coordinator room might be the only areas needed. Or you might want to offer local printing for every office, using cheap dot-matrix printers.

The computer lab area should serve present needs and allow for expansion in the future. It should include a user service area for the staff consultants and a place for printer stands and boxes of print paper, and bins for distribution of printouts.

Another room should also be considered as a control room. A reasonable size would be no less than 6 x 9 feet and would accommodate the network controlling equipment, such as file servers, CD-ROM servers, CD-ROM drive units, a workstation to access the server, a network backup tape system, network connectivity devices such as repeaters, UPSs (uninterrupted power supplies), documentation and manuals for the network operating system and CD-ROM databases, floppy disks, a lot of cables and wires, and tables and shelves. In general, it should accommodate all the equipment that will be used to control the network and any equipment that users are not supposed to access plus a desk for the network administrator, if needed.

A wiring closet might also be needed that will act as a wiring center for the network to facilitate the diagnosing of problems and expansion of the network in the future. It should be located in a central location in the building to facilitate office connections and other public service areas. This central wiring closet should be secure and have good air circulation. The closet will be used as a cable fan-out point and house the wiring hubs or concentrators, trans-ceivers, and other equipment that will attach cables to the backbone. If the wiring closet is large enough to accommodate the control equipment, then you will not need a separate room for the server.

A third room is needed for the coordinator of the network.

The next step is to determine the probable topology of the network and think about three items: connecting the wiring closet to the control room, wiring the workstations to the wiring closet, and laying out the cables in the service area and other offices in the building. For open areas, you better use telephone boxes attached to a pole that carries the cables from the ceiling to the floor. Because of electric interference, network cables should run in sep-arate channels from the electric power cables and wiring in elevator shafts.

Wiring the premises involves careful design that eventually will result in system flexibility. Such flexibility can produce an easy installation that will not be affected by departmental, user, or device moves from one location to another. Flexibility also involves terminating the cables at a specific point that will help in creating centralized expansion and distribution points in the building. These central points, or wiring closets as they are called, will be used to cross-connect cables through the floors and to run remote devices. The idea is to wire the building once. To simplify future installations and moves, every station and desk should be served by a data cable. To adapt to changes in communications and computer technology, it is advisable to use up-to-date systems. Because fiber optic has enormous potential, experts in the field recommend running fiber backbones and using twisted-pair cables to connect the nodes. Mixing UTP and fiber cable can maximize flexibility. Documenting cable paths, closet terminations, and floor layouts is very important. Labeling the cables after every change or modification is also very important.

To change the cabling type in an existing LAN, the existing LAN adapters can be used, but a transceiver must be used to translate between an adapter that is designed for a specific type of cable (such as coax cable) and the desired type of cable (such as UTP).

Design Process

Network design is not a committee assignment. The design has to reflect the objectives, but it also involves choices from among numerous options. Deci-sions have to be made about media, topology, access method, etc. This is best done by designating a single individual, probably an experienced consultant or a staff member, to be the network administrator.

You should review all the information you have collected so far from your meetings, observations, field visits, and conversations with different groups and individuals before you start the design of the network. You will also draw preliminary diagrams for the service sites selected. Once this phase is com-plete, you will be ready to design the network, estimate costs, and get approval for the project.

In order to design a network, you must either have some technical background or have a colleague on staff who knows the details. Otherwise, hire someone who knows network products that will work together. Usually, network designers try to avoid two things: a poor choice of topology and the use of inferior components. In fact, not all components are appropriate for a given job, and not all components work well together. Always depend on product reviews and the advice of an experienced consultant. Some vendors—including Andrew, Blackbox, and South Hills DataComm—provide free consultations during planning and design of networks.

Start the design with a sketch of the network physical topology and all the outside connections to the external networking resources. For example, if the network is small and confined to a limited area, you will not need a backbone; if the network is composed of subnetworks, you will. Draw the backbone first. Backbones must be the highest-performance components in the enterprise. They must be selected carefully because they will affect the speed of the whole network. The subnetworks are connected to the backbone directly, usually through a bridge, concentrator, or router.

Once you have defined the logical parameters (access and transport protocols such as CSMA/CD, passing token, etc.) and the physical diagrams, you will be ready to select the network operating system. After that, you will begin the process of selecting vendors for the various components of the network.

On large enterprises, simulation is required, while on small networks, simulation is not worth the cost involved because the risk of failure is limited.

Cost Estimates

Because cost estimates are basically based on parts and labor, they usually do not include the cost of staff and user training. If you are buying a complete system, CD-ROM vendors such as CBIS, EZ-Net, Meridian, and Online Computer Systems will help you estimate the costs of network equipment.

To estimate the costs, you will need information about the following:

> area the cabling system will cover
>
> number of trunk segments needed
>
> number of nodes (file servers, CD-ROM servers, repeaters, hubs, printers, and workstations)
>
> distance between stations and the overall length of the trunk segment and its type
>
> growth potentials of the network
>
> type of cable you can use in a building that complies with the fire code
>
> type of cable used in duct, plenum, or the space used for air handling
>
> type of computer applications that will run on the network.

Cost estimates can be itemized into categories, such as personnel, equipment, training, and software. They can also be arranged into areas of service, such as maintenance, management, upgrades, and replacement.

Implementing the Network

Once you receive the network-building parts for the first phase of the project, start with the installation of the network infrastructure such as cables, network interface cards, and remote programmable read-only memory (PROM). Try not to disturb staff or users, or to disrupt the flow of operations and services in your organization. Configure the server machines. Connect the CD-ROM drives per their manuals. Contact vendors for missing items. Install the log-in batch files and other important programs, such as applications software, network drivers, menuing system, metering system, and other utility programs. Do some testing after the installation of any software or hardware.

Keep the administrators informed of your progress and the constraints. After you test the system thoroughly, ask other people to test the network after explaining to them how the network is used. Try to implement some of the feedback of the testers, if they make sense. After extensive testing, you can bring the network online for public or office use. Explain to all users how to log-in and log-out, what applications are on the network, and how each is used.

An important issue is documentation. A well-documented network will be self explaining, as it will limit training to the necessities. Informative messages and a clear menu system will help all users very much. If logging in is required, users should be told how to log in properly.

CHAPTER **8**

Networks: Issues and Concerns

There are many issues to consider while planning, implementing, and operating a local area network. These issues are independent from the network operating system and the LAN type. Security, for example, is a major concern as no one wants the problem of a faltering system. For no reason whatsoever other than to prove a point, some users might try to beat the system by breaking into it. Others might attack the system to incapacitate it. Still others might try to copy software programs, infringing on the copyright law. What's more, some innocent or careless users could unknowingly inflict harm on the network. You should anticipate potential attacks against your network. But remember, protecting your network will add to the overall cost of the LAN.

Attacks are of many types and you should anticipate them. There are physical, active, and passive attacks. Where physical attacks are directed toward workstations, printers, and other LAN equipment, active attacks threaten to interfere with the proper functioning of the network. They include those that are directed mostly at data, such as erasing files or altering the data; infringing on the copyright law by unauthorized copying of data and program files; or introducing a virus. Power surges can wipe out the data on a file server. Also, the lack of procedures and guidelines to follow during emergencies can leave the user as well as the staff in a disarray. Passive attacks, on the other hand, include tapping into the network or gaining information about the system and the users without interfering with its proper operation.

This chapter will try to explain these issues as well as many others such as CD-ROM licensing, software metering, and menuing systems.

Security

People constitute the largest potential threat to any computer network as the majority of LAN security failures are due to human involvement. Because security measures in LANs depend heavily on the requirements of individual networks, the LAN host should carry out a risk analysis in order to decide which security measures to implement.

Most network architectures do not take aggressive precautions to provide for increased security. On the physical level, most networks use simple physical media (copper cables specifically) which are easy for unauthorized users to tap into the network. On the transmission level, the main loopholes are a result of using methods such as the broadcast principle for communication adopted by the Carrier Sense Multiple Access (CSMA), which allows every station on the network to hear and evaluate all data frames. So, the lack of physical security and the ease with which transmission may be disrupted both make it easy to gain illegal access to the LAN.

Security threats may include the following:

> monitoring traffic on the network and recording the electromagnetic emissions from the copper cables—the data obtained this way may be used to identify LAN users and to read passwords and data that are not encrypted

> connecting unauthorized stations to the network using vampire clamps or wall outlets without being noticed

> the continual broadcasting of connection requests using a LAN analyzer that can disrupt broadcasting on a network

> electronic vandalism by altering or deleting data and software programs

> physical vandalism and common theft

> fire and natural disasters such as earthquakes and floods.

The security measures that should be considered are of different levels: physical, logical, transmission, and data.

Physical Level

On the physical level, security measures may include hardware security. This relates directly to equipment that controls the network, including network servers, CD-ROM drives, tape backups, repeaters, transceivers, bridges, and routers.

> In general, equipment that is not supposed to be accessed directly by users should be locked in a secure place that has an alarm system. These rooms should not be accessed except by the supervisor and authorized personnel. Also, locking the keyboard and drive doors on the servers is recommended. If special rooms are not available, servers and other equipment should be housed in lockable cabinets.

The procedures for bringing the servers up and down should be understood and they should be undertaken by designated staff only.

Cable conduits as well as network wiring closets should be made inaccessible.

Equipment, such as workstations and printers, that is to be accessed by users should be secured using antitheft tools.

Network traffic as a whole could be monitored to detect irregularities and unauthorized connections using LAN analyzers or Time Domain Reflectometers (TDRs), which can find any unauthorized transceiver connections.

The topology and the media type can add more security to a LAN. For example, unlike in a bus structure, where all nodes are attached to the bus line and any signal is heard by every node on the network, in a star-shaped cabling, only one device is attached to a line, while the line starts at a hub.

There are a variety of methods on the market to lock equipment in place to restrain the hardware. A professional installer will provide equipment insurance against theft; in addition, aesthetics are preserved. Physical security applies to all equipment, including computers, monitors, keyboards, mouse devices, and printers. For example, the PadoLock system from Doss Industries of San Francisco consists of interlocking steel plates. One plate, containing a lock, is attached to the top of the table. Another plate is secured to the bottom of the computer system unit. The system unit is mounted onto the plate. The key is then turned to lock the two plates together. The monitor and the keyboard are attached to the plate through a steel cable. All keys should be locked in a secure place. The problem with this system is that if equipment is to be moved often from one place to another, the organization has to pay for removing the plates. However, unless the culprit carries the whole table with the computer system attached, it is very difficult to separate the equipment from the table on-site without the key. The installer of the security system should know the computer brand, as there are specific plates for each computer brand.

Other companies, such as Secure-It, supply a kit consisting of cables, locks, and fasteners through which to loop the cable through as many as six pieces of equipment. PC Security offers a system called the Grabber, which consists of steel plates and a steel cable and padlock. There are other systems that will prevent unauthorized power-ups such as the STOPPER from PC Security. In general, most cable or connect systems are lacking in aesthetic appeal and they do not prevent vandalism.

Logical Level

On the logical level, security measures may include the user interface and how the user accesses the network to utilize its resources. This level includes user identification, passwords, authentication, authorization, confidentiality, secrecy, and anonymity.

Transmission Level

On the transmission level, special attention should be made to encrypt users' information and passwords on the file server. This is very important, especially to secure remote connections against unauthorized intruders. Since remote connection is done off-site, the intruder who breaks into a system is sometimes hard to detect. There are steps that can be taken to protect the LAN against remote intruders.

On the physical level:

> Physical access can be prevented by placing these servers and other communications devices such as modems in locked rooms.

> Fault tolerance is another feature, which lets a server continue operation in the event of hardware failure. Other measures, such as redundant hot-pluggable power supplies, allow each PC board in the communications server to have its own power supply. This will allow the swapping of individual PC processors without disrupting the operation of the other processors.

On the logical level:

> In order to handle communications in large networks, filters should be used in bridges, routers, and brouters.

> Public- or private-key encryption of data should be considered to prevent the monitoring and decryption of the data signals by unauthorized intruders.

> The network operating system should restrict access to specific ports, set maximum connection times, and force dial-back, where an authorized user calls the host system and then hangs up. The host then calls the user back at a predefined phone number.

> Monitoring the activities of every user to detect unauthorized accesses to the LAN could be accomplished by using such software packages as the LANtrail from Horizons Technology, and Languard and Security Guardian, both from Command Software Systems.

> A dial-up number for remote access should never be advertised.

> In an academic environment, if a remote access service is offered to faculty, the faculty should be asked not to reveal the number and passwords to the students.

Data Level

Data protection against misuse is important. The following measures should be considered to protect the data:

Measures on the server side:

> Uninterruptible power supply (UPS) for every server computer

> Server automatic backup or even duplicated servers

> Redundant data management with duplicated hard disks

> Network backup

Measures on the workstation side:

Diskless stations, which may be loaded by remote booting, unless the CD-ROM software needs a hard disk for data overflow and temporary files

Access to the server is restricted via log-on with user names, passwords, station addresses, and time-out

At the file and directory levels, rights of users and security procedures should be specified

Surge protectors to defend LAN workstations and peripherals against power surges, which could damage sensitive electronic components or cause data loss.

In order to improve security, idle workstations should be automatically logged off. Software such as NetOFF System III, distributed by On Technology, closes applications and files for PCs and Macs. It can be used in Windows and DOS workstations on NetWare 3.x or 4.x, LANtastic, and Windows NT networks. After an idle period, NetOFF blanks the screen out and requires passwords to regain access. After another idle period, it logs users out.

LAN operating systems use various levels of data security. However, three security schemes are used by most LAN software operating systems. These are: file level and network directories, users and passwords, and groups of users.

Files and directories can be given specific attributes so that they cannot be deleted, or the files could be removed even by users who might be granted the right to perform a task in these directories.

Access to a network by users can be restricted within specific hours of the day. Usually, users are given names or account numbers. Their passwords are encrypted and changed periodically. Encrypting passwords at the server, and while they are transferred through the cables to the server, prevents unauthorized cable taps from revealing these passwords. In case a password is forgotten, there are software packages, such as ACCESSDATA/NTPASS from AccessData, that will decrypt passwords. There are other packages sold by the same vendor that will do the same for application programs, such as WordPerfect and Lotus 1-2-3.

While every user should go through an authorization process, the number of permissible incorrect log-ins should be specified before the system locks a user out.

The privileges that a user is granted include accessing specific files, subdirectories, or certain drives. A user can be granted the right to scan, read, write, edit, create, or even delete files in specified subdirectories, but the user should not be able to perform any tasks other than those which he or she is authorized to do.

Users can be divided into groups. A user may belong to one or more groups and each group has specific access rights. The user can be shifted from one group to another, if needed. For example, a workstation that belongs to the CD-ROM group will not be able to run other network applications except CD-ROMs.

Users should always be reminded to log out as soon as they finish a session. They also should be advised not to leave a workstation unattended. The

LAN supervisor should log out when leaving a workstation to prevent a user from accessing the system under the supervisor's name with full supervisory rights. Supervisors are advised to create a normal user account for themselves to perform nonsupervisory activities.

Diskless workstations, if needed, can provide useful security features for sensitive data, since users in nonsupervised areas cannot download data files to disk and remove them from the building. At the same time, users cannot introduce viruses at the workstation.

Data Integrity

To maintain data reliability on a network server, LAN vendors offer many techniques, such as disk mirroring, duplexing, and hot fix.

Disk mirroring

Disk mirroring, also known as disk shadowing, provides redundant disks of the same size. If one fails, the other disk takes over for it. Both disks receive the same updates at the same time.

Duplexing

In order to attain a higher level of fault tolerance, a duplexing technique is used. The duplexing technique requires having redundant disks plus redundant disk controllers. This arrangement is called disk duplexing or channel mirroring because the entire disk channel is replicated, including the disk and the disk controller.

Hot fix

The third technique is known as the hot fix. If during a writing process a bad area on the hard disk is encountered, the hot fix intercepts the writing process and redirects the data to a good disk sector.

Helpful Measures

For security, the following protection measures might be considered:

Accounts should have expiration dates
Users should be assigned passwords
Passwords should have expiration dates and periodic changes
Users can log in through specific stations at specific times
Specific disk space should be assigned to each user
Concurrent connections for each user should be defined
Audit trails should be gathered of all log-in and log-out requests, and of account lockouts
The system should be continually checked for intruders and account lockouts

Privileges and rights to access specific directories and use specific files should be clearly explained

Authorized users should not be able to explore outside their designated areas

Special equipment that can sense abnormalities in the cable signal should be used to discover cable taps

Uninterrupted power supplies for important pieces of hardware such as file servers should be used

Use of backup systems for data integrity.

The Virus Threat

Because networks are susceptible to intentional and unintentional virus infection, the threat of computer viruses is constant. Virus threats can paralyze the network operations. Not every antivirus software package can cure all of the viruses. In order to guard a LAN system against viruses, one has to understand what a virus can do. A virus is just a piece of code written to corrupt a computer file system or the disk-booting sector or the file-allocation table (FAT). The FAT is the DOS's map of the hard disk. DOS breaks down the disk into units called clusters, each one typically holding 2,048 bytes (corresponding to four 512-byte sectors). A single file comprises a number of clusters. The FAT map tells DOS which cluster forms each file. When the file allocation table is affected, the FAT entries point to the wrong clusters and the data in files become confused.

A virus can reproduce by modifying other programs to include a copy of itself. The first known virus was written in 1983 by Fred Cohen, a student at the University of Southern California who wanted to prove that computer code could replicate itself, attach to other files, and change the behavior of the computer. He later included his findings in a doctoral dissertation. Since then, the number of viruses has grown to more than 10,000.

File viruses invade executable files only (files with _.COM and _.EXE extensions, batch files, device drivers, and any file that can be executed). The file virus loads itself into memory when an infected file is executed and spread to uninfected files as those files are run. If it makes its way to the server, it begins to take effect immediately or it stays dormant and causes damage later during a specific period of time. Some viruses can damage the whole hard disk. Viruses can spread to LAN workstations, then affect users' floppy diskettes, and then even spread to other computers.

Examples of viruses that infect the disk's boot sector include Stoned, Monkey, Michelangelo, and Exebug. The following four viruses are examples that infect the files: Satan Bug, Maltese Amoeba, Tremor, and Dark Avenger.

Types of Viruses

In general, any program or code that is written to corrupt a computer system is called a virus. However, viruses use different techniques. Based on their techniques, viruses can be divided into the following types:

Bacteria

Also known as rabbits, typical programs in this category usually reproduce themselves exponentially until they fill up all the processor capacity, memory, or disk space, denying the user access to those resources.

Logic bomb

Also called time bomb, this can be either a program or a segment of code built into a program that is activated when a condition is met (e.g., a specific date). Time bombs can cause extensive damage. The most well known logic bomb was Michelangelo of 1991.

Password catcher

This is a program that looks innocent as it collects ID and password combinations, usually in a hidden file accessible only to the author. The collected ID/password is used later to access the system and mimic the original users, thus preventing authorized LAN users from accessing the system.

Repeat dialer

This is a program that continually calls the same number, thus placing it virtually out of service for any other caller.

Trapdoors

Also known as back-doors, these are helpful entry points for programmers while a program is still under development. They are used to facilitate debugging and enhancing the program code. But once a program reaches the production stage, these back-doors should be removed. However, some programmers do not close these holes and keep them to access the system later after it is delivered to the customer, and to break its security.

Trojan horse

Trojan horses are programs that look very useful but are actually hiding viruses and logic bombs. When the program runs and the code reaches a specific point, it releases its viruses and logic bombs.

War, or demon dialer

This is a program that tries to find dial-up ports in computer systems. By using a modem-equipped PC, a hacker provides a range of phone numbers that the program sequentially dials seeking a computer tone to prevent other remote users from accessing the network. (The term *hacker* refers to people who use computers in illegal and disruptive ways. Previously, the same term was used to denote a person who is a computer genius.)

Worm

A worm is a program that scans a system or an entire network for available unused disk space in which to run. Once it runs, it ties up all computing resources in a system or on a network and effectively shuts it down. Probably the most well-known worm was the November 2, 1988, Internet incident. In two days, an estimated 6,200 UNIX-based computer systems on the network were infected. That worm was planted by Robert T. Morris Jr., a Cornell computer science graduate student who was tried later, fined $10,000, and ordered to perform 400 hours of community service.

Sources of Viruses

Viruses infect any form of writable storage, including hard drives, diskettes, magnetic tapes and cartridges, optical media, and memory. The most frequent sources of contamination include

> running programs on an infected computer
>
> running an infected program on a LAN
>
> copying an unknown disk containing a carrier program
>
> bulletin boards with contaminated files
>
> booting with an infected disk
>
> intentional action by individuals.

Virus Symptoms

The following symptoms may indicate a system infection:

> unexplained system crashes
>
> programs that suddenly don't seem to work properly
>
> data files or programs mysteriously erased
>
> disks becoming unreadable
>
> changes in the dates and times of files such as COMMAND.COM
>
> programs showing the same date and time when the directory is displayed
>
> file size increase
>
> sudden decrease of free space
>
> numerous unexpected disk accesses from a program that has never allowed that before.

Preventing Infection

To prevent a virus infection is to prevent the virus from establishing itself within the system. LAN users should attend a virus awareness training session.

It is crucial that users realize the damage a virus can inflict on the LAN. To control viruses, LAN policies and procedures should include the following:

> encouraging users not to run freeware and shareware on the LAN
>
> running antivirus software regularly on the servers
>
> checking all workstations during log-in
>
> establishing a virus-response staff
>
> control of the infection once it is detected
>
> recovery from the virus, including backup and dump policies
>
> distribution of free antivirus software to the LAN users
>
> caution in testing and using unfamiliar software.

Antivirus Software

Several commercially available programs can help detect viruses and provide some degree of protection against them. The following is a list of antivirus packages that can run on LANs to protect from, detect, and remove viruses: Anti-Virus Plus from Techmar Computer Products, Certus from Certus International, Data Physician Plus from Digital Dispatch, Dr. Solomon's Anti-Virus Toolkit from Ontrack Computer Systems, Flu-Shot Plus from Software Concepts Design, the Norton AntiVirus from Symantec, SafeWord Virus-Safe from Enigma Logic, Vaccine from WorldWide Software, Vi-Spy from RG Software Systems, ViruCide from Parsons Technology, Virus-Pro from International Security Technology, ViruSafe from Xtree, Viruscan Version from McAfee Associates.

The following is a list of some antivirus NetWare Loadable Modules (NLMs) that will load onto a Novell NetWare operating system: Anti-Virus from Central Point Software, Anti-Virus Toolkit from Ontrack Computer Systems, Inocu-LAN from Cheyenne Software, LANDesk Virus Protect from Intel PC Enhancements Division, and NetShield from McAfee Associates.

You can download McAfee's server-based antivirus utility, which is fully certified by Novell, electronically through a network of bulletin boards, CompuServe, America Online, and Internet. The related files are CLEAN102.ZIP, NETSC102.ZIP, SCANV102.ZIP, and VSHLD102.ZIP.

Network Backup Storage Subsystems

The reasons to back up the network include the following:

> erasing files by mistake
>
> hard disk failure
>
> fire and theft
>
> power loss and power spikes
>
> hard disk's slowing down because of bad disk fragmentation.

Tape backup units are the most inexpensive way to back up network files (prices start at less than $1,000), compared to rewritable optical drives, which start at the $2,000 range. Data on the file server should be fully backed up on a regular basis and, of course, after each change of the files on the server. Tape cartridges should be numbered and marked with the current date. An extra tape cartridge should be stored in a fireproof safe or in a place outside the LAN premises.

When selecting a tape backup system, you should match the size of the tape with the size of the uncompressed files on the server. Some systems use a very large storage resource that provides large disk capacity as well as an optical jukebox and/or tape library. The following is a list of some backup systems: ARCserve from Cheyenne Software, Conner Backup from Conner Storage Systems, Enterprise from Epoch Systems, LANshadow from Horizons Technology, Mountain TapeWare from Mountain Network Solutions, Network Archivist from Palindrome, NetWorker from Legato Systems, ServerDat from GigaTrend, and Xpress Librarian from Emerald Systems.

CD-ROM Licensing

Providing multiple simultaneous access to the same CD-ROM disc is considered by some publishers as making illegal photocopies of a textbook. However, paying the full retail price for each additional user is considered by buyers as unfair. Many companies have no clearcut policies for networking their CD-ROM products, and it seems that there is no perfect solution. This makes CD-ROM multiuser licensing appear as lagging far behind CD-ROM networking technology. Technically speaking, it is possible to run any CD-ROM disc on a network; however, this does not make it legal. Until recently, most CD-ROM products were marketed and licensed as single-user systems. However, vendors have started to offer multiple-user licenses for network use. Many of them have not yet determined how to price their CD-ROM products. Some publishers do not charge an additional fee for use of their CD-ROM products on a network. Others charge a fee per node for multiple-workstation access above the base price of each CD-ROM disc.

In addition to charging a yearly subscription price, some companies charge a fixed-station license fee, including dial-in remote access. Still, some vendors equip their software with a monitor to count the number of users who can access any CD-ROM disc simultaneously. When the number of users reaches the limit, the system refuses access until someone exits an application. Some vendors use a device called a "dongle," or key, that looks like a plug. For the CD-ROM application to run, this dongle must be plugged into the printer's port. Other methods are used such as providing the end user with a specific number of access codes. Some single-user CD-ROM application software stops running if it senses the presence of a network operating system.

Vendors use many types of licensing CD-ROMs, including the following:

Concurrent Users

Accessing a specific disc concurrently, whether on-site or remotely, is limited to a specific number of users. Additional users—than the number allowed— will get a busy message. The problem with this approach is that some users will walk away from the workstation leaving the number of concurrent users unchanged. A time-out feature can be added to the application software or to the menuing system to drop out any unattended workstation after a specific period of time.

Licensed Workstations

This type of software license requires customers to purchase a license for every PC on the network that will use the software. This method specifies the number of workstations allowed to access a CD-ROM application. For example, 10 out of 50 workstations may be granted access to a specific CD-ROM application. The problem with this solution is that if these 10 workstations are used for other purposes than CD-ROMs, a user has to wait until one of the users terminates a session. The solution to this problem is to designate these 10 workstations exclusively for CD-ROMs. The disadvantage of this approach is that these 10 workstations may not be used all the time for CD-ROMs. To benefit from this approach, the number of exclusive CD-ROM workstations should be minimal based on the needs of the users.

Site License

This type of license allows an unrestricted number of network users to access a particular application, either organization-wide or within a "site" of an organization, such as a university or school library. Usually, site licenses are negotiated on a case-by-case basis. This method allows a one-time payment to cover use of the CD-ROM application on the network, no matter how many workstations are active at any time. However, although any CD-ROM server can theoretically handle more than 100 users, performance of many CD-ROM applications will significantly degrade once the system serves a specific number of concurrent users. There is no specific number as each application is different. Some applications will cause the system to be degraded when the number of concurrent users reaches 30, while some can cause the system to degrade when the number of concurrent users reaches only 4 users. The user has to observe the system to find out the exact number for each CD-ROM application.

License per User

This license requires customers to purchase individual licenses for each person on the network who will use the software. Those persons can use the application from any workstation.

Software License

This is a contract between the software user and the software vendor that gives the software user permission to access a given software product for a specific period of time, subject to conditions such as fees, number of users, and the software's operating environment. After the test period, the software will become inaccessible.

License per Server

Under this type of license, a single copy of the software on the file server is accessed by as many nodes as are attached to the server.

Operational Issues

Software Metering Tool

Software metering allows the control of the number of users within the program license limits. These programs monitor and manage user access to certain applications on the network server. In addition, some software-metering tools track the various software licenses to enforce the terms pertaining to each. LAN metering programs help in auditing network activities, regulating the number of users legally accessing networked programs, and establishing effective security. They also provide information on how the network is used and what applications are used most.

Metering tools will lock out anyone trying to use an application above the designated maximum user number. Direct Access Network menuing system, from Fifth Generation Systems, has built-in metering. Saber Meter, from Saber Software, is sold separate from the Saber Menuing System. Other metering packages include AppMeter from Funk Software, CentaMeter from Tally Systems, SiteLock from Brightwork Development, SiteMeter from McAfee Associates, SofTrack from On Technology, SoftWare Metering and Resource Tracking for NetWare from Frye Computer Systems, Turnstyle from Connect Computer, and WorkStation Manager from McCarty Associates. Some of these companies provide free, fully operable metering software that expires after a specific date.

Menuing Systems

One of the problems on networks is controlling access to applications on the LAN without sacrificing LAN security. As the number of applications on the LAN grows, so do the problems of adjusting the menu with every change. Adding or removing information from the menu usually becomes a painful task, and moving applications around will annoy many users. Network menu systems provide an integrated solution to managing network access. They provide control over what can be accessed. They also provide monitoring of application use, i.e., metering. There are many packages on the market, such as Automenu from Magee Enterprises, Direct Access Network from Fifth Generation Systems, EZ-MENU from Progressive Computer Services, Net-menu from NETinc., Saber Menu System from Saber Software, and Direct Access Network from Fifth Generation Systems.

You can download a shareware version of Automenu via ANONYMOUS FTP at:

```
risc.ua.edu subdirectory: /pub/network/misc/menus/auto47.zip
ux1.cso.uiuc.edu   subdirectory: /pc/execpc/automenu.zip
```

You can also download a freeware menu called MC Menu via ANONY-MOUS FTP at:

```
cs.dal.ca
     subdirectory:  /pub/comp.archives.comp.sys.novell
ftp.uni-kl.de
     subdirectory:  /pub/pc/novell
plaza.aarnet.edu.au
     subdirectory:  /micros/pc/garbo/net
wuarchive.wustl.edu
     subdirectory:  /mirrors4/garbo.wuasa.fi/net
```

Training Issues

As networks grow, support for users and the hardware they operate becomes an increasingly important issue. In a CD-ROM network, each user (staff and clients) may need to be trained in basic PC operations and CD-ROM search strategy as well as network usage. Deciding who performs this support is important. If the LAN supervisor is left with the task of training new users or helping existing users, he or she is drawn away from other tasks such as maintaining the efficiency of the network or the filing system. In libraries, for instance, training is left to the bibliographic instructors. At least six areas for training can be identified:

> development of search strategy
>
> use of equipment—system hardware and software
>
> use of Boolean and logical operators
>
> design and modification of search procedures
>
> terminology or vocabulary control
>
> database selection

Training methodology could include all or some of the following: handouts, workbooks, self-directed study, help available in the network, workshops, demonstrations, individual instruction, and lectures. It is recommended, however, that data on user preferences for training methodologies and the areas of training be gathered before designing an instruction program.

Managing Emergencies

Policies and procedures should be adopted to handle emergency situations relating to the operation of the network. These policies should be written down and they should cover issues such as climate control of the operations room, security, reporting of problems, guidelines and etiquette of the public area, responding to alarms, shutting down the network, bringing up the network, and names of authorized personnel assigned to respond to these issues.

The following are sample procedures and guidelines in a university setting. The network is running Novell NetWare, and the CD-ROM server is running OPTI-NET CD-ROM network management software. The LAN equipment is locked in a secured room, which is equipped with an alarm system. These procedures should be well understood by all LAN staff.

Responsibilities of the Network Administrator

The network administrator is responsible for the following:

> network maintenance on every level: servers, workstations, and the cabling system
>
> network security
>
> bringing the system up and down
>
> upgrading network management software
>
> updating the already installed CD-ROM databases
>
> reconfiguring the network architecture, including recabling and adding components
>
> installing newly added CD-ROM databases
>
> gathering and distributing statistical data about the use of the network
>
> attending conferences and keeping up-to-date information about technological changes.

User Manuals

Many libraries create easy-to-read short leaflets or quick reference LAN brochures. Such guides seem very helpful. Detailed manuals are also needed in the service area. These brochures should be brief and they should act as an overview of the services provided. CD-ROM LAN users are always interested in the following:

> a brief overview of the services offered and how to use these services
>
> how to construct an effective search strategy with examples
>
> how to construct a relevant search
>
> how to search individual CD-ROM databases
>
> how to print and download
>
> how to exit applications
>
> a description of the available CD-ROM databases
>
> how to connect to the mainframe and the outside world.

Outsiders

In some urban university environments, students from neighboring schools are allowed to use the university library. Those students will take advantage of the information center as well, thus depriving rightful students from using the center. Because of the limited number of available workstations and license restrictions, some CD-ROM centers apply different policies, for example, prohibiting outsiders from using the center by asking users to display their IDs all the time. Others issue account numbers to the rightful students to access the network.

Integrating the CD-ROM Applications

In a library, the staff should know how to integrate the services provided by the LAN into other library services. Consultation on regular software applications (word processing, spreadsheets, databases, and others) on the LAN could be left to LAN consultants, who are mostly students, while consultation on how to apply search strategies and use different CD-ROM applications could be provided by reference librarians.

Regular meetings between reference librarians and the LAN administrator will result in service improvement. The librarians can convey users' wish lists and their perception of the network to the LAN administrator. Reference librarians can also provide training sessions for new users.

Signage

Signs should only be made for essential services. Too many signs have the effect of discouraging the reader from reading them. Signage is very important at the following locations:

> service desk
>
> printers
>
> special workstations for the handicapped
>
> special workstations which provide specific services
>
> entrances and exits.

Hardware Cleaning

A small dust vacuum should be used to clean the keyboard. Cleaning solutions are messy and are not recommended for keyboards because of the metal grid contacts inside the keyboard. For the monitor, use monitor cleaners such as 3M Multipurpose Cleaning Solution and XPO Cleaner for Dry Erase Surfaces. Use Glare/Guard Optics Plus Cleaner from Optical Coating Laboratories for glare-guard screens. Also, cleaning kits are available from distributors such as MISCO and Global Computer Supplies.

CHAPTER **9**

Servers and Workstations

The main objective of any computer network is to share the available computer hardware and software, as well as other information resources, among users. These computing resources are usually made available through one or more computers on the network. These computers are known as servers. Not only the type of LAN is important when designing a computer network, but also the type of computer that will be assigned the role of server.

Based on how the hardware peripherals, the software programs, and other computing and information resources and services are made available to workstations (client PCs), networks can be configured as centralized (dedicated server LANs) or decentralized (peer-to-peer LANs).[1] In the centralized configuration, a dedicated server provides network services to all client PCs. Network users cannot use the server as a workstation to run their own programs. This is in contrast to the decentralized configuration, where all PCs in the network can assume the role of servers and workstations at the same time. This means that any PC can share its software, drives, and any hardware peripherals attached to it with any other PC in the network. In the meantime, that same computer can access any other computer on the network, in which case that computer becomes a client workstation.

Selecting a File Server

The file server is the PC that controls network activities such as file services, printing, data and program sharing, communication, and network security functions. Usually, the server is a PC with large memory capacity, a fast processor, large disk capacity, or large disk arrays for sharing file storage. If it includes disk arrays, it is called RAID (Redundant Array of Independent Disks), a concept developed at the University of California at Berkeley to improve the input/output performance, storage capacity, and reliability of hard disk drives. RAID computers are typically high-end PCs that run a network operating system and have high-capacity disks with a fast access time, high-powered processors, and fast buses with multiple slots.

Computer central processing units (CPUs), or microprocessors, are usually labeled with the numbers 8086, 8088, 80286, 80386, and 80486. The 80586 chip, however, was labeled P5, which is used in the Pentium computer.

Actually, any 286-, 386-, 486-, or Pentium-based computers can act as servers. You're advised, however, not to use 286-based machines unless there is no alternative. Be warned that 286-based machines are very slow and will not be able to handle the flow of operations properly. Also, specific network operating systems might not run on 80286-based servers. For example, Novell's NetWare 3.x will not run on an 80286 computer, while Windows for Workgroups requires at least 386 machines to run properly.

Many corporations are still using old computers such as the classic PCs, PC/XTs, and 286 computers. When 286 computers are used on a network, they operate under serious memory constraints. The extended memory size is limited to 16 Mb on 286 and 386SX computers. Upgrading the CPU of a 286 computer to 386 or 486 will cost at least $350, and the results are unpredictable. Still, you will have to upgrade the memory of these 286 computers. You may rather buy 386 or 486 computers in the beginning. Although you can use 286 PCs as workstations, their CPUs may not be able to keep pace with fast 16-bit network interface cards (NICs). The reason is that the adapter's device-driver software does much of the work of turning data into network packets in the background. And, of course, the CPU must be up to the task or your applications will be very slow, thus defeating the prime objective of your network, which is to provide better, faster, and easier service.

An 80286 file server can be selected for a very small LAN with five workstations or less, and one or two CD-ROM applications. If the LAN is expected to grow rapidly in applications and number of workstations, a 386 or 486 computer should be selected. Depending on the budget, 486 EISA (Enhanced Industry Standard Architecture) or Pentium computers should be considered for file servers and CD-ROM servers, while 486DX computers and their less-expensive version, 386SX computers, are considered for workstations. Power users may opt to use superservers equipped with multiprocessors. As a rule, the faster the CPU of the server, the faster the throughput of the LAN. So, selecting a 486 or a Pentium computer as a server will result in high throughput.

Because file servers are the heart of any network, some vendors might try to convince you to acquire expensive and specialized hardware when selecting a file server. Although the file servers have an impact on the network's overall performance, you should not feel compelled to acquire an expensive PC simply to keep up with technology or obtain unneeded power.

A server should have a big memory—at least 16 Mb of RAM and a large, fast hard disk (over 320 Mb). All in all, a server is usually recommended as the most powerful machine in the LAN. While powerful machines come with a high price tag, the prices of the less-powerful machines can be very attractive.

You may decide it is not worth paying for a superserver when the job can be handled reasonably by a less-powerful machine. Still, there are more reasonable alternatives on the market and you should look for a cost-effective computing platform.

If the server is supporting distributed data access, a 486/66-MHz processor with an EISA bus or a Pentium should be considered. These high-power machines with advanced buses can handle the disk and network I/O loads imposed by heavy database access.

Because peer-to-peer networks divide their computing resources among many machines, using expensive and powerful PCs with multiprocessors as servers is not a pressing issue, whereas a powerful machine is required to provide services to all client workstations in a server-dedicated network.

Selecting a file server should be done very carefully because upgrading an old file server is not a pleasant operation. Thus, scalability (the ability to upgrade the processor, memory, and other hardware and software components), reliability, and serviceability should be the main concerns. An important consideration is the feasibility of upgrading the RAM, the motherboard, and the hard disk. Does the server have a modular design that supports processor upgrades or replaceable processor modules—i.e., can a 80386 processor be upgraded in the future to 80486?

You should know that the only thing that cannot be upgraded in a computer is the bus. An 8-bit bus, for example, cannot be upgraded to a 16-bit bus. To avoid running into bus-throughput problems, it is recommended that an advanced EISA or Micro Channel bus be considered from the beginning, since these 32-bit bus machines promise higher throughput. However, investing in an expensive server with a Micro Channel or EISA interface does little good if the hard disks and controllers are not adequate, and if disk cache or memory cache is not used. Nevertheless, the computer's processing power and its interface bus will be crucial when the server runs more tasks.

Sometimes, the fastest computer selected as a file server might not be approved by the developer of the LAN operating system. To avoid inconvenience, it always pays to contact the developer of the network operating system for its list of approved PCs and networking components. Although this does not mean that any other PC cannot be used as a file server, it is better to watch for incompatibility. For instance, a nondedicated Novell NetWare 2.2 file server must be 100 percent IBM-compatible to operate properly in this mode; otherwise, it will lock up after NetWare runs on it. Also, an approved PC for NetWare 2.2 does not necessarily run properly on NetWare 3.11. When selecting a file server, always consider the number and types of applications, the number of CD-ROM drives and CD-ROM databases, the projected number of users, the total amount of possible disk space to be used, and whether or not the file server will be used as a communications server. As these requirements grow, internetworking could be removed from the file server to be installed in separate bridges or routers—or get a separate communications server.

In addition to processor speed (expressed in megahertz), you should also consider memory-access time (expressed in milliseconds), bus type (Industry Standard Architecture, EISA, and Micro Channel), and bus speed (8-bit, 16-bit, and 32-bit). Maintenance of the server and workstations is important; the user should look into who will do the maintenance operations: the vendor, the maker of the computer, or an outside contractor; the quality of the service provided by any one of those should be investigated. It is worthy to look into the results of the surveys conducted by many computer magazines on the quality of services provided by various vendors.

Disk caching is very important to use with these systems, since most LAN operating systems and CD-ROM operating software depend heavily on memory cache for better performance. For example, on a Novell NetWare network, the memory of the server should not be less than 12 Mb, plus 1.2 Mb for each SCSI CD-ROM drive attached to the server. Thus, if you connect 28 SCSI CD-ROM drives to a Novell NetWare network, you will need a server with almost 48 Mb to handle the 28 CD-ROM drives. In other situations, CD-ROM management software such as OPTI-NET cannot accept memory cache over 8 Mb. Such information should be known so you do not buy more memory than you actually need.

Bus Slots

To avoid buying an expansion chassis to increase the number of bus slots in the future, you should consider a file server with as many empty bus slots as possible. An expansion chassis is an expensive solution to adding more slots to an already crammed PC server, in comparison with simply purchasing a server that has enough adapter slots from the start.

For better performance, you should consider high-speed buses like Micro Channel Architecture or EISA, since these architectures are capable of moving data quickly to and from other components in the server. Depending on the bus installed inside a computer, PCs can be specified as ISA 8/16-bit bus, EISA 32-bit bus, and Micro Channel Architecture 32-bit bus.

The bus of any computer is the communications channel used to transfer data between I/O devices, memory, disk storage, and the CPU. A computer with an EISA bus is more expensive than a computer with an ISA bus. Micro Channel Architecture is used in IBM PS/2 computers.

For analogy, a system bus is like a road, and the data that move over that bus are the traffic. If the bus has more lanes, or a faster throughput capacity, more traffic can move in a given length of time. The question is how much capacity the user needs before the bus is saturated under heavy traffic. The reason for asking this question is that as long as the traffic on the LAN is not heavy, data can move on an ISA bus just as quickly as on an EISA or Micro Channel Architecture bus. But once the capacity of the network is increased and the performance is degraded, then an EISA or Micro Channel bus will be needed. This bus performs better than an ISA bus; however, its cost is higher.

ISA bus

The ISA bus is used in most PCs. ISA enables expansion devices like network interface cards, CD-ROM interface cards, video adapters, and modems to send and receive data to and from the PC's microprocessor and memory 16 bits at a time. Expansion devices are plugged into sockets in the PC's motherboard. ISA is sometimes called the AT bus, because it was originally introduced with the IBM PC-AT in 1983. The first ISA had an 8-bit path. With the introduction of the IBM PC-AT, the ISA was expanded from an 8-bit data path to a 16-bit data path. This bus is the standard for all 80286 PCs, most 80386 computers, and some 80486 computers. Any card on an AT bus uses a different interrupt line to signal the CPU when it wants access to the bus. Each card should have a unique IRQ interrupt. Only 11 interrupts are available in the ISA bus. When configuring a server using an ISA computer, the user might run out of interrupts when adding many different interface cards and using all the serial and parallel ports. Even though the processor speed may be 33 MHz, when data reach the 8-MHz ISA bus from the processor, it will slow down. As applications move to true-color graphics, full-motion video, and 3D rendering, ISA will not be able to handle them efficiently.

EISA bus

EISA, an extension of the 16-bit ISA bus standard, allows expansion devices like network interface cards, video adapters, and modems to transfer data across the PC bus 32 bits at a time. EISA was introduced in 1988 and serves as an alternative to IBM's Micro Channel Architecture. To support ISA cards, an 8-MHz clock rate is used, but the bus can provide direct memory access rates of up to 66 Mbits/sec. Because EISA has a separate I/O and processor bus, the I/O bus can maintain a low clock rate to support ISA boards while the processor bus runs at higher rates. EISA machines can provide high-speed disk I/O to multiple users. The connector inside the computer accepts both ISA and EISA boards.

Micro Channel Architecture bus

The Micro Channel Architecture bus was developed by IBM to help resolve the difficulties of combining fast processors with the relatively slow ISA bus. Micro Channel is not compatible with ISA buses. Micro Channel Architecture provides a 32-bit interface that is faster than ISA and is a better match for 80386 and 80486 processors. Micro Channel Architecture is designed to handle both memory and I/O transfers through multiplexing, which allows several processes to share the bus simultaneously. Multiplexing splits the bus into several channels that can each be used by different processes. If processor-intensive applications will be run at the server, superservers may be a better choice due to their superior throughput and multiprocessor capabilities.

Bus Selection

The selection of a computer with a specific bus type (ISA, EISA, or Micro Channel) depends on budget, expected performance, type of service needed, and availability of parts. For example, a 486/33-MHz file server with standard 8-MHz ISA bus is a poor choice for a large CD-ROM LAN. For a large LAN, the user should select a file server with an EISA or Micro Channel bus. Although the price difference between ISA and EISA computers is almost $500, as a rule the ISA is the choice for most standalone systems and network workstations. EISA and Micro Channel, on the other hand, offer advantages for network servers, computer-aided design, multimedia, multitasking, and certain high-end graphics programs. Usually faster computer processors (80386, 80486, or the Pentium) guarantee faster memory access. An advanced bus such as EISA, on the other hand, will not improve performance, unless the user adds a caching disk controller or a software disk cache.

On a network, the EISA bus in the file server offers high performance, especially when coupled with caching capabilities. It is usually selected by professional network installers, and many computer manufacturers support it. EISA bus computers are capable of running 16-bit LAN cards in addition to the expensive 32-bit EISA cards, but with less performance.

Hard Disk Considerations

With the average price of hard disks at almost $.50 per megabyte, several manufacturers are offering 340-Mb hard drives as the basic standard. The following are some guidelines when considering the hard disk:

For the power users, performance should take precedence over price since for hard disks of 1.8 Gb and above the average price is almost $.28 per megabyte. If fast access to large files is the top priority, the key specifications would be the usable data-transfer rate and rotational speed. If database searches and CD-ROMs are the main application, the crucial number will be the average seek time.

Some buyers are turning to RAID systems to gain the fault tolerance necessary for mission-critical applications. However, RAID is expensive for small- to medium-size networks at a cost ranging from $4 to $17 per megabyte.

When considering the disk performance of a file server, the user should be concerned with four important factors: seek time, latency, access time, and rotational speed. Time is usually measured in milliseconds, meaning that the lower the number, the better the performance—e.g., access time of 18 milliseconds is faster than that of 22 milliseconds. The seek time is the time it takes to move the head across the platter to a particular track to read or write data. Users should ask whether this number indicates read-seek time, write-seek time, or an average of the two. Some vendors may list the average read-seek time, which is faster than the write-seek time. Latency is the time it takes for a drive to vertically position the head over the track to begin data transmission. Access time is the sum of the seek time and the average latency. Access time of the server's hard disk should be 10 milliseconds or less. Basically, as the capacity and the number of disk surfaces in a drive increase, the access time improves. Rotational speed is the speed of the drive, and is measured in rotations per minute. Most general-purpose drives operate at about 5,400 rpm; high-performance drives run at 7,200 rpm and above.

Disk Standards

Encoding methods and disk interfaces are available in several standards. Considered here are the Enhanced Small Device Interface (ESDI), Integrated Drive Electronics (IDE), and the Small Computer Systems Interface (SCSI) drives. The original hard disks used Seagate Technology's ST-506 technology, which worked with XT- and AT-class computers. With high-performance systems, one must make sure that the hard disk drive conforms to the storage technology: ESDI, IDE, or SCSI.

ESDI is one step up from ST-506 technology. ESDI systems are faster and have more storage capacity than ST-506 drives. ESDI reduces the amount of communication between the drive and the controller, which in turn increases efficiency. Because the CPU manages ESDI, ESDI is suitable for single-tasking environments with a capacity requirement of 2 Gb. One controller supports a maximum of two disk drive attachments. These types of drives and controllers are very fast and hold a lot of data. ESDI is a high-speed interface and currently capable of 24 Mbits/sec in transfer rate as a specified top-end limit. Most drives running ESDI are limited, however, to a maximum of 10 to 15 Mbits/sec data-transfer rate.

IDE drives have transfer rates that can be two to three times greater than those of ESDI drives. The maximum throughput of IDE drives can reach 3 to 4 Mb per second. IDE drives are cheaper because IDE technology combines the disk and the controller on the same unit. Most IDE drives are medium capacity, from 40 Mb to 200 Mb. However, IDE hard disks have reached 1 Gb and work well in 1.8-Gb configurations.

SCSI is basically an enhanced version of the IDE interface. While IDE connects only hard disks, SCSI connects hard disks as well as other peripherals. See chapter 2.

Print Servers

File-server performance can be increased if the print service is taken off the network file server and assigned to a dedicated print server. In a very busy network, a powerful EISA or Micro Channel Architecture computer can be dedicated to the task of printing. Computers acting as print servers make printers available for shared use—in some cases up to five for each print server. Print servers store incoming jobs as files in a special subdirectory called a "print spool" on a hard disk drive. When the full print job has arrived in the print spool, its file waits in a queue for the first available printer.

Almost all networking software products allow the print server to run on the file server or on a separate computer. There are five ways to attach a print server to a network:

Printer Attached Directly to File Server

This seems suitable and cheap for a small network. There are some restrictions, however: while parallel printer cables cannot run more than 30 feet, serial printer cables can run a little farther. While the parallel port offers faster connection, it does not match a direct network connection. Therefore, serial printers are slower than parallel printers. However, the total length of the parallel cable can reach 1,200 feet through the use of devices such as Printer-LINK from Primax Electronics.

Printer Attached to a Dedicated Print Server

In this configuration, a dedicated PC is assigned the role of a print server. This PC can be any old PC, where one printer or more can be attached to it. This solution will relieve the file server of many of the print queues. However, by placing this PC in the public area, it might be mistaken for a workstation and users might turn it on and off, thus causing the loss of print jobs.

Printer Attached to a Specialized Print Server

Specialized print servers are small. Once it is attached to the network cable, a print server can be mounted on the side of any printer. The number of printers that can be attached to this server vary from manufacturer to manufacturer. Specialized print servers include ASP Computer Products' JetLAN/P, Castelle's LANpress, Datacom Technologies' Series 8000, Digital Products' NetSprint, Extended Systems' PocketPrintServer, Lantronix's EPS2 Multiprotocol Print Server, Artisoft's Central Station, Rose Electronics' LANJet or MicroServ, MiLAN Technology's Fastport, and Intel's NetPort.

Printer Attached to a Local Workstation

In this configuration, a printer is attached to a workstation that runs a TSR (terminate-and-stay-resident) program, which allows the network to use this printer for network print jobs. The problem with this approach is that the amount of memory left after loading the TSR program might not be enough to run any CD-ROM applications.

Printer Connected Directly to the LAN Cable

A network printer interface card is attached to the printer's high-speed I/O bus, and connected directly to the network cable. Examples of such printers include Compaq's Papermarq 15 and 20, C-Tech's C-Itoh ProWriter CI-8 Laser Printer, HP's LaserJet 4Si and LaserJet 4Si MX, and Lexmark's IBM 4039 Laserprinter 10D and IBM 4039 Laserprinter 10R.

Communications Servers

Data communications over the phone lines are handled in two ways:

> *Asynchronous communication* a character-based method that transmits at limited speeds of up to 14.4 Kbits/sec—compared to the speed of the LAN, which could reach 10 Mbits/sec. Asynchronous data transmission is characterized by varying amounts of time between each bit that is sent. Asynchronous can be used over a standard phone line. However, when higher speeds are needed, special (dedicated) lines are leased from the local phone company.

> *Synchronous communication* a block-oriented method that transmits at up to 64 Kbits/sec. The main difference is that synchronous

communication is faster because it eliminates the need to transmit stop and start bits.

Communications servers use asynchronous communications to enable remote users to access the LAN (dial-in) or local users to access remote devices (dial-out) over a dial-up telephone line and modem—but with limitations. Asynchronous communications servers are also called "dial-in/dial-out servers," or "modem servers." During a dial-up, remote users usually use the public switched telephone network for remote connections. The phone line connects a single user at a remote workstation to a LAN, or it connects LANs to other LANs for occasional use, such as the delivery of store-and-forward electronic mail. Actually, modems are required at each end of the transmission (the user side and the LAN side) to convert computer digital signals to analog signals that can be sent over telephone lines, and then back again to computer signals. The software that runs in the communications servers translates between the network and whatever communications speeds, data alphabets, and protocols the external connections use. Among the popular uses of communications servers are remote computing, file transfer, CD-ROM access, computer conferencing, electronic mail, network administration, management and diagnostics, customer support, user training and teaching, and groupware applications.

There are two basic dial-in solutions:

> *Remote-control servers*   process all data locally on the LAN and send only keystrokes and screen changes to the remote client. Remote-control software is best for applications residing on the network.
>
> *Remote-client servers*   process all data on the remote PC, sending all network traffic across the dial-up line. Remote-client software is best for applications residing on the client PC and the data residing on the LAN.

Remote-Control Servers

Remote control is probably the most efficient way to remotely connect to a network. Remote-control software processes all data locally on the LAN and transmits only keyboard and screen changes to the remote client. It is ideal if applications reside on the LAN and if they run on the network in a non-client/server mode. The general problem with remote control is that every client should have a copy of the client software installed in the remote PC, which is compatible with the host-version software.

Remote-control software may run in three configurations, but with some loss of transparency: single PC, multiprocessing remote-control servers, or multitasking remote-control servers.

Single PC

With remote control, a remote computer (called the remote, viewer, or guest) dials in to, and takes control of, another PC (called host or support) on the network, as if the remote user were sitting at the other PC, typing on its keyboard and viewing its screen. Thus, a user in Los Angeles can dial in to a PC in New York. All processing takes place on the controlled PC in New York, with only keystrokes and screen information going through the phone line to Los Angeles. Because of limitations in the hardware, however, graphics programs may not run properly. CD-ROM applications can be accessed remotely using the same techniques. The hardware and software needed are shown in Table 9–1.

Remote users can redirect printing from the controlled PC's printer to the remote-control PC's printer. The advantage to this is that the controlled PC executes applications at a local level at network speed and sends the remote user the results (usually screens) in a compressed mode. During communication, it is required that each remote caller assume control of a host computer on the network. The remote computer receives its video from the host computer, and the host receives all keyboard and mouse input from the remote user. The display screen at the remote site looks exactly like the screen on the networked PC. Using high-speed modems, though, remote users will notice little speed difference than if they were actually at the host computer. Some of the more popular remote access software packages are Procom for LAN, Norton Lambert's Close-up, Symantec's pcANYWHERE IV LAN, Ocean Isle Software's ReachOut, Triton Technologies' Co/Session LAN, SoftKlone Distributing's Takeover, Microcom's Carbon Copy Plus, Blast's Blast Professional, Digital Communications Associates' Remote, and Central Point Software's Commute. All can run Windows applications remotely.

Multiprocessing Remote-Control Servers

Setting up one computer to handle one call is easy, but large networks need to allow many remote users to call simultaneously. Instead of dedicating many PCs to handle remote access, some manufacturers have developed multiprocessing remote-control servers, which are also known by different names, such as multiple CPU servers and remote-client servers.

The heart of the remote-control server is a single-board PC, which is a microcomputer implemented on a single adapter board.

The remote-control server is attached by a cable to the network through a network adapter card. All processing takes place on the board, with only keystrokes and screen information going through the phone line to the remote PC. With remote-control servers, the remote PC acts more or less as a terminal.

Table 9–1. *Requirements for remote PC dial-up*

LAN site	Remote user site
Host PC (the controlled PC) connected to modem	Remote PC connected to modem
Modem connected to phone jack	Modem connected to phone jack
Communications software (host edition); e.g., Carbon Copy, pcANYWHERE, and Co/Session	Communications software (remote edition)
Network interface card connected to the LAN cable	

The remote-control server typically contains two or more such adapters. Each remote dial-in user "takes over" one of the single-board PCs.

Communications servers with multiple CPU systems are dedicated computers in chassis with high-speed modems installed in them. They act as nodes on the network, separate from the file and print servers. Software running on the communications server makes its serial ports or internal modems available to other workstations on a first-come-first-served basis. Some communications servers include PC processor boards, which are attached to the LAN and respond to commands entered by remote users. Dedicated communications servers are recommended because services involving dial-up lines and modems are inherently less reliable than basic file, print, or routing services, which can be handled by the file server.

For dial-in and dial-out services, many communications servers combine remote-control and standard asynchronous communications service functions in a single box—e.g., LAN Central System-Asynchronous Communications Server (LCS-ACS) from Cubix and Telebit, ChatterBox/Network Resource Server (NRS) from J&L Information Systems, and CAPserver from Evergreen Systems. Processor boards for these servers are sold for less than $1,500. To share just one or two modems, LANModem may be the most economical choice for situations where large numbers of modems are not required.

In most remote-access servers, processor units are replaceable. For example, an 80386 processor board can be replaced with an 80486. The trouble with this strategy is that processor boards are expensive and there's not much use for them once they're replaced. Some vendors (e.g., J&L) have addressed this problem by putting the board's processors and video circuitry on separate daughterboards so that users can upgrade the processor or video rather than replacing the entire board.

Some of the well-known remote-control software packages are Procom for LAN, pcANYWHERE, Co/Session, and Carbon Copy, to name a few. These packages provide basic remote-control functions as well as modem-pooling and Windows capabilities.

Multitasking Remote-Control Servers

In order to service their clients, multitasking remote-control servers use a multitasking operating system to simulate multiple processors. They use the Virtual 86 mode of 386- and 486-based computers. They share the same network adapter and use intelligent multiport serial cards to handle simultaneous phone calls. Like multiprocessor remote-control servers, they can cost more than $2,000 per line, and a functional system might cost over $40,000. Products in this category include LANMaster IncomServ from Vestra-Subco, Access Server from Novell, and 386/Multiware from Alloy Computer Products.

Features of Remote-Control Packages

The following features are essential to running a smooth remote-control operation. Any package should provide multilevel passwords, password retry limitations, remote PC boot off the host PC, screen blanking, restricted-time online capability, and host callback. It should be able to run host sessions in an unattended mode. It should include a variety of terminal emulations, support multiple file transfer protocols, print on remote as well as host printer, support serial and LAN connections, support DOS and Windows environments, run with a pool of modems or communications servers and support rates of up to 115,200 bits/sec. It should also support error-correction file transfer protocol and have a compression utility and a chat mode for online discussions.

Remote-Client or Remote-Node Access

Remote-client products are ideal for client/server applications. They are simple to use and relatively inexpensive compared to remote-control multiprocessor asynchronous communications solutions. They provide transparent access to the LAN. A remote-client also known as "remote-node connection" gives users the same "look" as being locally connected to the network—but not the same "feel." The remote PC is treated as an actual node on the office network. This connection is much slower than a remote-control connection because all Internetwork Packet eXchange (IPX) traffic, including executable files, must pass over the telephone lines. Remote-client software processes all data on the remote PC, sending all network traffic across the dial-up line. Remote-client software is best if the applications reside on the node and the data reside on the LAN, so executing network-based applications is not recommended. As long as all executable files are located on the remote user's computer, remote client is a good way for users to access data files.

With remote-client access, remote users run some communications protocols on PC computers, e.g., IPX/SPX (Internetwork Packet eXchange/Sequenced Packet eXchange), TCP/IP (Transmission Control Protocol/Internet Protocol), or AppleTalk (for Macintosh computers) across a phone line. System 7 or higher is required for the remote Macintosh, however. All data files and applications pass through the telephone line. In a client/server configuration, there will be no speed degradation. In a non-client/server configuration, speed degradation is noticed. The reason is that the client station requests data from the server only when needed. There are several remote-client access packages on the market, such as LANModem from Microtest, DCA Remote LAN Node (RLN) from Digital Communications, and NetModem from Shiva. A single modem in this category can cost between $1,500 and $2,000. Remote-node access servers include Cubix Connect, COMMUNIQUE from Integrated Workstations, NRS-ChatConnect from J&L Information Systems, ACS for NetWare Connect from Microdyne, LAN Access Server from Gateway Communications, and Communication Server 386 from U.S. Robotics.

Some network operating systems have developed remote-access modules. For example, Novell developed NetWare Connect, which is a set of NetWare Loadable Modules (NLMs). These modules support the following three main functions: dial-out, remote control, and remote node. Any workstation on the same NetWare network as a NetWare Connect server can establish a dial-out connection. Using the NetWare Asynchronous Services Interface (NASI) Connection service or the Network Computing Service (NCS), a logical connection is established between NetWare Connect and the workstation, which can then access a modem on the network and dial-out.

Modems

Modems are used for remote access. There are different types of modems on the market. Understanding their types and how they transmit will help in selecting the right modem for the services intended. Modems translate electronic signals into audible tones (MOdulation) that are translated back into electronic signals (bits) when they are received by another modem (DEModulation), hence the word modem. The speed of data transmission is measured in bits per second (bits/sec). The most common modems operate at speeds of 2,400, 4,800, 9,600, and 14,400 bits/sec.

A modem may be internal or external. An internal modem must be installed inside the computer in any empty expansion slot. External modems offer status lights and easy portability. Internal modems might be slightly faster than the external because they eliminate the external modem's slow serial interface. There are other issues to consider when buying modems, such as price (the higher the speed, the higher the price), warranty, and the bundled software.

Communication between two modems can happen in three different ways:

Simplex transmission means that information is transferred in one direction from the sender to the receiver.

Half-duplex transmission means that information is transferred in both directions, but only one direction at a time.

Duplex transmission means that information can be transmitted in both directions simultaneously.

The names of modem standards introduced by the CCITT start with a "V," followed by a dot. Old standards were introduced by Bell Telephone. Microcom introduced many standards, including Microcom Networking Protocol MNP (4), a proprietary error correction standard and MNP (5), a data-compression standard.

Modem standards are confusing because of their number structure. When selecting a modem, however, one has to pay attention to such numbers. For example, V.42 modems are not faster than V.32 modems because these are two different standards (V.32 is a modulation standard, while V.42 is an error correction standard that is incorporated in most V.32 modems). Modem standards cover three main areas: modulation standards, error correction standards, and data-compression standards.

Modulation standards include the following:

Bell 103 is a Bell Telephone standard for communication at 300 bits/sec

Bell 212A is a Bell Telephone standard for communication at 1,200 bits/sec

V.21 is a CCITT-approved standard for communication at 300 bits/sec

V.22 is a CCITT-approved standard for communication at 1,200 bits/sec

V.22bis is a CCITT-approved standard for full-duplex signaling rates of 1,200 and 2,400 bits/sec. LANModem provides two ports, one with a built-in V.32bis 9.6 Kbits/sec modem ("bis" is a French word that denotes a second version of a standard)

V.23 is a CCITT-approved standard for communication at 1,200 bits/sec in one direction and 75 bits/sec in the other

V.29 is a CCITT-approved standard for communication at 9,600 bits/sec half-duplex

V.32 is a CCITT-approved standard for asynchronous and synchronous communication that governs full-duplex signaling at 4,800 and 9,600 bits/sec

V.32bis is a CCITT-approved standard for asynchronous and synchronous communication that allows signaling at 4,800-, 7,200-, 9600-, 12,000-, and 14,400-bits/sec full-duplex modems

V.32terbo, a de facto standard, was implemented by more than 20 vendors while they were waiting for the CCITT to make a decision on V.34. V.32terbo provides connection speeds of up to 19,200 bits/sec.

V.Fast has been formally named by ITU-T (formerly the CCITT) as V.34. V.Fast doubled the throughput of V.32bis to reach 28,800 bits/sec and almost maximizes the capabilities of today's existing voice-grade phone lines.

Error correction standards include the following:

MNP (2), (3), and (4) are three levels of the public-domain Microcom Network Protocol error-control scheme.

V.42 is a CCITT-approved standard that incorporates a fallback to MNP (2), (3), and (4) as an alternative method for error correction, in case the other modem is not V.42-compliant. V.42 standard prevents a noisy line from causing data loss. This standard provides an error-corrected session between one modem and the other modem on the telephone line.

Data-compression standards include the following:

MNP (5), Microcom's proprietary, licensed protocol, capable of transmitting data in two-thirds of the original time

V.42bis is a CCITT-approved standard that allows a data transmission in one-third of the original time, and at up to a 4-to-1 compression ratio.

Workstations

Virtually any type of IBM-compatible personal computer can be used as a workstation. Computers such as the IBM XT, AT 286, any 386SX or DX, and any 486 computers and Apple Macintoshes can be used on the same network. When selecting workstations, one should keep in mind that in today's networks, most of the processing takes place in the workstation. The workstation must have the capability required to handle all application programs and services provided to the network users. When a workstation is chosen, it should be clear that software developers depend heavily on the power provided in the microprocessors of new computers to handle the complicated features of their programs in a timely fashion. The amount of computer memory (discussed in the next chapter) and the type of video system depend on the requirements of the applications the LAN will provide to its users. If CD-ROM applications are run through Windows, for example, then workstations with at least 8 megabytes of memory are needed. Because of the lower prices of computers, the ideal choice is a 386 with 8 Mb of memory, VGA color monitor with a low level of radiation emission, at least an 80-Mb hard disk, and a floppy disk drive. The 386DX and 386SX make good workstations. However, the cheap and cost-effective 386SX computer—a limited edition of the DX computer—runs at 16 MHz, while the DX computers are manufactured with different speeds such as 20 MHz, 25 MHz, 33 MHz, 40 MHz, 50 MHz, and 66 MHz. Both DX and SX can run applications under DOS, Windows, and OS/2 operating systems. Because many CD-ROM applications write temporary files to disks, a local hard disk increases the workstation performance and reduces network traffic. At least one floppy drive is needed in the workstation to encourage users to download data from CD-ROM databases onto floppy diskettes in order to take the load off the network printer.

Diskless workstations, often called "LAN workstations," are specialized PCs without disk drives. Because they barely have parts in them, they are less expensive than regular PCs. They are typically installed where security and cost are of major concern. Diskless workstations cannot boot DOS on their own. This is accomplished through firmware—i.e., software encoded on memory chips and installed on the network adapter card, known as boot PROM. On the file-server hard disk, the LAN administrator copies different versions of DOS (depending on the type of computer used as a workstation) and saves them in different directories. For example, if the network is using three different types of workstations—such as Compaq (which uses DOS 5.0), Zenith (which uses DOS 4.0), and Gateway 2000 (which uses DOS 6.0)—then all three DOS versions should be copied to the hard disk of the file server in three different directories. There is a matching list that links the workstation node address with the boot file it is to use. In the boot file, the type of DOS used by the workstation is specified and a proper search path is set to the same DOS version stored on the server. When booting, each computer—depending on its unique address—will boot from the directory assigned to it.

There are some drawbacks associated with diskless workstations. Often diskless workstations have their network adapter cards integrated into their system motherboards. If the network adapter card needs upgrading, the whole system board must be changed. It is better to choose a workstation that does not have the network adapter card integrated into the system board, or at least one that allows the LAN administrator to disable the old NIC and install a new NIC in its place. This integration might also have included the video adapter and the RAM, which means that the user cannot upgrade the video type and amount of RAM installed on the workstation.

A serious drawback of using diskless workstations in a CD-ROM network is that most CD-ROM application programs need a temporary storage area to store temporary files. If the workstation does not have a hard disk, the CD-ROM software will store the temporary files on the hard disk of the file server, thus adding more strain on the file-server operations.

Note

1. Both configurations—dedicated server and peer-to-peer—are not strictly defined as they were three or four years ago. Although both terms are still used, they have lost much of their meaning. Some network operating systems allow a dedicated server to run local applications—Novell's NetWare file server is an example. Even Microsoft LAN Manager, which is considered a high-end NOS, like Novell's NetWare, allows peer-to-peer source sharing. At some point, NetWare and LAN Manager were traditionally thought of in the context of dedicated server systems. Also, on peer-to-peer networks, dedicated servers can exist.

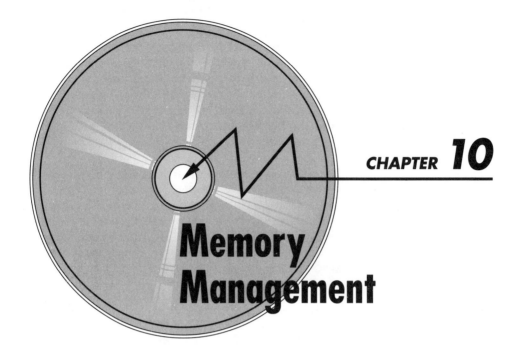

CHAPTER 10

Memory Management

Adding memory to a computer usually makes it more powerful, since it can run larger programs and hold more data. However, even the most powerful computer won't run properly if its memory is not optimized. Optimization of the system's memory is a complex operation that can be done manually using DOS version 5.0 or higher, or, better, it can be done through specialized memory manager software. The optimization process includes the evaluation of the hardware and the software until the most efficient way to use DOS memory is found. Many large application programs, especially CD-ROM database programs, that once fit in the memory of a stand-alone computer won't fit now in the memory of the same computer that has been connected to a network. The reason is that in a network, a computer has to load a variety of workstation support programs before it can function properly as a workstation. This hardly leaves any room in the workstation's memory for large programs to run—a situation known as RAM CRAM. This is because most of the programs cannot work outside the conventional memory of the workstation, which is limited to the first 640K. Unless the memory of the workstation is managed properly, all large programs will not be able to load and run properly.

Memory Basics

Memory is the place where the microprocessor (or CPU) stores programs and manipulates data generated during a computer session. Also, data keyed in by the user is mapped into the memory of the computer. The design of the microprocessor dictates the amount of memory a computer can use directly. This amount of memory is referred to as the microprocessor accessible space. The first IBM PC used an 8088 microprocessor that can directly address up to 1,024K, or 1Mb, of memory. The 1,024K is divided into 16 64K segments (fig. 10–1).

The memory segments of a typical IBM-compatible computer are numbered 0–9 (10 segments) and then A–F (6 segments). Segments 0–9 are designated for RAM—this is where most of the programs run. The size of this area is 640K (10x64), which is the standard memory. Because the 640K division starts at address zero, this area is often referred to as low memory, base memory, or conventional memory. Segments A–F are called upper memory, because they start right above the 640K of the conventional memory. They are reserved for special RAM locations, such as video display ROM (read-only memory), the PC's BIOS (Basic Input/Output System) ROM, and hard drive controller ROM. The size of the upper memory is 384K (6x64). The unused locations in the upper memory are marked "reserved." Although most PCs do not use segment E, IBM PS/2 system is using it for its ROM.

The architecture of the first megabyte of memory has not changed since the introduction of the first PC. No matter how large the RAM in any PC might be, the conventional memory occupies the first 640K while the upper memory occupies the area between 640K and 1,024K.

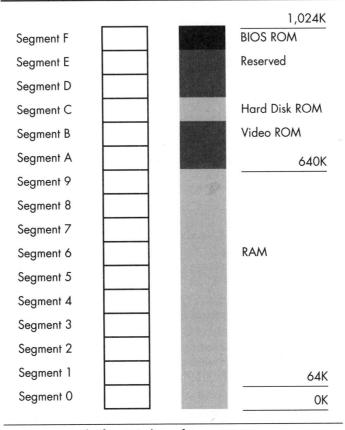

Segment F		1,024K BIOS ROM
Segment E		Reserved
Segment D		
Segment C		Hard Disk ROM
Segment B		Video ROM
Segment A		640K
Segment 9		
Segment 8		
Segment 7		
Segment 6		RAM
Segment 5		
Segment 4		
Segment 3		
Segment 2		
Segment 1		64K
Segment 0		0K

Figure 10–1. *The first megabyte of memory*

In the early days of personal computers, most machines could access only 64K of memory. This limitation did not present a problem since the software programs of the day considered 64K plenty of room. This was dramatically changed when IBM introduced the first PC. Although the sophisticated CPU of the first PC (the Intel 8088) could address one megabyte of memory, early PCs did not contain this much memory. Programmers started to exploit the new capabilities of the PC, and users quickly discovered problems. The 8088 CPU cannot access all the addresses of the one megabyte of memory. In addition, some of those addresses were unavailable to users, as they were reserved for the CPU to communicate with hardware devices like the disk drives and video display.

Memory Limitations

Most of low DOS memory is available for application programs. DOS itself uses some of this 640K. In order to become a fully functional workstation in a network, a computer has to load many types of software, such as the following:

> DOS resources—e.g., COMMAND.COM
>
> network drivers and shell programs—e.g., NetWare's IPXODI.COM and NETx.COM
>
> terminate-and-stay-resident programs (TSRs)—e.g., screen savers, menu-ing programs, printer emulators, and special key combinations
>
> device drivers (programs that control other programs or hardware)—e.g., a mouse driver or a CD-ROM driver such as HITACHI.SYS
>
> the Microsoft CD-ROM Extensions (MSCDEX), if needed.

The problem is that the size of the workstation support programs could reach well over 170K in the conventional memory. Consequently, in order to run any application program on the workstation, the size of this program has to fit into the remaining area in the conventional memory. This is true only when the microprocessor works in a mode known as the real mode.

Real Mode

The number of lines connecting the microprocessor with the bus that carries memory addresses determines the number of bytes that a microprocessor can access to read and write. The number of bytes is equal to 2 to the power of the number of address lines. The number of address lines in old PCs (8086/88) is 20 lines, meaning that their microprocessors can address 2^{20} (or 1,048,576) locations in memory, or 1 Mb of RAM. This mode, in which all 20 address lines are active is known as the real mode. The 80286 and 80386SX computers contain 24 address lines each and can address 2^{24} (or 16 Mb of memory). The 80386DX and 80486 computers contain 32 address lines each and can address 2^{32} (or 4 Gb of RAM). Only when running in a special mode, called protected mode, can the 286, 386, and 486 computers use all of their address lines.

Protected Mode

Because DOS is not capable of running in the protected mode, the processors of these computers (286, 386, and 486) adjust themselves to emulate the 8086 processor and use only the first 20 address lines. Thus, the real mode limits access in these computers to the first megabyte of memory. The upper memory (384K) of the 1 Mb real-mode address space is reserved for the hardware use. Thus, DOS and DOS applications are confined to the leftover area, which is equal to 640K (the conventional memory). Standard DOS programs cannot be larger than 640K. However, DOS extender technology provides for DOS programs to be bigger than 640K and run in protected mode (in an extended area above 1,024K, known as the extended memory). Some examples are IBM Interleaf, Paradox 386, Lotus 1-2-3 Release 3.0, and AutoCAD.

Virtual 86 Mode

The 386 and 486 computers can run in a third mode similar to the real mode, called Virtual 86 mode. In the Virtual 86 mode, DOS can gain access to more than 1 Mb of RAM by shifting some programs from the 640K area to the 384K area. This way, the user can load some programs, TSRs, device drivers, and other DOS resources in the upper memory of 386 and 486 computers. This can be done manually if DOS 5.0 or higher versions are used by altering the following two files: CONFIG.SYS and AUTOEXEC.BAT. The first file the computer looks for when booted is the CONFIG.SYS file. It then looks for the AUTOEXEC.BAT file. Another way is to use memory manager software (e.g., 386MAX from Qualitas, QEMM-386 from Quarterdeck Office Systems, and NetRoom from Helix Software). The memory manager takes advantage of the Virtual 86 mode in order to create more room in the 640K area to run large application programs.

In order to manage the memory of the computer, it is helpful to know something about two important memory chips: the ROM (Read-Only Memory) and the RAM (Random Access Memory) chips.

Read-Only Memory (ROM)

The system ROM usually occupies segment F, the last 64K in the upper memory between 960K and 1,024K. The information in the ROM chip is stored permanently by the manufacturer on the system board (motherboard), and it is retained inside the chip even when the PC is turned off. The ROM's contents can only be read and cannot be written over. The ROM chip contains the nervous system of the microcomputer, the BIOS (Basic Input/Output System). The BIOS includes the basic subroutine programs that perform the computer self-checkup every time the computer is turned on, in addition to subroutines that provide communication links between the keyboard, video display, disk drives, and serial and printer ports for the microprocessor. Each BIOS is customized by the PC's manufacturer to work with all the components inside the computer. Many adapter cards, such as network adapter cards and video cards, contain ROM chips to communicate with the computer. The ROM chips of these adapters might contain routines designed to supplement and sometimes replace routines in the system board BIOS.

Computer ROM BIOS is important, since older BIOSs of older computers might create problems when running in a network—e.g., running older Phoenix BIOSs and older American Megatrends' BIOSs under Novell's NetWare network operating system.

Not all ROMs are read-only. There are special types of ROMs that can be erased, such as the EPROM (erasable programmable ROM), which can be erased only if it is exposed to high-intensity ultraviolet light; the EEPROM (electrically erased PROM), which can be erased by electrical signals; and the Flash EPROM or flash memory, which is an inexpensive kind of ROM that can be erased electrically and updated without replacing the chip. An example of a ROM chip that can be programmed is the PROM (programmable read-only memory), which is used on the network interface cards to boot workstations remotely.

Random Access Memory (RAM)

Computer memory is commonly referred to as RAM. RAM can be written to, read from, or erased by the user. The data in this memory are wiped out once the computer is turned off. RAM is a temporary storage area for programs and data that the microprocessor uses as its work area. This memory is located in memory chips on the system board of a computer or on add-in memory boards. The computer memory can be increased by installing more memory chips directly on the system board. This is where software programs run and where the users enter data when using word processors, spreadsheets, and databases. RAMs are manufactured in many designs. The most common and least expensive is the dynamic RAM, or DRAM. To hold the data, the DRAM uses a technique called "memory refreshing." Through this technique, the DRAM reenergizes itself periodically by passing a current though its memory cells every few milliseconds. Because this technique slows down the performance of the DRAM, it is therefore cheap and is used to build the memory of the majority of the PCs on the market. Static RAM, or SRAM, is more expensive and much faster than the DRAM because it does not have to periodically reenergize itself. Since it is almost four times faster than DRAM, SRAM is mostly used to build memory cache on 386 and 486 computers. Video RAM, or VRAM, is a special type of RAM that is built on many video adapter cards to allow the PC processor to display data on the screen, and to allow the video display circuitry of the board to paint the screen. The complementary metaloxide semiconductor (CMOS) RAM is another type of RAM that is used to retain the configuration of a PC by means of a small battery.

Memory chips are manufactured in various types. These types are important when increasing the memory of your computer. Any computer uses just one type, and the types cannot be mixed in one computer. The three well-known types of RAM chips are the DIP (dual in-line package), the SIMM (single in-line memory module), and the SIP (single in-line package). While older 8088-based computers used 200-nanosecond chips, most 386 computers require DRAM chips with access times of 80 nanoseconds or less. As a rule, the lower the number, the faster the chip and the more expensive it will be. So, the 200-nanosecond chip is slower and cheaper than the 100-nanosecond chip. When increasing the size of the memory, you should not add faster chips to a PC than what the manufacturer recommends.

The DIP has two parallel rows of prongs. A SIMM, which usually contains an entire bank of RAM chips soldered onto one card, features an edge connector. The SIMM fits into special slots, usually located on the system board. A SIP looks very much like a SIMM except that it has a tiny row of legs in place of the edge connector.

Memory Types

Any PC can have as many as three principal types of memory: conventional, extended, and expanded. In addition, most computers have an upper memory area. Different techniques are used to access each type of memory.

Conventional Memory

Conventional memory is the basic type of memory found on all computers. It is limited to the area between 0 and 640K in a computer, with a 640K RAM installed. It is 512K if the computer has only 512K of RAM installed. The 640K limit is related to the 1-Mb limit of the 8088 or 8086 CPU used in first-generation IBM PC computers. When 80286 computers were introduced, the first megabyte (the conventional memory plus the upper memory area) became known as real-mode memory. When operating in real mode, the 80286 CPU has inherited the same limitations of old computers by emulating the 8088 or 8086 CPU. Using the MEM command at the DOS prompt (DOS 5.0 and higher versions) will display information on how the various types of memory are used.

Upper Memory

Upper memory occupies the area between 640K and 1,024K. Actually, any PC with 1 megabyte of RAM is composed of the following:

> 640K Conventional RAM
>
> 384K Upper memory (used by the computer hardware)
>
> 384K Extended memory
> _____
>
> Total   1,408K (1.4 Mb of RAM)

Although the upper memory is reserved for standard system hardware, it contains vacant areas that may be used to load additional hardware, such as network adapters. The available sections may be used to access additional memory by using one of two interfaces: the Expanded Memory Specification (EMS) or the eXtended Memory Specification (XMS). There are device drivers, such as MS-DOS's HIMEM.SYS and EMM386.EXE utilities, that let MS-DOS applications use the additional memory. There are many good utilities that can provide graphical representation of the upper memory area, such as UMASCAN, which accompanies Jeff Prosise's DOS 5 Memory Management, and DISCOVER.EXE, which is included with Multimedia Cloaking software from Helix Systems.

Extended Memory

Memory beyond the first megabyte (above 1,024K) address space is called extended memory. It is available only on systems with 80286 or higher processors. Extended memory is fast and efficient. However, many programs are designed to use conventional memory and cannot run in extended memory. The reason is that the numbers of addresses that identify locations in extended memory to programs are beyond the addresses most programs can recognize. Generally, all programs can recognize addresses in the 640K of conventional memory, but they need special instructions to recognize the higher addresses in extended memory.

Different methods of accessing extended memory have been developed. For instance, many applications use DOS extenders that let MS-DOS applications use extended memory in the protected mode. DOS extenders are often built into MS-DOS applications such as spreadsheets and desktop publishing programs. Under certain utilities, a system can provide extended memory through eXtended Memory Specification (XMS) standard. The XMS standard defines the following three memory areas:

> *Upper Memory Blocks (UMBs)*   UMBs are sections of upper memory that have RAM mapped into them by a memory manager. UMBs can be used by MS-DOS and MS-DOS applications.
>
> *High Memory Area (HMA)*   The first 64K of memory above the 1-megabyte boundary (1,024K to 1,088K).
>
> *Extended Memory Blocks (EMBs)*   Extended memory beyond the HMA.

To use extended memory, an extended memory manager such as HIMEM. SYS (included with MS-DOS 5.0 and higher versions) should be installed through the CONFIG.SYS file. The extended memory size is limited to 16 Mb on the 286 and 386SX. On 386DX or 486 computers, the size of the extended memory can be as much as 4 Gb. No extended memory is present on old 8086 or 8088 PCs. The first 64K of extended memory, known as HMA (high memory area), starts at the very end of the first one megabyte and is accessible by any HMA-aware software. Extended memory (XMS) is managed from the high memory area. DOS 5 and higher versions use the driver HIMEM.SYS to communicate with the first 64K of the XMS region (fig. 10–2). The HMA can be used only by a single program and may not be used simultaneously by multiple programs.

Expanded Memory

Expanded memory is accessed through available sections of upper memory using the LIM/EMS standard. Soon after the introduction of IBM's PC-AT in

Extended memory area (XMA) is 16 Mb on 286 and 386SX. It can reach 4 Gb on 386DX and 486 computers.	1,088K
High memory area (HMA) is 64K. It starts at 1,024K–1,088K.	1,024K
Upper memory (384K) is composed of six upper memory blocks. The size of each block is 64K. This area is reserved for hardware. It starts right above the 640K conventional memory area.	640K
Conventional memory	
HIMEM.SYS	0K

Figure 10–2. *Extended memory (XMS)*

1984, it became obvious that the 640K limit on memory was not enough to run long spreadsheets and other memory-demanding programs. By the end of 1984, Lotus and Intel were joined by Microsoft (LIM) to develop a specification that would permit all PCs to access more than 640K of RAM. They released version 3.2 of this specification in early 1985 under the name LIM/EMM (Lotus/Intel/Microsoft Expanded Memory Manager). LIM/EMM version 3.2 could provide up to 8 Mb of expanded memory. EMS Version 4.0 was released in 1987 and could support up to 32 Mb. In fact, the EMM laid the basis for accessing memory that lies outside the processor's normal address space.

Any PC from the earliest 8088-based computer to the 80486 can use EMS to access memory beyond one megabyte. Before the introduction of the 80386 computers, users had to install an EMS expanded memory board, such as Intel Above Board, then load the LIM/EMM software driver that lets application programs access that memory. The EMM divides all the RAM on the board into a series of 16K blocks called "logical pages." Then it divides a 64K region of the upper memory (between 640K and 1 Mb) into four evenly spaced 16K blocks called "physical pages" (fig. 10–3). This 64K region is called the "page frame." To access expanded memory, an application program requests a specified number of logical pages from the EMM, then maps them individually to physical pages in the page frame. Once a logical page is linked to a physical page, a program can read from and write to that memory location as if it were conventional memory. When new information is needed, the program issues another call to the EMM to replace the logical pages currently mapped to the page frame with new logical pages.

The hardware necessary for expanded memory is now built into the 80386 and higher processors. MS-DOS's EMM386.EXE driver can provide access to the upper memory area to build the EMS page frame and use extended memory to simulate expanded memory. Data which are supposedly stored in expanded memory are in reality stored in extended memory.

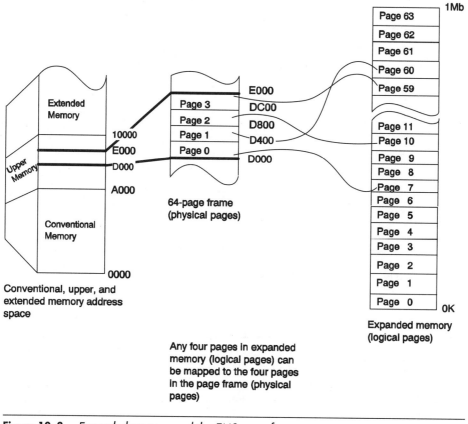

Figure 10–3. *Expanded memory and the EMS page frame*

To use expanded memory, a program has to be specifically written to make calls to the expanded memory manager so it can map expanded memory pages in and out of the page frame. Another advantage of expanded memory is that some DOS drivers can be placed in this memory by the CONFIG.SYS file. These drivers include RAMDRIVE.SYS (uses switch /a), SMARTDRV.SYS (uses switch /a), and FASTOPEN.EXE (uses switch /x). Only in DOS 4.0, BUFFERS can be installed in expanded memory. In DOS 5 and DOS 6, buffers can be installed in extended memory. DOS refers to the expanded memory controlled by EMM386.EXE as EMS memory.

Cache Memory

The access rate of a typical double-speed CD-ROM drive ranges between 180 and 400 milliseconds (ms). It is considered slow if you compare it with the access speed of a hard disk drive—10 to 18 ms. But on a network, you will notice increased performance due to the use of the CD-ROM drive cache and the server computer memory cache.

Before deciding to buy more RAM for the CD-ROM server to increase the disk caching for better performance, it is a good idea to consult the developer of the CD-ROM network management software because some CD-ROM redirectors do not use RAM over 16 Mb. Some cannot go beyond 8 Mb.

While the internal components of PCs have made exponential jumps in performance, disk drives are still lagging behind in terms of speed and data-transfer rate. There are many techniques to improve computer performance. However, the most important technique used for multimegabyte transfer rates in today's computers is caching. In networks, the amount of memory available for cache can make the difference between a sluggish network server and one that performs efficiently. Most network operating systems set their own cache buffers to improve performance of the operating system in the file server. These cache buffers are established in the common memory, not in the high-speed memory used by the processor. LAN operating systems use cache buffers for quick access to commonly accessed files, such as LAN drivers, disk drivers, utilities, directory names, and the file-allocation tables.

The user controls the number and size of cache buffers through the LAN operating system. It is best not to exceed the recommended values as the search performance would be degraded due to too many cache buffers. So, if the size of each cache buffer is set to 4K, then 1,000 buffers consume approximately 4 Mb of RAM.

Current techniques allow for two types of caching to improve system performance:

> Memory cache on the CPU, both internal and external, will increase RAM performance.

> Disk cache on the disk drive and on the disk controller will improve disk efficiency.

Memory Cache

Cache memory is a section of expensive and high-speed static memory (SRAM) that stores data retrieved from the relatively inexpensive, slower dynamic memory (DRAM) used for system memory. The mode of transferring data from RAM to cache is known as "cache writes." In this mode, data are temporarily stored in the cache memory in anticipation of future use by the CPU. If requested data are found in the cache memory, the data are transferred directly to the CPU at zero wait states (the CPU does not have to slow down to wait for memory to transfer data), thereby greatly improving performance of the system. This memory is managed by the cache memory controller.

Memory cache decreases the time required to fetch the text instruction in the program code. It provides a small amount (usually 32K, but this figure can reach more than 512K) of fast SRAM (the cache) that is logically located between the processor and the DRAM (main memory). SRAM in the cache usually has an access time of as much as 35 nanoseconds to as little as 15 nanoseconds, compared to the 70 to 120 nanoseconds' access time of the DRAM used in the main memory of today's computers. This increased access speed allows swift CPUs to access data in cache at zero wait states. The larger the cache memory in a computer, the more expensive the computer will be.

A cache is made effective by the tendencies of most programs to access the same few memory locations over and over, and to access neighboring locations of those accessed recently. Once those few locations have been loaded into fast cache, most accesses are made from the cache, not from the slower main memory, thus increasing system performance.

Cache circuitry ensures that the portions of main memory that are most often used are copied into the cache, making the majority of the memory access to fast memory in the cache, and not to the slower main memory. Whenever the processor attempts to read a memory location in a system that uses a memory cache, the memory subsystem checks to see if the contents of that location are stored in the cache. If so, the data are transferred from the cache at a fast SRAM speed, referred to as a cache hit. If the data are not in the cache, the processor must wait until the data can be transferred from the slower main memory; this is called a "cache miss." While more cache RAM always helps, it can reach a point of diminishing returns, where doubling or tripling the cache size can improve the hit rate by only one or two percentage points. In most cases the increased cost for extra cache memory might not be worth such a marginal performance increase.

Disk Caching

Disk cache can improve system performance by decreasing the time it takes for applications to access data from the fixed disk. Applications that require several disk reads, such as databases and CD-ROM–based information, can improve performance when a cache is used. Reading cached information from memory is much faster than reading it from hard disks or from CD-ROM discs. Many disk drives offer a cache ranging from 64K to as much as 1 Mb. Drives with a larger cache will perform significantly better. When the computer is powered up, disk-caching software allocates to itself a buffer of expanded or extended memory (from 512K to several megabytes). Some caches take a specific amount of memory for the buffer; others take all the memory that's available and later release it to programs that need it for processing.

When a program is loaded, the CPU goes to the hard disk for data. The cache intercepts the request, and then finds the needed files—either program or data files. Next, it reads them into its buffer for the CPU to access directly. The CPU treats the disk cache as if it's a hard drive. This technique is used for successive readings; if data needed are not there, the cache retrieves them from the disk and stores them, then feeds them to the CPU. As the cache fills up, it releases the data that have been in the buffer the longest. Users can get reading hits in two ways. When the information requested is in a logical, sequential pattern, the drive, anticipating the next move, will fetch the data before asked for it. The second and more common occurrence comes about because people tend to access the same data over and over. The drive will just hold the data in the cache because it's easier to get it from there.

During clock cycles when the CPU would otherwise be idle, the cache reads more data into the buffer from sectors near the files that have already been read. This second-guessing anticipates that data in nearby sectors may soon be needed—a feature that works best with defragmented disks.

Some caches intercept commands to the system's memory management software. If a program requires more memory—to index a complex database, for example—the cache tells the memory manager to free up caching memory so that the program can carry the task. When a program saves data, some caches intercept the data and defer writing it to disk until the CPU is idle. If the data file is still in the cache, only the sectors that have changed are written to disk. Some caches also hold pending writes and perform them in an order that minimizes the movements of the disk and drive head.

The following are the most important approaches for disk caching:

Disk-controller caching approach

The disk-controller vendors are offering either an IDE or a SCSI interface with cache as an option. SCSI-2 interface with cache is included in Distributed Processing Technology's SmartCache III PM2021 ($285), while IDE interface with cache is included in the DC-200 from Promise Technology ($149). IDE and SCSI controllers with cache improve performance by as much as 65 percent.

Software caching approach

Hard disk software caching is cheaper than hard disk controller caching. PC-Kwik's Super PC-Kwik costs $79, and Symantec's Norton Speedrive costs $99. In the meantime, SmartDrive disk cache software is standard software from Microsoft and has been included in MS-DOS since version 4.01 and Windows 3.1. As of MS-DOS 6.2, the SMARTDRV device driver has CD-ROM caching capabilities in addition to caching hard disks. It is recommended that users upgrade to MS-DOS 6.2, since Microsoft set the default of SMARTDRV device driver in DOS 6.0 with write-caching turned on. The problem with the SMARTDRV driver of MS-DOS 6.0 is that if users stopped working and almost immediately turned off their PCs, there wouldn't be enough time for the cache to transfer data to the hard drive, resulting in data loss. In MS-DOS 6.2, the write-caching is turned off.

The performance of a CD-ROM drive can be boosted if the CD-ROM driver (e.g., HITACHI.SYS) is loaded before you load SMARTDRV. Also, you can increase the number of buffers to 12 or 14 if you have more than 4 Mb of RAM by editing the line in the AUTOEXEC.BAT file that loads MSCDEX.EXE so that the number following the /M: switch is 12 or 14, instead of 8 or 10.

The products to speed up CD-ROM access include:

> CD Speedway from IMSI
> CD AllCache from Charis Engineering, available for Mac, PC, and Windows
> OPTI-CDcache from Online Computer Systems.

CONFIG.SYS

FILES=

The "FILES=" statement in the CONFIG.SYS file specifies how many files can be opened concurrently. If a number is not specified, the default number is 8.

However, DOS does not allow FILES to load in the HMA. Each file in this statement consumes about 59 bytes of conventional memory. Unless the user expects to open a large number of files at the same time, "Files=" should use a number between 10 and 30. If an application needs a higher number, the user can always change this statement.

BUFFERS=

The "BUFFERS=" command in the CONFIG.SYS file specifies the number of buffers that MS-DOS reserves for file transfers. The number should be between 1 and 99. Buffers are DOS disk cache. The amount of space reserved by the "BUFFERS=" command depends on the size of the disk sectors, which is usually .5K. So, BUFFERS=20 would use 10K of memory for the buffers. The greater the number of buffers, the faster the system runs. However, past a certain value, increasing the number of buffers only uses more memory without increasing the speed. The MS-DOS manual offers the following guidelines for the effective buffer sizes for different sizes of hard disks:

Hard disk size	Buffer size
Less than 40 Mb	20
40 through 79 Mb	30
80 through 119 Mb	40
More than 120 Mb	50

These guidelines constitute a problem because buffers are usually loaded either in the conventional memory or in the high memory. Only when DOS is loaded high, and the buffers are below a critical number, will the buffers automatically load in high memory. To figure out the critical number for an 80486DX-33 computer running under DOS 6.0 with 4 Mb memory and 312K hard disk drive, the "BUFFERS=" in the CONFIG.SYS file was assigned different values. Many TSR programs were also present. The computer was rebooted after every change. The MEM command was used with the following switch "/D" each time after rebooting the computer with the new buffer values. The size of the buffers and the "largest executable program size" were recorded as shown in Figure 10–4:

BUFFERS=	Where loaded	Size in conventional memory	Largest executable program size
50	Conventional Memory	26,608 bytes 26K	546928 534K
45	Conventional Memory	23,962 bytes 23K	549584 537K
44	High Memory	512 bytes 1K	570944 558K
41	High Memory	512 bytes 1K	570944 558K
40	High Memory	512 bytes 1K	573024 560K
39	High Memory	512 bytes 1K	573024 560K
36	High Memory	512 bytes 1K	573024 560K
25	High Memory	512 bytes 1K	573024 560K

Figure 10–4. *The size of buffers and the largest executable program size associated with them*

For this computer, the ideal number of buffers is 40. The size of the largest program that can run on this computer is almost 573,024 bytes (560K). When increasing the buffers to 41, the buffers were still loaded in high memory, but a strange thing happened: the largest executable program size had been reduced from 573,024 bytes (560K) to 570,944 bytes (558K). It turned out that the COMMAND.COM file, which was loaded in high memory, had moved part of it (2,080 bytes, to be exact) to the conventional memory, thus reducing the largest executable program size in the conventional memory to 570,944 bytes. Any number below 40 had no effect on the largest executable program size. But when the buffers were increased to 45, DOS forced the buffers to load in conventional memory, and the largest executable program size dropped from 558K to 537K.

DOS does not divide the buffers between conventional and upper memory; they have to be in one memory or the other. If you are using DOS 5, issuing the command "MEM /P" at the DOS prompt will give the size of the files and device drivers in hexadecimal notation. If the hex number associated with the buffers (listed under I/O in the upper memory) is 200h (hex), then the buffers are loaded high; otherwise, they are loaded low in the conventional memory.

SMARTDrive

SMARTDrive is a disk-caching program for computers that have a hard disk and extended or expanded memory. This driver can improve the performance of the hard disk by a factor of 10 by converting some of the extended or expanded memory into disk caching called SMARTDrive cache. The disadvantage of using SMARTDrive is that it uses almost 27K of the conventional memory if loaded low. Although a larger cache is faster, increasing the size of the cache to over 2,048K might not improve the caching process after all. However, the smallest number should not be set less than 256K.

If SMARTDrive or another cache driver is used, the set "BUFFERS=" should be assigned the value of 1 or 2, leaving the SMARTDrive to do the buffering. However, SMARTDrive caches only data on hard disks, not on the floppy disks. There are other programs that can cache hard as well as floppy disk data such as Microsoft's Super PC-Kwick Disk Accelerator. MS-DOS 6.2 includes support for read-caching CD-ROM drives.

SMARTDRV.SYS can be loaded into upper memory by adding a command to the CONFIG.SYS file similar to the following:

```
DEVICEhigh=C:\DOS\SMARTDRV.SYS 1024
```

This command sets aside 1,024K or 1 Mb of extended memory to be used as disk cache to buffer disk data. Loading SMARTDrive with the /A switch locates the cache in expanded memory:

```
DEVICEhigh=C:\DOS\SMARTDRV.SYS 1024 /A
```

If you turn the computer off before the information in the disk cache is written to your hard disk, the information could be lost. To prevent this, add the /C parameter to write any cached information to the hard disk before it is lost:

```
DEVICEhigh=C:\DOS\SMARTDRV.SYS 1024 /C
```

```
Microsoft SMARTDrive Disk Cache version 4.1
Copyright 1991,1993 Microsoft Corp.

Room for 256 elements of 8,192 bytes each
There have been 7,585 cache hits
 and 2,149 cache misses

Cache size: 2,097,152 bytes
Cache size while running Windows: 2,097,152 bytes

                Disk-Caching Status
   drive   read-cache   write-cache   buffering
   A:       yes          no            no
   B:       yes          no            no
   C:*      yes          yes           no
   H:       yes          yes           no

   * DoubleSpace drive cached via host drive.

   For help, type ''Smartdrv /?''.
```

Figure 10–5. *Number of cache hits and misses*

The information in Figure 10–5 is displayed by issuing the following command: SMARTDRV /S.

Multimedia Cloaking, however, has a replacement for **SMARTDRV** that loads in the extended memory, thus freeing the conventional as well as the upper memory of almost 44K.

LASTDRIVE=

When MS-DOS starts, it reserves space in memory for a table that contains information about each logical disk drive attached to the system. The user can increase the number in the CONFIG.SYS file by using the DOS command "LASTDRIVE = x," where x is a letter in the range A to Z, depending on the number of drives attached to the system. The default number DOS assigns is five logical drives (A, B, C, D, and E). Each drive requires almost 88 bytes. If the system has only two floppy drives (A, B), one hard disk drive (C), and one logical CD-ROM drive, using "LASTDRIVE = D" will save 88 bytes in the conventional memory. Always follow the rules of the CD-ROM networking manager and the network operating system you are using. For example, on a Novell NetWare, the LASTDRIVE could equal "F" or a higher letter.

STACKS=

This command sets the amount of RAM that MS-DOS reserves for processing hardware interrupts. It can limit the number and size of interrupt stacks that

MS-DOS uses. The syntax for this command is "STACKS=n,s," where n speci-fies the number of stacks. Valid values for "n" are 0 and numbers in the range of 8 through 64. "S" specifies the size in bytes of each stack. Valid values for "s" are 0 and numbers in the range of 32 through 512. By default, MS-DOS uses zero interrupt stacks for IBM PC, IBM PC-XT, IBM PC-Portable, and compat-ible machines; and nine stacks for IBM PC-AT, IBM PS/2, and compatible ma-chines. Setting STACKS=0,0, however, will prevent DOS from allocating the default stacks (9,128), which consume almost 3,280 bytes. If STACKS=0,0 causes DOS to crash because of an "Internal stack overflow" error message, stacks should be increased and the system should be reset after each change.

FCBS=

A file-control block (FCB) is a data structure that stores information about a file. FCBS command should be used only if a program requires it. Most newer programs do not require this command in the CONFIG.SYS file. Some pro-grams that use file control blocks to perform file operations may require a higher FCBS setting. The range is between 1 and 255. The FCBS default is 4. Setting the "FCBS = 1" would minimize the space DOS sets aside to cache information contained in file-control blocks. If an application crashes because it cannot open a file, this statement should be removed in order to use the default setting.

SHELL

Environment variables are used to control the behavior of some batch files and TSR programs and to control the way MS-DOS appears and works. The com-mands that set up the environment include the following: SET, INCLUDE, PROMPT, PATH, COMSPEC, DIRCMD; all can be used in the AUTOEXEC.BAT file. The SHELL command used in the CONFIG.SYS file is the preferred method of using the COMMAND.COM command to permanently increase space for the environment table. The SHELL command specifies the name and location of the command interpreter the user wants MS-DOS to use; the com-mand interpreter is the program responsible for displaying the command DOS prompt. The default command interpreter for MS-DOS is COMMAND.COM. MS-DOS searches the root directory first for COMMAND.COM. If the com-mand interpreter is not in the root directory, the user has to specify its exact location in the CONFIG.SYS file.

The COMMAND.COM command accepts switches to define the size of the environment, but the SHELL command itself does not. So, the switches can be included with the SHELL command in the CONFIG.SYS file. The follow-ing switches can be used: /e: (specifies the environment size in bytes) and /p: (makes the new copy of the command interpreter permanent). The default number of bytes of the environment for DOS 3.1 is 128 bytes. The default number value for higher versions of DOS is 256 bytes. Valid values for DOS 5 and DOS 6 are 160 to 32,768. It is better to start with a low number, like 160. If the system issues an "Out of environment space" when running a batch file or SET command, the number can be increased in increments of 16. This is an example: SHELL=C:\COMMAND.COM /P /E:160. During installation, some programs assign a high number. The number might be higher than the program really needs. After changing the size of the environment, the computer must be rebooted to reflect the new value.

SETVER

If the following message is displayed when attempting to run certain programs—"Incorrect DOS version"—the SETVER statement should be added to the CONFIG.SYS file. Many programs designed to run with a previous version of MS-DOS will run correctly under higher MS-DOS versions. In some cases, however, a program might not run correctly unless its name is included in the MS-DOS version table; this is true for some CD-ROM software. The table indicates to the program that it is running with the MS-DOS version for which it was designed, even though it is running with an MS-DOS higher version. By interpreting the higher MS-DOS version as the earlier version, the program will probably run correctly. However, using SETVER will not solve the problem if the program is not compatible with the higher MS-DOS version. SETVER.EXE loads into memory the MS-DOS version table, which lists names of programs and the number of the MS-DOS version with which each program is designed to run. To display or modify the version table, use the SETVER command.

Before the SETVER command can be used, the version table must be loaded into memory by a device driver command in the CONFIG.SYS file as follows:

```
DEVICEhigh=C:\DOS\SETVER.EXE
```

This command will load the driver in the upper memory. Here is how it works: Suppose a program file named MYPROG.EXE that runs with MS-DOS version 3.30 needs to run under MS-DOS version 5.0. To run MYPROG.EXE, the SETVER command must be set first to create an entry in the version table that will cause MYPROG.EXE to interpret MS-DOS version 5.0 as version 3.30:

```
SETVER MYPROG.EXE 3.30
```

To delete the MYPROG.EXE entry from the version table (without otherwise affecting the MYPROG.EXE file), the following command is used:

```
SETVER MYPROG.EXE /DELETE
```

To list the contents of the version table on drive C, type the following command:

```
SETVER C:
```

Memory Management Solutions

Whether MS-DOS or specialized memory management software is used, memory management is done through two programs on the PC; these are CONFIG.SYS and AUTOEXEC.BAT files. Editing of these two files might become a daily ritual until all application programs on the network work together in harmony. The DOS editor EDIT.COM can be used for editing these files. But before editing these two files, the user is advised to make a DOS bootable floppy disk just in case the computer won't start from the hard disk. The MEM command and its associated parameters (the parameters of DOS 5 and DOS 6 are different) will display the result of any changes you do to these two files.

Maximizing conventional memory is important in running memory-hungry programs that cannot take advantage of extended or expanded memory. Both Microsoft Windows and DOS 5 have changed the requirements for memory management. In the Windows environment, efficient use of memory is critical for optimal system operation. For one thing, Windows' capacity and speed can be improved by freeing conventional memory before starting Windows. This will also help DOS applications running under Windows.

As we have seen, any computer, even the 8088, has 640K of conventional memory used by the MS-DOS operating system and applications, and 384K reserved for hardware. Some of the 384K area remains unused; 128K is earmarked for video RAM, but on most systems, at least 32K of that will remain empty. System ROM takes 64K (128K on PS/2s), and video adapters take 32K ROM. The size of unused space in high memory can be as much as 192K. To access expanded memory (EMS), a memory manager has to use 64K of that address space for the EMS page frame. Memory managers can remap memory addresses of the 386 chip and move extended memory into the unused area between 640K and 1 Mb. The user can then load TSRs and drivers into these high areas, which are called upper memory blocks (UMBs). One of the main uses of the UMBs is to get large network drivers out of the conventional memory.

Most memory managers give more than 600K of conventional memory. Some include utilities that free up space normally claimed by the video adapter—up to 96K with EGA (Enhanced Graphics Adapter) or VGA (Video Graphics Array) and 64K with mono. However, the system will give up this space again if graphics are used. If the TSRs and device drivers have a user-controlled placement option, then they can be placed in high memory. Also, memory managers that use page frames can squeeze large programs into crowded high memory. NetRoom, for example, uses 386 "virtual machine" technology to create about 500K outside the conventional memory to load TSRs and device drivers. This technique works well with network drivers and TSRs that do not require direct interaction (pop-up features). QEMM-386's Stealth feature swaps the BIOS ROMs in and out of memory to make room for TSRs, thus providing a lot of upper memory space—but it does not work with all TSRs. 386MAX reclaims the space consumed by unused ROMs to let more TSRs and device drivers load in upper memory. Several memory managers free up conventional memory by mapping ROMs from peripherals such as printers and scanners into RAM. Memory Commander provides faster video BIOS that runs from external memory.

Memory management packages strive to manage space in some typical ways by:

> moving TSRs and device drivers from the conventional memory (the first 640K) into unused address space
>
> controlling extended and expanded memory
>
> utilizing memory above 640K

> copying and remapping the BIOS ROM to fast RAM, which can speed up video and some disk operations

> recovering shadow RAM on certain machines (computers with shadow RAM capability are able to relocate the system and/or video BIOS from slower ROM chips to faster RAM to improve system performance).

When an expanded memory board is added on some older computers that have only 512K of conventional memory, there will be a gap between 512K and 640K, since the address space of the extended memory board starts at 1,024K. Some memory managers fill this gap by mapping extended memory in 512K to 640K space.

Memory managers must establish a link between programs in the high memory area (HMA) and the portion of DOS that runs in the first 640K. For example, DOS 5.0, installs HIMEM.SYS in HMA to act as a link between lower memory and programs stored in the upper memory block (UMB). A typical computer (a non-PS/2) with EGA/VGA and no additional ROM adapter will have as much as 192K of unused high memory. Generally, memory managers identify this space and try to free as much space in the conventional memory (fig. 10–6).

Knowing what to accomplish before installing any of the memory managers is highly recommended because it can become very tricky during installation. The following list includes some memory managers that can be used in workstations. The sizes of free memory mentioned in this list are approximate and they will vary among systems. Also, vendors claim numbers that are obtained from specific configurations, not necessarily the number a user can obtain. There are many memory management programs, including the following:

ATLast from RYBS Electronics

ATLast is designed as a memory optimizer for loading device drivers, TSRs, and DOS tables into available UMB space. It works best as an adjunct to DOS 5.0's own high memory and extended memory services, but it can work with older DOS versions from 3.3. ATLast also works on 8088-, 8086-, or 286-based PCs equipped with NEAT shadow RAM or a third-party EMS 4.0 expansion board.

	Extended memory		
64K	High memory area (HMA)	1,088K	
64K	System ROM	1,024K	
160K	Unused memory (network cards, ROM)	960K	High DOS memory
32K	Video adapter	800K	
128K	Video RAM	768K	
640K	Conventional memory (for applications)	640K	

Figure 10–6. *Memory map*

DOS 5.0 Memory Management Kit from Biologic

This kit has a memory analysis, optimizing, and reporting capabilities.

DR DOS from Digital Research

DR DOS has more memory management features than MS-DOS. It can provide almost 627K free memory after TSRs, drivers, and DOS are loaded high; 723K maximum free contiguous memory for text-mode programs; and 541K free memory for Windows enhanced-mode DOS session.

Memory Commander from V Communications

Memory Commander provides a huge conventional memory area for DOS. It can provide almost 621K free memory after TSRs, drivers, and DOS are loaded high; 842K maximum free contiguous memory for text-mode programs; and 593K free memory for Windows enhanced-mode DOS session.

MS-DOS 5.0 from Microsoft

MS-DOS 5.0 can free the conventional memory and load TSRs and drivers into upper memory using HIMEM.SYS and EMM386.EXE device drivers. However, all these operations are done manually. MS-DOS 5 can load part of it in the HMA on most 80386 PCs, thus saving about 40K of the conventional memory. Because these two files come free with MS-DOS, you should use them first to see if you can run any program on your network without memory problems. If you experience difficulties, then you should try other commercial programs mentioned in this section.

HIMEM.SYS

The HIMEM.SYS is the Extended Memory Specification (XMS) that permits DOS and application programs to access upper memory, extended memory, and the High Memory Area (HMA) without interfering with each other. This file is part of MS-DOS. The size of the memory area occupied by DOS varies from one DOS version to another, as shown:

DOS Version	Size
DOS 4.01	90K
DOS 5.0	56K
DOS 6.0	57K

Adding the following two statements to the CONFIG.SYS file will free the conventional memory by transferring a large portion of DOS from the conventional memory to the HMA.

```
DEVICE = C:\DOS\HIMEM.SYS
DOS = HIGH
```

The first command should be mentioned before any other statements that will try to load other files or drivers high. The second command can be anywhere in the CONFIG.SYS file.

Unless the computer is at least 286, DOS cannot be loaded high. The compatibility issue should be observed. After using HIMEM.SYS, if the following message is displayed when the computer is turned on, it usually indicates that the PC is 100 percent AT-compatible.

```
Installed A20 handler number 1
64K High Memory Area is available
```

The A20 handler contains the code of the computer, which HIMEM.SYS is using to access the HMA, the first 64K of extended memory. If, however, an error such as "Unable to control A20 line" is displayed, then the DOS manual should be checked for the correct type of machine to be used. The command HELP HIMEM.SYS will also display a machine list and their codes. A line such as the following can be added to the CONFIG.SYS file:

```
DEVICE=C:\DOS\HIMEM.SYS /MACHINE:7
```

In this example, MACHINE:7 is assigned to Toshiba 1600 and 1200XE computers.

The settings in the CONFIG.SYS and the AUTOEXEC.BAT files have a dramatic effect on the size of the conventional memory left to run application programs. To avoid problems, it is recommended that you start with a very small CONFIG.SYS and AUTOEXEC.BAT, then move forward by adding device drivers and other TSRs (one at a time), reboot the computer, then check the memory by using the MEM command and its parameters. This way, it will be easy to determine which command caused the problem.

EMM386.EXE

The EMM386.EXE driver converts unused space in the upper memory area to UMB RAM, or converts XMS memory to EMS 4.0 expanded memory, or both, so you can load driver programs into the upper memory area. The two files that cannot be loaded high are HIMEM.SYS and EMM386.EXE. So, you cannot issue a command such as the following:

```
DEVICEhigh=C:\DOS\HIMEM.SYS
```

The statement to install this driver should come right after the installation of HIMEM.SYS as follows:

```
DEVICE=C:\DOS\HIMEM.SYS
DEVICE=C:\DOS\EMM386.EXE
DOS=HIGH, UMB
```

You have to check the MS-DOS manual for the parameters associated with HIMEM.SYS and EMM386.EXE.

Netroom from Helix Software

Netroom is good when the network drivers are larger than 200K. It can provide large areas outside the 640K area to load those large network drivers. It can provide almost 622K free memory after TSRs, drivers, and DOS are loaded high; 685K maximum free contiguous memory for text-mode programs; and 565K free memory for Windows enhanced-mode DOS session.

Multimedia Cloaking from Helix Software

Although Multimedia Cloaking is not a memory manager, but rather a RAM CRAM memory solution, it can solve some serious problems. The author has used it to daisy-chain 16 CD-ROM drives, with results that are far beyond the reach of any other memory manager in this group. The problem was that every daisy-chained CD-ROM drive requires 8K of memory. Since the LASTDRIVE would equal "s," the required space in memory would be 8x16, or 128K. This is in addition to the space required for MSCDEX.EXE (36K), CD-ROM device driver (16K), mouse driver (55K), and other TSRs and device drivers.

Multimedia Cloaking, which works well with MS-DOS EMM386.EXE, includes three utilities: CD-ROM driver to replace Microsoft's MSCDEX (you can still use MSCDEX if you choose), a disk cache like DOS SMARTDrive that also handles CD-ROM caching, and a small-footprint mouse driver. All three drivers take up only 8K of conventional memory and zero K of upper memory, while the rest of the utilities run under 32-bit protected mode in extended memory. You can win back about 22K of RAM in the conventional memory and 50K of RAM in the upper memory, which can be used for network drivers or other TSRs. If combined with Netroom (also from Helix), QEMM-386, or 386MAX, the results are even higher.

QEMM-386 from Quarterdeck Office Systems

QEMM-386 is one of the popular memory managers that can increase the UMB space by more than 80K. It can provide almost 620K free memory after TSRs, drivers, and DOS are loaded high; 683K maximum free contiguous memory for text-mode programs; and 613K free memory for Windows enhanced-mode DOS session.

QMAPS from Quadtel

QMAPS has a good utilities package. It can provide almost 620K free memory after TSRs, drivers, and DOS are loaded high; 679K maximum free contiguous memory for text-mode programs; and 597K free memory for Windows enhanced-mode DOS session.

QRAM from Quarterdeck Office Systems

QRAM is used in 8086-, 8088-, and 80286-based PCs with LIM/EMS 4.0 or EMS expanded memory board. For computers without expanded memory, QRAM works with Chips and Technologies' NEAT chip set with shadow RAM.

386MAX for 386 AT computers and BlueMAX for PS/2 from Qualitas

386MAX is well designed, and its memory optimizer is very powerful. It is easy to use and includes an online tutorial and system analysis program for tuning the system. It can provide almost 622K free memory after TSRs, drivers, and DOS are loaded high; 684K maximum free contiguous memory for text-mode programs; and 605K free memory for Windows enhanced-mode DOS session. It provides an excellent tutorial on memory management, as well as system analysis tools. 386MAX also incorporates a program loader for 8086-, 8088-, and 286-based PCs with shadow RAM or EMS 4.0 support. A companion product, BlueMAX is used for 386- and 486-based PS/2 Micro Channel computers. It provides exclusive BIOS compression technology that can give PS/2s an extra 80K or more in contiguous high DOS.

These packages usually contain optimization programs that examine memory configuration and automatically make the necessary modifications—e.g., MS-DOS' MEMMAKER, QEMM-386's OPTIMIZE, and 386MAX's MAXIMIZE. During installation, most of these memory managers make several passes (usually three). During the first pass, the program places its own drivers in CONFIG.SYS and then reboots the system. During the second pass, it attempts to load device drivers and TSRs high and then reboot the system. During the final pass, the program reconstructs CONFIG.SYS and AUTOEXEC.BAT files, then reboots the system one more time.

Using Memory Management Solutions

How to Start

Before acquiring a memory manager, you should do the following:

> Figure out how much memory the TSRs and device drivers use. System reporting utilities such as **MS-DOS MEM/C** or **MEM/C/P** or Quarterdeck's Manifest can be used.

> Find out which areas of the upper memory blocks (UMB) are used by the hardware's ROM BIOS and whether or not the memory manager can recover any of that space. The user has to ask if the memory manager can fix and recover the E segment; refer to Figure 10–1.

> Verify if the software running on the system needs EMS. Unless programs running on the system need EMS, the user can save 64K of the UMB region by not establishing the page frames. However, QEMM-386's Stealth and 386MAX's FlexFrame will establish EMS as they need a page frame to run.

> Finding out the memory requirement for each software program and CD-ROM software on the network will help in selecting the proper memory manager.

Avoiding Conflicts with Network Adapter Cards

The shared RAM data buffer on a network adapter card occupies an area between 640K and 1,024K. Because the NIC is usually initialized after loading the memory software manager through the CONFIG.SYS file, it is impossible to detect this RAM buffer. But if a third-party manager is to be installed, it should be done so after logging on to the network. This may enable the setup program to detect the shared adapter RAM. If, however, a memory manager is installed and the network become inaccessible, the network card manual should be examined to find out what address range the card occupies. Then use an Exclude parameter—such as x=mmmm-nnnn, which is used with MS-DOS—on the memory manager's line in CONFIG.SYS to prevent it from using the area the RAM buffer needs. To exclude addresses in the range E000-EC00, the following line can be used in the CONFIG.SYS file: DEVICE=C:\DOS\ EMM386.EXE X=E000-EC00.

Some networks have a command that will display what address range the network card is using. Novell's IPX will do so when IPXI. is typed. Sometimes the system locks while booting due to an address conflict. If this happens, holding down the Alt-key will reboot the computer without loading the memory manager.

Unloading Device Drivers

Device drivers are of two types: block drivers and character drivers. Block drivers include CD-ROM drivers and RAM disks; they transfer data in the form of blocks. Character drivers include communications drivers and ANSI.SYS; they transfer data as individual characters. Not all the drivers in any CONFIG. SYS file are used at all times. So, it is a good idea to load them when needed and unload them afterward. The problem is that most of these utilities require some RAM. Dynamic Memory Control (from Adlersparre & Associates), for example, can deal with both types of drivers. It can deal with drivers for CD-ROMs, scanners, fax boards, and miscellaneous printer control software. It can even load and unload Quarterdeck's QEMM-386. Others can deal with just one type of driver and not the other, such as Rod Pullmann's DEVICE.ZIP (which can be downloaded from CompuServ's IBMSYS, Library 1) and Jim Kyle's DEVLOD.ARC (which can be downloaded from CompuServ's DDJFO-RUM, Library 0). Both can deal only with character drivers. Other utilities can be downloaded from PC MagNet's UTILFORUM, such as TSRCOM.ZIP in Library 16; INSTALL/REMOVE is available as INSTAL.ARC in Library 2.

CHAPTER 11

Network Standards and Specifications

The continuous efforts of such organizations as the Institute of Electrical and Electronics Engineers (IEEE), American National Standards Institute (ANSI), and International Standards Organization (ISO) have made it possible for hardware components manufactured by different developers to interact on the same network. Today, there are varieties of network standards to meet any organization's need for sharing computing resources. Any organization can choose from among many types of wiring: from the most expensive cabling systems such as fiber-optic to the least expensive such as twisted-pair wiring. There are also several types of network technologies to choose from, such as Ethernet, ARCNET, token ring, and Fiber Distributed Data Interface (FDDI). New network technologies based on hardware solutions have emerged. These new technologies use high-speed data transmissions of over 100 Mbits/sec, such as FDDI, Asynchronous Transfer Mode (ATM), Fiber Channel, and Fast Ethernet.

Network technology is changing rapidly before many organizations are even ready to network their computing resources. In spite of the technological changes, any network is basically composed of network interface cards (NICs) installed in computers and hooked by cables, then run by a network operating system (NOS). Wireless networks follow that scheme as well, but they usually use antennas instead of cables for communication.

Your network should be built according to the standards approved by the IEEE, such as Ethernet and token ring, or ANSI, such as FDDI. These network standards are flexible and widely supported by the network industry. Other standards exist; ARCNET, for example, is a proprietary standard supported by Datapoint Corporation. LAN selection depends heavily on present and future applications, the size of the LAN, and the financial resources. An organization may decide to build a powerful and expensive LAN using FDDI fiber-optic cabling for the backbone and FDDI over copper for the nodes and desktop components. Another organization may decide to build a very simple and inexpensive, yet efficient, network over thin coaxial or twisted-pair wiring.

Network Protocols and Standards

A network protocol is just a set of rules, standards, and procedures designed to handle the exchange of information among computers in a network setting. A typical protocol defines the rules for configuring the network, the means by which computers identify one another, the data signals and the form that the data should take in transit, the method by which information is processed once it reaches its final destination, the procedures for handling damaged or lost data packets, and approaches to problem-solving. Although each network protocol runs in a specific environment using a specific type and length of cable, the network industry is moving toward a concept known as "protocol independence," meaning that the physical network (the medium, i.e., the cabling system) should not concern itself with the protocols being carried.

There are many committees that have been established by such organizations as the IEEE and ANSI. The main function of these committees is to develop the protocols and standards, but it is the industry that develops the network products that conform to those standards. One of the active committees is the IEEE 802. Committee 802 is a very active organization that developed a variety of standards for many LAN topologies. This committee uses decimal numbers to identify its protocol standards. For example,

IEEE 802.0 LAN and MAN

IEEE 802.1 Higher Level Interface

IEEE 802.2 Logical Link Control

IEEE 802.3 covers the use of the CSMA (Carrier Sense Multiple Access) media access control scheme over bus topology as it is used on Ethernet networks.

IEEE 802.3 10Base-2 deals with the use of "thinwire" on thin Ethernet.

IEEE 802.3 10Base-5 covers the "thickwire" on thick Ethernet. The transmission rate of both the thin and the thick wires is 10 Mbits/sec. Base refers to baseband, 2 and 5 refer to the length of cable segments (which should not exceed 200 meters for the thin wire and 500 meters for the thick wire)—hence the type 10Base-2 and 10Base-5.

IEEE 802.3 10Base-T deals with Ethernet on twisted-pair wiring.

IEEE 802.4 specifies the token bus access method.

IEEE 802.5, also called ANSI 802.1-1985, specifies the 4- or 16-Mbits/sec token ring architecture. It defines the access protocols, cabling, and interface for token ring LANs.

IEEE 802.6 Metropolitan Area Networks

IEEE 802.7 Broadband Technical Advisory Group

IEEE 802.8 Fiber Technical Advisory Group

IEEE 802.9 Integrated Voice/Data

IEEE 802.10 Interoperable LAN Security

IEEE 802.11 Wireless LAN

IEEE 802.12 100Base-VG

IEEE 802.14 100Base-T

ANSI X3T9.5 covers the 100 Mbits/sec FDDI specification over dual counter-rotating rings.

Networks built in accordance with these standards will operate in the most efficient way. Other proprietary standards exist—e.g., the 2.5-Mbits/sec ARC-NET standard, marketed by Datapoint.

The four well-known network technologies that will be discussed in this chapter are Ethernet, token ring, ARCNET, and FDDI. Many network vendors, such as Black Box and Andrew, will help you select the right network components for your LAN.

Ethernet

Ethernet is the most popular LAN technology in use today. Ethernet, in all its variations, operates in a bus topology and uses Carrier Sense Multiple Access/Collision Detection (CSMA/CD) as an access method. This widely used standard is often described by its formal standard designation, IEEE 802.3. The Ethernet topology was developed in 1980 by Digital Equipment, Intel, and Xerox (DIX). Ethernet II, or V2.0, is the current specification, which differs from IEEE 802.3 in the way the data frames are formed. (A data frame is a group of bits that make up a basic block of data for a transmission on a network.) Novell and other companies use the IEEE 802.3 as a default, but they support both specifications. Ethernet uses a 10-Mbits/sec signaling rate; however, 100-Mbits/sec speeds can be achieved—e.g., 100VG-AnyLAN Ethernet and 100Base-X Ethernet.

Ethernet exists in a multitude of topologies. In the following list, only the first three Ethernet topologies are popular. The first number represents the speed, base means baseband, broad means broadband, and the last number when multiplied by 100 equals the length in meters of the cable segment.

10Base-5

Coaxial cable (RG-11) with maximum segment lengths of 500 meters that can be extended to 2,500 meters using repeaters; uses baseband transmission methods.

10Base-2

Coaxial cable (RG-58 A/U) with maximum segment lengths of 185 meters (approximately 200 meters—hence the number 2) that can be extended to 1,000 meters using repeaters; uses baseband transmission methods.

10Base-T

Twisted-pair cable with maximum segment lengths of 100 meters. While the 10Base-T uses a hub to form a physical star topology, it uses a CSMA/CD access method in a logical bus topology.

1Base-5

Twisted-pair cable with maximum segment lengths of 500 meters and transmission speeds of up to 1 Mbit/sec.

10Broad-36

Coaxial cable (RG-59 A/U CATV type) with maximum segment lengths of 3,600 meters between two connected stations; uses broadband transmission methods.

10Base-F

Supports fiber-optic cable backbones of up to 4 kilometers with transmission at 10 Mbits/sec. The star plays the same role as the hub in 10Base-T LANs. The EIA/TIA (Electronic Industry Association/Telecommunications Industries Association) has approved this cable for cross-connects between campus buildings in its Commercial Building Wiring standard.

100Base-X

A new Ethernet standard that supports 100 Mbits/sec throughput and uses the existing CSMA/CD access method over hierarchical twisted-pair wiring configurations.

100VG-AnyLAN

A new Ethernet standard that supports 100 Mbits/sec throughput and uses a new demand priority access method over hierarchical twisted-pair wiring configurations.

With the exception of the newly developed Ethernet 100VG-AnyLAN, Ethernet topology is a linear bus with a CSMA/CD access method.

On Ethernet, the network stations or nodes are connected together with cables at intervals to one long main cable, referred to as the trunk segment cable (fig. 11–1). All trunk segments in a network form the network trunk cable. This network trunk cable is the backbone of the whole network. 10Base-T is configured as a star topology in which each workstation is attached by cable to a central hub.

Thick-Ethernet (10Base-5) Cable Network Hardware

Thick-Ethernet cabling allows a great number of nodes to be installed on the network. The basic hardware components of the thick Ethernet include the following:

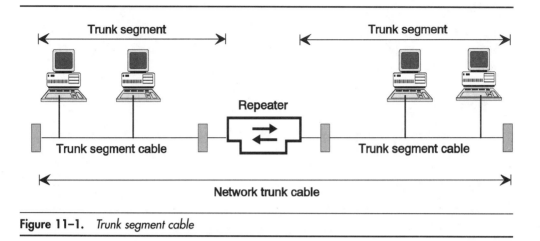

Figure 11–1. *Trunk segment cable*

Network Interface Card (NIC)

A network interface card is inserted in each file server, CD-ROM server, and station. These cards will be cabled to allow communication among stations. Most NICs support either thick or thin Ethernet cabling. The NIC should have a female DIX-type connector for the attachment of the thick Ethernet transceiver cable. It usually has a socket for the remote-boot PROM (programmable read-only memory) chip, which is sold separately. A combo NIC will also support twisted-pair wiring. In the PC world, the ISA (Industry Standard Architecture) still is the dominant bus architecture. Most of the ISA computers sold today use a 32-bit bus and a 16-bit bus, with perhaps one or two 8-bit slots. Many 16-bit NICs can operate in 8-bit slots in older computers.

There are different types of NICs, such as the following:

8-bit NICs These cards are slow and usually fit into 8-bit expansion slots inside the computer. They are usually used in old PCs.

16-bit NICs These cards are faster than the 8-bit NICs. They are designed to fit into 16-bit expansion slots inside the computer. They are usually used in AT machines. Many of the cards are dual 16-/8-bit cards. These dual cards can work well in AT-class machines, in either 8- or 16-bit slots, and in older 8-bit XT-class machines. However, if used in 8-bit slots, the 16-bit NIC runs at a fraction of its speed potential. It has to be noted that cards designed as 8-bit NICs and installed in 8-bit slots run faster than 16-/8-bit dual cards installed in 8-bit slots.

32-bit NICs In heavy-traffic LANs, because these cards are faster than the 16-bit NICs, they are usually installed in file servers and CD-ROM servers. They are designed to work with EISA (Extended Industry Standard Architecture) or ISA (Industry Standard Architecture) machines. They fit into 32-bit expansion slots inside 386 and 486 computers.

PS/2 computers that use Micro Channel Architecture require different types of NICs, such as the NE/2, which resembles the 16-bit interface card, and the NE/2-32, which resembles the 32-bit interface card.

Repeater

A repeater is an optional device. You need a repeater when you join two Ethernet trunks to extend the length of the LAN and to strengthen the network signals. A repeater attaches to the transceiver on each cable trunk with a transceiver cable.

Transceiver

On a thick-Ethernet cable, stations communicate on the network through transceivers which are attached to the trunk segment cable. A transceiver has three connectors: two are the thick Ethernet in/out connectors, and the third is used to attach the workstation to the transceiver by using a transceiver cable, known also as a drop cable.

A transceiver may be attached to an Ethernet cable in one of two ways:

Standard N Connectors Here, the Ethernet coaxial cable at the interface point is cut in two ends and the transceiver contacts are linked together via a coaxial cable coupling (screw connections).

TAP Connectors Known also as clamping, the TAP (terminal access point) does not interrupt the LAN operation. Here, a point probe is pressed into the inner conductor of the coaxial cable, while at the same time contact with the outer conductor is established via a clamp. The probe and the clamp are linked to the transceiver.

Transceiver cable

Also called drop cable, this thick cable attaches the stations to external transceivers.

DIX connectors

A DIX connector plug, which is shaped like the letter "D," is mounted on one end of the transceiver cable, while a DIX connector socket is mounted on the other end of the cable. The DIX plug will be attached to the network interface card and by the slide lock on the NIC. The DIX socket will be attached to the external transceiver.

Thick-Ethernet trunk cable

Thick-Ethernet cable is a 50-ohm, 0.4-inch diameter coaxial cable. Most dealers sell precut lengths of cable with a standard N-series connector plug attached to each end. Bulk quantities are also available from vendors, but the N-series connectors have to be mounted on the cable using a stripping and crimping tool. The following are connection components:

N-Series Male Connector Plugs An N-series male connector plug should be installed on both ends of the thick-Ethernet cable.

N-Series Barrel Connectors The N-series barrel connector joins two lengths of thick-Ethernet cable segments.

N-Series Terminators An N-series 50-ohm terminator is attached to each N-series male connector plug on each end of the thick-Ethernet cable. Only one terminator should have grounding capability.

Thick-Ethernet Cable Network Layout

Figure 11–2 illustrates the thick-Ethernet cable network layout.
     The following are specifications and limitations of the 10Base-5 standard:

Maximum trunk segment length is 500 meters (1,640 feet).

Maximum number of trunk segments is five (three coax segments with network stations and two link segments without network stations used for distance). They can be joined using four repeaters.

Maximum network trunk cable length of joined segments is 2,460 meters (8,200 feet).

Transceivers are connected to the trunk segment.

Maximum number of stations connected to one trunk segment is 100. A repeater or a bridge is considered a station. No more than 100

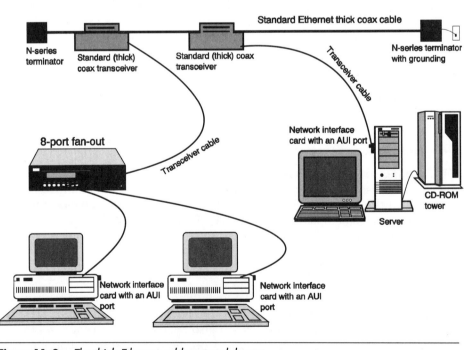

Figure 11–2. *The thick-Ethernet cable network layout*

transceiver connections are allowed per segment, including workstations, repeaters, and bridges connections.

Minimum distance between transceivers: 2.5 meters (8.2 feet). The annular rings on the thick-Ethernet cable mark where to tap in a transceiver MAU (medium attachment unit). The transceiver attaches to the AUI (Attachment Unit Interface) port on an Ethernet adapter card through a transceiver cable. The AUI port looks like the monitor port on a PC.

The maximum workstation-to-transceiver distance is 50 meters (164 feet).

Both ends of each trunk segment should be terminated with a 50-ohm N-series terminator. Only one of these terminators must be grounded to prevent loopbacks.

Barrel connector splices should be kept to a minimum.

A maximum of two inter-repeater links is allowed between devices; the maximum length of cable when repeaters are used is 4 kilometers (2.5 miles). Link segments are not trunk segments; they are point-to-point segments connecting two repeaters. No station may be connected to a link segment.

Only transceivers with their SQE (signal quality error) test disabled should be used with repeaters. SQE is also known as heartbeat.

Impedance of the cable is 50 ± 2 ohms.

Thin-Ethernet (10Base-2) Cable Network Hardware

Thin Ethernet, also known as Thinnet, is a good choice to build smaller and less expensive networks with a maximum of 30 stations per cable segment. The medium used for this type of network is known as the cheapernet. It is suitable for local area networks which are limited to a single story, several rooms, etc. Thinnet supports a 10-Mbits/sec data rate in the baseband transmission technology. Since cheapernet only differs from the standard Ethernet 10Base-5 type in the physical layer, and is thus compatible in the other LAN layers and uses the same data rate (10 Mbits/sec), an Ethernet 10Base-5 segment may be linked to a cheapernet using a suitable repeater. The basic hardware components include the following:

Network interface card (NIC)

A NIC is inserted into each file server, CD-ROM server, and station. When cabled, these cards allow communication among stations. Unlike in the standard Ethernet, a separate transceiver is not needed in 10Base-2 technology since the NIC comes with a built-in transceiver. If the card is for a diskless workstation, it will require a remote-boot PROM (programmable read-only memory) chip to be installed on a socket on the NIC.

Most of the cards have thick-Ethernet AUI connectors as well as the thin-Ethernet BNC or the twisted-pair RJ-11 connection. The BNC looks like a TV cable connector, while the RJ is similar to a phone jack. Some cards have the three types of connectors (AUI, BNC, and RJ-11), while others have only one connector.

Repeater

A repeater is an optional device. You need a repeater when you join two Ethernet trunks. You install a repeater also to strengthen the signals between them. A repeater attaches to the transceiver on each cable trunk with a transceiver cable. A message transmitted on a LAN must pass through no more than two repeaters before either reaching its destination or passing through a LAN bridge.

Thin-Ethernet cable

The industry-standard RG-58 A/U or RG-58 C/U (thin coaxial Ethernet) 50-ohm coaxial cable is used. Most dealers sell precut lengths of 20 feet with a standard BNC connector plug attached to each end. Bulk quantities are also available, but the BNC connectors have to be installed using a crimp tool.

BNC connector jacks and plugs

A BNC jack on the NIC is connected to the trunk segment cable. The BNC connector plugs attach to both ends of thin-Ethernet cable and connect the cable to T-connectors and barrel connectors.

BNC barrel connectors

Needed to join together two lengths of cable segments.

BNC T-connectors

These have two jacks opposite each other; they are used to connect two lengths of cable. The third plug attaches to the BNC connector jack on the network interface card in a node. You will need one for every workstation in the network. One end on the T-connector on the last workstation will be connected to the cable, while the other end will be terminated by a BNC terminator.

BNC terminators

A BNC 50-ohm terminator is needed to be installed on only one of the two jacks on a T-connector when no other length of cable is attached to that jack. To properly install an Ethernet network, one regular BNC should be used on one end, and just one BNC terminator with grounding wire should be used at the other end of the last T-connector.

Thin-Ethernet Cable Network Layout

Figure 11–3 illustrates the thin-Ethernet cable network layout.

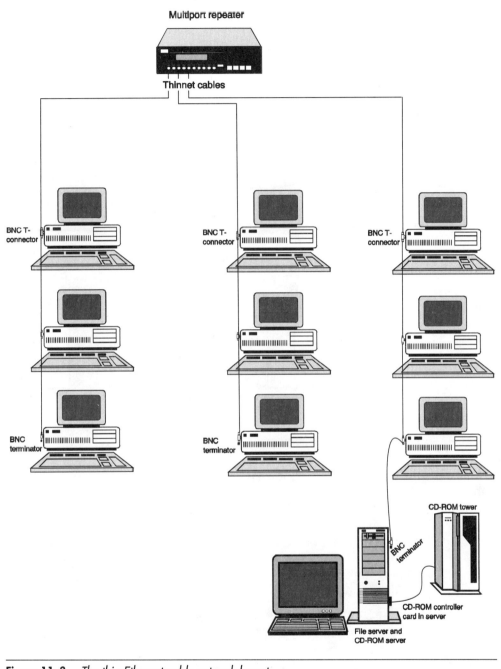

Figure 11-3. *The thin-Ethernet cable network layout*

Figure 11-4 illustrates a simple Ethernet Thinnet network that can run using a CD-ROM network management software such as OPTI-NET (DOS version) and IPX protocol that comes with the network interface card. Such a network does not need repeaters or hubs. This network can support up to 30 nodes.

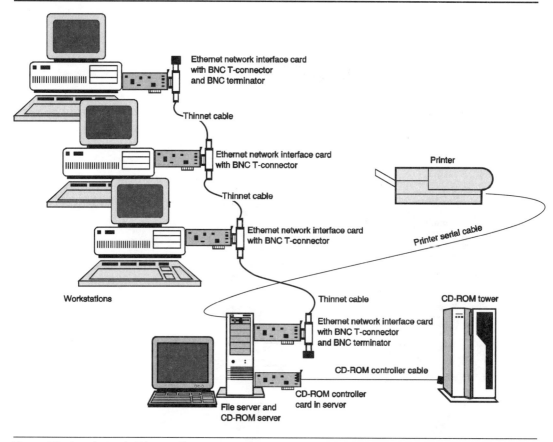

Figure 11–4. *A simple Ethernet Thinnet network*

The following are specifications and limitations of the 10Base-2 standard:

Maximum trunk segment length is 186 meters (607 feet) without repeaters.

Maximum number of trunk segments is five (three coax segments with network stations and two link segments without network stations) using four repeaters.

Maximum network trunk cable length is 925 meters (3,035 feet).

Maximum number of stations connected to one trunk segment is 30. Repeaters, bridges, routers, and servers are considered nodes.

The total number of nodes on all segments cannot exceed 1,024.

Minimum distance between BNC T-connectors is 0.5 meters (1.6 feet).

Devices are typically connected with T-connectors.

The first and last device on each segment should be terminated on one side of its T-connector with a 50-ohm resistor. One of these resistors must be grounded.

Barrel-connector splices should be kept to a minimum.

T-connectors must be plugged directly into the Ethernet network interface card. No cable is allowed between the NIC and the T connector.

If a BNC transceiver is used to connect a device, then the maximum length of a transceiver cable is 50 meters (164 feet).

A maximum of two inter-repeater links is allowed between devices; the maximum length of cable when repeaters are used is 4 kilometers (2.5 miles). Link segments are not trunk segments; they are point-to-point segments connecting two repeaters. No station may be connected to a link segment.

Combined Thin/Thick-Cable Networks Hardware

If the trunk segment exceeds 607 feet (the maximum length of the thin-Ethernet trunk segment), but is less than 1,640 feet (the maximum length of all trunk segments), a thin/thick-Ethernet cable network can be created by using a combination of thin and thick coax cables on a single trunk segment. This way, you can extend the length of the thin trunk segment (607 feet) to 1,640 feet. Such layout may expand the network over a long distance before a repeater is required. Reducing the amount of thick cables used on the network will also save money. A thin-cable trunk segment can be joined to a thick-cable trunk segment with a repeater. This way, a maximum of five dissimilar trunk segments can be joined with four repeaters. Thin and thick cables can also be joined in the same trunk segment (fig. 11–5).

The maximum length of the thin cable that can be used in a thin/thick combination network is equal to: (1,640 minus overall length of the trunk segment) / 3.28 (a fixed number). For example, if the trunk segment is 1,000 feet, you can use 195 feet of thin cable and 805 feet of thick cable (1,640-1,000)/3.28=195).

The hardware needed is the same as the hardware used in both thin- and thick-Ethernet cables. However, in order to join a thin trunk segment to a thick trunk segment, you need the following two adapters: (1) N-series jack to BNC jack and (2) N-series plug to BNC jack.

Thin/Thick-Ethernet Cable Network Layout

Figure 11–6 illustrates the thin/thick-Ethernet cable network layout.

Twisted-Pair Ethernet (10Base-T) Cable Network Hardware

Twisted-pair Ethernet (10Base-T) is an implementation of the 802.3 Ethernet standard over unshielded twisted-pair (UTP) wiring: the same wiring and RJ-45 connectors used with modern telephone systems. The standard is based on a physical star topology, with each node connected to a central wiring center, and a maximum cable segment length of 100 meters (330 feet). 10Base-T uses a physical star topology while it uses the CSMA/CD access method as the logical bus topology.

10Base-T is based on a point-to-point cable scheme known as the "star" topology. In this topology, each workstation is connected to a central hub,

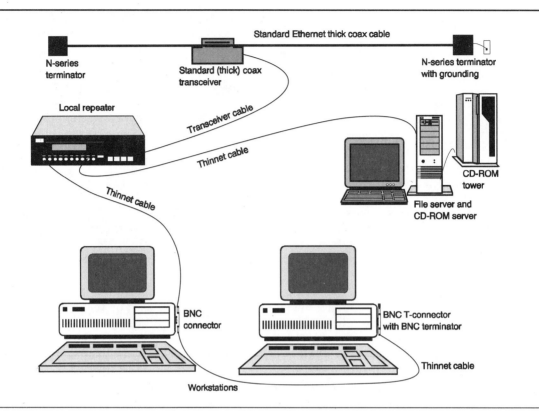

Figure 11–5. *Repeaters can be used to change cable type from Standard Ethernet to thinnet cable.*

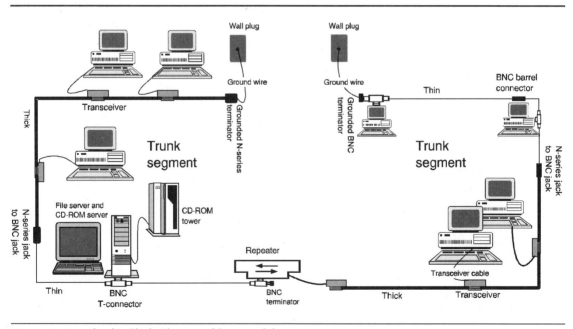

Figure 11–6. *The thin/thick-Ethernet cable network layout*

known as the repeater hub. The cable length between the NIC and the so-called repeater hub may be up to 100 meters. Here, the transceiver is built on the NIC. Twisted-pair wiring is relatively inexpensive and easy to wire. As of October 1990, the IEEE 802.3 standard for Ethernet networks of type 10Base-T specifies a 10 Mbits/sec CSMA/CD LAN with 100-ohm unshielded twisted-pair (UTP) conductors. Since maintenance is always done at the central repeater hub, it is easier to manage a 10Base-T Ethernet with its star topology than a bus Ethernet. This is true because 10Base-T contains a "link integrity test" which is implemented at the repeater module. If the test signal transmitted from the hub to the NIC fails, the hub removes the station from the 10Base-T network. The basic hardware components include the following:

Hub

Also called concentrator, a hub often uses up to 12 ports. It is needed to build the star configuration.

Network interface card

An Ethernet card with a DIX-type 15-pin connector or 10Base-T RJ-45 connector is required.

Transceiver

If the NIC has a built-in transceiver, you do not need a separate transceiver. The transceiver has an RJ-45 connector on one side and a DB-15 connector on the other.

Transceiver cable

The transceiver cable attaches the transceiver to the back of the network interface card.

Twisted-pair Ethernet cable

This cable can be shielded or unshielded and can be up to 100 meters long. You will need an RJ crimp tool if you are installing the cable yourself. Unshielded cable category 3, 4, or 5 with 24 AWG (American Wire Gauge) cable is recommended.

RJ-45 connectors

Used most often because they are inexpensive and easy to install.

Punchdown block connector cable

If existing telephone cable is to be used, a 50-pin Telco cable that connects the hub directly to a telephone punchdown block simplifies the installation. Check with the hub vendor.

Wallplate

A wallplate is a connector with an RJ plug. If a phone connection is also required, dual plates can be purchased.

Twisted-Pair Ethernet Cable Network Layout

Figure 11–7 illustrates the layout of the twisted-pair cable network.
The following are specifications and limitations of the 10Base-T standard:

> Maximum length of a 10Base-T link segment from a transceiver to hub cannot exceed 100 meters (328 feet) without repeaters.

> Maximum number of trunk segments is 1,024, connecting 1,024 workstations.

> Maximum number of repeaters or hubs is four (five segments with three tapped).

> Twenty-two to 26 AWG unshielded twisted-pair cable is used (24 AWG recommended). Level 3, 4, or 5 unshielded twisted pair should be used. For best results, use level 4 or 5. The diameter of the cable conductor should be 0.4 to 0.6 mm.

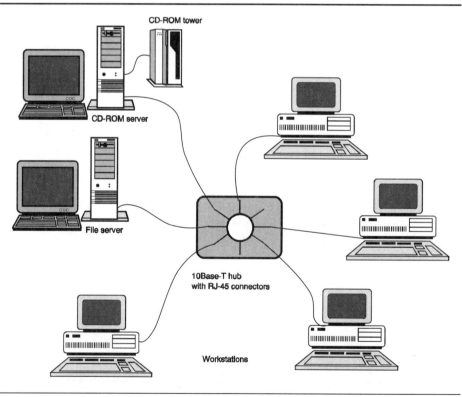

Figure 11–7. *The twisted-pair cable network layout*

Cable resistance in the range of 5–10 MHz should be between 85 and 111 ohms.

Eight-pin plugs (type RJ-45) are specified as connectors, where only four pins are used by 10Base-T, namely pins 1 and 2 for transmit and pins 3 and 6 for receive data. Each pair is crossed over so that the transmitter at one end connects to the receiver at the other end.

A transceiver and a 15-pin transceiver cable may be attached to each workstation. Some cards have built-in transceivers.

Devices are connected to a central hub in a star configuration.

Hubs usually have an AUI (Attachment Unit Interface) port for attaching to an Ethernet backbone.

Devices with standard AUI connectors may be attached by using a twisted-pair transceiver (MAU).

A hub typically connects 12 stations. Up to 12 hubs can be concatenated to expand the number of workstations.

Hubs can be attached to coaxial or fiber-optic backbones to become part of larger Ethernet networks.

Fiber-Optic Ethernet

FOIRL (Fiber-Optic Inter-Repeater Link) and 10Base-FL are the two current standards for Ethernet operations. Both use the same cables (50- to 100-micron multimode) and they are link-compatible (fig. 11–8).

The following are specifications and limitations of the 10Base-F standard:

The maximum length of a 10Base-FL segment is 1.2 miles (2 kilometers).

The maximum length of an FOIRL segment is 0.6 mile (1 kilometer).

The cable used is 50-, 62.5-, or 100-micron duplex multimode fiber-optic cable (62.5 micron is recommended).

Devices are connected to a central concentrator or repeater in a star configuration.

Devices with AUI connectors should be attached via a fiber transceiver.

Repeaters may be cascaded to create large networks.

Table 11–1 includes a summary of the characteristics of the three types of Ethernet networks: thick-, thin-, and UTP-Ethernet networks.

ARCNET

ARCNET, a proprietary standard, was developed in 1977 (Ethernet was developed in 1980) by Datapoint Corporation to provide a so-called "interprocessor bus" for use with their Attached Resource Computer (ARC) system. First used by Datapoint on its own business computing systems, the first ARCNET chip was not introduced to the public until 1982. It lost its popularity because it is

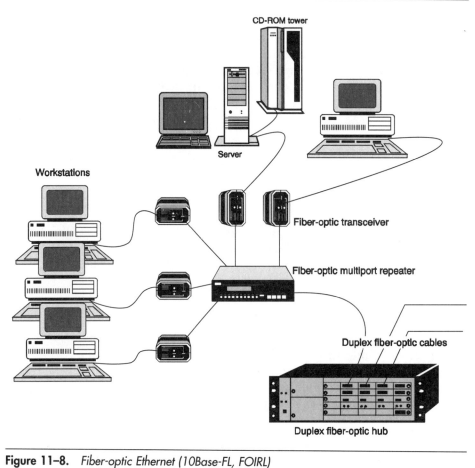

CD-ROM tower

Server

Workstations

Fiber-optic transceiver

Fiber-optic multiport repeater

Duplex fiber-optic cables

Duplex fiber-optic hub

Figure 11–8. *Fiber-optic Ethernet (10Base-FL, FOIRL)*

not an IEEE or ANSI national standard. However, many vendors are still supporting it. ARCNET transfers data at a speed of 2.5 Mbits/sec over a token-passing protocol using RG-62 coaxial cable, but can also support other cable types, including twisted-pair and fiber optics (fig. 11–9).

Token passing is a network-access method that puts a data token signal on the cable that stations look to for requests, commands, or data. Stations give information only to empty tokens. Node addresses are set manually with switches on the board in ARCNET systems. The maximum number of nodes is 255.

When ARCNET is installed with a large number of users on a very busy system, its performance tends to drop fairly fast. ARCNET also offers little in the way of large system connectivity and therefore is suited for small to mid-size organizations. Another version, called ARCNET Plus, increases the speed of this type of LAN to 20 Mbits/sec. The maximum number of nodes on ARC-NET Plus has been increased to 2,047. Thomas Conrad currently offers TCNS (Thomas Conrad Networking System), a 100-Mbit/sec implementation of ARC-NET over fiber, coaxial, or UTP. Although this is a proprietary solution, it does offer a high-speed option for graphic workstation applications like computer-

Table 11–1. *Summary of the characteristics of three types of Ethernet networks*

Characteristics	Thick Ethernet	Thin Ethernet	Unshielded Twisted-Pair
Signaling techniques	Baseband	Baseband	Baseband
Data rate	10 Mbits/sec	10 Mbits/sec	10 Mbits/sec
Maximum cable segment length	500 meters	185 meters	100 meters
Maximum network length with repeaters	2,500 meters	1,000 meters	2,500 meters using thick coaxial backbone
IEEE standard	10Base-5	10Base-2	10Base-T
Attachments per segment	100	30	1
Topology	Bus	Bus	Star
Transmission medium	RG-11 coax	RG-58 coax	UTP
Attachment spacing	2.5 meters, minimum	0.5 meter, minimum	N/A
Connector type	DB-15	BNC and T-connectors	RJ-45 (8-pin connector) 1, 4, 5, 6 straight through
Maximum number of stations per network	1,024	1,024	1,024
Impedance rating of cable	50 ohms (cable ends are terminated)	50 ohms (cable ends are terminated)	75-150 ohms
Media access protocol	CSMA/CD	CSMA/CD	CSMA/CD

aided design (CAD), digital imaging, distributed databases, electronic publishing, and automated manufacturing.

The basic hardware components of ARCNET networks include the following:

Network Interface Cards

ARCNET NICs are available from vendors, including Standard Microsystems Corporation (SMC) and Thomas Conrad. If the card is for a diskless workstation, it will require a remote-boot PROM (programmable read-only memory) chip to be installed on a socket on the NIC.

You have to set the node address on the NIC for each workstation. Each workstation is assigned a unique address in the range of 1 to 255. It is important to write this station number on the outside faceplate of each card as

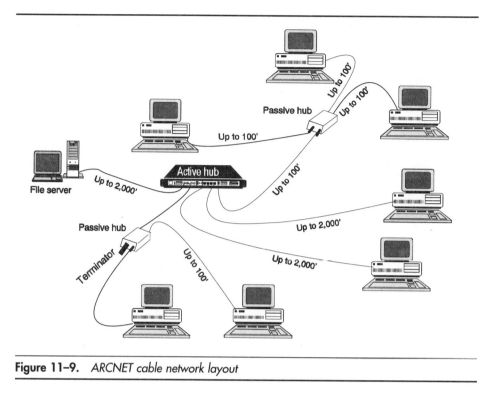

Figure 11–9. *ARCNET cable network layout*

well as in a logbook for future reference. The token passes to workstations from the lowest number to the highest number in a loop.

ARCNET Cabling

The type of cable used is the RG-62 A/U 93-ohm coaxial cable. Fiber-optic cabling can also be used in ARCNET networks. You attach coaxial cable segments to active hubs, passive hubs, and network interface cards with BNC-type connectors. Many vendors sell precut standard lengths. Bulk cable is also available, but you must mount the BNC connectors yourself using a coaxial cable stripping and crimping tool.

Active Hubs

Active hubs are used to split, relay, condition, and amplify signal strength. Usually, active hubs have eight ports. Workstations can be a maximum of 2,000 feet from active hubs. It is not necessary to terminate unused ports on an active hub since they are self-terminating.

Passive Hubs

Passive hubs are used to split and relay network signals. They have four ports, which are standard BNC connectors to which network cables can be attached.

Workstations cannot be farther than 100 feet from a passive hub. Each unused port on a passive hub must be terminated.

BNC Terminators

A 93-ohm BNC terminating plug must be placed on all passive hub ports that are not in use.

BNC Coaxial Twisted-Lock Connector Plugs

Attached to both ends of any length of cable.

BNC T-Connectors

A T-connector is attached to the BNC connector on the back of an ARCNET interface card when it is used in a bus topology. The T-connector provides two cable connections for signal-in and signal-out. You will need a T-connector for each workstation, plus two for each repeater being used.

BNC Connector Jacks

Attached to any BNC connector plug found on passive and active hubs and NICs. The following rules and limitations apply to ARCNET networks:

> Maximum length from one network end to the other end is 6,000 meters (20,000 feet, or 3.8 miles).

> Maximum number of stations is 255.

> Maximum length from station to station is 600 meters (2,000 feet).

> Maximum length from station to active hub is 600 meters (2,000 feet).

> Maximum length from station to passive hub is 30.5 meters (100 feet).

> Maximum length from active hub to active hub is 600 meters (2,000 feet).

> Maximum length from active hub to passive hub is 30.5 meters (100 feet).

> Maximum stations on single eight-port active hub are 64 if coax bus is used, 80 stations if twisted-pair bus is used.

> Any unused port on a passive hub must be terminated with a 93-ohm terminator. However, on active hubs it is recommended but is not necessary to terminate any unused ports.

> When stations are wired in a bus configuration, the maximum trunk length of the bus segment is 305 meters (1,000 feet), or 400 feet if twisted-pair is used.

> Passive hubs cannot connect to other passive hubs.

> Passive hubs are used to connect active hubs at a maximum distance of 30.5 meters (100 feet).

If a station is removed from the network, its cable should be removed and a terminator installed on the hub.

Most active hubs have eight ports; each port supports eight nodes if coax-bus is used, 10 nodes if twisted-pair bus is used.

Up to three workstations can be grouped around a four-port passive hub. One connection leads back to an active hub or file server. Each workstation cannot be farther than 30.5 meters (100 feet) from the hub.

Table 11–2 summarizes the configuration rules for the coax and the twisted-pair bus wiring designs.

Token Ring

The token ring standard provides a consistent data flow and can deliver a performance that is much higher than ARCNET or Ethernet. According to the IEEE 802.5 standard, the signaling rate occurs at 4 to 16 Mbits/sec, depending on the hardware used. Tokens are passed from network node to the next highest node address instead of being broadcast into the cabling, as they are in Ethernet. Considering the performance token ring offers, one may wonder why it is not the most commonly used standard. Token rings' drawbacks are cost and cabling. In most cases, the cost of token ring equipment nearly doubles that of Ethernet and triples that of ARCNET. While Ethernet adapters can cost as little as $100 each, token ring adapters tend to cost twice that amount. Token ring was initially designed to work with shielded twisted-pair (STP) cabling, but UTP has become an accepted alternative. IBM's type 1 and type 6 cables are difficult to work with, and token ring UTP greatly reduces the cable distances allowed when designing a system. However, token ring is a good choice for connecting PCs and mainframes. Figure 11–10 illustrates a 16-Mbits/sec type 1 token ring network.

Types of Token Ring Cables

The IEEE standards for token ring cables apply to IBM's Token Ring system. Consult vendors for outdoor cables. Refer to IBM Token Ring networks publications on the subject. Refer also to other vendors' publications, such as Black Box, Andrew, Star-Tek, and Nevada-Western. These vendors have excellent catalogs and planning guides for non-IBM token ring products.

Table 11–2. *Coax and the twisted-pair bus wiring designs*

Characteristics	Coax Bus	Twisted-Pair Bus
Maximum stations per bus	8	10
Maximum length of bus	1,000 feet	400 feet
Maximum distance between nodes	100 feet	100 feet
Maximum stations on single eight-port active hub	64	80

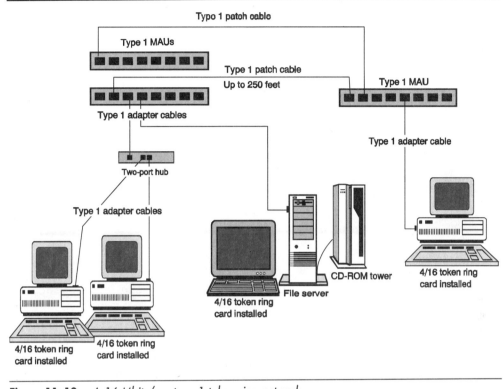

Figure 11-10. *A 16-Mbits/sec type 1 token ring network*

Type 1 cable

Uses two individually shielded 22-AWG solid copper wires in the twisted-pairs, as opposed to stranded wire in type 6. Each pair is foil-shielded, then covered overall by tinned copper braid. It is suitable for 4- or 16-Mbits/sec applications and is typically used for data transmission. The cost per foot for the PVC cable is about $.46, while the cost per foot for the plenum cable is about $1.05.

Type 2 cable

Combines two 22-AWG, individually shielded twisted data-pairs and four 26-AWG unshielded twisted-pair solid wiring in the same sheath for voice transmission. It is suitable for 4- or 16-Mbits/sec applications for the connections between the lobe (the length of cable linking a node to a Multistation Access Unit (MAU)) and the main ring path (the main cable that connects the MAUs together in a token ring configuration). It is available for phone service and data. The cost per foot for the PVC cable is about $.66, while the cost per foot for the plenum cable is about $1.41.

Type 3 cable

Uses four unshielded, solid, twisted-pairs of wire for voice or data. It is an IBM version of twisted-pair telephone wire. It is suitable for 4-Mbits/sec token ring

LANs but not for most 16-Mbits/sec networks. It is typically used for baluns (devices that usually allow coax cables to be connected to twisted-pair cables). A special jumper cable, consisting of type 6 wire, a filter, and a data connector must be used to connect type 3 wire to a MAU. The cost per foot for the PVC cable is about $.09, while the cost per foot for the plenum cable is about $.21.

Type 4 cable

No specifications published, but it will be used to connect IBM PS/2 model 40 computers together.

Type 5 cable

Uses two 100/140-micron (one-millionth of a meter corresponding to approximately 1/25,000 of an inch) strands of glass-fiber core wrapped with a buffer and surrounded with fibers. This fiber-optic cable is used for the main ring path to link MAUs for greater main-ring distances or to connect networks between buildings. Because of power-surge problems, type 5 cable is recommended for use between buildings. The cost per foot of the PVC cable is about $1.50, while the cost per foot for the plenum cable is about $1.70.

Type 6 cable

Uses two 26-AWG stranded (not solid), shielded, twisted-pairs wrapped in a PVC jacket for greater flexibility. It typically connects to a LAN adapter. It is more flexible than type 1. It is suitable for 4- or 16-Mbits/sec applications. It is usually used to run from the wallplate to the PC, or from the patch panel to the MAU. Type 6 cable can be substituted for type 1 or type 2 cable. But the distances will be reduced by two-thirds. To determine the length needed in type 1 or type 2, multiply the length of type 6 by 3/2. For example, 100 feet of type 6 will be equivalent to 150 feet of type 1 or type 2. The cost per foot for the PVC cable is about $.42.

Type 7 cable

No specifications published.

Type 8 cable

A special-design 26-AWG twisted-pair data-grade wire with a plastic ramp cover to fit under the carpet without being lumpy.

Type 9 plenum cable

Similar to type 6 cable with a plenum fire-resistant jacket, it is used between floors in a building. It is suitable for 4- or 16-Mbits/sec applications. Type 9 cable is best used for shorter cable runs from MAU to PC where plenum cable is needed. Type 9 cable can be substituted for type 1 or type 2 cable. To determine the length needed, multiply the length of type 9 cable by 3/2. For example, 100 feet of type 9 will be equivalent to 150 feet of type 1 or type 2. The cost per foot for the plenum cable is about $.79.

Token Ring Adapters

Token ring interface cards are available in two models: 4 Mbits/sec and 16 Mbits/sec. If 16 Mbits/sec is used on the 4-Mbits/sec network, it will function at 4 Mbits/sec. If the card is for a diskless workstation, it will require a remote-boot PROM (programmable read-only memory) chip to be installed on a socket on the NIC.

For standard-bus (ISA) stations, you can use interface cards such as:

IBM Token Ring PC Adapter (full-length, 8-bit ISA)

IBM Token Ring PC Adapter II (half-length, 8-bit ISA)

IBM Token Ring 16/4 Adapter (three-quarter-length, 8-bit ISA).

For Micro Channel Architecture PS/2 stations, you can use interface cards such as:

IBM Token Ring PC Adapter/A

IBM Token Ring 16/4 Adapter/A

IBM Token Ring 16/4 Busmaster Server Adapter/A.

The IBM Token Ring Network 16/4 Busmaster server adapter/A is a 24-bit Micro Channel adapter. You can use up to eight busmaster server adapters in a Micro Channel file server. This adapter can be inserted in a 16- or 32-bit expansion slot, but it will not support a file server with more than 16 Mb of memory and more than 8 Gb of disk storage.

While IBM sells the largest number of token ring adapters, other companies sell token ring adapters that are widely accepted in the industry. These companies include Compaq, Intel, Madge, Olicom, and Proteon.

Other Token Ring Components

A Multistation Access Unit (MAU)

A MAU is a wire concentrator that connects eight or more workstations to the ring via drop cables called "lobe cables." On either side of the MAU are the "ring-in" and "ring-out" ports. These ports are used to concatenate MAUs. The ring-in port from one MAU is connected to the ring-out port of another MAU.

Token ring network adapter cables

Eight feet long each. One end connects to the adapter port, the other to the MAU or to a patch cable. Token ring cables typically have a nine-pin connector on one end to attach to the NIC and a special type A data connector that plugs into the MAU or to a patch cable. For an IBM system, you should use type 6 cable.

Patch cables with a connector

These patch cables can be connected to each other, to adapter cables, or to a MAU. For an IBM system, you should use type 6 cable of any length up to 150 feet. Patch cables extend the distance of a workstation from a MAU device.

Data connector

The data connector is the plug that terminates all twisted-pair wiring. Type 1 cable uses IBM cabling system type A data connectors. Two data connectors can mate together by a 180-degree rotation of one "genderless" connector. When two connectors are used, one of the connections is contained in a face-plate. There are three types of connections used on a token ring network: genderless, DB-9, and RJ-11. The genderless, or "hermaphroditic," is used to connect a workstation to a MAU. This connector is physically located on the MAU end of the cable connection. DB-9 is the connector that attaches to the workstation. For an unshielded-pair cable, the connector used is the RJ-11 on both ends of the cable.

Media filters

These filters are required at the workstations when type 3 telephone twisted-pair cable is used. They convert cable connectors and reduce noise.

Patch panels

A patch panel is useful for organizing cable between the MAU and a telephone punchdown block. A standard telephone connector is used to connect the patch panel to the punchdown block. Another method is to wire the MAU directly to the punchdown block.

The following are specifications and limitations of the token ring networks:

Maximum number of stations on one ring is 260 for shielded type 1 cable.

Maximum number of stations on one ring is 72 for UTP telephone type 3 cable.

Maximum distance from a workstation to a MAU when you use type 1 cable is 101 meters (330 feet), assuming that the cable is one continuous segment.

Maximum workstation-to-MAU distance (not including the eight-foot adapter cable) is 45 meters (150 feet) when cable segments are joined by using patch cable.

Maximum patch cable distance between two MAUs is 45 meters (150 feet).

If copper repeaters are used, they can extend the allowable distance between MAUs to up to 750 meters (2,460 feet).

If fiber repeaters are used, they can extend the allowable distance between MAUs to up to 2.5 miles (4 kilometers).

If multiple MAUs or repeaters are used, they should be housed to-gether and cabled locally in a single chassis.

Maximum number of MAUs is 12.

Maximum patch cable distance connecting all MAUs is 120 meters (400 feet).

Patch cables are used if a station is located farther than eight feet from the MAU.

The MAUs in the token ring network must be connected in "ring" using patch cables through the ring-out and ring-in receptacles on the MAU.

All 16/4 adapters on each physical ring should use the same data rate: either 4 Mbits/sec or 16 Mbits/sec.

Fiber Distributed Data Interface (FDDI)

The Fiber Distributed Data Interface (FDDI), developed under the American National Standards Institute (ANSI) X3T9.5 working group, is a physical layer standard comprising 100 Mbits/sec using fiber-optic media in a dual-ring topology that supports 500 nodes over a maximum distance of 100 kilometers (65 miles). FDDI uses a token-passing scheme and has evolved to become the backbone network of choice that can link the existing subnetworks in any organization.

The importance of the FDDI is derived from being a national standard. This means that as long as the manufacturers follow this standard, all FDDI computers, workstations, and peripheral equipment will connect, regardless of the manufacturer. The FDDI standard defines two physical rings that simultaneously send data in different directions. The dual counter-rotating rings offer fault tolerance. If a link fails, the ring reconfigures itself so it can continue to serve all nodes. FDDI uses 62.5/125-micron fiber with a 0.275 numerical aperture for both the computer and the building wiring environment. Although FDDI is employed to provide connectivity among buildings and departments over a fiber backbone, FDDI networks are expanding to include workstations as well.

With increasing use of video and multimedia, even 100 Mbits/sec would become saturated. Asynchronous Transfer Mode (ATM) switching hubs or Fast Ethernet may be more suitable for network backbone requirements. New hubs may contain Ethernet ports for workstations and FDDI ports for servers or superservers.

The three FDDI transmission modes include, first, asynchronous token-passing ring, in which any station can access the network by acquiring the token. However, time-sensitive applications such as video will suffer delays because there is no traffic prioritization. The second method, synchronous token-passing ring, allows prioritization of time-sensitive traffic so packets, like voice and video, can arrive on time. This standard is in the making by ANSI. The third method, circuit-based mode, is used in FDDI-II to provide a dedicated communication channel between two stations.

At the physical layer of the OSI model, FDDI specifies:

a dual-fiber ring, with a total LAN circumference of about 62.5/125-micron multimode optical fiber

a distance of about 1.2 miles (2 kilometers) over single-mode fiber, with a duplex connector at each end

500 nodes are allowed to be connected on a single ring.

Users can be attached to one or both of the rings, using one of the following two methods: single-attachment stations (SAS) or dual-attachment stations (DAS). The SAS method is less expensive than the DAS method. The connection among SAS nodes is a single cable sheath; in the case of DAS, the connection among DAS nodes consists of two cable sheaths, each containing two fiber-optic or copper cables. One sheath acts as the primary connection and the other as the secondary connection, which is typically used as a backup link in normal operation. If the primary connection fails, the secondary interconnect can be patched to the primary in an attempt to reestablish the link. Typically, FDDI is employed as a backbone among intelligent wiring hubs, where the hubs are connected in the dual-attachment configuration and individual stations are connected to the hub in single-attachment configuration.

Unlike conventional token ring, FDDI allows data packets from more than one station to share the ring simultaneously. FDDI provides a higher bandwidth and longer distances than shielded and unshielded twisted-pair cable. Because of its high bandwidth and speed (100 Mbits/sec), it is ideal for medical imaging and for CAD/CAM (Computer-Aided Design and Computer-Aided Manufacturing) applications. FDDI-II is a new standard that has emerged to support multimedia applications that use graphics, text, and sound. FDDI-II operates at 100 Mbits/sec.

For good installation, all glass multimode graded index fiber is highly recommended. Today, building-to-building links make up the majority of fiber-optic installations. Intrabuilding cable should meet the 1990 National Electrical Code flammability requirements designated by Underwriters Laboratories, Inc. The code designates that each cable must meet one of three levels of safety—plenum, riser, or general purpose—and be labeled as such on the outer jacket. Interbuilding cable-fiber count is specified at 24 to 144 fibers (design is in multiples of six). For indoor applications, a cable-fiber count of 12 to 36 fibers is recommended. Most of the users choose FDDI primarily as a backbone to connect Ethernet and token ring LANs through bridges and routers.

Prices of fiber-optic cables and adapters are becoming cheaper because of competition among vendors. Prices usually vary depending on whether the LAN has dual-ring capability.

Many companies have designed other architectures based on the FDDI industry. Cabletron Systems, Crescendo Communications, Digital Equipment Corporation, IBM, and Microdyne have produced LANs that are based on the 100-Mbits/sec FDDI standard but use unshielded twisted-pair (UTP) wire. This technology has become the ANSI Twisted-Pair–Physical Medium Dependent standard. This standard defines an FDDI network that runs over category

5 data-grade cable and IBM type 1 STP cable. All features of the FDDI are provided except the distance of the cable. UTP supports 100 meters (330 feet) between nodes, while fiber supports 2 kilometers between nodes.

It is possible for sites that have installed Ethernet 10Base-T with category 5 UTP data-grade, twisted-pair cable to upgrade to the FDDI/UTP copper-wire standard following the FDDI/UTP standard, not the 10Base-T standard. However, network backbones that link distant LANs will still use fiber-based FDDI. Specifications also exist to use shielded twisted-pair Distributed Data Interface.

LocalTalk Networks

Basically, LocalTalk is a physical bus topology that is wired with twisted-pair telephone wire in a daisy-chain configuration (fig. 11–11). LocalTalk cable segments can span 1,000 feet and support 32 stations, but performance degrades rapidly on busy networks of 20 or more nodes. When performance degrades, LocalTalk can be subdivided by installing bridges. Additional networks can be attached using repeaters, bridges, or routers. Transmission speeds are 230.4 Kbits/sec, which is too slow for multiuser databases and the transferring of large files. Bridges can be used to filter traffic and keep excess traffic from overloading the network. Companies such as Farallon Computing and Black Box can help in designing and building AppleTalk networks.

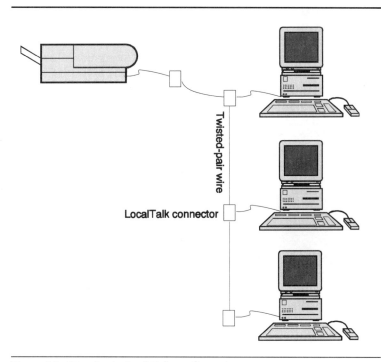

Figure 11–11. *Basic AppleTalk configuration*

PhoneNET Talk is Farallon Computing's solution for adding an MS-DOS or Windows machine to an AppleTalk network. The PhoneNET Talk package includes the PhoneNET Talk Local Talk adapter card and installing software. Although you can access any AppleShare file server and any networked laser printer or Image Writer, you cannot share a hard disk on the PC. Also, it consumes a lot of memory—almost 100K.

Table 11–3 summarizes LocalTalk and PhoneNET adapter configurations. The following are LocalTalk network specifications:

The total length of the network cannot exceed 1,000 feet.

Stations can be added to the network without bringing the whole system down.

You do not need special software to access peripheral devices as Macintosh computers have built-in LocalTalk support. However, in some systems like Macintosh System 7, file-sharing services such as AppleShare are included.

You can attach LocalTalk to other network segments such as EtherTalk and TokenTalk.

Other protocols such as IPX and TCP/IP are not supported, except with special third-party equipment.

Through LocalTalk cards and special software, non-Macintosh computers (Intel-based systems) can access peripherals and share files on the network.

When building an AppleTalk network, instead of using direct twisted-pair cables, you can use the existing telephone cable. You can always use the extra wires in the cable for data transmission. These wires are attached to a phone equipment closet. The leads from the wall connector attach to a punchdown block which can be connected to a hub with a patch panel or 50-wire cables. This way, each branch of the hub, which is considered a separate network, can be 1,000 feet and have as many as 32 workstations.

Because Apple original connector modules have built-in terminators, they self-terminate if the connector is not used. However, in some designs, you must plug in a terminator at the end of a cable or daisy-chain wire.

Table 11–3. *LocalTalk and PhoneNET adapter configurations*

Adapter	Topology	Nodes	Maximum Length
LocalTalk	Daisy chain	32	1,000 feet
PhoneNET	Daisy chain	24	1,800 feet
PhoneNET	Backbone	32	4,500 feet
PhoneNET	Passive star	32	4,500 feet or four branches of 1,125 feet
PhoneNET	Active star	48	12 ports which can support four branches, each with lengths of up to 3,000 feet per port

Signaling Speed and LAN Throughput

There is a difference between the signaling speed and the throughput of a LAN. The signaling speed is the theoretical maximum rate at which the data can be transmitted, while throughput is the actual measure of the ability of a LAN to pass data signals. Like signaling speed, throughput is measured in bits per second (bits/sec), kilobits per second (Kbits/sec), or Megabits per second (Mbits/sec).

Usually the advertised throughput of a LAN is the throughput that has been achieved under laboratory conditions, which is different from the actual throughput in real situations (table 11–4). The advertised speed usually is the speed of the transmission rate over the cable. What these numbers do not show is the factors that limit effective throughput on a PC-based LAN, such as data-transfer rate of a hard disk drive, the transfer rate of the computer's data bus, and the efficiency of the networking software. For example, the advertised throughput of an Ethernet LAN is 10 Mbits/sec. Under heavy traffic load, the response time might degrade to reach a 2.5-Mbits/sec level, which is very slow. Likewise, the throughput of a 16-Mbits/sec token ring network might degrade to reach a 5–6-Mbits/sec level. From the computer side, a 16-MHz 386SX computer may have 1-Mbit/sec throughput on any LAN.

If you keep adding more stations to a network, the network will run out of bandwidth and the response time will be greatly affected. Installing graphics or multimedia applications on a LAN will also reduce the response time of that LAN. Because of these problems and others, the network industry is searching for effective standards and technologies to increase LAN bandwidths as well as data transmission and throughput rates. Many companies are now selling high-speed LANs such as ATM, FDDI, and FDDI over Copper. However, the average cost per node is high. Table 11–5 includes some of the high-speed LAN standards, which are either on the market or planned for the future. Adapters and hubs for the ATM, FDDI, and FDDI over Copper are already on the market, sold by such vendors as: ACE/North Hills Electronics, Cabletron Systems, Chipcom Corporation, Digital Equipment, Fibermux, Fibronics, Hewlett-Packard, IBM, Interphase, Lannet, Madge Networks, Network Peripherals, Optical Data Systems, Proteon, Standard Microsystems, Sun Microsystems, SynOptics, 3Com, and Ungermann-Bass.

Table 11–4. *A comparison between signaling speed and throughput of common LANs*

	Signaling Speed	Throughput
Ethernet	10 Mbits/sec	1 to 3 Mbits/sec
Token ring	4 Mbits/sec	1 Mbit/sec
Token ring	16 Mbits/sec	8 Mbits/sec
FDDI	100 Mbits/sec	25 to 70 Mbits/sec
LocalTalk	230 Kbits/sec	90 Kbits/sec

Table 11–5. *High-speed networks*

Standard	Standards Group	Application	Data Rates	Cable Type	Average Cost Per Node
ATM	ATM Forum IETF, ITU-TSS	Desktop, LAN backbone, MAN, WAN (for data, voice, and multimedia)	25 Mbits/sec, 52 Mbits/sec, 155 Mbits/sec, 622 Mbits/sec, 2,488 Gbps/ planned	Types 3 and 5 UTP, STP	$4,400 (155 Mbits/sec)
FDDI	ANSI	Desktop, LAN, backbone (for data and some multimedia)	100 Mbits/sec	Fiber Optic	$3,600 (workstations), $2,575 (PCs)
FDDI over Copper	ANSI	Desktop (for data and some multimedia)	100 Mbits/sec	Type 5 UTP, STP	$1,800 (PCs)
FDDI-II	ANSI	Desktop, LAN, backbone (for data and multimedia)	100 Mbits/sec	Fiber Optic	N/A
FFOL	ANSI	Desktop, LAN, backbone, MAN (for data, voice, and multimedia)	150 Mbits/sec– 2.4 Gbps	Fiber Optic	N/A
Fiber Channel	ANSI	Desktop, LAN, backbone (for data)	133 Mbits/sec, 266 Mbits/sec, 530 Mbits/sec, 1 Gbps	Thin and Thick Coax; STP	$2,575
High-Speed Token Ring	IEEE	Desktop, LAN, backbone (for data and multimedia)	Undecided	Undecided	N/A
ISICHRONOUS Ethernet	IEEE	Desktop, LAN, backbone (for data and multimedia)	16 Mbits/sec	Types 3, 4, and 5 UTP and STP	$220-$240
Fast Ethernet (100BASE-VG)	IEEE	Desktop (for data and some multimedia)	100 Mbits/sec	Types 3, 4, and 5 UTP and STP	$400
Fast Ethernet (CSMA/CD)	IEEE	Desktop (for data and some multimedia)	100 Mbits/sec	Types 3, 4, and 5 UTP and STP	$600

ATM = Asynchronous Transfer Mode
CSMA/CD = Carrier Sense Multiple Access with Collision Detection
FFOL = FDDI Follow On LAN
ITU-TSS = International Telecommunications Union-Telecommunications Standard Sector (Formerly CCITT)

Each network standard uses different architecture: either shared media or switched technology. ATM, for example, is based on the switching architecture. This new architecture uses a switch in place of the hub in the wiring closet. The switch establishes dedicated LAN segments to individual nodes, thus preserving the LAN bandwidth instead of sharing it among the nodes. To understand this sharing concept, consider that in a 10-Mbits/sec Ethernet network supporting 20 PCs, each PC will use only 0.5-Mbits/sec bandwidth, which means that the bandwidth is proportional to the number of nodes (20/10) on the network. If the 10-Mbits/sec Ethernet is replaced with a 155-Mbits/sec ATM switching technology, the bandwidth to each user could reach 155 Mbits/sec—310 times that available on the 10-Mbits/sec Ethernet network.

The following five high-speed LANs implement the token-passing architecture:

FDDI (100 Mbits/sec)

FDDI over Copper (100 Mbits/sec)

FDDI-II is geared to multimedia (100 Mbits/sec)

FFOL (FDDI Follow On LAN) is eventually meant to replace FDDI and will operate at 2.4 Gbits/sec

High-speed token ring.

The following three standards are intended to succeed Ethernet:

Fast Ethernet (100BASE-VG)

Fast Ethernet (100 Mbits/sec CSMA/CD, which operate at 100 Mbits/sec over copper)

Isochronous Ethernet, which is 16 Mbits/sec and is meant for multimedia.

More network technologies are yet to come. They are expected to handle data and multimedia applications. They include the Full-Duplex Ethernet (20 Mbits/sec / shared media), the Switched Ethernet (10 Mbits/sec), the Switched FDDI (100 Mbits/sec), and the Switched Token Ring (16 Mbits/sec / switched). The average cost per node will range between $1,200 and $7,000.

APPENDIX **A**

Installation of SCSI Host Adapters

Basic Steps

There are essentially three steps to successfully networking CD-ROM drives, regardless of the type of network.

1. It is important that you test the CD-ROM drives to make sure that they work properly and that they can be accessed without any problems. Install the CD-ROM interface card and cables, and connect the CD-ROM drives. Use the appropriate CD-ROM device driver software for the types of drives you are using. For example, use a SCSI/ASPI driver for SCSI adapters. Install MSCDEX (version 2.21 or higher) or its equivalent—e.g., CorelSCSI!'s CORELCDX, if needed. This step is done before you install the network interface card and before you start networking the CD-ROM drives.

During this step, you might encounter some error messages. The most encountered error messages range from CDR100 to CDR104. If the error persists, the reinstallation of the Microsoft Extensions software might correct the problem.

Error	Message and Cause of Error
CDR100	*Unknown error*
CDR101	*Not ready reading drive X. Abort, Retry, Fail?*

CDR101   The following are some causes of this error: no disk in the drive, an upside-down disk, a disk was not allowed enough time to "spin up" before a command was issued, a damaged disk, an incompatible disk, a scratched or dirty disk, or a damaged caddy.

If the error persists after correcting the situation, reinstall MSCDEX.

CDR102   *EMS memory no longer valid*

CDR103   *CD-ROM not High Sierra or ISO 9660 format reading drive D. Abort, Retry, Fail?*

The causes of this error can be:

The CD-ROM disc is recorded in Macintosh's HFS (hierarchical file system) or in the UNIX file system.

MSCDEX is loaded from Windows.

The disk is not in the ISO 9660 or High Sierra format.

CDR104   *Door open*
          Not enough drive letters available

You have to count the drives and change the line LASTDRIVE=X in the CONFIG.SYS file, where X is the highest letter used. So, if you have two hard drives or partitions (C: and D:) and four CD-ROM drives, the statement LASTDRIVE=H will be sufficient to suppress this error.

Device driver not found: CDROMDRV
No valid CD-ROM drivers selected

Some possible causes of this error include the following:

The SCSI device driver or the CD-ROM device driver failed to load.

The driver is corrupted.

A syntax error exists in the CONFIG.SYS file's DEVICE=line (make sure there is no space before or after the equal sign).

Check the spaces, slashes, and spelling.

The wrong device driver name was specified when MSCDEX was loaded.

Check your CONFIG.SYS and AUTOEXEC.BAT files for errors. If you don't find any, reinstall Microsoft Extensions.

2. Install the network interface card (or cards) in the file server and load the network software, then test to see if you can still access the CD-ROM drives.

3. Make sure that you can access the CD-ROM drives from any workstation in the network.

Physical and Logical Drives

During installation, you might be asked to provide information about the physical and logical drives. As the name implies, a physical drive is the actual drive or the hardware you have installed and attached to the machine server with cables and interface cards. Network software uses a different addressing and naming scheme to refer to physical devices. The name of a CD-ROM drive Z: on a file server, for example, might be D: or E:. These names are logical drives or logical devices.

The number of logical devices might exceed the number of physical devices—e.g., a hard disk drive might include one partition (C:) or more partitions (C: and D:). These two partitions are two logical devices occupying one physical device. Another example: logical drive D: can be used to serve, for example, 28 physical CD-ROM drives. Each workstation in the network might access the same or a different CD-ROM database. However, each database will run on one drive (logical drive D:) or more (logical drives D:, E:, etc.). These logical drives will take the same name in any workstation. So, workstation 1 will run database 5 on logical drive D:, while workstation 20 runs database 9 on logical drive D: also. If a database is composed of more than one disk, any workstation will run that database on logical drives D:, E:, F:, etc.

To overcome the limitation in the number of letters of the alphabet, some systems assign logical names, such as ERIC1, ERIC2, ART, etc.

Installation of SCSI Host Adapter

Plugging in a single device to a SCSI host adapter is a straightforward operation. Plugging in multiple devices is not an easy job. Most makers of SCSI adapters conform to the de facto standard the ASPI (Advanced SCSI Programming Interface) developed by Adaptec or the so-called Common Access Method (CAM), which is followed by Future Domain. ASPI cannot be used with CAM. Only one driver software program is used.

Before buying, make sure that the SCSI adapter will work with the SCSI device. Most SCSI CD-ROM drive vendors will provide you with the right adapter for their CD-ROM drive units. Also, special device drivers are usually supplied with the drive unit for CD-ROM SCSI boards. These drivers are on the diskette that comes with the CD-ROM drive. The diskette contains many device drivers intended for different types of computers and intended for different types of interface boards. You have to select the right one for the system in hand.

Usually, start by attaching one device at a time, test the system, then attach the next device. This way will save a lot of guessing if anything went wrong.

General Rules

To reduce signal reflections on the SCSI bus, identify which two SCSI devices (including the host adapter) will form the physical endpoints of your SCSI bus. The SCSI bus is the cable chain that connects the SCSI host adapter and devices together. The SCSI bus cannot exceed the SCSI length limitation of 18 feet, including internal ribbon cables, if any. Once you have identified the first and last physical SCSI devices on the ends of the SCSI bus chain, you must terminate them. These devices must have a set of resistors, called "terminators," either installed or disabled. All other SCSI devices installed between the ends of the SCSI bus must have their terminators either removed or disabled. Improper termination of a device will result in general bus failure.

Internal Devices Only

When only internal devices are connected to the host adapter, the last device connected to the SCSI ribbon cable and the host adapter itself should be terminated (fig. A–1).

External Devices Only

When only external devices are connected to the host adapter, both the last device on the external chain of the devices and the host adapter itself should be terminated (figs. A–2 and A–3).

Internal and External Devices

When both internal and external SCSI devices are connected to the host adapter, the last external device and the last internal device should be terminated (fig. A–4).

Terminating the Host Adapter

Usually, the installed bus terminators on the host adapter are enabled by default. Host adapter termination should be disabled only if you attach SCSI devices to both internal and external connectors, since the host adapter would

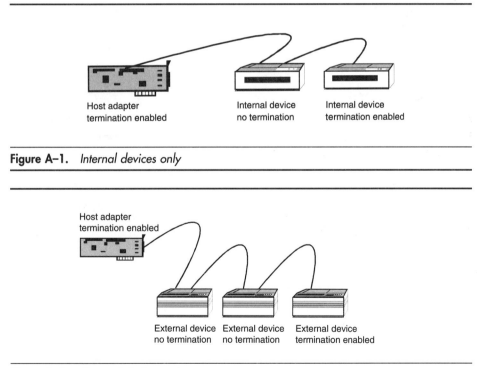

Host adapter
termination enabled

Internal device
no termination

Internal device
termination enabled

Figure A–1. *Internal devices only*

Host adapter
termination enabled

External device External device   External device
no termination   no termination   termination enabled

Figure A–2. *External devices only*

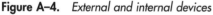

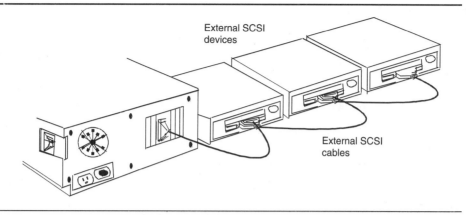

Figure A–3. *Connecting multiple external devices only*

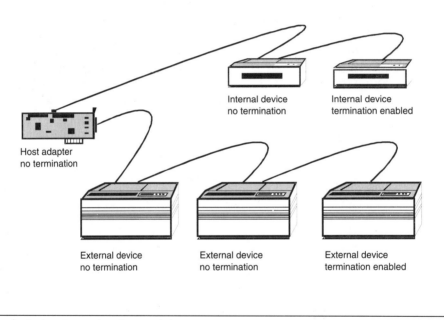

Figure A–4. *External and internal devices*

then be in the middle of the SCSI bus. When using an EISA computer system, enabling or disabling host adapter termination is software-selectable only and is done through your computer's EISA configuration utility.

SCSI ID Setting

Every device attached to a SCSI adapter (up to seven devices) is assigned a unique number from 0 to 6. The default value for your host adapter is SCSI

ID 7. The boot drive, if connected, usually is 0, while 1 is assigned to the second hard disk drive, if installed. Repeat this setting for each additional SCSI board in your computer. If you are not using internal devices, you may use 1 for the first external device.

A software driver is needed for every SCSI device attached, other than the first two hard disks. ASPI systems require that ASPI driver software be installed ahead of any other SCSI driver in the PC.

Step 1

Before making connections, turn off the power to all equipment to be connected and remove the PC's cover. Prepare the host SCSI adapter. If there is only one hard disk drive, use the default settings of the host adapter. The interrupts and memory address of the adapter should not conflict with other adapters in the PC. If two hard disks are in the PC, one of them has to be removed along with its controller or host adapter until the SCSI controller works. Make sure that the SCSI terminator resistors are in place. Match the adapter to any empty expansion slot. Plug the adapter into the slot.

Step 2

Apply the termination rules (above) to the hard drives. Set the SCSI ID number on the drive to the value required by the host adapter's BIOS (internal drives have jumpers or dip switches that allow you to set the SCSI ID number). The first drive will be 0. Connect the drive to one end of the SCSI ribbon and the host adapter to the other end. Plug the power connector into the drive.

Step 3

Keep the PC uncovered. Switch on the PC. If the drive is unformatted, boot from a floppy and format the disk, then install the required software.

Step 4

Install the second SCSI hard drive, if any. Set the SCSI ID of the drive to 1. Remove the termination resistor from this drive because it will be placed in the middle of the SCSI daisy chain. The chain will be in the following order:

- 0 First SCSI hard drive
- 1 Second SCSI hard drive
- 7 Host SCSI adapter

Switch off the PC and install the drive by attaching it to any connector in the middle of the SCSI cable.

Step 5

The first two hard drives will not need device driver software, but any additional devices will need drivers. You will need to install the ASPI driver and the software drivers used by each individual SCSI device you add to the system. The ASPI or CAM driver must precede any other SCSI drivers listed in the CONFIG.SYS file. Any system must use either ASPI or CAM. However, CAM-based host adapters can work without adapters; if the system is running under an OS/2 operating system, you do not need to install the drivers. Install the drivers in the CONFIG.SYS file, one at a time. This way, you will recognize any problems right away.

Step 6

Any internal devices added should follow the same procedures as above. Connect them in the middle of the chain. You will need to match the SCSI ID required by the software that will use the devices.

A third device will install like a second internal device. Remove the terminations from the device and set the SCSI device ID to the value required by its software (but not 0 or 1 used by the first two hard drives). Plug the device into any of the connectors in the middle of the internal SCSI cable and into a power connector. Install its driver, and test the new device with its software.

Once you add an external device, the terminator will shift from the host adapter to the external device. Switch off the PC, pull out the host adapter, and remove the three termination resistor packs from it. Reinstall and reconnect the host adapter.

Now set the SCSI ID for the external SCSI device. Use the number required by the software that will use the device (do not use either 0 or 1). Plug one end of an external SCSI cable into the host adapter and the other end into one of the two SCSI connectors on the external SCSI device. You can use either of these connectors—they are electrically identical. Now attach a terminating plug to the other SCSI connector on the external device. Install the driver associated with the new SCSI device.

Switch on the external SCSI device, then reboot your PC. Test the new device. Ensure that your internal SCSI devices and any other SCSI peripherals already installed are still operating before you proceed with the next external device.

Step 7

Continue the daisy chain until all SCSI devices are installed and working. Installing additional external devices follows naturally. First, set the SCSI ID numbers of each new unit to any unused value from 2 to 6. Unplug the termination from the last device in the SCSI chain, and connect a new SCSI cable in its place. Plug the other end of this cable into the next SCSI device, then plug the termination into the other connector on the new device. Install its driver, reboot, and test the device.

SCSI Extenders

The extender is a device you can add to the system to extend the number of SCSI devices you can attach to a single SCSI host adapter. Without the extender, most host adapters support only 7 devices (e.g., 7 CD-ROM drives).

With the extender, they can support up to 49 drives. The software that controls the drives must support this design. For example, SCSI Express from Micro Design International only supports the attachment of CD-ROM drives manufactured by Micro Design to an external bus. An IBM host adapter can only support a maximum of 15 devices. So, the primary benefit of the SCSI extender is the significant increase of available online CD-ROM drives. The transfer rate of a SCSI extender per SCSI-2 adapter is 10 Mbytes/sec.

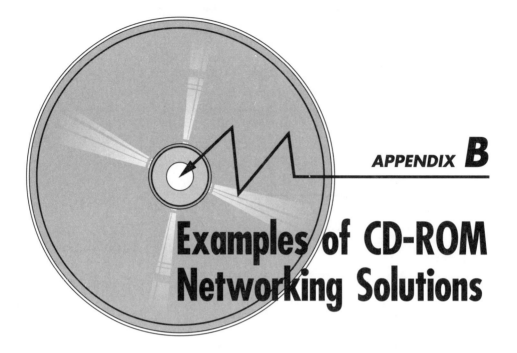

APPENDIX **B**

Examples of CD-ROM Networking Solutions

The following highlights networking CD-ROM drives using SCSI Express, Windows for Workgroups, LANtastic, and LocalTalk to build CD-ROM networks. The reader is referred to chapter 11 for the specifications of different types of networks. Your CD-ROM server should have enough memory—at least 1.2 Mb for each SCSI CD-ROM drive attached.

Installing the SCSI Express CD-ROM Drives with Extenders

SCSI Express was developed by Micro Design International (MDI). It is built on the concept that multiple SCSI devices (hard disk, WORM, Rewritable, CD-ROM, etc.) can coexist on the same SCSI adapter, regardless of whether that adapter is for ISA, EISA, or MCA bus computers. The SCSI Express package includes software drivers and utilities designed to work with Micro Design's full line of storage subsystems. You have to check with the company if you have hardware produced by another vendor.

In this example, we assume that a Novell NetWare network already exists and it is operational. We also assume that you are connecting 21 CD-ROM drives to one SCSI-2 host adapter card using the extender technology (actually, you can connect up to 49 drives to a single SCSI-2 host adapter). MDI recommends that you use Micro Design SCSI Express 600CDXEXT CD-ROM drives. The 21 SE600CDXEXT CD-ROM drives will be divided into three stacks, 7 drives each. The 7 drives are as follows: one drive unit that will connect to the Extender Y SCSI cable, and three two-drive units.

1. Before making connections, turn off the power to all equipment to be connected.
2. Plug in the male/female connector of the Extender Y SCSI cable to the lower SCSI connector at the rear of each single drive unit (fig. B–1).
3. Connect the single connector end of the Extender Y SCSI cable of the third stack to the host adapter installed in the CD-ROM server.
4. Plug an active terminator into the upper SCSI connector on the rear of the CD-ROM drive at the end. Up to six additional MDI CD-ROM drives may be connected to the port of each extender.
5. Locate the pushwheel switches on the rear of each drive.
6. The right switch sets the target ID (TID) for the SCSI extender. The extender is usually shipped from the factory with a default TID of 1.
7. The left switch sets the logical unit number (LUN) for this CD-ROM drive. The extender is shipped from the factory with a default LUN setting of 5.
8. Set the switches as explained in Figure B–2.
9. Connect AC power cables of each stack to an AC outlet.

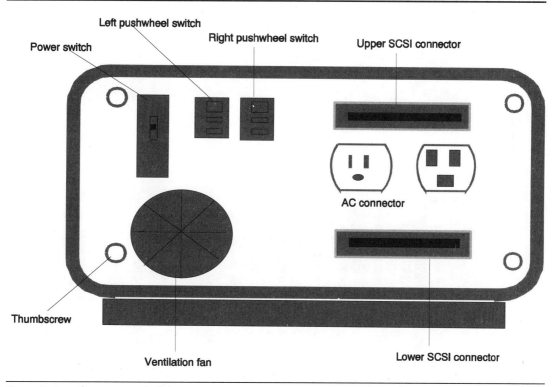

Figure B–1. *The rear panel of the SCSI Express 600CDXEXT CD-ROM drive. The male/female connector of the Extender Y SCSI cable should be connected to the lower SCSI connector.*

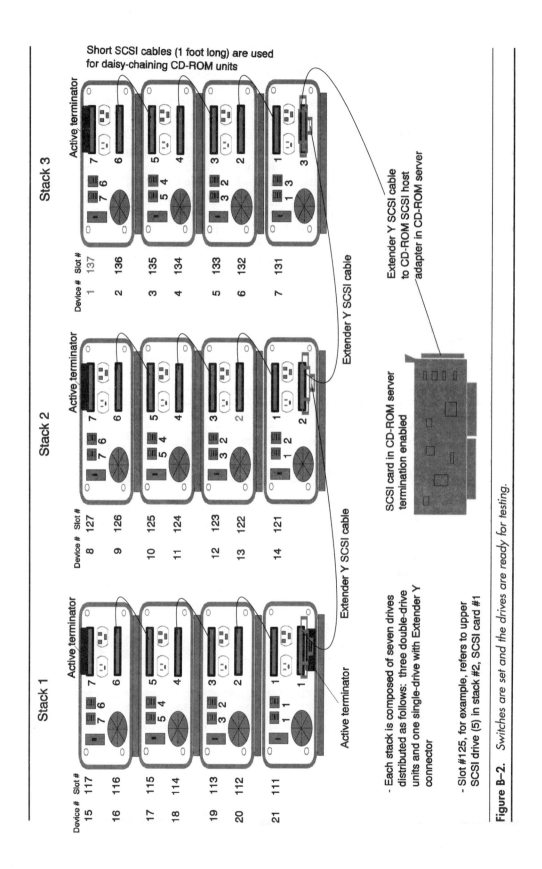

Figure B–2. Switches are set and the drives are ready for testing.

Installation of SCSI Express on Novell NetWare 386

Bring the server up and mount the SYS volume. If you have NetWare version 3.11 or 3.12, you can load the SCSI Express Installation Utility by typing:

```
:LOAD drive:INST31x
```

If you have NetWare version 4.0 or above, type:

```
:LOAD drive:INST40
```

where *drive:* refers to the drive letter of the floppy drive containing the SCSI Express software.

The Initialization Configuration Options screen will be displayed. You can change the default configuration at this time. Once the installation configuration is saved by pressing <F10>, the Host Adapter Configuration screen appears next.

The Host Adapter Configuration screen displays all supported host adapters detected on the screen. Press <F10> to save the host adapter configuration.

The Configure Devices screen appears next. It displays all of the SCSI CD-ROM and other mass-storage devices you might have. Each device is identified by a device line, except for jukeboxes; they are identified by multiple lines, one per changer and one per internal drive.

Each device line is composed of the following:

ID: displays the device's address

Name: name of the manufacturer

Group: name of the jukebox group

Type: device type (CD for CD-ROM, WO for WORM, etc.)

Driver: driver assigned to the device (CDDRV for SCSI Express CD-ROM drives)

Once you save the Configure Devices, the file-processing status bar appears. The utility creates the SCSI Express directory on SYS:SYSTEM and DOS partition and copies over files. The Save Configuration Files Options screen appears. Select Save Configuration Files if you are satisfied with the configuration. As a result, the necessary modifications will be made to STARTUP.NCF and AUTOEXEC.NCF for you. These two files might look like Figures B–3 and B–4.

```
#STARTUP.NCF
LOAD ISADISK PORT=1FO INT=E
LOAD C:\NETWARE\EXPRESS\XLIB31X
LOAD C:\NETWARE\EXPRESS\BTHA PORT=334 SGSEGS=32
LOAD C:\NETWARE\EXPRESS\BTHA PORT=230 SGSEGS=32
LOAD C:\NETWARE\EXPRESS\AHA 2740 SLOT=3 SGSEGS=32
LOAD C:\NETWARE\EXPRESS\ASPITRAN
```

Figure B–3. *The STARTUP.NCF file*

```
#AUTOEXEC.NCF
FILE SERVER NAME CDROM-1
SET REPLY TO GET NEAREST SERVER=OFF
IPX INTERNAL NET 1905949
LOAD DIRLPFIX.NLM
LOAD EAINFIX.NLM
LOAD MAXCDCFX.NLM
LOAD WORMROFX.NLM
SET VOLUME LOW WARN ALL USERS=OFF
SEARCH ADD C:\NETWARE
SEARCH ADD C:\NETWARE\EXPRESS
LOAD NE3200 SLOT=5 FRAME=ETHERNET_802.3 NAME=ENET_8023
BIND IPX TO ENET_8023 NET 11247059
LOAD REMOTE XXX1
LOAD TPX
MOUNT ALL
```

Figure B–4.   *The AUTOEXEC.NCF file*

If the installation is successful, you will be instructed to restart the server after exiting from the utility.

Preparing a CD

To mount a CD-ROM volume, you must first create a File Set for it. You create a File Set for each physical disc. Each time you receive an update for a CD-ROM disc, you must create a File Set for the new disc.

1. Insert a disc into the CD-ROM drive (use caddies if the drives require them)
2. At the CD-ROM server console, type: : LOAD CDUTIL
3. Select the first item from the Main Menu: Select CD-ROM Drive
4. A pop-up list of drives appears
5. Select the CD-ROM drive you want to create a File Set for from the list
6. The Main Menu reappears. Select Create File Set. The utility scans the disc. It displays a File Set Information form with the following information: File Set Name, Volume Name, Trustee List, Owner, and Name Spaces.
7. You can change the default names or accept them. For example, if you are mounting ABI Inform 1994 disc, you may assign names such as:

> File Set Name: ABI1994 (1 to 8 characters) <Enter>
> Volume Name: ABI1994 (1 to 15 characters) <Enter>

Trustee List, Owner, and Name Spaces are NetWare concepts.

When finished, save the File Set Information form. The utility will prompt you to mount the volume. Select Yes if you want to mount the volume now;

otherwise, select No. You can mount the volume from the Main Menu or at NetWare prompt as follows, provided you have mounted CDUTIL:

If you have NetWare 3.11, type: MOUNT *vID*

If you have NetWare 3.12 or 4.0 or greater, type:

SCAN FOR NEW DEVICES
MOUNT *vID*

Replace *vID* with the name of the volume: e.g.; MOUNT ABI1994

You can dismount a volume and remove a File Set either from the Main Menu or at the NetWare prompt as follows, provided you have mounted CDUTIL: :DISMOUNT *vID*

To remove a File Set, type: :CDDRV RM *FileSet.*

The search and retrieval software for CD-ROM databases will be installed on the NetWare file server like any other application. Figure B–5 is a simple batch file that will work from a workstation to access two SilverPlatter ERIC discs using SCSI Express and Novell NetWare 3.11.

```
@echo off
REM batch file to access SilverPlatter ERIC database
CLS

ATTACH ServerName/UserName >NUL
IF ERRORLEVEL == 1 GOTO EXIT

LINK INS D: ServerName/VolumeName1: >NUL
LINK INS E: ServerName/VolumeName2: >NUL

K:
CD \APPS\CDROM\SPIRS >NUL
ECHO .
ECHO .
ECHO .
ECHO PLEASE WAIT...LOADING ERIC

K:\APPS\CDROM\SPIRS\SPIRS.EXE

H:
Link Del D: >Nul
Link Del E: >Nul

:EXIT
LOGOUT ServerName >NUL
CLS
```

Figure B–5. *Simple batch file*

Windows for Workgroups (WFW)

Windows for Workgroups is one of the most appealing solutions to sharing CD-ROM applications, especially if you are using applications that run under Windows. WFW lets a Windows workstation share its disk drives, including CD-ROM and printers. It is easy to install since the installation is essentially transparent as WFW determines your hardware setup and configures itself with minimum intervention from you. Once installed, sharing a CD-ROM drive with WFW is almost completely transparent to the user. WFW is compatible with Novell NetWare.

Installing a CD-ROM Drive with WFW

During installation, WFW adds the /S (share) switch to the MSCDEX command line. If you are using MSIPX, Microsoft's special WFW-compatible driver to access the NetWare file server and to allow other stations to share your drive, you must place MSCDEX after NetStart, but before MSIPX in the AUTOEXEC. BAT file.

Sharing CD-ROM Drives with Other Users

Once WFW is installed, use the File Manager to announce the CD-ROM drives to other network users.

1. In the toolbar at the top of the screen, click on the icon for the drive (floppy, hard, or CD-ROM) you want to share. A file list from the CD-ROM in that drive will be displayed.
2. Click on the Share button (this button shows a little hand and a file folder) to allow other users to share the specified drive. The Share Directory dialog box appears.
3. Fill in the Share Directory dialog box with the following information:
   - *Share Name:*   This is the name that others on the network see when they browse for the drive.
   - *Path:*   The Path line is filled in for you.
   - *Comment:*   You can add any comments for others to see.
   - *Reshare at Startup:* If this box is marked, the share will happen the next time you start WFW.
   - *Access Type:*   This button determines what sort of access users have to the drive (read-only or full access). You can also allow access through a password.
4. Click on the OK button to activate the share.

Accessing Other Drives on the Network

To access drives attached to other WFW workstations, use the File Manager:

1. Click on the Connect button (the first button) on the toolbar. The Connect Network Drive dialog box appears.
2. Fill in the appropriate options in the Connect Network Drive dialog box.

3. Click on the arrow of the Drive combo box to choose the drive letter assigned to the shared CD-ROM drive.
4. Ignore the Path combo box as it is filled in automatically.
5. If selected, the Reconnect at Startup check box will automatically reconnect you the next time you start Windows.
6. From the Showed Shared Directories on list box, click on the icon that identifies the computer and the drive or CD-ROM drive you want to access.
7. Once you select a computer, a dialog box appears in the bottom displaying any directories available on that computer. If you click on the CD-ROM drive's share, the Path combo box will be filled in automatically.
8. Click on the OK button. Now you can access information on the CD-ROM you chose.

Sharing CD-ROM Drives on LANtastic

LANtastic is a peer-to-peer networking software program that runs under DOS. It has a Windows interface that can be installed after LANtastic for DOS is installed. After Windows loads, LANtastic for Windows drivers are activated.

1. The installation of LANtastic should be a straightforward operation. However, the only thing you have to do after installation is to remove the MSCDEX command from the AUTOEXEC.BAT file and insert it into the STARTNET.BAT file between the LANtastic REDIR and SERVER command lines.
2. Through the file named NET_MGR, access LANtastic's Network Resource Manager. A list of resources is displayed on the screen. Press the Insert key and type an identifying name for the CD-ROM drive such as CDROM_1. Then type the DOS drive name; e.g., D: or E:, as the true link, and exit.

Accessing Another CD-ROM Drive

To connect a workstation to the shared drive, access LANtastic's Peer NET program.

1. From the Main Functions menu, select Network Disk Drives and Printers.
2. Specify the DOS drive name (D:, E:, etc.) for the CD-ROM drive.
3. From the list of available servers, select the server that contains the CD-ROM drive you want to access, then select the CD-ROM drive from the list of available drives on the selected server.
4. Press the Escape key to exit to the DOS prompt.

CD-ROM Drives on a Mac Network

The CD-ROM drives are named volumes on the Mac. Almost all Macs are SCSI-based. When another user picks your machine in their Chooser, they see the CD-ROM's name in the list of volumes.

Make sure that the drive works on the local machine before you try to share it across the network.

Check the drive's documentation to see how you can set the address. If your CD-ROM drive is the only device in the chain, set it for SCSI ID 1.

1. Attach the drive to your SCSI bus.
2. Make sure that the bus is properly terminated.
3. Connect your CD-ROM drive to its power supply.
4. Connect the audio-out connectors from the CD-ROM drive to the Mac's audio-input port.
5. Start your Mac and run the installer program from the floppy drive.
6. Restart your Mac. If there is a disc in the CD-ROM drive, the CD-ROM drive icon should show up on your desktop along with your hard drive icons.

To access your computer from another computer:

1. Open the Chooser.
2. Pick the AppleShare icon.
3. Pick your machine from the list of servers on the right side of the Chooser.
4. Enable File Sharing on the machine and wait a minute or so before you reopen the Chooser.
5. In the Volumes dialog box, which has the name of the server at the top, click the CD-ROM's volume name.
6. Click OK. The drive's icon should appear on your desktop.

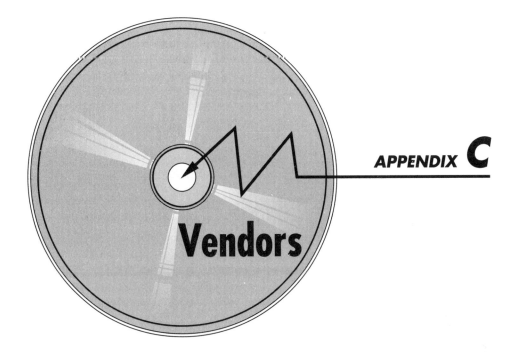

APPENDIX **C**

Vendors

3Com Corp.
5400 Bayfront Plaza
Santa Clara, CA 95052
(408) 764-5000

AccessData Corp.
125 South 1025 East
Lindon, UT 84042
(801) 785-0363,
(800) 658-5199
Fax: (801) 224-6009

Acme Electric
20 Water St.
Cuba, NY 14727
(716) 968-2400,
(800) 325-5848
Fax: (716) 968-1420

Actrix Systems, Inc.
6315 San Ignacio Ave.
San Jose, CA 95119
(408) 281-4321,
(800) 422-8749
Fax: (408) 578-4102

Adaptec
691 S. Milpitas Blvd.
Milpitas, CA 95035
(408) 945-8600,
(800) 934-2766

Adlersparre & Associates, Inc.
1803 Douglas St., #501
Victoria, BC, Canada V8T 5C3
(604) 384-1118
Fax: (604) 384-3363

Advanced Computer
  Communications
10261 Bubb Rd.
Cupertino, CA 95014
(408) 864-0600
Fax: (408) 446-5234

Advanced Graphic Applications, Inc.
90 Fifth Ave.
New York, NY 10011-7696
(212) 337-4200,
(800) 347-2871

Advanced Network Systems, Inc.
16257 Monterey Rd.
Morgan Hill, CA 95037
(408) 779-2209,
(800) 333-6381
Fax: (408) 776-8511

Alcom Corp.
1616 N. Shoreline Blvd.
Mountain View, CA 94043
(415) 694-7000,
(800) 873-1329
Fax: (415) 694-7070

Alloy Computer Products, Inc.
165 Forest St.
Marlboro, MA 01752
(508) 481-8500

Alpha Technologies
3767 Alpha Way
Bellingham, WA 98226
(206) 647-2360,
(800) 322-5742
Fax: (206) 671-4936

American Power Conversion
132 Fairgrounds Rd.
West Kingston, RI 02892
(401) 782-2515,
(800) 800-4272

AMP, Inc.
P.O. Box 3608
Harrisburgh, PA 17105-3608
(800) 522-6752

Andrew
19021 120th Ave. N.E.
Bothell, WA 98011
(206) 485-8200,
(800) 776-6174

Apple Computer, Inc.
20525 Mariani Ave.
Cupertino, CA 95014
(408) 996-1010

Artisoft, Inc.
2202 N. Forbes Blvd.
Tucson, AZ 85745
(602) 670-7100,
(800) 233-5564
Fax: (602) 670-7101

ASP Computer Products
160 San Gabriel Dr.
Sunnyvale, CA 94086
(408) 746-2965,
(800) 445-6190
Fax: (408) 746-2803

Banyan Systems, Inc.
115 Flanders Rd.
Westboro, MA 01581
(508) 898-1000

Beame & Whiteside
706 Hillsborough St.
Raleigh, NC 27603-1655
(919) 831-8989

Best Power Technology
P.O. Box 280
Necedah, WI 54646
(608) 565-7200,
(800) 356-5794
Fax: (608) 565-2221

Beyond
38 Sidney St.
Cambridge, MA 02139
(617) 621-0095,
(800) 845-8511
Fax: (617) 621-0096

BICC Communications
103 Millbury St.
Auburn, MA 01501
(508) 832-8650

Biologic
7950 Blue Gray Circle
Manassas, VA 22110
(703) 368-2949

Black Box Corp.
P.O. Box 12800
Pittsburgh, PA 15241
(412) 746-5500,
(800) 552-6816
Fax: (800) 321-0746

Blast, Inc.
P.O. Box 808
107-B West Salisburry St.
Pittsboro, NC 27312-9903
(919) 542-3007,
(800) 242-5278
Fax: (919) 542-0160

Boffin Limited
2500 West County Road 42
Burnsville, MN 55337
(612) 894-0595

Brightwork Development, Inc.
766 Shrewsbury Ave.,
Jerral Center West
Tinton Falls, NJ 07724
(201) 530-0440,
(800) 552-9876

Buffalo Products
2805 19th St. S.E.
Salem, OR 97302
(503) 585-3414,
(800) 345-2356
Fax: (503) 585-4505

C-Tech Electronics
2515 McCabe Way
Irvine, CA 92714
(714) 833-1165,
(800) 347-4528
Fax: (714) 757-4533

Cabletron Systems, Inc.
35 Industrial Way
P.O. Box 5005
Rochester, NH 03867-0505
(603) 332-9400

Caculus, Inc.
1761 W. Hillsboro Blvd.
Deerfield Beach, FL 33442
(305) 481-2334,
(305) 481-1866

Castelle
3255-3 Scott Blvd.
Santa Clara, CA 95054
(408) 496-0474,
(800) 289-7555
Fax: (408) 496-0502

CBIS, Inc.
5875 Peachtree Industrial Blvd.
Bldg. 100, Suite 170
P.O. Box 921206
Norcross, GA 30092
(404) 446-1332,
(800) 344-8426
Fax: (404) 446-9164

CE Software, Inc.
P.O. Box 65580
1801 Industrial Circle
Des Moines, IA 50265
(515) 221-1801,
(800) 523-7638
Fax: (515) 221-1806

Central Point Software, Inc.
15220 NW Greenbrier Pkwy., #200
Beaverton, OR 97006
(503) 690-8088,
(800) 445-4208

Cheyenne Software, Inc.
3 Expressway Plaza
Roslyn Heights, NY 11577
(516) 484-5110,
(800) 243-9462
Fax: (516) 484-3446

Chi Corp.
31200 Carter St.
Solon, OH 44139
(216) 349-8600

Chinon America, Inc.
615 Hawaii Ave.
Torrance, CA 90503
(310) 533-0274,
(800) 441-0222
Fax: (310) 533-1727

Chipcom Corp.
Southborough Office Park
118 Turnpike Rd.
Southborough, MA 01772
(508) 460-8900,
(800) 228-9930
Fax: (508) 460-8950

Cirtus International Corp.
13110 Shaker Sq.
Cleveland, OH 44120
(216) 752-8181,
(800) 722-8737

Cisco Systems
1525 O'Brien Dr.
P.O. Box 3075
Menlo Park, CA 94025
(415) 326-1941,
(800) 533-NETS
Fax: (415) 326-1989

Citrix Systems, Inc.
210 University Dr.
Suite 700
Coral Springs, FL 33071
(305) 755-0559,
(800) 437-7503
Fax: (305) 341-6880

Clovis, Inc.
25 Porter Rd.
Littleton, MA 01460
(508) 486-0005
Fax: (508) 486-3755

Command Software Systems, Inc.
1061 E. Indiantown Rd.
Suite 500
Jupiter, FL 33477
(407) 575-3200
Fax: (407) 575-3026

Compaq Computer
2055 SH 249
Houston, TX 77070
(713) 370-0670,
(800) 345-1518
Fax: (713) 374-4583

Connect Computer Co.
9855 West 78th St., #270
Eden Prairie, MN 55344
(612) 944-0181

Conner Storage Systems
36 Skyline Dr.
Lake Mary, FL 32746
(407) 263-3500,
(800) 5-CONNER
Fax: (407) 263-3555

Contact East, Inc.
335 Willow St.
North Andover, MA 01845-5995
(800) 225-5334
Fax: (800) 225-5317

Corel Systems Corp.
1600 Carling Ave.
Ottawa, Canada K1Z 8R7
(613) 728-3733,
(800) 836-7274
Fax: (613) 761-9176

Cubix Corp.
2800 Lockheed Way
Carson City, NV 89706-0719
(702) 883-7611,
(800) 829-0550
Fax: (702) 882-2407

D-Link Systems
5 Musick
Irvine, CA 92718
(714) 455-1688,
(800) 326-1688
Fax: (714) 455-2521

Da Vinci Systems
4200 Six Forks Rd., Suite 200
Raleigh, NC 27609
(919) 881-4320,
(800) 328-4624
Fax: (919) 787-3550

Data Interface Systems, Inc.
P.O. Box 4189
Austin, TX 78765
(512) 346-5641,
(800) 351-4244

Datacom Technologies, Inc.
11001 31st Pl. W.
Everett, WA 98204
(206) 355-0590,
(800) 468-5557
Fax: (206) 290-1600

DataDisc
Route 3, Box 1108
Gainesville, VA 22065
(703) 347-2111
Fax: (703) 347-9085

DAVID Systems, Inc.
701 E. Evelyn Ave.
Sunnyvale, CA 94088
(408) 720-8000
Fax: (408) 720-1337

Deltec Electronics
2727 Kurtz St.
San Diego, CA 92110
(619) 291-4211,
(800) 854-2658
Fax: (619) 291-2973

Digital Communications Associates
1000 Alderman Dr.
Alpharetta, GA 30202-4199
(404) 442-4000,
(800) 348-3221

Digital Dispatch, Inc.
55 Lakeland Shores Rd.
Lakeland, MN 55043
(612) 436-1000,
(800) 221-8091

Digital Equipment Corp. (DEC)
146 Main St.
Maynard, MA 01754
(508) 493-5111,
(800) 344-4825
Fax: (508) 493-8780

Digital Products, Inc.
411 Waverly Oaks Rd.
Waltham, MA 02154
(617) 647-1234,
(800) 243-2333
Fax: (617) 647-4474

Digital Research, Inc.
BOX DRI, 70 Garden Ct.
Monterey, CA 93942
(408) 649-3896,
(800) 274-4374

Distributed Processing Technology
140 Candace Dr.
Maitland, FL 32751
(407) 830-5522,
(800) 322-4378

DMA, Inc. (Dynamic Microprocessor
   Association)
1776 Jericho Turnpike
Huntington, NY 11743
(516) 462-0440
Fax: (516) 462-6652

Document Imaging Systems Corp.
   (DISC)
541 Weddell Dr.
Sunnyvale, CA 94089-2114
(408) 734-5287
Fax: (408) 734-2692

DynaTek Automation Systems
15 Tangiers Rd.
Toronto, ON M3J 2B1
(416) 636-3000
Fax: (803) 879-2030

East Coast Software, Inc.
118 Rock Rd.
Booters Town, Co Dublin, Ireland
(353) 1-283-1166
Fax: (353) 1-283-1232

Eastman Kodak Company
901 Elmgrove Rd.
Rochester, NY 14653-5200
(800) 235-6325 (USA),
(800) 465-6325

Educational Solutions
4683 American Rd.
Rockford, IL 61109
(800) 443-3229

Emerald Systems Corp.
12230 World Trade Dr.
San Diego, CA 92128
(619) 673-2161,
(800) 767-2587
Fax: (619) 673-2288

Enigma Logic, Inc.
2151 Salvio St., #301
Concord, CA 94520
(415) 827-5707,
(800) 333-4416

Epoch Systems
8 Technology Dr.
Westboro, MA 01581
(800) 873-7624
Fax: (508) 366-6853

Evergreen Systems
120 Landing Ct., Suite 120
Novato, CA 94945
(415) 897-8888
Fax: (415) 897-6158

Extended Systems
9675 W. Glen Ellyn St.
Boise, ID 83794
(208) 322-7575,
(800) 235-7576
Fax: (208) 377-1906

Exzel Corp.
2003 E. 5th St., #3
Tempe, AZ 85281-3064
(602) 894-0795,
(800) 325-7334

EZ-Systems
24 Graf Rd.
Newburyport, MA 01950
(508) 465-6060,
(800) 533-7756
Fax: (508) 465-6633

Farallon Computing
2470 Mariner Sq. Loop
Alameda, CA 94501
(510) 814-5100
Fax: (510) 814-5020

Fifth Generation Systems, Inc.
10049 N. Reiger Rd.
Baton Rouge, LA 70809
(504) 291-7221,
(800) 873-4384

FlexSys Corporation (FSC)
See EZ-Systems

Fresh Technology Group, Inc.
1478 N. Tech Blvd., #101
Gilbert, AZ 86234
(602) 497-4200

Frye Computer Systems, Inc.
19 Temple Pl.
Boston, MA 02111
(617) 451-5400,
(800) 234-3793

Funk Software, Inc.
222 Third St.
Cambridge, MA 02142
(617) 497-6339

Future Domain Corp.
2801 McGaw Ave.
Irvine, CA 92714
(714) 253-0400,
(800) 879-7599

Future Echo
9559 Irondale
Chatsworth, CA 91311
(818) 709-2091
Fax: (818) 709-0489

Gandalf Data, Inc.
1020 South Noel Ave.
Wheeling, IL 60090
(800) 426-3253
Fax: (708) 541-6803

Gandalf Systems Corp.
Cherry Hills Industrial Center
Building 9
Cherry Hill, NJ 08003
(609) 424-9400,
(800) GAN-DALF
Fax: (609) 751-4376

Gateway Communications, Inc.
2941 Alton Ave.
Irvine, CA 92714
(714) 553-1555,
(800) 367-6555
Fax: (714) 553-1616

GigaTrend
2234 Rutherford Rd.
Carlsbad, CA 92008
(619) 931-9122,
(800) 743-4442
Fax: (619) 931-9959

Global Computer Supplies
11 Harbor Park Dr.
Port Washington, NY 11050
(516) 625-6200,
(800) 845-6225
Fax: (800) 227-1246

The Global Solution
4165 E. La Palma Ave.
Anaheim, CA 92807
(714) 961-7000,
(800) 232-1347
Fax: (714) 961-0102

Grapevine LAN Products, Inc.
8519 154th Ave. NE
Redmond, WA 98052
(206) 865-9773
Fax: (206) 232-8705

Hays Microcomputer Products, Inc.
P.O. Box 10503
Atlanta, GA 30348
(404) 840-9200

Helix Software
47-09 30th St.
Long Island City, NY 11101
(718) 392-3100,
(800) 451-0551

Hewlett-Packard Co.
100 Mayfield Ave.
Mountain View, CA 94043
(415) 968-5600

Hewlett-Packard
Network Printer Div.
300 Hanover St.
Palo Alto, CA 94304
(800) 527-3753

Horizons Technology, Inc.
Software Products Group
3990 Ruffin Rd.
San Diego, CA 92123
(619) 292-8320
Fax: (619) 565-1175

ICOT Corp.
P.O. Box 5143
San Jose, CA 95150
(408) 433-3300,
(800) 762-3270

INCOM USA
116 Village Blvd., Suite 200
Princeton, NJ 08540
(609) 951-2259
Fax: (609) 520-1702

Inmac
2465 Auqustine Dr.
P.O. Box 58031
Sanata Clara, CA 95052-8031
(800) 547-5444

Insight Direct
1912 W. 4th St.
Tempe, AZ 85281
(602) 902-1176,
(800) 927-7848
Fax: (602) 902-1180

Insignia Solutions, Inc.
1300 Charleston Rd.
Mountain View, CA 94043
(415) 694-7600,
(800) 848-7677
Fax: (415) 694-3705

Intecom, Inc.
601 Intecom Dr.
Allen, TX 75002
(214) 727-9141

Integrated Workstations, Inc.
1648 Mabury Rd.
San Jose, CA 95133
(408) 923-0301,
(800) 832-6526
Fax: (408) 923-0427

Intel
5200 N.E. Elam Young Pkwy.
Hillsboro, OR 97124
(800) 538-3373
Fax: (800) 525-3019

Intercomputer Communications
  Corp.
8230 Montgomery Rd.
Cincinnati, OH 45236
(513) 745-0500
Fax: (513) 745-0327

International Business Machines
  (IBM)
Old Orchard Rd.
Armonk, NY 10504
(914) 765-1900,
(800) 426-2468

International Security Technology,
  Inc.
515 Madison Ave., #3200
New York, NY 10022
(212) 288-3101

Invisible Software, Inc.
1142 Chess Dr.
Foster City, CA 94404
(415) 570-5967

J & L Information Systems
9238 Deering Ave.
Chatsworth, CA 91311
(818) 709-1778
Fax: (818) 882-1424

JetFax, Inc.
978 Hamilton Ct.
Menlo Park, CA 94025
(415) 324-0600
Fax: (415) 326-6003

JVC Information Products
17811 Mitchell
Irvine, CA 92714
(714) 261-1292
Fax: (714) 261-9690

Kubik Enterprises, Inc.
18873 Allandale Ave.
Saratoga, CA 95070
(604) 261-4191
Fax: (604) 261-4174

LANshark Systems, Inc.
6502 E. Main St.
Reynoldsburg, OH 43068
(614) 866-5553
Fax: (614) 866-4877

Lantronix
26072 Merit Cir., Suite 113
Laguna Hills, CA 92653
(714) 367-0050

Legacy Storage Systems
25A S St.
Hopkinton, MA 01748
(508) 435-4700,
(800) 966-6442
Fax: (508) 435-3080

Legato Systems, Inc.
260 Sheridan, #415
Palo Alto, CA 94036
(415) 329-7880
Fax: (415) 329-8898

Lexmark International
740 New Circle Rd.
Lexington, KY 40511
(606) 232-2000

Logical Engineering
5364 Ehrlich Rd., Suite 250
Tampa, FL 33625
(813) 264-5236
Fax: (813) 264-5140

LogiCraft, Inc.
22 Cotton Rd.
Nashua, NH 03063
(603) 880-0300,
(800) 880-5644
Fax: (603) 880-7229

Lotus Development Corp.
55 Cambridge Pkwy.
Cambridge, MA 02142-1295
(617) 577-8500,
(800) 343-5414
Fax: (617) 693-3512

McAfee Associates
2710 Walsh Ave., Suite 200
Santa Clara, CA 95051-0963
(408) 988-3832
Fax: (408) 970-9727

McCarty Associates, Inc.
929 Boston Post Rd.
Old Saybrook, CT 06475
(203) 388-6994

Magee Enterprises
P.O. Box 1587
Norcross, GA 30091
(800) 662-4330

Maximum Storage, Inc.
5025 Centennial Blvd.
Colorado Springs, CO 80919
(719) 531-6888,
(800) 843-6299
Fax: (719) 531-0227

Maxoptix
3342 Gateway Blvd.
Fremont, CA 94538
(510) 353-9700,
(800) 546-6695
Fax: (510) 353-1845

MCR Corp.
1700 S. Patterson Blvd.
Dayton, OH 45479
(800) 225-5627

Meridian Data, Inc.
5615 Scotts Valley Dr.
Scotts Valley, CA 95066
(408) 438-3100,
(800) 767-2537
Fax: (408) 438-6816

Micro Design International, Inc.
6985 University Blvd.
Winter Park, FL 32792
(407) 677-8333,
(800) 228-0891
Fax: (407) 677-8365

Microboards of America
308 Broadway
P.O. Box 130
Carver, MN 55315
(612) 448-9800
Fax: (612) 448-9806

Microcom, Inc.
500 River Ridge Dr., No. 8
Norwood, MA 02062
(617) 551-1000,
(800) 822-8224
Fax: (617) 551-1006

Microdyne Corp.
207 S. Peyton St.
Alexandria, VA 22314-2812
(703) 739-0500,
(800) 255-3967
Fax: (703) 739-0572

MicroNet Technology, Inc.
80 Technology Dr.
Irvine, CA 92718
(714) 453-6100
Fax: (714) 453-6101

Microsoft Corp.
One Microsoft Way
Redmond, WA 98052-6399
(800) 426-9400
Fax: (206) 936-7329

MicroSolutions
132 W. Lincoln Hwy.
DeKalb, IL 60115
(815) 756-3411,
(800) 296-1214
Fax: (815) 756-2928

Microtest, Inc.
3519 E. Shea Blvd.
Phoenix, AZ 85028
(602) 971-6464,
(800) 526-9675

MiLAN Technology
894 Ross Dr., Suite 101
Sunnyvale, CA 94089
(408) 752-2770,
(800) 606-4526
Fax: (408) 752-2790

Miramar Systems
121 Gray Ave., Suite 200B
Santa Barbara, CA 93103
(805) 966-2432,
(800) 862-2526
Fax: (805) 965-1824

Misco and Powerup
1 Misco Plaza
Holmdel, NJ 07733
(800) 876-4726

Morton Management
12079 Tech Rd.
Silver Spring, MD 20904
(301) 622-5600,
(800) 548-5744
Fax: (301) 622-5438

Motorola, Inc.
Altair Products Operations
3209 N. Wilke Rd.
Arlington Heights, IL 60004
(708) 632-4723

Mountain Network Solutions, Inc.
360 El Pueblo Rd.
Scotts Valley, CA 95067
(408) 438-6650,
(800) 458-0300
Fax: (408) 438-7623

NEC Technologies
1255 Michael Dr.
Wood Dale, IL 60191
(800) 632-4636
Fax: (800) 366-0476

Net-Source, Inc.
1265 El Camino Real, #101
Santa Clara, CA 95050
(408) 246-6679

NETinc
P.O. Box 271105
Houston, TX 77277
(713) 974-1810
Fax: (713) 781-0257

Network Systems Corp.
7600 Boone Ave. N.
Minneapolis, MN 55428
(612) 424-4888

Next Computer
900 Chesapeake Dr.
Redwood City, CA 94063
(415) 366-0900,
(800) 848-6398

Norton-Lambert Corp.
P.O. Box 4085
Santa Monica, CA 93140
(805) 964-6767
Fax: (805) 683-5679

Novell, Inc.
122 East 1700 South
Provo, UT 84606
(801) 429-3098,
(800) 453-1267

Novell, Inc.,
Communications Products Division
890 Ross Dr.
Sunnyvale, CA 94089
(408) 747-4000,
(800) 453-1267

NSM Consumer Electronics
694 Fort Salonga Rd.
Northport, NY 11768
(516) 261-7700
Fax: (516) 261-7751

OAZ Communications, Inc.
44920 Osgood Rd.
Fremont, CA 94539
(510) 226-0170,
(800) 638-3293
Fax: (510) 226-7079

Ocean Isle Software, Inc.
1201 19th Pl.
Vero Beach, FL 32960
(407) 770-4777,
(800) 677-6232
Fax: (407) 770-4779

On Technology Corp.
One Cambridge Center
Cambridge, MA 02142-1604
(617) 374-1400,
(800) 767-6683
Fax: (617) 374-1433

Online Computer Systems, Inc.
20251 Century Blvd.
Germantown, MD 20874
(301) 428-3700,
(800) 922-9204
Fax: (301) 428-2903

Ontrack Computer Systems, Inc.
6321 Bury Dr.
Eden Prairie, MN 55346
(612) 937-1107,
(800) 752-1333

Optical Access International, Inc.
500 W. Cummings Park Rd.
Woburn, MA 01801
(617) 937-3910,
(800) 433-5133
Fax: (617) 937-3950

Optical Data Systems, Inc.
1101 E. Arapahoe Rd.
Richardson, TX 75081
(214) 234-6400
Fax: (214) 234-1467

Optus Software, Inc.
100 Davidson Ave.
Somerset, NJ 08873
(908) 271-9568
Fax: (908) 271-9572

Orange Micro
1400 N. Lakeview Ave.
Anaheim, CA 92807
(714) 779-2772
Fax: (714) 779-9332

Ornetix Network Products
1249 Innsbruck Dr.
Sunnyvale, CA 94089-9808
(408) 744-9095,
(800) 965-6650
Fax: (408) 744-1068

Ornetix Technologies, Inc.
Department SWI
55 Reid St.
South River, NJ 08882
(212) 764-2385,
(800) 347-8439
Fax: (212) 768-2301

Palindrome Corp.
600 East Diehl Rd.
Naperville, IL 60563
(708) 505-3300
Fax: (708) 505-7917

Parsons Technology, Inc.
One Parsons Dr.
P.O. Box 100
Hiawatha, IA 52233-0100
(319) 395-9626,
(800) 223-6925

PC-Kwik Corp.
15100 S.W. Koll Pkwy.
Beaverton, OR 97006
(503) 644-5644,
(800) 274-5945

PC Security
420 Lexington Ave., Suite 1714
New York, NY 10179
(212) 949-1825

Penril DataComm Networks
1300 Quince Orchard Blvd.
Gaithersburg, MD 20878
(301) 921-8600,
(800) 473-6745
Fax: (301) 921-8376

Performance Technology, Inc.
800 Lincoln Center
7800 IH 10 West
San Antonio, TX 78230
(210) 979-2000,
(800) 327-8526
Fax: (210) 979-2002

Philips LMS
4425 Arrows West Dr.
Colorado Springs, CO 80907
(719) 593-7900,
(800) 777-5674
Fax: (719) 593-4597

Photonics Corp.
2940 N. First St.
San Jose, CA 95134
(408) 955-7930

Pinnacle Micro, Inc.
19 Technology Dr.
Irvine, CA 92718
(714) 727-3300,
(800) 553-7070
Fax: (714) 727-1913

Pioneer New Media Technologies
2265 E. 220th St.
Long Beach, CA 90810
(800) 444-6784

Plextor
4255 Burton Dr.
Santa Clara, CA 95054
(408) 980-1838,
(800) 886-3935
Fax: (408) 986-1010

Primax Electronics
254 Hacienda Ave.
Campbell, CA 95008
(408) 379-6482

Procom Technology, Inc.
2181 Dupont Dr.
Irvine, CA 92715
(714) 852-1000,
(800) 800-8600
Fax: (714) 852-1221

Procomp USA, Inc.
6777 Engle Rd., Suite L
Cleveland, OH 44130
(216) 234-6387
Fax: (216) 234-2233

Progressive Computer Services, Inc.
P.O. Box 7638
Metairie, LA 70010-7638
(504) 831-9717,
(800) 628-1131
Fax: (504) 834-2160

Promise Technology
1460 Koll Cir.
San Jose, CA 95112
(408) 452-0948,
(800) 888-0245

Protege Corp.
4165 East La Palma Ave.
Anaheim, CA 92807
(714) 961-7000
Fax: (714) 961-0102

Proteon, Inc.
9 Technology Dr.
Westborough, MA 01581
(508) 898-2800
Fax: (508) 366-8901

Pure Data, Inc.
1740 South I-35
Carrolton, TX 75006
(214) 242-2040
Fax: (214) 242-9487

Puzzle Systems
16360 Monterey Rd., Suite 250
Morgan Hill, CA 95037
(408) 779-9909
Fax: (408) 779-5058

QD Products
1260 Karl Ct.
Wauconda, IL 60084
(708) 487-3333,
(800) 323-6856
Fax: (708) 487-2689

Quadtel Corp.
3190-J Airport Loop Dr.
Costa Mesa, CA 92626
(714) 754-4422,
(800) 748-5718

Qualitas, Inc.
7101 Wisconsin Ave. Suite 1386
Bethesda, MD 20814
(301) 907-6700,
(800) 676-0386
Fax: (301) 907-0905

Quarterdeck Office Systems
150 Pico Blvd.
Santa Monica, CA 90405
(310) 392-9851
Fax: (310) 314-4219

Racal Interlan
155 Swanson Rd.
Boxborough, MA 01719
(508) 263-9929,
(800) 526-8255

Rapid Data Systems
1050 Northgate Dr.
San Rafael, CA 94903
(415) 499-3354,
(800) 743-3054

RG Software Systems, Inc.
6900 E. Camelback Rd., #630
Scottsdale, AZ 85251
(602) 423-8000

RightFAX
4400 E. Broadway
Suite 312
Tucson, AZ 85711
(602) 327-1357
Fax: (602) 321-7469

Rose Electronics
10850 Wilcrest, Suite 900
Houston, TX 77099
(713) 933-7673,
(800) 333-9343
Fax: (713) 933-0044

RTIS
20251 Century Blvd.
Germantown, MD 20874
(301) 428-3700,
(800) 922-9204
Fax: (301) 428-2903

RYBS Electronics, Inc.
2590 Central Ave.
Boulder, CO 80301
(303) 444-6073

Saber Software Corp.
5944 Luther Ln., Suite 1007
Dallas, TX 75209
(214) 361-8086,
(800) 338-8754
Fax: (214) 361-1882

Santa Cruz Operation, Inc.
400 Encinal St.
Santa Cruz, CA 95061
(408) 425-7222

Shiva Corp.
One Cambridge Center
Cambridge, MA 02142
(617) 252-6500,
(800) 458-3550
Fax: (617) 252-4852

SilverPlatter Information, Inc.
100 River Ridge Dr.
Norwood, MA 02062
(617) 769-2599,
(800) 343-0064
Fax: (617) 969-5554

SIRS
P.O. Box 2348
Boca Raton, FL 33427-2348
(407) 994-0079,
(800) 232-7477
Fax: (407) 994-4704

SmartStorage
100 Burtt Rd., Suite 201
Andover, MA 01810
(508) 623-3300

SMC, Standard Microsystems Corp.
80 Arkay Dr.
Hauppauge, NY 11788
(516) 435-6255,
(800) 992-4762
Fax: (516) 273-3123

SMS Data Products
1501 Farm Credit Dr.
McLean, VA 22101-5004
(703) 883-4398
Fax: (703) 356-4831

SoftKlone Corp.
327 Office Plaza Dr., #100
Tallahassee, FL 32301
(904) 878-8564,
(800) 634-8670

Software Concepts Design
594 Third Ave.
New York, NY 10016
(212) 889-6431

The Software Link
3577 Parkway Ln.
Norcross, GA 30092
(404) 448-5465,
(800) 451-5465

Software Publishers Association
  (SPA)
1111 19th St. N.W.
Suite 1200
Washington, DC 20036
(202) 452-1600

Solid Systems, Inc.
5610 Guhn Rd.
Houston, TX 77040
(713) 895-0500,
(800) 324-0500
Fax: (713) 690-2722

Sony Electronics, Inc.
3300 Zanker Rd.
San Jose, CA 95134
(800) 352-7669

South Hills Datacomm
760 Beechnut Dr.
Pittsburgh, PA 15205
(412) 921-9000,
(800) 245-6215
Fax: (412) 921-2254

Specialized Products Co.
3131 Premier Dr.
Irving, TX 75063
(214) 550-1923,
(800) 866-5353
Fax: (800) 234-8286

Spry
316 Occidental Ave. S.
Seattle, WA 98104
(206) 447-0300

Star-Tek
71 Lyman St.
Northboro, MA 01532
(508) 393-9393

SunSelect
Two Federal St.
Billerica, MA 01821
(508) 442-2300

SunSoft, Inc.
6601 Center Dr. West, Suite 700
Los Angeles, CA 90045
(310) 348-8649
Fax: (310) 348-8609

Supro Network Software, Inc.
P.O. Box 18
Warsaw, Ontario, Canada K0L 3A0
(705) 652-1572

Symantec Corp.
10201 Torre Ave.
Cupertino, CA 95014
(408) 253-9600,
(800) 441-7234
Fax: (408) 252-4694

Symmetrical Technologies
600 Herndon Pkwy.
Herndon, VA 22070
(703) 834-1800

SynOptics Communications, Inc.
4401 Great America Pkwy.
Santa Clara, CA 95052
(408) 988-2400
Fax: (408) 988-5525

TAC Systems, Inc.
1031 Putman Dr.
Huntsville, AL 35816-2271
(205) 721-1976
Fax: (205) 721-0242

Tally Systems Corp.
112 Etna Rd.
Lebanon, NH 03766
(603) 643-1300,
(800) 262-3877

TEAC America, Inc.
7733 Telegraph Rd.
Montebello, CA 90640
(800) 888-4923

Techmar Computer Products, Inc.
98-11 Queens Blvd., #2C
Rego Park, NY 11374
(718) 997-6666,
(800) 922-0015

Telebit Corp.
1315 Chesapeake Terrace
Sunnyvale, CA 94089
(800) 835-3248
Fax: (408) 745-3310

Tera Technologies, Inc.
7755 SW Cirrus Dr.
Beaverton, OR 97005
(503) 643-4835

Texel Corp.
4255 Burton Dr.
Santa Clara, CA 95054
(800) 886-3935
Fax: (408) 986-1010

Thomas-Conrad Corp.
1908R Kramer Ln.
Austin, TX 78758
(512) 836-1935,
(800) 332-8683
Fax: (512) 836-2840

Tiara Computer Systems, Inc.
1091 Shoreline Blvd.
Mountain View, CA 94043
(415) 965-1700,
(800) 638-4272
Fax: (415) 965-4807

Todd Enterprises, Inc.
224-49 67th Ave.
Bayside, NY 11364
(718) 343-1040,
(800) 445-8633
Fax: (718) 343-9180

Toshiba America
9740 Irvine Blvd.
Irvine, CA 92718
(714) 583-3000,
(800) 334-3445

Tracs International
731 6th Ave. S.W., #220
Calgary, Alberta T2P 0T9
Canada
(403) 263-4800
Fax: (403) 233-8076

TransFAX Corp.
6133 Bristol Pkwy., #275
Culver City, CA 90230
(310) 641-0439
Fax: (310) 641-4076

Traveling Software, Inc.
18702 N. Creek Pkwy.
Bothell, WA 98011
(206) 483-8088,
(800) 662-2652

Trellis
225 Turnpike Rd.
Southboro, MA 01772
(508) 485-7200,
(800) 793-3390
Fax: (508) 485-3044

Triton Technologies
200 Middlesex Turnpike
Iselin, NJ 08830
(908) 855-9440,
(800) 322-9440
Fax: (908) 855-9608

UMI (University Microfilms, Inc.)
300 North Zeeb Rd.
Ann Arbor, MI 48106-1346
(313) 761-4700,
(800) 521-0600
Fax: (313) 662-4554

Ungermann-Bass, Inc.
3900 Freedom Cir.
P.O. Box 58030
Santa Clara, CA 95052
(408) 496-0111
Fax: (408) 970-7300

Univel
2180 Fortune Dr.
San Jose, CA 95131
(800) 486-4835

US Marketing, Inc.
1608 17th Ave. South
Nashville, TN 37212
(615) 269-9071

US Robotics, Inc.
8100 N. McCormick Blvd.
Skokie, IL 60076-2999
(708) 982-5010,
(800) 342-5877
Fax: (708) 982-5235

US Robotics Software
5615 Corporate Blvd.
Baton Rouge, LA 70808
(504) 923-0888,
(800) 242-5278

US Sage, Inc.
1215 N. Hwy. 427, #135
Longwood, FL 32750
(407) 331-4400,
(800) 999-6770

V Communications, Inc.
4320 Stevens Creek Blvd., #275
San Jose, CA 95129
(408) 296-4224

Vestra-Subco, Inc.
1401 N. 14th St.
Temple, TX 76501
(817) 771-2124,
(800) 441-6189

Virtual Microsystems
1825 Grant St., Suite 700
San Mateo, CA 94402
(415) 573-9596,
(800) 722-8299
Fax: (415) 572-8406

Walnut Creek CD-ROM
4041 Pike Ln., Suite D-241
Concord, CA 94520
(510) 674-0783,
(800) 786-9907
Fax: (510) 674-0821

Wavetek
9145 Balboa Ave.
San Diego, CA 92123
(619) 279-2200

Wellfleet Communications, Inc.
8 Federal St.
Billerica, MA 01821
(508) 670-8888

Winchester Systems, Inc.
400 W. Cummings Park
Woburn, MA 01801
(617) 933-8500

WordPerfect Corp.
1555 N. Technology Way
Orem, UT 84057-2399
(801) 225-5000,
(800) 451-5151
Fax: (801) 222-5077

WorldWide Software, Inc.
20 Exchange Place, 27th Fl.
New York, NY 10005
(212) 422-4100,
(800) 999-6031

Xtree Co.
4330 Santa Fe Rd.
San Luis Obispo, CA 93401
(805) 541-0604,
(800) 477-1587

Yamaha Corporation of America
Systems Technology Division
981 Ridder Park Dr.
San Jose, CA 95131
(408) 437-3133
Fax: (408) 437-8791

Young Minds, Inc.
1910 Orange Tree Ln., Suite 300
P.O. Box 6910
Redlands, CA 92375-0910
(800) 964-4964

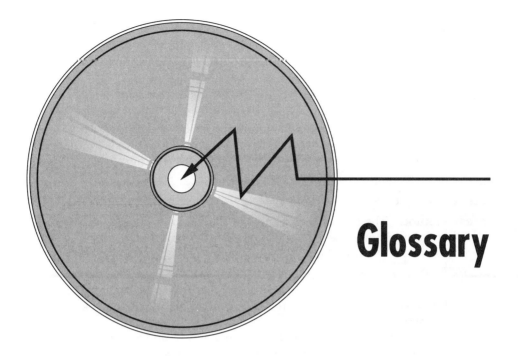

Glossary

1Base-5   An IEEE specification matching the older AT&T StarLAN product. It designates a 1-Mbit/sec signaling rate, a baseband signaling technique, and a maximum cable-segment distance of 1 x 100 meters (100 meters).

10Base-2   An uncommon reference to the Ethernet standard known as cheapernet, thin Ethernet, or thinnet variations. It is an IEEE specification for running Ethernet over thin coaxial cable. It designates a 10-Mbits/sec signaling rate, a baseband signaling technique, and a maximum cable-segment length of 185 meters (607 feet), or nearly 2 x 100 meters (200 meters), where stations are daisy-chained.

10Base-5   An IEEE specification for running Ethernet over thick coaxial cable. The cable system is specified by DEC (Digital Equipment Corporation) and Xerox. It designates a 10-Mbits/sec signaling rate, a baseband signaling technique, and a maximum cable-segment length of nearly 5 x 100 (500 meters, or 1,640 feet). It is an uncommon reference to the Ethernet standard known as Thicknet or thick Ethernet.

10Base-F   Fiber Ethernet, used between workstations and a concentrator. It is an IEEE specification that designates a 10-Mbits/sec signaling rate, and an estimated distance of 2.2 kilometers.

10Base-T   Implementation of the IEEE 802.3 Ethernet standard on unshielded twisted-pair wiring. It designates a 10-Mbits/sec signaling rate using baseband signaling technique. It uses a star topology, with stations connected to a multiport hub. The maximum contiguous length of a 10Base-T cable segment is usually limited to 100 meters (328 feet) because of the extreme signal interference on the unshielded cabling, although 200 meters is nominally supported for distances between a hub and a workstation. There are two versions. One supports bidirectional signaling with dual-pair (four-wire) telephone wiring, thus allowing hardware to see collisions. The other version uses single-pair to support daisy-chaining of multiple workstations.

3270 The generic name for the family of interoperable IBM system components—terminals, printers, and terminal cluster controllers—that can be used to communicate with a mainframe by means of the Systems Network Architecture (SNA) or other protocols. All of these components have four-digit names, some of which begin with the digits 327.

access key *See* software key

access manager *See* license manager

access method The set of rules by which the network controls the flow of information among the nodes. Generally, the way that network devices access the network medium. CSMA/CD and token passing are two access methods.

access time The time (in milliseconds) that the drive takes to find the right track in response to a request (the seek time), plus the time it takes to get to the right place on the track (the latency). IBM PC-XTs used 80- to 110-ms drives, while ATs used 28- to 40-ms drives, and 80386- and 80486-based systems use 10- to 20-ms drives. Floppy disk access times are almost 200 milliseconds. CD-ROM drive access times, however, are in the 250- to 1000-ms range.

active hubs Active hubs amplify transmission signals to extend the cable length. *See also* passive hubs

Adaptive Differential Pulse Code Modulation (ADPCM) An audio-compression method that stores the amplitude difference between successive digital samples instead of the raw sample data. Because ADPCM permits some data loss, it is often called "lossy compression." A component of CD-ROM XA, recommended in the MPC Level 2 specifications. It usually offers a 4:1 compression ratio.

address Data structure used to identify a unique entity, such as a particular process or network location.

ADPCM *See* Adaptive Differential Pulse Code Modulation

American National Standards Institute *See* ANSI

ANSI (American National Standards Institute) An organization that develops and publishes standards for codes, alphabets, and signaling schemes. It ensures that standards written by recognized industry groups such as the IEEE societies are developed through a process that is fair to all involved.

AppleShare File Server Apple's own file server program. AppleShare runs on a Mac (usually a IIci or better) and lets other Macs use files and printers attached to the server.

AppleShare Workstation The software that a Mac uses to connect to shared network resources, such as printers and file servers. AppleShare Workstation comes as part of the Macintosh system software.

AppleTalk A series of related communications protocols introduced and maintained by Apple Computer. At one time, AppleTalk also referred to the cabling system now known as LocalTalk. AppleTalk runs over LocalTalk as well as Ethernet or token ring. Among the services included in AppleTalk are Filing Protocol (AFP) and AppleTalk Print Services (ATPS).

AppleTalk Filing Protocol (AFP)   The network data-transport protocol used by Apple Computer to let Macintosh computers communicate over a network.

application layer   The seventh layer of the ISO/OSI model. It performs network services like file transfer, terminal emulation, and electronic mail.

application program interface (API)   Any standardized set of software interrupts, calls, and data formats used to initiate network services.

archival storage   The long-term storage of infrequently used data.

ARCNET   Attached Resource Computing Network, a network architecture marketed by Datapoint Corporation and other vendors. It uses a token-passing bus architecture, usually on coaxial cable. It is generally implemented on the chips and connectors on the network interface card. ARCNET provides intercommunication among networked devices at a rate of 2.5 Mbits/sec.

ARPANET   Advanced Research Projects Agency Network. A network originally sponsored by the Defense Advanced Research Projects Agency (DARPA) to link universities and government research centers. The TCP/IP protocols were pioneered on ARPANET.

Asynchronous Transfer Mode (ATM)   Also known as cell relay, ATM is a method used by Broadband Integrated Service Digital Network (BISDN) for transmitting voice, video, and data over high-speed LANs. Speeds of up to 2.2 gigabits per second are possible. ATM has found wide acceptance in the LAN and wide area network (WAN).

asynchronous transmission   A method of data transmission that uses start bits and stop bits to coordinate the flow of data so that the time intervals between individual characters do not need to be equal. Parity may also be used to check the accuracy of the data received.

ATM   *See* Asynchronous Transfer Mode

Attachment Unit Interface   *See* AUI

attenuation   Loss of communication signal energy, or the decrease in power of a signal transmitted over a wire, measured in decibels.

audio CD   A compact disc designed to play only audio.

AUI (Attachment Unit Interface)   A 15-pin socket used by some Ethernet devices. AUI connections adapt between two different cabling types and work with a wide range of wiring schemes.

auto-answer   The ability of a modem to answer incoming phone calls automatically.

auto-dial   The ability of a modem to dial a telephone number automatically.

back end   A node or software program that provides services to a front end. *See also* client, server

backbone   A high-speed link joining together several networks. It is the portion of the network that handles the bulk of traffic.

backbone network   A network to which several, usually smaller networks are attached. The smaller networks typically serve departmental workgroups and may be located on separate floors of a building with a vertical backbone network spanning the floors.

balun (BALanced UNbalanced)   An impedance-matching device that connects a balanced line and an unbalanced line. It converts impedance of one interface to the impedance of a second interface. An example would be a twisted-pair line (balanced) to a coaxial cable (unbalanced).

bandwidth   The range (band) of signal frequencies that are transmitted on a channel. The difference between the highest and lowest frequencies is measured in cycles per second hertz (Hz). Analog circuits typically have a bandwidth limited to that of the human voice (about 300 Hz to 3,000 Hz). A telephone can transmit sound frequencies between 400 Hz and 4,000 Hz; it therefore has a bandwidth of 3,600 Hz. Networks with a bandwidth of 10–100 Mbits/sec are quite common. The higher the transmission rate, the greater the bandwidth requirement. Fiber-optic and coaxial cables have excellent bandwidths.

base address   The first address in memory, often used to describe the beginning of a network interface card's I/O space.

baseband network   A technique for transmitting signals in which the entire bandwidth of the transmission medium is used by a single digital signal, so that computers in a baseband network can transmit only when the channel is not busy. The information is transmitted as pulses rather than as variations in a carrier signal. A baseband network can operate over relatively short distances (up to 3.2 kilometers, or 2 miles, if network traffic is light) at speeds of from 50 Kbits/sec to 16 Mbits/sec. Ethernet, AppleTalk, and most PC LANs use baseband techniques.

baud   A measure of the number of signal changes that can be accommodated by a transmission medium. A voice-grade telephone line can support a maximum baud rate of 2400. Baud is frequently misconstrued to represent the bit rate that can be transmitted by a given modem. The proper measure, however, is bits-per-second (bits/sec). For data rates exceeding 2400 bits/sec, multiple bits are encoded for each signal change by combining modulation techniques; a 9600-bits/sec modem encodes 4 bits for each signal change by utilizing a combination of amplitude modulation and phase modulation. In this case, each baud will equal 4 bits.

BIOS (basic input/output system)   Pronounced "bye-os." A set of instructions that lets the computer's hardware and operating system communicate with applications and peripheral devices, such as hard disks and printers. These instructions are stored in the ROM (read-only memory) as a permanent part of the computer. If you are experiencing difficulties after adding new hardware components to a computer, your computer's BIOS may be out-of-date.

bit   Contraction of BInary digiT. A bit is the basic unit of information in the binary numbering system, representing either 0 (for off) or 1 (for on). Bits can be grouped to form larger storage units; the most common grouping is the 7- or 8-bit byte.

bit mapped   A screen display in which the image on the screen is generated and refreshed using a binary matrix (bit map) at a specific location in memory.

BITNET (Because It's Time Network)   A low-cost, low-speed academic network consisting primarily of IBM mainframes and 9600-bits/sec leased lines. Remote job entry (RJE) is the primary means of performing work on this network, which has merged with CSNET (Computer+Science Network) to form CREN (Corporation for Research and Educational Networking).

BNC   A connector for coaxial cable used with thin Ethernet (Thinnet) and ARCNET (RG-62) cabling.

BNC connector   Standard connector used to connect IEEE 802.3 10Base-2 coaxial cable to a transceiver.

Books   CD-ROM standards are described in several industry-accepted manuals identified by color, such as Yellow Book, Red Book, Green Book, and Orange Book.

boot PROM (Programmable Read-Only Memory)   A memory chip allowing a workstation to communicate with the file server and to read a DOS boot program from the server. A boot PROM is usually installed on the network interface card (NIC) to allow a workstation to boot from the network file server. A boot PROM is needed if the workstation does not have a disk drive or hard disk to boot from.

bridge   A device that connects and passes data packets between two network segments. Bridges enable nodes on one network to communicate with nodes on another network. Bridges operate at Level 2 of the ISO's OSI Reference Model (the data-link layer) and are upper-layer protocol-insensitive.

broadband network   A technique for transmitting a large amount of information, including voice, data, and video, over long distances using the same cable. Broadband is based on the same technology used by cable television. The information is transmitted as waves rather than as signals. The transmission capacity is divided into several distinct channels that can be used concurrently by different networks. The individual channels are protected from each other by channels of unused frequencies. A broadband network can operate at speeds of up to 20 Mbits/sec. Also called *wideband transmission.*

broadband signaling   A data-transmission technique that permits simultaneous transmission of multiple signals over a single cable at different frequencies. Broadband networks can carry video, radio, and other signals, in addition to data.

brouter (bridge/router)   A device that combines the functions of a bridge and a router. Brouters can route one or more protocols, such as TCP/IP, and bridge all other traffic. Some devices called brouters are in fact multiport bridges.

buffer   An area of RAM (usually 512 bytes plus another 16 for overhead) in which DOS stores data temporarily. On a CD-ROM drive, a buffer is 64K to 256K of memory that acts as a temporary storage area for data read off a disc before it is sent to the computer.

buffered repeater   A device that amplifies and regenerates signals so that they can travel farther along a cable. This type of repeater also controls the flow of messages to prevent collisions.

buffering   A network interface card's ability to receive/process additional network packets. Some NICs have built-in buffering capability.

bundle   Two or more products and/or services that are licensed and/or priced as a unit rather than being licensed and/or priced separately.

bus   An electronic pathway along which signals are sent from one part of a computer to another. A computer contains several buses, each used for a different purpose. The address bus allocates memory addresses; the data bus carries data between the processor and memory, while the control bus carries signals from the control unit.

bus network   In networking, a topology that allows all network nodes to receive the same message through the network cable at the same time. *See also* ring network, star network, token ring network

byte   Contraction of BinarY digiT Eight. A group of 7 or 8 bits, also known as an octet. A byte usually holds a single character, such as a number, letter, or symbol. Bytes are usually grouped into kilobytes (1,024 bytes), megabytes (1,048,576 bytes), and gigabytes (1,073,741,824 bytes) for convenience when describing hard disk capacity, computer memory size, or the size of a computer file.

cache   Pronounced "cash." A special area of memory managed by a cache controller that improves performance by storing the contents of frequently accessed memory locations and their addresses. When the processor references a memory address, the cache checks to see if it holds that address. If it does, the information is passed directly to the processor.

caddy   The removable case used by some CD-ROM drives to hold a disc while it is being read.

callback modem   A special modem that does not answer an incoming call, but instead requires the caller to enter a code and hang up so that the modem can return the call.

campus network   A network that connects local area networks from multiple departments inside a single building or a set of buildings. Campus networks are LANs which do not include wide area network (WAN) services, even though they may extend for several miles.

capacitance   The measure of a component's ability to store an electrical charge.

carrier   An analog signal of fixed amplitude and frequency that is combined with a data-carrying signal to produce an output signal suitable for transmitting data.

Carrier Sense Multiple Access with Collision Detection   *See* CSMA/CD

carrier signal   A tone or radio signal upon which data ride.

CAU   *See* controlled access unit

CAV   *See* constant angular velocity

CBIS   A NetBIOS-compatible CD-ROM network product produced by CBIS, Inc.

CCITT Comité Consultatif Internationale de Téléphonie et de Télégraphique (Consultative Committee on International Telephone and Telegraph) An organization, based in Geneva, that develops worldwide data communications standards. Three main sets of standards have been established: CCITT Groups 1–4 standards apply to facsimile transmissions, the CCITT V Series of standards apply to modems and error detection and correction methods, and the CCITT X Series of standards apply to local area networks (LANs). Recommendations are published every four years. Each update is identified by the color of its cover; the 1988 edition was known as the Blue Book, and the 1992 update has a white cover.

CCITT Groups 1–4 *See* CCITT

CCITT V Series *See* CCITT

CCITT X Series *See* CCITT

CDDI Copper Distributed Data Interface. An extension of the FDDI to provide a cheaper way to link desktops to FDDI-equipped wiring centers using copper STP and UTP wiring. *See also* Fiber Distributed Data Interface

CD-I (Compact Disc-Interactive) Defines how CD-I data are recorded on CD-ROM XA discs. Also known as the Green Book.

CD-NET A CD-ROM networking product produced by Meridian Data that is based on the Novell NetWare.

CD-ROM Acronym for compact disc read-only memory. A high-capacity optical storage device that uses compact disc technology to store large amounts of information. A single 4.72-inch disc can hold up to 600 megabytes on one side. Also known as the Yellow Book.

CD-ROM Extended Architecture (CD-ROM XA) Originally backed by Microsoft, the XA standard combines elements from several books, most notably the Green Book. ADPCM-compressed digital audio can quadruple—at minimum—the audio capacity of an XA disc. XA also permits the interleaving of audio, video, and arbitrary data like text, which a compatible player will play in proper synchronicity. Special software drivers, as well as hardware components, are generally required.

CD-ROM server A computer on the network that makes CD-ROM optical discs available to other workstations on the network. In some schemes, notably peer-to-peer networking arrangements, the optical server may be the same machine as the file server.

CD-ROM XA *See* CD-ROM Extended Architecture

central processing unit *See* CPU

channel An individual path between sender and receiver that carries one stream of information. A two-way path is a circuit.

cheapernet Industry term used to refer to the IEEE 802.3 10Base-2 standard or the cable specified in that standard. *See also* thin Ethernet

client This term can be applied to both LAN nodes or software programs that request services from another network node, usually a server. Client nodes are often termed "workstations" to distinguish them from servers. *See also* back end, server

client/server architecture A computing architecture that distributes processing between clients and servers on the network. Clients request information from the servers. The servers store data and programs, and provide network-wide services to clients.

clock-doubling A mechanism used by some Intel processors that allows the chip to process data and instructions internally at twice the speed used by the rest of the system. For example, the Intel 80486DX2 operates at 50 MHz internally, but operates at 25 MHz when communicating with other system components.

clock rate *See* clock speed

clock speed The internal speed of a computer or processor, normally expressed in megahertz (MHz). Also known as clock rate. The following table provides information about clock speed for different types of Intel processors.

	8088	80286	80386DX	80486DX	Pentium
Date of Introduction	June 1989	Feb. 1982	Oct. 1985	April 1989	March 1993
Number of Transistors	28,000	134,000	275,000	1.25 million	3.1 million
Initial Speed in Millions of Instructions per Second	0.37	1.2	6	20	100
Clock Speed	4.77 MHz	6 MHz	16-66 MHz	16-100 MHz	60+ MHz

CLV *See* constant linear velocity

coaxial cable A communications cable made of a center conductor surrounded by plastic insulation and then a second shaft of fine-wire screening.

collision A condition that occurs when two or more stations try to transmit data at the same time on a network.

communications server A server equipped with one or more modems, which can be shared by users for outgoing calls.

compact disc-recordable (CD-R) CD-R machines that press discs in one or more sessions used to be the sole domain of plants that manufacture software and music discs. What cost $75,000 a few years ago now sells for under $4,000.

computing environment *See* platform

concentrator Any communications device that allows a shared transmission medium to accommodate more data sources than there are channels currently available within the transmission medium, such as a wiring hub. This piece of hardware connects a cable end to a hardware device or another cable. A hub is a central connecting point for cables. A concentrator is a type of hub. However, a hub is referred to as a product that only supports Ethernet, token ring , or FDDI, while a concentrator may support all or combinations of these. *See also* hub

concurrent use license A type of software license that allows access to a special number of simultaneous users.

connectivity   The ability of any given computer or application to cooperate with other network components, purchased from other vendors, in a network environment where resources are shared.

constant angular velocity (CAV)   An unchanging speed of rotation. Hard disks use a CAV encoding scheme, where the disk rotates at a constant rate. This means that sectors on the disk are at the maximum density along the inside track of the disk. As the read/write heads move outward, the sectors must spread out to cover the increased track circumference, and therefore the data-transfer rate falls off. *See also* constant linear velocity

constant linear velocity (CLV)   A changing speed of rotation. CD-ROM disk drives use a CLV encoding scheme to make sure that the data density remains constant. Information on a compact disc is stored in a single, spiral track, divided into many equal-length segments. To read the data, the CD-ROM disk drive must increase the rotational speed as the read head gets closer to the center of the disc, and decrease as the head moves back out. Typical CD-ROM data-access times are in the order of 0.3 to 1.5 seconds—much slower than those of a hard disk. *See also* constant angular velocity

consumptive use license   A type of software license where the use of a software product consumes license units in a nonreusable manner.

controlled access unit (CAU)   An intelligent MAU (Multistation Access Unit), or multiport wiring hub for a token ring network, that allows ports to be switched on and off.

conventional memory   The amount of memory accessible by DOS in PCs using an Intel processor operating in real mode, normally the first 640K. The designers of the original IBM PC made 640K available to the operating system and applications, and reserved the remaining space for internal system use, the BIOS, and video buffers. 640K may not seem like much memory space now, but it was 10 times the amount of memory available in other leading personal computers available at the time. Since then, applications have increased in size to the point where 640K is inadequate. *See also* expanded memory, extended memory, high memory area, memory management

copy   The original or any duplications in any form made from it. It also means to make a duplicate copy of a software program.

copyright   The protection given under law to the expression of an idea. Copyright protection is extended to software.

CPU (Central Processing Unit)   That part of a computer system that contains the circuitry and storage that interprets and executes instructions, handles interrupts, and performs timing and other machine-related functions.

CPU designation   The serial number or the exact identification of a CPU.

CPU license   A type of software license that allows the operation of a software product on a specific designated CPU.

CPU redesignation   A change in the designation of a CPU on which a product is authorized to operate.

CREN   The Corporation for Research and Educational Networking. The result of a merger of BITNET and CSNET (Computer+Science Network).

CSMA/CD (Carrier Sense Multiple Access with Collision Detection) A baseband protocol with a built-in collision-detection technique. In this scheme, the station listens to the activities on the cable; if the cable is not in use, the station is permitted to transmit its messages. This protocol is combined with collision detection. When two stations transmit at the same time, they both stop and signal that a collision has occurred. Each then tries again after waiting a predetermined time period, usually several microseconds. *See also* token passing, token ring network

CSNET Computer+Science Network. A large internetwork consisting primarily of universities, research institutions, and commercial concerns. CSNET has merged with BITNET to form CREN.

daisy chain A form of bus topology in which LAN nodes are cabled to one another. Each node should have two ports: one for the input and one for the output.

datagram A unit of information which contains a source and destination address, along with data. It is a logical grouping of information sent as a network-layer unit over a transmission medium without prior establishment of a virtual circuit. The terms "frame," "message," "packet," and "segment" are also used to describe logical information groupings at various layers of the OSI Reference Model and in various technology circles. IP datagrams are the primary information units in the Internet.

data-link layer The second of the seven layers of the ISO/OSI model. This layer validates the integrity of the flow of data from one node to another. Its main services are addressing, error detection, and flow control.

DECnet Also DNA (DECnet Network Architecture). A group of communications products (including a protocol suite) developed and supported by Digital Equipment Corporation (DEC) compatible with Ethernet and a wide range of systems. The most recent iteration is DECnet Phase V, which is largely based on the OSI protocols.

dedicated line A communications circuit used for one specific purpose, and not shared among other users. In a telephone leased line, the line often does not pass through interexchange switching equipment and the line is leased on a flat monthly fee regardless of how much data are transmitted. Also called a private line or a leased line.

dedicated server A computer that operates exclusively as a server. A dedicated file server is a computer that provides resources to other nodes on the network. It performs specialized network tasks such as storing files. This server cannot be used by users as a workstation. In order to perform, it has to be left uninterrupted. *See also* server

demodulation In communications, the process of extracting the data from a modulated carrier signal; the reverse of modulation. *See also* modem

demonstration license A type of software license that allows the software product to be used for marketing or promotion purposes only.

device driver A small program that allows a computer to communicate with and control a device. When you connect CD-ROM drives or install a network interface card, you need device drivers to establish a connection with these peripherals.

dial-up line   A communications circuit that can be accessed from the public telephone network.

direct memory access (DMA)   A technique for moving data directly between main memory and a peripheral.

disk server   A network node that provides shared access to a magnetic disk drive or an optical disc drive. Commonly known as a "file server."

diskless workstation   A networked computer that lacks local disk-storage capability. A diskless workstation boots and loads all its programs from the network file server.

distributed processing   A type of computing in which processing, storage, control, and/or input/output functions are allocated among interconnected processors. There are several types of distributed processing:

> **client/server computing**   A type of distributed processing in which a client requests service or information from a server that performs the service and/or returns the requested information to the client.

> **cooperative processing (or computing)**   A type of distributed processing in which processing, storage, control, or input/output functions are allocated among interconnected processors, each cooperating synchronously to perform the total task.

> **peer-to-peer computing**   A type of distributed processing with no distinction between nodes as to roles or services performed. Program control is at each node, and management of shared resources is distributed to all nodes equally.

distributed server   A LAN configuration in which there are many file servers spread throughout the network, as opposed to a central file server.

domain   A jurisdiction of servers and clients controlled and managed by a single server.

double-speed drive   A CD-ROM drive that reads data at 300 Kbits/sec, compared to a single-speed drive that reads data at 150 Kbits/sec.

download   The process of capturing data being received from another computer or from a CD-ROM disc in memory or on disc. In communications, to transfer a file or files over a network or using a modem.

downtime   The amount of time that a computer system is not working due to a hardware or software failure.

DR-DOS   A DOS-compatible operating system originally developed by Digital Research (DR), now owned by Novell, that runs on Intel processors.

DRA (Data Research Associates)   A major integrated library system vendor that runs software developed for DEC hardware platforms.

DRANet   A proprietary computer network run by DRA that links library systems into a central DRA computer system for database access. DRANet can access CD-ROM networks.

drop cable   A short cable used in thick Ethernet to connect a network device to an MAU (Multistation Access Unit). Maximum cable length is 50 meters (165 feet). *See also* MAU

dumb terminal   A combination of keyboard and screen that has no local computing power and is used to input information to a large, remote computer, often a mainframe or a minicomputer. The remote computer provides all the processing power for the system. *See also* intelligent terminal

duplix circuit   A telecommunications circuit that allows the transmission of data in both directions at the same time.

e-mail   *See* electronic mail

EBCDIC (Extended Binary Coded Decimal Interchange Code)   The data alphabet used in all IBM computers except the PC; it determines the composition of the 8-bit string of 0's and 1's representing each character (alphabet, numeric, or special symbols).

EISA (Extended Industry Standard Architecture)   A 32-bit PC bus system that serves as an alternative to IBM's Micro Channel Architecture (MCA). The 32 bits is an adaptation of the 8- and 16-bit data buses originally developed by IBM and now standard in almost all PCs that use Intel 8086, 80286, 80386, and 80486 microprocessors. The EISA architecture is a joint development by an industry consortium headed by Compaq and is compatible with the IBM AT bus; MCA is not.

electronic mail   The use of networks to transmit messages, texts, and reports. Also called *e-mail.*

emulator   A device built to work exactly like another device—hardware, software, or a combination of both. For example, a terminal emulation program lets a PC pretend to be a terminal attached to a mainframe computer.

end user   A person (or organization) who accesses a software product for his or her own use.

Enhanced Expanded Memory Specification (EEMS)   A revised version of the original Lotus-Intel-Microsoft Expanded Memory Specification (LIM/EMS) that lets DOS applications use more than 640K of memory space. *See also* memory management

enterprise   A corporate organization including the parent, its subsidiaries, and/or affiliates.

enterprise license   A type of software license that allows use of a software product throughout all or part of an enterprise.

Enterprise Network Services (ENS)   A software product based on Banyan Systems' StreetTalk Directory Service for VINES which brings NetWare Directory Services (NDS) features to NetWare 2.x and 3.x networks. ENS includes StreetTalk Directory Assistance, the Banyan Security Service, Banyan Network Management, and support for IPX/SPX.

enterprise-wide network   A network that connects every computer in every location of a business group, organization, or corporation.

EPROM (erasable programmable read-only memory)   An integrated reusable chip that can be programmed to record and maintains its contents until erased, usually under ultraviolet light.

Ethernet A popular local area network design, the product of Xerox Corporation, characterized by 10-Mbits/sec baseband transmission over a shielded coaxial cable and employing CSMA/CD protocol on a bus topology as the access-control mechanism; standardized by the IEEE as specification IEEE 802.3. Referring to the Ethernet design or as compatible with Ethernet.

EtherTalk A network communications protocol used by Apple Computer that lets Macintosh computers communicate over an Ethernet network.

exa- (E) A prefix meaning one quintillion or 10^{18}. In computing, the prefix means 1,152,921,504,606,846,976, or the power of 2 closest to one quintillion (2^{60}).

exabyte (EB) 1 quadrillion kilobytes, or 1,152,921,504,606,846,976 bytes.

expandability The ability of a system to accommodate expansion. In hardware, this may include the addition of more memory, more or larger disk drives, and new adapters. In software, expandability may include the ability of a network to add users, nodes, or connections to other networks.

expanded memory A DOS mechanism by which applications can access more than the 640K of memory normally available to them. The architecture of the early Intel processors restricted the original IBM PC to accessing 1 Mb of memory, 640K of which was available for applications; the remaining 384K was reserved for system use, the BIOS, and the video system. At that time, 640K was more than 10 times the amount of memory available in other personal computers. However, as both applications and DOS grew, they began to run out of room. The Expanded Memory Specification LIM 4.0 is the standard method of accessing expanded memory. This specification lets programs running on any of the Intel 8086 family of processors access as much as 32 Mb of expanded memory. The expanded memory manager (EMM) creates a block of addresses into which data (held in memory above the 1-Mb limit) is swapped in and out as needed by the program. In other words, a 64K segment of addressable memory creates a small window through which segments of expanded memory can be seen, but only one segment at a time. *See also* conventional memory, memory management

expanded memory manager (EMM) A device driver that supports the software portion of the Expanded Memory Specification (EMS) in an IBM-compatible computer. *See also* memory management

Expanded Memory Specification (EMS) The original version of the Lotus-Intel-Microsoft Expanded Memory Specification (LIM/EMS) that lets DOS applications use more than 640K of memory space. *See also* Enhanced Expanded Memory Specification, expanded memory, memory management

extended memory Memory beyond 1 megabyte (Mb) on computers using the Intel 80386 and later processors not configured for expanded memory. PCs based on the early Intel processors could access only 1 Mb of memory, of which 640K was available for applications, and the remaining 384K was reserved for DOS, BIOS, and video settings. Later processors could access more memory, but it was the 80386 with its ability to address 4 gigabytes of memory that really made extended memory usable. Also, the Microsoft

Windows memory manager HIMEM.SYS lets Windows use all of the extended memory installed in a computer. Extended memory is particularly valuable when using OS/2, which can take full advantage of its benefits. *See also* conventional memory, Expanded Memory Specification, memory management

fault tolerance   A design method that ensures continued system operation in the event of individual failures by providing redundant elements.

FDDI   *See* Fiber Distributed Data Interface

Fiber Distributed Data Interface (FDDI)   An ANSI-defined standard X3T9.5 for transmission at 100-Mbits/sec token-passing network using dual counterrotating rings over fiber-optic cable. FDDI uses wiring hubs, and the hubs are prime candidates to serve as network monitoring and control devices. Another specification has emerged using copper STP and UTP wiring known as CDDI (Copper Distributed Data Interface) or FDDI over Copper.

fiber-optic cable   A pair of thin strands of glass or plastic surrounded by an insulating fiber. Fiber-optic cable is lighter and smaller than traditional copper cable, is immune to electrical interference, offers better security, and has better signal transmitting. Fiber cables are an excellent choice for high-speed building backbones.

file server   *See* dedicated server, disk server, server

File Transfer Protocol   *See* FTP

firmware   A set of memory chips that maintain their contents without electrical power. The set includes ROM (Read-Only Memory), PROM (Programmable Read-Only Memory), EPROM (Erasable Programmable Read-Only Memory), and EEPROM (Electrically Erasable Programmable Read-Only Memory).

flash memory   A special form of read-only memory (ROM) chip that can be erased at signal levels commonly found inside a computer. Once it is programmed, the chip does not lose its contents even if it is pluged into another computer.

floating license   A type of software license where the software product is not tied to a specific CPU or site.

fractional T1   One portion of a T1 circuit. A T1 circuit has a capacity of 1.544 Mbits/sec, the equivalent of 24 64-Kbits/sec channels. Customers can lease as many of these 64-Kbits/sec channels as they need; they are not required to lease the entire 1.544-Mbits/sec circuit.

frame   A logical grouping of information sent as a link-layer unit over a transmission medium. The terms "packet," "datagram," "segment," and "message" are also used to describe logical information groupings at various layers of the OSI Reference Model and in various technology circles.

frame relay   A data communication method for wide area networks slowly replacing X.25. Like X.25, frame relay transmits variable-length packets of data at speeds of up to 2 Mbits/sec.

Frankfurt Group   An industry consortium that has devised a CD-ROM file format standard to replace ISO 9660. It is likely to be adopted as ISO 13490.

frequency-division multiplexing The technique of transmitting multiple signals on the same medium.

front-end application An application running on a networked workstation that works in conjunction with a back-end application running on the server. Examples are electronic mail and database programs.

FTP (File Transfer Protocol) The TCP/IP protocol used to log in to a network, list files and directories, and transfer files. FTP supports a range of file types and formats, including ASCII, EBCDIC, and binary files.

full-text database A database that contains the complete text of the original sources. The sources can be books, journals, directories, newspaper articles, court decisions, etc.

gateway A combination of hardware and software that acts as a connection between two dissimilar networks. Typically, the gateway is a box or card with cables coming in from both networks. Logically, the gateway takes messages, strips each transmission down to a level in which the systems are the same, and then builds up the message in the form needed by the system receiving them. Often used to allow access to mainframe computers and minicomputers. It also allows access to wide area networks, such as X.25.

Gb *See* gigabyte

Gbits/sec Gigabits per second.

Gbytes/sec Gigabytes per second.

GHz *See* gigahertz

giga- A prefix meaning one billion or 10^9. *See also* gigabyte

gigabyte (Gb) One thousand megabytes (1,000,000,000 bytes), 2^{30}, or 1,073,741,824 bytes.

gigahertz (GHz) One billion cycles per second.

global network An international network that spans all departments, offices, and subsidiaries of the corporation.

graphical user interface (GUI) Pronounced "gooey." A graphics-based user interface that allows users to select files, programs, or commands by pointing to pictorial representations on the screen rather than by typing long, complex commands from a command prompt.

Green Book The Green Book defines CD-Interactive (CD-I), an entire hardware and software standard developed by Philips for use in its consumer line of CD-I players. CD-I discs may contain a mix of audio, video, and text that can be "streamed" in synchronicity. Note that both multisession Photo CD and CD-ROM XA use parts of the Green Book standard.

half-duplex (HDX) In asynchronous transmissions, the ability to transmit on the same channel in both directions, but only in one direction at a time.

hertz (Hz) The frequency of electrical vibrations (cycles) per second. One Hz equals one cycle per second.

heterogeneous network A network that consists of workstations, servers, network interface cards, operating systems, and applications from many different vendors, all working together as a single unit. The network may also use different media and different protocols over different network links. *See also* homogeneous network

HFS (hierarchical file system)   The file system used by the Apple Macintosh.

high memory area (HMA)   In an IBM-compatible computer, the first 64K of extended memory above the 1-megabyte (Mb) limit of 8086 and 8088 addresses. Programs that conform to the Expanded Memory Specification (EMS) can use this memory as an extension of conventional memory. However, only one program, such as DOS, Microsoft Windows, or an application, can use or control HMA at a time. If DOS is loaded into the HMA, approximately 50K more conventional memory becomes available for use by applications. *See also* expanded memory, extended memory, memory management

High Sierra Specification   The unofficial CD-ROM file format standard that was eventually modified and accepted as the ISO 9660 standard. It was called High Sierra because it was defined at a meeting held in the High Sierra Hotel near Lake Tahoe, Nevada, in November 1985.

hit rate   The rate at which the computer finds information it requires in cache memory.

homogeneous network   A network that consists of one type of workstation, server, network interface card, and operating system, with a limited number of applications, all purchased from a single vendor. All nodes use the same protocol and the same control procedures. *See also* heterogeneous network

host   The central or controlling computer in a networked or distributed processing environment, providing services that other computers or terminals can access via the network.

hub   A hub is a central connecting point for cables. It serves as the meeting point in a star wiring arrangement. A hub modifies transmission signals, thus allowing the network to be extended to accommodate additional workstations. A concentrator is a type of hub. Both wiring hubs and concentrators are useful for their centralized management capabilities. However, a hub is referred to as a product that only supports Ethernet, token ring, or FDDI, while a concentrator may support all or combinations of these. *See also* active hubs, concentrator, passive hubs

Hz   *See* hertz

IDE (Integrated Drive Electronics)   A popular hard disk interface standard used for disks in the range of 40 megabytes to 1.2 gigabytes and requiring medium to fast data-transfer rates. The electronic control circuit is located on the drive itself, thus eliminating the need for a separate hard disk controller card.

IEEE (Institute of Electrical and Electronics Engineers)   Pronounced "eye-triple-ee." IEEE is a membership organization, founded in 1963, including engineers, students, and scientists. IEEE also acts as a coordinating body for computing and communications standards, particularly the IEEE 802 standards for thc physical and data-link layers of local area networks (LANs), following the ISO/OSI model.

IEEE standards The Institute of Electrical and Electronics Engineers (IEEE), acting as a coordinating body, has established a number of telecommunications standards, including Group 802:

IEEE 802.1: An access-control standard for bridges linking 802.3, 802.4, and 802.5 networks

IEEE 802.2: A standard that specifies the data-link layer for use with 802.3, 802.4, and 802.5 networks

IEEE 802.3: 10Base-2 deals with the use of "thinwire" on thin Ethernet

IEEE 802.3: 10Base-5 covers the "thickwire" on thick Ethernet

IEEE 802.4: A standard that defines bus topology networks using token passing

IEEE 802.5: A standard that defines ring networks using token passing

IEEE 802.6: An emerging standard for metropolitan area networks (MANs)

IEEE 802.7: Broadband Technical Advisory Group

IEEE 802.8: Fiber Technical Advisory Group

IEEE 802.9: Integrated Voice/Data

IEEE 802.10: Interoperable LAN Security

IEEE 802.11: Wireless LAN

IEEE 802.12: 100Base-VG

IEEE 802.14: 100Base-T

impedance An electrical property of a cable that combines capacitance, inductance, and resistance, measured in ohms. Impedance can be described as the apparent resistance to the flow of alternating current at a given frequency. Excessive impedance can cause data errors. Each transmission protocol and network topology specifies its own standards for impedance.

Integrated Services Digital Network *See* ISDN

intellectual property Ideas, processes, or works of authorship, including designs, methods, inventions, and know-how, which are protected as patents, copyrights, trademarks, and/or trade secrets.

intelligent terminal A terminal with built-in memory and processing for performing more complex functions than a "dumb terminal" performs.

interconnection Defines a situation in which two computer systems can communicate but without consideration of how the interaction between the applications processes is controlled.

interface An interconnection point, usually between pieces of equipment.

International Standards Organization (ISO) An international standard-making body, based in Geneva, that establishes global standards for communications and information exchange. ANSI is the United States member of ISO. The seven-layer International Standards Organization/Open Systems Interconnection (ISO/OSI) model for computer-to-computer communications is one of the ISO's most widely accepted recommendations. *See also* ISO/OSI model

internet   *See* internetwork

Internet   A collection of networks and gateways including ARPANET (Advanced Research Projects Agency Network) and NSFnet (National Science Foundation net). Internet uses TCP/IP protocols. In general, Internet refers to any computer systems connected by TCP/IP. When capitalized it refers to the worldwide Defense Advanced Research Projects Agency (DARPA) network that connects thousands of research institutions, universities, corporations, and government laboratories. Internets can be independent of the DARPA Internet, but they all use TCP/IP to connect dissimilar systems such as VMS and UNIX systems.

internetwork   A collection of networks interconnected by routers that functions generally as a single network. Sometimes called an internet, which is not to be confused with the Internet (with capital I).

Internetwork Packet eXchange   *See* IPX

Internetwork Packet eXchange/Sequenced Packet eXchange   *See* IPX/SPX

internetworking   The connection of two or more computer networks, so that nodes on one network can communicate with nodes on the other network. This might involve connecting LANs and WANs. The term may refer to products, procedures, and technologies.

interoperability   The ability of hardware and software produced by different vendors to exchange information.

interrupt request (IRQ)   Hardware lines that carry a signal from a device to the processor. This computer signal or instruction causes an interruption of a program for an I/O task. IRQs are set by means of hardware switches or settings on adapter cards, such as network adapter cards, to be connected to a unique and specific I/O task in order to avoid conflicts between machine devices that are connected to the computer. Not all LAN adapter cards use hardware interrupts (IRQs); some (like LANtastic) use software-selected interrupts.

IP (Internetwork Protocol)   The TCP/IP session-layer protocol that regulates packet forwarding by tracking internet addresses, routing outgoing messages, and recognizing incoming messages.

IP address   The address used to define the computer node number according to the TCP/IP protocol.

IPX (Internetwork Packet eXchange)   This network transport software protocol is used to move requests and data across NetWare LANs between server and/or workstations. IPX packets are encapsulated and carried by the packets used in Ethernet and the similar frames used in token ring networks.

IPX/SPX (Internetwork Packet eXchange/Sequenced Packet eXchange)   Two network protocols. IPX is network protocol for moving information across the network; SPX works on top of IPX and adds extra commands. In the OSI model, IPX conforms to the network layer and SPX is the transport layer.

IRQ   *See* interrupt request

ISDN (Integrated Services Digital Network)   A CCITT standard for a worldwide digital communications network intended to replace all current systems with a completely digital transmission system. Computers and other devices connect to ISDN via simple, standardized interfaces. When complete, ISDN systems will be capable of transmitting voice, video, audio, and data.

ISO   *See* International Standards Organization

ISO/OSI model (International Standards Organization/Open Systems Interconnection model)   A networking reference model defined by the ISO that divides computer-to-computer communications into seven connected layers. Such layers are known as a protocol stack. Each successively higher layer builds on the functions of the layers below, as follows:

> **Application layer 7:**   The highest level of the model. It defines the way that applications interact with the network, including database management, electronic mail, and terminal-emulation programs.

> **Presentation layer 6:** Defines the way that data are formatted, presented, converted, and encoded.

> **Session layer 5:** Coordinates communications and maintains the session for as long as it is needed, performing security, logging, and administrative functions.

> **Transport layer 4:** Defines protocols for structuring messages and supervises the validity of the transmission by performing some error checking.

> **Network layer 3:** Defines protocols for data routing to ensure that the information arrives at the correct destination node.

> **Data-link layer 2:** Validates the integrity of the flow of data from one node to another by synchronizing blocks of data and controlling the flow of data.

> **Physical layer 1:** Defines the mechanism for communicating with the transmission medium and interface hardware.

ISO 9660   The international file-format standard for most of today's CD-ROMs. It is an updated version of the High Sierra format, which was developed in 1985 and later adopted by the International Standards Organization (ISO).

ISO 10149   The official ISO designation for the Yellow Book CD-ROM standard.

ISO 13490   *See* Frankfurt Group

jumper   An electrically conductive part that is used to connect two or more points on a circuit board. Commonly used to select among options, or determine whether a particular option is on or off. When the jumper is installed, the circuit is shorted (closed). When the jumper is removed, or connected only to a single pin, the circuit is open.

K   *See* kilo-

Kb   *See* kilobit

KB   *See* kilobyte

Kbit   *See* kilobit

Kbits/sec   Kilobits per second

Kbyte   *See* kilobyte

key   *See* software key

kHz   Kilohertz, 1000 cycles per second.

kilo-   A prefix indicating 1,000 in the metric system. Because computing is based on powers of 2, in this context, kilo usually means 2^{10}, or 1,024. To differentiate between these two uses, a lowercase k is used to indicate 1,000 (as in kHz), and an uppercase K to indicate 1,024. *See also* mega-

kilobaud   One thousand bauds. A unit of measurement of the transmission capacity of a communications channel. *See also* baud

kilobit (Kb or Kbit)   1,024 bits (binary digits). *See also* megabit

kilobits per second (Kbits/sec)   The number of bits, or binary digits, transmitted every second and measured in multiples of 1,024 bits per second. Used as an indicator of communications transmission rates. *See also* megabits per second

kilobyte (K, KB, or Kbyte)   1,024 bytes. *See also* exabyte, megabyte, gigabyte, petabyte, terabyte

kilohertz   *See* kHz

kiosk   A boothlike device that uses a computer and often a CD-ROM drive to allow users to access information without human assistance.

Kodak Photo CD   Based on the Orange Book standard, Photo CDs store digitized 35mm photographs recorded at Kodak processing centers. Some early CD-ROM XA drives were Photo CD-compatible, since XA and Photo CD share some aspects of the Green Book standard. Today's Photo CD drives are all multisession and not necessarily XA-compatible, though once XA hardware is defined, high-end CD-ROM drives are likely to be compatible with both XA and multisession Photo CDs.

LAN   *See* local area network

LAN Manager   A network operating system, developed by Microsoft and 3Com, that runs on 80386 and 80486 computers. The file-server software is a version of OS/2; client PCs can be OS/2, DOS, UNIX, or Macintosh. Disk mirroring, disk duplexing, and UPS (uninterruptible power supply) monitoring functions are available. The network operating system supports IPX/SPX, TCP/IP, and NetBEUI.

LAN Server   A network operating system from IBM, based on a version of OS/2, that runs on 80386 and later Intel processors. LAN Server supports Microsoft Windows, DOS, UNIX, and Macintosh clients as well as FTP, IPX/SPX, and NetBIOS protocols.

LANtastic   A popular peer-to-peer network operating system from Artisoft that runs with DOS or Microsoft Windows and supports Microsoft Windows, DOS, Macintosh, and UNIX clients. LANtastic supports up to 300 users, includes built-in CD-ROM and electronic-mail support, and can connect into the NetWare environment.

lead-in area   The place on a CD-R or CD-ROM disc where the final table of contents is written.

lead-out area   The place on a CD-R or CD-ROM disc that tells the drive that there are no more data to be read.

leased line   *See* dedicated line

license   A permit or right to do something that would otherwise be prohibited. It also refers to the contract granting such permission, including all rights and obligations. *See also* software license agreement

license agreement   *See* software license agreement

license key   *See* software key

license manager   A control mechanism, usually a software program, used to allow access to a software product within the terms of a license. Also called access manager.

licensee   The party in a software agreement receiving the license rights granted.

licensor   The party in a software agreement granting the license rights.

local area network (LAN)   Network of computers within a relatively small geographical area (usually not larger than a small campus of buildings) governed by strict rules. Control of access and structure (topology), enabling resources, data and applications are shared among a number of end users. Compared to WANs, LANs are usually characterized by relatively high data rates and relatively low error rates.

LocalTalk   The shielded, twisted-pair (STP) wiring and connectors available from Apple for connecting Macintosh computers using the built-in Apple-Talk network hardware. LocalTalk is Apple's proprietary 230-Kbits/sec baseband CSMA/CA (Carrier Sense Multiple Access with Collision Avoidance) network protocol.

location   An identified physical address.

loopback device   Part of a cable tester that directs a signal transmitted through a cable back to the cable tester for test purposes.

m   *See* milli-

M   *See* mega-

MAC   *See* media-access control

magneto-optical (MO)   A writable and readable optical-storage technology that is used mostly for archival storage.

mainframe computer   A large, fast multiuser computer system designed to manage large amounts of data and complex computing tasks. Mainframes are normally installed in large corporations, universities, or military projects and can support hundreds, even thousands, of users. *See also* minicomputer

MAN   *See* metropolitan area network

MAU (Multistation Access Unit)   A multiport wiring hub for token ring networks that can connect up to eight lobes to a ring network. IBM refers to a MAU that can be managed remotely as a controlled access unit.

Mbits/sec   *See* megabits per second

MCA (Micro Channel Architecture)   The basis for IBM Micro Channel bus, used in high-end models of IBM's PS/2 series of personal computers.

media-access control (MAC)   The lower component of the data-link layer that governs access to the transmission media. The logical-link layer is the upper component of the data-link layer. MAC is used in CSMA/CD and token ring local area networks (LANs) as well as in other types of networks.

medium attachment unit   A transceiver that attaches to the AUI (Attachment Unit Interface) port on an Ethernet adapter card and provides electrical and mechanical attachments to fiber-optic, twisted-pair, or other media.

mega- (M)   A prefix meaning one million in the metric system. Because computing is based on powers of 2, in this context mega usually means 2^{20}, or 1,048,576—the power of 2 closest to one million.

megabit (Mbit)   A little over one million ($2^{20} = 1,048,576$) bits of data (binary digits 0 or 1). It can describe the amount of data that can be transported across a network link in a particular length of time. *See also* bit, megabits per second

megabits per second (Mbits/sec or Mbps)   A measurement of the amount of information moving across a network or communications link in one second, measured in multiples of 1,048,576 bits.

megabyte (Mb)   Usually 1,048,576 bytes. Megabytes are a common way of representing computer memory or hard disk capacity.

megahertz (MHz)   One million cycles per second. A processor's clock speed is often expressed in megahertz. The original IBM PC operated an 8088 running at 4.77 MHz; the more modern Pentium processor runs at 66 MHz; and the MIPS R4400 runs internally at 150 MHz.

memory cache   An area of high-speed memory on the processor that stores commonly used code or data obtained from slower memory, eliminating the need to access the system's main memory to fetch instructions. The Intel 82385 cache controller chip was used with fast static RAM on some systems to increase performance, but more modern processors include cache-management functions on the main processor. The Intel 80486 contains a single 8-kilobyte (K) cache to manage both data and instruction caching. The Pentium contains two separate 8K caches, one each for data and instructions. *See also* cache

memory management   The way in which the computer handles memory. In a DOS-based PC, you may find the following kinds of memory:

> **Conventional memory:** The area of memory below 640K.

> **Upper memory:** The 384K of memory between 640K and 1 megabyte (Mb); also known as reserved memory. This space is used by system hardware such as the video adapter. Unused portions of upper

memory are known as upper memory blocks (UMBs). On an 80386 (or later) processor, UMBs can be used for device drivers or terminate-and-stay-resident programs.

Extended memory: The memory above 1 Mb on 80386 (or later) processors. Extended memory needs an extended memory manager, such as HIMEM.SYS.

High memory area: The first 64K of extended memory.

Expanded memory: Memory above conventional memory that can be used by certain DOS applications. Expanded memory requires an expanded memory manager. Many of the design decisions made in the original PC, and in early versions of DOS, define these apparently random memory boundaries.

metering software   Software that keeps track of software or database usage.

metropolitan area network (MAN)   A public high-speed network (100 Mbits/sec or more) capable of voice and data transmission over a range of 25 to 50 miles (40 to 80 kilometers). It spans a metropolitan area. Generally, a MAN spans a larger geographical area than a LAN, but a smaller geographical area than a WAN.

MHz   *See* megahertz

Micro Channel Architecture   *See* MCA

milli- (m)   A prefix meaning one-thousandth in the metric system, often expressed as 10^{-3}.

millisecond (ms or msec)   A unit of measurement equal to one-thousandth of a second. In computing, hard disk and CD-ROM drive access times are often described in terms of milliseconds; the higher the number, the slower the disk system.

minichanger   A sort of jukebox with a mechanical assembly that can hold a small number of CD-ROM disc caddies and automatically plays one disc at a time.

minicomputer   A medium-sized computer running a multitasking operating system capable of managing more than 100 users simultaneously, suitable for use in a small company or a single corporate or government department. *See also* mainframe computer, workstation

MIPS (million of instructions per second)   A measure of the processing speed of a computer's central processing unit (CPU).

Mode 1 and Mode 2   In CD-ROM, these terms refer to the organization of data in a sector. Mode 1 employs error detection code and error correction code (EDC/ECC) to ensure that data are always retrieved accurately. Mode 2, used for audio and video, forsakes error correction since errors do not necessarily render such data ineffective. Mode 2 is further split into Form 1 (corrected) and Form 2 (uncorrected), allowing for the interleaving of corrected and uncorrected data in alternating sectors on the same track. This lets XA drives "stream" text, audio, and video data together in synchronicity. MPC Level 2 requires the support of all modes and forms.

modem   A MOdulation/DEModulation device that allows a digital device to be connected to an analog transmission network and vice versa.

modulation   In communication, the process used by a modem to add the digital signal onto the carrier signal, so that the signal can be transmitted over a telephone line. *See also* demodulation

MPC (multimedia PC)   A standard created by the Multimedia Marketing Council that establishes the minimum acceptable requirements for running multimedia applications on Windows-based PCs.

MS-DOS   Acronym for Microsoft Disk Operating System. MS-DOS, like other operating systems, allocates system resources—such as hard and floppy disks, the monitor, and the printer—to applications that need them. MS-DOS is a single-user, single-tasking operating system, with either a command-line or shell interface. Over 20,000 different applications run under MS-DOS on an estimated 100 million computers. Over the years, Microsoft has released several major upgrades: (Version 1.0, Aug. 1981), (Version 2.0, March 1983), (Version 3.0, Aug. 1984), (Version 3.1, Nov. 1984), (Version 3.2, Dec. 1985), (Version 3.3, April 1987), (Version 4.0, Nov. 1988), (Version 5.0, June 1991), (Version 6.0, Spring 1993), (Version 6.2, Fall 1993).

msec   *See* millisecond

multichanger   A sort of jukebox with a mechanical assembly that can hold a large number of CD-ROM disc caddies (sometimes over 1,000 discs) and automatically plays many discs at a time.

multicustomer license   A type of software license that allows the licensee to process its own data from one or more of its customers.

multimedia   The use of multiple types of data—audio, video, text, graphics—in a single application.

multimedia PC   *See* MPC

multimode   Essentially, an optical fiber designed to carry multiple signals, distinguished by frequency or phase, at the same time. *See also* single mode

MultiPlatter   A proprietary CD-ROM networking product produced by SilverPlatter, based on a Novell LAN. In 1993, SilverPlatter ceased distribution and maintenance on CD-ROM LAN products to concentrate on database and search engine development. SilverPlatter's efforts resulted in the production of ERL systems. *See* "Client-Server Alternative: The Electronic Reference Library" in chapter 6.

multiplexing   Putting multiple signals on a single channel. *See also* frequency-division multiplexing

multisession   The ability to record a disc in more than one session, or the ability to read a partially recorded disc. Older CD-ROM drives can only read the first recorded session on a disc, while multisession drives can access data across all available sessions. Most of today's CD-ROM drives use multisession primarily to read Photo CDs that have been written to more than once.

multispeed   This describes a drive's ability to spin the disk at different speeds. The faster rotation typically doubles the average data-transfer rate of a CD-ROM drive by sending more data to the buffer in a given amount of time. Multispeed drives automatically switch between modes, slowing down in the case of Red Book audio, since the data are recorded to play back properly at 150 Kbytes/sec.

Multistation Access Unit   *See* MAU

multitasking   The ability of a computer to perform more than one task simultaneously.

N connector   The large-diameter connector used with thicknet Ethernet cable.

narrowband network   *See* baseband network

NDIS (Network Driver Interface Specification)   Originally developed by Microsoft and 3Com, NDIS is used by LAN Manager and VINES for LAN adapter drivers. NDIS helps different operating systems and adapters to work together and provide a way to use multiple protocol stacks in the same host.

NetBEUI (NetBIOS Extended User Interface)   Microsoft's extension to NetBIOS. NetBEUI is used by LAN Manager, Windows for Workgroups, and Windows NT networks.

NetBIOS (Network Basic Input/Output System)   A specification to link a network operating system with specific hardware. Similar on some layers to IP and IPX. Some vendors use their own implementations of NetBIOS.

NetWare   A popular group of network operating systems developed by Novell. NetWare products are available for various computer platforms, including PC-AT compatibles and Macintosh computers.

NetWare Loadable Module (NLM)   Software that adds features to or enhances Novell NetWare. NLMs are applications and drivers that run on a NetWare server and can be loaded or unloaded while the server is running.

network   A continuing connection of hardware and software between two or more computers that facilitates sharing of files and resources. It allows computers to transmit data over both local and long distances.

Network Driver Interface Specification   *See* NDIS

Network File System (NFS)   A distributed file-sharing system developed almost a decade ago by Sun Microsystems. NFS allows a computer on a network to use the files and peripheral devices of another networked computer as if they were local. NFS is platform-independent and runs on mainframes, minicomputers, reduced instruction set computing–based workstations, diskless workstations, and personal computers.

network interface card (NIC)   A circuit board that acts as an access unit placed in one of the microcomputer's expansion slots that permits direct connection to a network cable. It contains the necessary hardware and software, which allow a node to communicate across the network. It cooperates with the network operating system to transmit data to and receive it from the network. Some NICs can be attached externally to a computer.

Network layer Layer 3 of the OSI Reference Model. It handles data routing across the network.

network operating system (NOS) A set of control programs designed to manage LAN resources and activities. The control programs allow interconnection between the various servers, workstations, and peripherals on the network.

network topology *See* topology

NETX A network shell program that determines if a command or request is for the local workstation disk operating system (DOS) or NetWare network operating system.

NFS *See* Network File System

NIC *See* network interface card

NLM *See* NetWare Loadable Module

node A connection or switching point on the network such as servers, workstations, and special devices. The term usually refers to computers but may also apply to bridges, routers, and brouters. A node must be intelligent to handle the communications control functions.

NOS *See* network operating system

ODI (Open Data-link Interface) A Novell specification, released in 1989, that allows multiple network interface card device drivers and protocols to share a single network interface card without conflict. ODI makes it easy to use a NOS with various LAN adapters and lets you use multiple protocol stacks in the same host.

OEM (Original Equipment Manufacturer) A term normally used to describe a reseller arrangement, under which the manufacturer of a software product grants rights to the reseller to market the product, usually under a separate label.

ohm Resistance to the flow of electrons. One ohm (Ω) is the resistance in a circuit when one volt maintains a current of one amp. Terminators for different network topologies have different ohm ratings.

one-third stroke A more accurate method to measure the performance of CD-ROM and other optical drives. This process requires that a search is done across one-third of the disc, not track to track.

Open Data-link Interface *See* ODI

open system A computer system that can communicate with any other open system, regardless of the specific components utilized or the source of those components.

optical media Storage media that use laser beams to record and read data. CD-ROM discs are examples of optical media.

OPTI-NET A CD-ROM networking product produced by Online Computer Systems. OPTI-NET is NetBIOS-compatible.

Orange Book Covers write-once, multisession media like Photo CD. It makes no provision for the drives themselves.

OS/2   A 32-bit multitasking operating system for Intel 80386 (or later) processors. It was developed jointly by Microsoft and IBM as the successor to DOS, and Windows was developed as a stopgap measure until OS/2 was ready. However, after its release, Microsoft chose to back Windows. In spring 1992, IBM released OS/2 version 2.0, which won many industry awards for its technical achievements.

OSI reference model   Open Systems Interconnection reference model. A model for networks developed by the International Standards Organization specifying how computers should communicate over a network. The model divides the network functions into seven connected layers. Each layer builds on the services provided by those under it. The OSI model describes what happens when a terminal talks to a computer or one computer talks to another. The system was designed to facilitate the creation of a system in which equipment from different vendors can communicate.

packet   A logical grouping of information that includes a header and usually user data and commands. This unit of information is formatted into packets prior to transmission.

packet driver   A software interface that allows client programs to use a standard approach for communicating with the network hardware of a PC workstation. Packet drivers insulate client software from the differences that exist between network hardware manufactured by different vendors.

packet switched data network (PSDN)   *See* packet switched network

packet switched network   A network where data are transmitted as individual packets which are switched according to addressing information contained within them as they traverse the network. X.25 has been the main standard for packet switching, now being supplanted by the frame relay.

parity   In communications, a simple form of error checking that uses an extra or redundant bit after the data bits but before the stop bit or bits.

passive hubs   Passive hubs split the transmission signal, allowing additional workstations to be added. *See also* active hubs

PBX   *See* private branch exchange

PCI (peripheral component interconnect) bus   A high-speed local bus standard.

PCMCIA (Personal Computer Memory Card International Association)   A not-for-profit association, formed in 1989, with more than 320 members in the computer and electronics industries, which developed a standard for credit-card-size, plug-in adapters designed for portable computers.

PDN   *See* public data network

peer-to-peer   An architecture in which two or more nodes can communicate with each other directly, without the need for any intermediary devices. In a peer-to-peer system, a node can be both a client and a server. *See also* peer-to-peer network

peer-to-peer network   A network architecture in which drives, files, and printers on each PC can be available to every other PC on the network, eliminating the need for a dedicated file server. Each PC can still run local applications. Traditionally, peer-to-peer systems are often used in relatively small networks, with 2 to 10 users, and can be based on DOS, OS/2, or UNIX. Popular peer-to-peer network operating systems include Novell's Personal NetWare and Artisoft's LANtastic.

personal-use license A type of software license that authorizes use by a specific person.

peta- A metric system prefix for one quadrillion, or 10^{15}. Abbreviated P. In computing, peta is equal to 1,125,899,906,842,624, or 2^{50}.

petabyte In computing, usually 2^{50}, or 1,125,899,906,842,624 bytes. Abbreviated as PB.

physical layer The first layer and lowest of the seven layers of the ISO/OSI model. It deals with the network medium—cables, connectors, and so on—that is used to connect the equipment.

platform The hardware and/or operating system context for a software product. Also called computing environment.

plenum cabling Cabling with a fire-resistant jacket. There are two types of outer coverings used for cables: PVC (polyvinyl chloride) and a fire-resistant material, typically made of a fluoropolymer material, which is usually a Teflon coating. PVC is common and low in cost but gives off poisonous smoke and fumes when it burns. When shopping for cabling to use within walls, between floors, or in suspended ceilings, make sure you buy cables meeting the CMR (Communications Riser Cable) or CMP (Communication Plenum Cable) specifications of the National Electric Code.

port The point at which a communications circuit terminates at a network, serial, or parallel interface card.

presentation layer Layer 6 of the OSI reference model. This layer handles format, code, and syntax conversion of the data exchanged between two application-layer entities.

print server A server that handles printing for all users on a network. A print server collects print jobs sent by applications running on other networked PCs, places them in a print queue on the hard disk, and routes them to one or more printers attached to the print server.

private branch exchange (PBX) A telephone system serving a specific location to connect calls among offices in the same complex, and to switch calls between the site and a larger phone network. Many PBX systems can carry computer data without the use of modems.

private line *See* dedicated line

PROM *See* boot PROM

protected mode In Intel 80286 and higher processors, protected mode provides hardware support for multitasking and virtual memory management. In 80286 computers, the CPU in the protected mode can address 16 Mb of memory directly. In 80386 computers and higher, the CPU in the protected mode can address up to 4 Gb of memory. In UNIX and OS/2 environments, the CPU runs in the protected mode. *See also* conventional memory

protocol A protocol is a set of rules and procedures that products should follow to perform activities and exchange information over a computer network. Protocols enable products from different vendors to communicate on the same network.

PSDN (packet switched data network) *See* packet switched network

public data network (PDN) Any government-owned or -controlled commercial packet switched network (e.g., X.25) offering wide area services to MANs and WANs.

public domain software Software for which intellectual property rights have expired or have been waived by the owner.

PVC (polyvinyl chloride) An extensively used insulator in cable coatings and coaxial cable foam compositions. *See also* plenum cabling

quad-speed drive A CD-ROM drive that reads data at 600 Kbytes/sec, four times the single-speed rate.

queue In printing, a temporary storage facility for data scheduled to print.

RAM (random access memory) Memory in the computer where data are temporarily stored and which is lost when the computer is turned off.

random access Describes the ability of a storage device to go directly to the required memory address without needing to read from the beginning every time data are requested. Although the term is common, a more accurate term is "direct access."

reboot To restart the computer and reload the operating system, usually after a crash.

Red Book The Red Book covers compact disc-digital audio (CD-DA), or standard CD-Audio, the same format as music compact discs.

redirector A software module loaded onto all the workstations on a network that intercepts application requests for file- and printer-sharing services and diverts them to the file server for action. Redirectors are often DOS terminate-and-stay-resident (TSR) programs.

regenerative repeater *See* repeater

remote access Use of a software product from an off-site location.

remote boot A technique used to boot a workstation from an image file on the file server rather than from a local drive attached directly to the workstation.

remote user A user who logs in to the network using a modem and telephone line from a site located some distance away from the main network.

repeater A device that amplifies and regenerates signals from one network segment to another similar network segment. Protocols must match on both segments. The repeater provides service at first level (the physical layer) of the ISO/OSI model. While in digital transmission, a repeater is a piece of equipment that receives a pulse train, amplifies it, retimes it, and then reconstructs the signal for retransmission; in fiber optics, a repeater is a device that decodes a low-power light signal, converts it to electrical energy, and then retransmits it via an LED (Light Emitting Diode) or laser light source. Known also as a "regenerative repeater."

response time The time lag between sending a request and receiving the data. Response time can be applied to a complete computer system, as in the time taken to look up a certain customer record, or to a system component, as in the time taken to access a specific cluster on disk.

right to use Specific privileges granted to the licensee under a software license.

ring network A network topology in the form of a closed loop or circle, with each node in the network connected to the next. Messages move in one direction around the system. When a message arrives at a node, the node examines the address information in the message. If the address matches the node's address, the message is accepted; otherwise, the node regenerates the signal and places the message back on the network for the next node in the system. It is this regeneration that allows a ring network to cover greater distances than star networks or bus networks do. Ring networks use some form of token-passing protocol to regulate network traffic. *See also* bus network, star network, token ring network

RJ-11/RJ-45 Designations for commonly used modular telephone connectors. RJ-11 is the standard four-wire connector used in most voice connections (phone lines). RJ-45 is the standard eight-wire connector for IEEE 802.3 10BASE-5 (StarLAN) networks. Also used as phone lines in some cases.

Rock Ridge Extensions CD-ROM file format extensions to ISO 9660 that accommodate the UNIX file structure.

ROM (read-only memory) A memory chip used for storing permanent instructions and data.

router A device that selects the best path for the transmission of information between two LANs.

routing The process of choosing which path or route is the best for a datagram. There are two types of routing: direct and indirect. Direct is when the sending and receiving hosts are in the same network. Indirect is when the sending and receiving hosts are in different networks and the datagram is sent first through a local gateway.

RS-232C An electrical standard for the interconnection of equipment established by the Electrical Industries Association, the same as the CCITT code V.24. RS-232C is used for serial ports.

SCSI (Small Computer System Interface) A high-speed (up to 4 Mbytes/sec) parallel interface defined by the ANSI X3T9.2 Committee. SCSI is the preferred method of connecting CD-ROM drives to computers. SCSI-2 comes in three varieties: fast, wide, and fast wide.

seat A term used to describe a physical device or workstation.

Sequenced Packet eXchange *See* SPX

server A computer and/or program that accepts, controls, and executes requests for processing or data from other computers and/or client programs in a network. A server provides shared access to network resources and handles special chores, such as disc storage, printing, or communications. The server acts as an interface between the LAN and the peripheral devices. It is used to store files for access by client stations. The server receives requests for peripheral services and manages the requests so that they are answered in an orderly, sequential manner. The term can be applied to both software programs or actual computing devices that provide services to a client. *See also* back end, client, dedicated server, peer-to-peer

session layer   The fifth of seven layers of the ISO/OSI model. It establishes, coordinates, and maintains session activity among applications, including application-level error control, dialog control, and remote procedure calls.

shareware   A software distribution method in which copies are freely made, exchanged, and tried, but if the software is placed into service, the user is honor-bound to pay a fee to the software developer.

shielded twisted-pair cable (STP)   A type of cabling used in some LANs, such as IBM Token Ring. STP provides greater protection against electromagnetic interference than the unshielded twisted-pair cable. *See also* unshielded twisted-pair cable

shielding   A protective enclosure for a transmission medium that is designed to minimize interference.

shrink-wrap software   A software distribution method whereby the license terms are deemed accepted when the user breaks a shrink-wrap seal or opens an enclosed sealed envelope containing the software.

signal quality error   *See* SQE

signaling   The process of sending a transmission signal over a physical medium for purposes of communication.

SIMM (single in-line memory module)   A narrow printed circuit board that holds eight or nine memory chips.

Simple Network Management Protocol   *See* SNMP

single mode   Describes an optical wave guide designed to propagate light of only a single wavelength and perhaps a single phase. Essentially, an optical fiber that allows the transmission of only one light beam, or data-carrying light wave channel, and is optimized for a particular light wave frequency. *See also* multimode

single session   A drive that cannot read a disc that has been recorded in multiple sessions. That drive can only read the first recorded session.

single-speed drive   A CD-ROM drive that reads data at a rate of 150 Kbytes/sec.

site   A location or set of locations, such as an office, factory, group of offices or factories, university, or other defined boundary.

site license   A type of software license that authorizes the use of a software product at a named site. *See also* site

smart modem   A modem (modulator/demodulator) that contains sophisticated electronics to provide internal processing capabilities such as auto-answer, auto-dial, setting or changing the speed of transmission, or the ability to be programmed from a communications software package. Other capabilities often include internal error detection, data compression, or the buffering of incoming or outgoing data.

SMB (server message block)   A formatted message used to request and reply to requests for file and print services in network systems.

SMTP (Simple Mail Transfer Protocol)   SMTP describes an electronic mail system with both host and user sections. Many companies sell host software, especially for UNIX, that will pass mail to other proprietary mail systems, such as IBM's PROFS. The user software is often included as a utility in TCP/IP packages for the PC.

SNA (Systems Network Architecture)   Developed in the 1970s, SNA is IBM's scheme for connecting its computerized products so that they can communicate and share data.

SNMP (Simple Network Management Protocol)   A structure for formatting messages and transmitting information between reporting devices and data collection programs; developed jointly by the Department of Defense, industry, and the academic community as part of the TCP/IP protocol suite.

software key   Password or authorization code provided by the licensor that enables a software product to be accessed, installed, or executed. Also known as "access key" and "license key."

software license agreement   A contract between the software vendor (licensor) and the software user (licensee) granting the licensee permission to use a given software product subject to certain conditions and obligations. Also called license agreement.

software product   Software programs, data, and supporting documentation.

SPX (sequenced packet exchange)   An enhanced set of commands implemented on top of IPX to create a true transport-layer interface. SPX provides more functions than IPX, including guaranteed packet delivery.

SQE (signal quality error)   A signal sent from transceivers back to the network controller card to indicate whether the collision circuitry is functional. Also called heartbeat, because when it is observed with the oscilloscope, the signal looks like it is a blip.

star network   A network topology in the form of a star. At the center of the star is a wiring hub or concentrator, and the nodes or workstations are connected to a common central switch by point-to-point links. *See also* bus network, ring network

STP   *See* shielded twisted-pair cable

StreetTalk   The distributed global naming and directory service for Banyan's VINES network operating system.

subnetwork   A LAN that is part of a larger network. In most cases, a subnetwork is connected to another subnetwork by a bridge or brouter.

Systems Network Architecture   *See* SNA

T1   Bell System terminology referring to a digital carrier facility used for transmission of data through the telephone hierarchy. The rate of transmission is 1.544 Mbits/sec. It may be used as a communication link between remote LANs or in LAN gateway implementations.

tap   A connector that couples to a cable without blocking the passage of signals down the cable.

T-connector A coaxial connector, shaped like a T, that connects two thin Ethernet cables while supplying an additional connector for a network interface card.

TCP (Transmission Control Protocol) The connection-oriented, transport-level protocol used in the TCP/IP suite of protocols. It is used to bundle and unbundle sent and received data into packets, to manage the transmission of packets on a network, and to check for errors.

TCP/IP (Transmission Control Protocol/Internet Protocol) Originally developed for the Defense Advanced Research Projects Agency (DARPA) of the Department of Defense (DOD) to internetwork dissimilar systems. The TCP protocol controls the transfer of data and the IP protocol provides the routing mechanism. This set of communications protocols has evolved since the late 1970s. It allows the transfer of data between two computers having dissimilar architectures and operating systems. Because programs supporting these protocols are available on so many different computer systems, they have become an excellent way to connect different types of computers over networks. The complete implementation of the TCP/IP includes Transmission Control Protocol (TCP), Internet Protocol (IP), Internetwork Control Message Protocol (ICMP), User Datagram Protocol (UDP), and Address Resolution Protocol (ARP). Standard applications are File Transfer Protocol (FTP), Simple Mail Transfer Protocol (SMTP), and Telnet, which provides virtual terminal on any remote network system. TCP/IP runs on a large number of VAXs and UNIX-based computers and is supported by many hardware vendors from PCs to mainframes.

Teflon Trade name for fluorinated ethylene propylene. A nonflammable material used for cable foam and jacketing. *See also* plenum cabling

Telnet A terminal emulation protocol, part of the TCP/IP suite of protocols, that provides remote terminal-connection services. The most common terminal emulations are for Digital Equipment Corporation's VT-52, VT-100, and VT-220 terminals. Many companies offer additional add-in emulations. This program and its protocol creates a terminal session between host and local UNIX computers.

tera- (T) A prefix meaning 10^2 in the metric system, 1,000,000,000,000; commonly referred to as 1 trillion.

terabyte (TB) In computing, usually 2^{40}, or 1,099,511,627,776 bytes.

terminal emulation The use of a PC or other computer to imitate the functions of a specific type of computer terminal. By executing different terminal-emulation software, a PC can communicate as an IBM 3270 or 3101 terminal; as a DEC VT-52, VT-102, or VT-220; or as other types of terminals. In enterprise networks, terminal emulation is often used with communication servers and gateways to enable workstations to act as terminals on attached mainframes and minicomputers.

terminate-and-stay-resident program (TSR) A DOS program that stays loaded in memory, even when it is not actually running. A TSR can be invoked quickly to perform a specific task.

terminator A resistor that is used at each end of a coaxial Ethernet segment or a chain of SCSI devices to ensure that signals do not reflect back and cause errors.

thick Ethernet Also known as Standard Ethernet, thick Ethernet is a form of Ethernet network that uses 50-ohm RG-11 coaxial cable as its cabling system. This relatively stiff cable is 1 centimeter (0.4 inch) thick, and can be used to connect network nodes up to a distance of approximately 1,006 meters (3,300 feet). Thick Ethernet is primarily used for facility-wide installations. Standard Ethernet installations conform to the IEEE 802.3 standard for 10Base-5 networks. Transceivers are usually connected to the coaxial cable and through flexible multiwire cable; those transceivers are connected to the nodes. *See also* thin Ethernet

thicknet *See* thick Ethernet

thin Ethernet An Ethernet network utilizing RG-58 coaxial cable as its cabling system. Thinnet conforms to the IEEE 802.3 standard for 10Base-2 networks. The cable is 5 millimeters (0.2 inch) thick. It is used to connect network nodes up to a distance of approximately 305 meters (1,000 feet). Thin Ethernet is primarily used for office installations. Sometimes it is referred to by its commercial name, Cheapernet. *See also* thick Ethernet

thinnet *See* thin Ethernet

third party Anyone other than the licensee or licensor.

throughput The amount of data that a system can process in a given amount of time, from input to output.

tier The categorization of a software product for pricing purposes based on machine size, configuration, access limitations, or other attributes.

timeout In some systems or applications, if a device does not respond, a timeout condition occurs, thus preventing a procedure from hanging up the computer. Timeouts are also used in communications to detect transmission failures. Some timeouts are fixed, such as the amount of time an operating system will attempt to access a modem or printer; others can be specified by the user. Sometimes, after a specific period of time a terminal or I/O device will perform some predetermined action, such as going back to the main menu screen.

time-sharing The technique of sharing the computing resources of a powerful computer among several users. The computer performs multitasking to service each user in turn. This is the traditional model of interactive computing used in mainframe and minicomputer environments in which the processing power is concentrated in a central computer.

token A special electrical signal, consisting of a distinctive bit pattern, that allows access to a transmission medium in some networks.

token passing An access protocol in which a special message bit (token) circulates among the network nodes giving them permission to transmit. Possession of the token gives a network node the right to transmit data for a specific period of time. The token can be used by one station at a time, thus preventing multiple nodes from transmitting on the network simultaneously. Fiber Distributed Data Interface (FDDI), token ring, and token bus networks all use token passing to avoid packet collisions. *See also* CSMA/CD

token ring network A local area network (LAN) with a ring structure that uses token passing to regulate traffic on the network and avoid collisions. On a token ring network, the controlling computer generates a token that controls the right to transmit. This token is continuously passed from one node to the next around the network. When a node has information to transmit, it captures the token, sets its status to busy, and adds the message and the destination address. All other nodes continuously read the token to determine if they are the recipient of a message. If they are, they collect the token, extract the message, and return the token to the sender. The sender then removes the message and sets the token status to "free," indicating that it can be used by the next node in sequence.

Token Ring network IBM's implementation of the token ring network architecture. It uses a token-passing protocol transmitting at 4 or 16 Mbits/sec. Using standard telephone wiring, a Token Ring network can connect up to 72 devices; with shielded, twisted-pair (STP) wiring, each ring can support up to 256 nodes. Although it is based on a closed-loop ring structure, a Token Ring network uses a star-shaped cluster of up to eight nodes, all attached to the same wiring concentrator or Multistation Access Unit (MAU). The MAUs are then connected to the main ring circuit. A Token Ring network can include personal computers, minicomputers, and mainframes. The IEEE 802.5 standard defines token ring networks.

topology The map or plan of the network. It describes how the nodes are connected. The physical topology describes how the wires or cables are laid out, and the logical or electrical topology describes how the messages flow. The most common are rings (where messages pass through each station in turn), star (where messages pass through a central node), and bus (where each message is presented to all nodes at the same time).

TP *See* twisted-pair cable

track-at-once The process of recording an entire CD-R disc at once in a single session.

transceiver A communication device capable of transmitting and receiving. In thick Ethernet networks, the transceiver is a separate device that provides a physical and electrical interface between network nodes and the trunk cable. In thin Ethernet network installations, it is included on the network interface card. This unit monitors the cable for activity to avoid data collisions. Sometimes referred to as a medium attachment unit. *See also* AUI, drop cable

transmission media Plural of medium; the cabling or wiring used to carry network signals. Typical examples are coax, fiber-optic, and twisted-pair wire.

transport layer The fourth of seven layers of the ISO/OSI model. It handles communication across the network. It is responsible for reliable network communication among end nodes. It implements flow and error control and often uses virtual circuits to ensure reliable data delivery.

triple-speed drive   A CD-ROM drive that reads data at 450 Kbytes/sec, three times the single-speed rate.

trunk line   *See* backbone network

TSR   *See* terminate-and-stay-resident program

twisted-pair cable (TP)   A transmission medium consisting of two insulated wires twisted around each other over the length of the cable to preserve signal strength. It is used for some networks and for telephone lines. One of the wires is used for the transmission and the other for the reception of data. Twisted-pair is easier to work with than coaxial cable. Twisted-pair can be shielded or unshielded.

twisted-pair Ethernet   Implementation of the Ethernet LAN that employs shielded or unshielded twisted-pair wiring as its transmission media. It follows the 10Base-T specification of the IEEE 802.3 standard.

UNIX   Pronounced "you-nix." A 32-bit, multiuser, multitasking, portable operating system, originally developed by AT&T. Since the purchase of UNIX Systems Labs, UNIX has been owned by Novell. UNIX was developed by Dennis Ritchie and Ken Thompson at Bell Laboratories in the early 1970s and has since been enhanced, particularly by computer scientists at the University of California, Berkeley. Networking, in the form of the TCP/IP set of protocols, has been available in UNIX from its early stages. In November 1989, UNIX System Release V 4.0 was released. UNIX is available on a huge range of computational hardware, ranging from a PC to a Cray supercomputer, and is also available in other related forms. For example, AIX runs on IBM workstations, A/UX is a graphical version that runs on powerful Macintosh computers, and Solaris from SunSoft runs on Intel processors.

unshielded twisted-pair cable (UTP)   A type of cabling used in some LANs, including twisted-pair Ethernet. The cable contains two or more pairs of twisted copper wires. The greater the number of twists, the lower the interference. UTP is offered in voice grade and data grade. The advantage of UTP is the ease of installation and the low cost of materials. Its drawbacks are limited signaling speeds and shorter maximim cable-segment lengths. *See also* shielded twisted-pair cable

usage-based license   A type of software license with charges based on a measure of resource utilization.

user   A person, entity, device, or process that accesses, operates, or maintains a software product.

user-based license   A type of software license that defines a specific number of users, or that designates users by name.

UTP   *See* unshielded twisted-pair cable

V series   *See* CCITT

VINES   A network operating system from Banyan Systems. VINES (a contraction of VIrtual NEtworking Software) is based on a special version of the UNIX System V operating system. VINES offers many options for connecting to minicomputers, mainframes, and other network file servers. It supports up to four network interface cards per server. Workstations can run DOS, Microsoft Windows, UNIX, or OS/2, and they can store native form files on the server. Macintosh computers can also attach to the network. VINES offers special support for very large LANs and wide area networks (WANs) with multiple file servers. *See also* Enterprise Network Services, StreetTalk

virus A program intended to damage a computer system without the user's knowledge or permission.

wait state When a system's memory is slower than the CPU, the system's CPU delays (or "waits") for a portion of the processing cycle to avoid outrunning the memory. Some CPUs run with one or more wait states. Others run zero wait states, which means that the CPU does not have to slow down and wait for memory.

WAN *See* wide area network

warrantee A guarantee or enforceable promise. Typical warranties include warranties of media, warranties of title, and warranties of specifications.

wide area network (WAN) A network spanning a greater distance than a LAN. It usually makes use of telecommunications links. These may be dial-up links or permanent links leased from a telecommunications carrier. WANs connect computers over an area as wide as the entire world.

wireless LAN A method of connecting a node or group of nodes into the main network using a technology other than conventional cabling. The following methods are in use: infrared line of sight (high-frequency light waves), high-frequency radio (high-frequency radio signals), or spread-spectrum radio. Data rates are usually less than 1 Mbit/sec. Wireless LANs are not always completely wireless. They may be used to replace the cabling on certain network segments or to connect groups of networks that use conventional cabling.

wiring closet Specially designed room or cabinet used for wiring data and voice networks. Wiring closets serve as a central junction point for wiring and wiring equipment that is used for interconnecting services.

workstation A microcomputer attached to a LAN and operating as a LAN node. Workstations are primarily used to run application software, as opposed to servers, which provide shared access to network resources.

WORM (write once, read many) An optical storage technology used primarily for archival storage. On WORM discs, data can be recorded but not erased or written over.

X.25 An international standard defining packet switched communication protocol for a private network. The recommendation is prepared by the CCITT. Along with other CCITT recommendations, the X.25 recommendation defines the physical-, data-link-, and network-layer protocols necessary to interface computers with X.25 networks. The standard defines the packet format for data transfers in a public data network.

X Series *See* CCITT

X Windows A windowing environment developed at MIT for UNIX workstations. X Window is an open and nonproprietary system, designed to be independent of both the display hardware and the underlying operating system. It is supported by all the major workstation vendors. The Open Software Foundation (OSF) implementation is known as Motif; Sun and Hewlett Packard use a version called OpenLook.

Xmodem   A popular file transfer protocol that divides data for transmission into blocks. Each block consists of the start-of-header character, a block number, 128 bytes of data, and a checksum. An extension to Xmodem, called Xmodem-CRC, adds an error-checking method by using a cyclical redundancy check (CRC) to detect transmission errors. *See also* Ymodem, Zmodem

Yellow Book   The Yellow Book describes the way data are physically organized on CD-ROMs, taking into account pits and lands, sector size, the spiral arrangement, and the speed at which data are read. Yellow Book CD-ROM applications may be PC- or Macintosh-compatible, although a growing number of discs contain separate software "engines" to run on both platforms seamlessly.

Ymodem   A variation of the Xmodem protocol. This popular file transfer protocol divides the data to be transmitted into blocks. Each block consists of the start-of-header character, a block number, 1 kilobyte of data, and a checksum. Ymodem also incorporates the capabilities to send multiple files in the same session and to abort file transfer during the transmission. Ymodem's larger data block results in less overhead for error control than required by Xmodem; however, if the block must be retransmitted because the protocol detects an error, there are more data to resend. *See also* Xmodem, Zmodem

Z39.50   A NISO standard entitled "Information Retrieval Service Definition and Protocol Specification for Library Applications." This standard offers a protocol that provides for the exchange of messages between computers for the purpose of information retrieval. It has important applications for library and information service vendors, and it gives guidelines for the format of queries, provides for the transfer of database records, and defines other record types. This standard is designed as an application layer (layer 7) protocol within the Open Systems Interconnection (OSI) protocol suite but is also being mapped into the TCP/IP protocol suite. The ISO equivalent standard is usually referred to as "ISO Search and Retrieval" (SR).

zero-wait state   *See* wait state

Zmodem   A popular file transfer protocol which is similar to Xmodem and Ymodem but is designed to handle larger data transfers with fewer errors. Zmodem also includes a feature called "checkpoint restart," which allows an interrupted transmission to resume at the point of interruption, rather than starting again at the beginning of the transmission. *See also* Xmodem, Ymodem

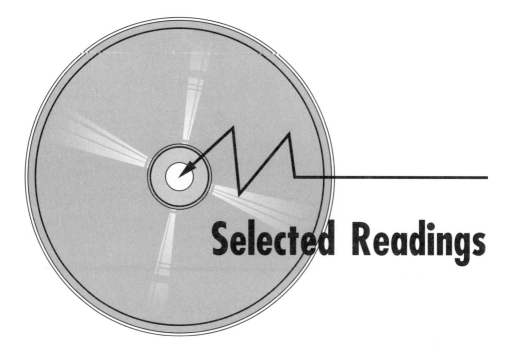

Selected Readings

Atkinson, Roderick D., and John R. Yokley. "Multiplatform CD-ROM Networking." *CD-ROM Professional* 6 (3): 73–81 (May 1993).

Ayre, Rick, and Laura Cox. "The Well Tuned PC: A Guide to Memory Management." *PC Magazine* 11 (13): 227+ (July 14, 1992).

"Backing Up Your Data: Network Backup Evolves." *PC Magazine* 12 (16): 277–312 (September 28, 1993).

Bailey, Charles W., et al. *The Public-Access Computer Systems Review, Volume 1, 1990.* Chicago: Library and Information Technology Association, 1992.

Barry, Simon. "Nine Memory Managers Open Up New Frontiers." *PC Magazine* 11 (3): 207–57 (February 11, 1992).

Bell, Steven J. "Providing Remote Access to CD-ROM: Some Practical Advice." *CD-ROM Professional* 6 (1): 43–47 (January 1993).

Bosak, Steve, and Jeffrey Sloman. *The CD-ROM Book.* 2d ed. Indianapolis: Que Corp., 1994.

Boss, Richard W. "Accessing Electronic Publications in Complex LAN Environments." *Library Technology Reports* 28 (3) (May-June 1992).

Brueggeman, Peter. "Memory Management for CD-ROM Workstations, Part 1." *CD-ROM Professional* 4 (5): 39–43 (September 1991).

Burgard, Michael J., and Kenneth D. Phillips. *DOS-UNIX Networking and Internetworking.* New York: Wiley, 1994.

Burke, David. "What You Need to Know before Networking CD-ROMs." *Computers in Libraries* 14(6): 16–22 (June 1994).

Chorafas, Dimitris N. *Beyond LANs: Client/Server Computing.* New York: McGraw-Hill, 1994.

———. *Local Area Network Reference.* New York: McGraw-Hill, 1989.

Cobb, Stephen. *Complete Book of PC and LAN Security.* Blue Ridge Summit, Pa.: Wendcrest Books, 1992.

Comer, Douglas. *Internetworking with TCP/IP. Volume 1: Principals, Protocols, and Architecture. Volume 2: Design, Implementation, and Internals.* New York: Prentice-Hall, 1991.

Conkling, Thomas W., and Bonnie Anne Osif. "CD-ROM and Changing Research Patterns." *Online* 18 (3): 71–74 (May 1994).

Cummings, Syndi, and Tad Giorgis. "Peer-to-Peering through Windows." *LAN Times* 10 (17): 87 (August 23, 1993).

Davis, Peter T. *Complete LAN Security and Control.* Blue Ridge Summit, Pa.: TAB Books, 1994.

Derfler, Frank J., Jr. *Guide to Connectivity.* Emeryville, Calif.: Ziff-Davis Pr., 1991.

———. "Networking Acronyms and Buzzwords (Guide to Networking Terminology)." *PC Magazine* 7 (11): 99–105 (June 14, 1988).

———. "Peer Pressure: Peer-to-Peer Networks." *PC Magazine* 13 (8): 237–74 (April 26, 1994).

Derfler, Frank J., Jr., and David Greenfield. "Peer-to-Peer LANs: Friend or Foe?" *PC Magazine* 12 (13): NE51+ (July 13, 1993).

Desmarais, Norman, ed. *CD-ROM Local Area Networks: A User's Guide.* Westport, Conn.: Meckler Publishing, 1991.

Drew, Heywood, et al. *Connectivity: Local Area Networks.* Carmel, Ind.: New Riders Publishing, 1992.

Dyson, Peter. *Novell's Dictionary of Networking.* Alameda, Calif.: Sybex, 1994.

Freed, Les, and Frank J. Derfler, Jr. *Guide to Using NetWare.* Emeryville, Calif.: Zeff-Davis Pr., 1991.

Glass, Brett. "Memory Managers." *PC World* 10 (7): 189–95 (July 1992).

Hannah, Stan A., and Joseph B. Miller. "Memory Management for the Stand-Alone and Networked PC." *Computers in Libraries* 15(3): 12–18 (March 1995).

Harper, Jim. "A DOS Redirector for SCSI CD-ROM: Putting the Pieces Together." *Dr. Dobbs Journal* 18 (3): 44–49 (March 1993).

Heath, Steve. *Effective PC Networking.* Newton, Mass.: Butterworth-Heinemann, 1993.

Hegering, Heinz-Gerd, and Alfred Lapple. *Ethernet: Building a Communications Infrastructure.* Redwood City, Calif.: Addison-Wesley, 1993.

Hoffs, Signe, and others. *CD-I Designers Guide.* New York; London: McGraw-Hill, 1992.

Hunter, Philip. *Local Area Networks: Making the Right Choices.* Redwood City, Calif.: Addison-Wesley, 1993.

Internetworking Technology Terms and Acronyms. Menlo Park, Calif.: Cisco Systems, 1992.

Kahl, Brewster, and Art Medlar. "An Information System for Corporate Users: Wide Area Information Servers." *Online* 15 (5): 56–60 (September 1991).

Karney, James. "Sharing a CD-ROM." *PC Magazine* 13 (4): 171–78 (February 22, 1994).

Koren, Judy. "Multiuser Access to CD-ROM Drives without a CD-ROM LAN, Part 1." *CD-ROM Professional* 5 (4): 59–66 (July 1992).

———. "Providing Access to CD-ROM Databases in a Campus Setting: Networking CD-ROMs via a LAN, Part II." *CD-ROM Professional* 5 (5): 83–94 (September 1992).

"LAN Links Take Form of Repeaters, Bridges, Routers and Gateways." *PC Week* 6 (4): C23 (January 30, 1989).

Learn, Larry L. "Networks: A Review of Their Architecture and Implementation." *Library Hi Tech* 6 (2): 19–49 (1988).

———. "Networks: The Telecommunications Infrastructure and Impacts of Change." *Library Hi Tech* 6 (1): 13–31 (1988).

Levy, Joseph R. *Welcome to Networking: A Guide to Local Area Networks.* New York: MIS Press, 1993.

Li, Sing. "Writing Non-SCSI CD-ROM Device Drivers." *Dr. Dobbs Journal* 19 (3): 102–10 (March 1994).

McCormick, John A. *Computers and the Americans with Disabilities Act: A Manager's Guide.* New York: McGraw-Hill, 1994.

McCoy, John H., and Wuhsiung Lu. "Network Access to CD-ROMs: Client/ Server Software for Extending CD-ROM Access across a NetBIOS-Based Network." *Dr. Dobbs Journal* 18 (8): 72–76 (August 1993).

Machovec, George S. "TCP/IP and OSI: Networking Dissimilar Systems Implications for Libraries." *Online Libraries and Microcomputers* 7 (6–7): 1–4 (June 1989).

———. *Telecommunications and Networking Glossary.* Chicago: Library and Information Technology Association, American Library Association, 1990.

———. *Telecommunications, Networking and Internet Glossary.* Chicago: Library and Information Technology Association, American Library Association, 1993.

McQueen, Howard. "CD-ROM Servers: An Overview." *CD-ROM Professional* 6 (5): 54–57 (September 1993).

Mahy, Rohan, and Kent Paul. "PC to Mac." *LAN Magazine* 7 (13): 50–63 (December 1992).

Maki, Ken. *Integrating Macs with Your PC Network.* New York: Wiley, 1994.

Microsoft Windows for Workgroups & MS-DOS 6.2. Redmond, Wash.: Microsoft Pr., 1993.

Miles, J. B. "CD-ROM Drives." *Government Computer News* 12 (17): 86–91 (August 16, 1993).

———. "Tape Storage Subsystems." *Government Computer News* 12 (13): 75–80 (June 21, 1993).

Miley, Michael. "Peer-to-Peer Gains Ground: LAN Administrators Are Pleased with Recent Performance and Reliability Improvements." *InfoWorld,* no. 15 (15): 53–54 (April 12, 1993).

Moholt, Pat. "The Influence of Technology on Networking." *Special Libraries* 80 (2): 113+ (Spring 1989).

Nadeau, Michael. *Byte Guide to CD-ROM.* Berkeley, Calif.: Osborne McGraw-Hill, 1994.

Naugle, Matthew. *Local Area Networking.* New York: McGraw-Hill, 1991.

———. *Network Protocols Handbook.* New York: McGraw-Hill, 1994.

Needleman, Raphael. *InfoWorld: Understanding Networks.* New York: Brady Computer Books, 1990.

Nemzow, Martin A. W. *The Ethernet Management Guide.* 2d ed. New York: McGraw-Hill, 1992.

"Network Connections: 100 Ethernet Cards; Byte/NSTL (National Software Testing Laboratories) Lab Report." *Byte* 18 (9): 172–91 (August 1993).

Niedermiller-Chaffins, Debra. *Inside Novell NetWare.* Carmel, Ind.: New Riders Publishing, 1991.

Novell Installation Supplements; NetWare. Provo, Utah: Novell, 1991.

Parker, Dana. "The Rainbow of Standards." *CD-ROM Professional* 6 (3): 151–54 (May 1993).

Parker, Dana, and Bob Starrett. *Guide to CD-ROM.* Carmel, Ind.: New Riders Publishing, 1992.

Peltier, Thomas. "The Virus Threat." *LAN Magazine* 7 (4): 19–20 (April 1992).

Perlman, Radia. *Interconnections, Bridges, and Routers.* Redwood City, Calif.: Addison-Wesley, 1992.

Process Software Corporation. *TCP/IP Defined: A Practical Guide to TCP/IP Networking Terms and Concepts.* Framingham, Mass.: Process Software Corp., 1992.

Prosise, Jeff. *PC Magazine DOS 5 Memory Management with Utilities.* Emeryville, Calif.: Ziff-Davis Pr., 1992.

———. *PC Magazine DOS 6 Memory Management and Utilities.* Emeryville, Calif.: Ziff-Davis Pr., 1993.

Rhodes, Peter D. *LAN Operations: A Guide to Daily Management.* Reading, Mass.: Addison-Wesley, 1991.

Roth, William. *Personal Computers for Persons with Disabilities: An Analysis, with Directories of Vendors and Organizations*. Jefferson, N.C.: McFarland, 1992.

Saffady, William. "Local Area Networks: A Survey of Technology." *Library Technology Reports* 26 (1) (January/February 1990).

Santifaller, Michael. TCP/IP and NFS Internetworking in a UNIX Environment. Redwood City, Calif.: Addison-Wesley, 1991.

Sasser, Susan B., Mary Ralston, and Robert McLaughlin. *Troubleshooting Your LAN*. New York: MIS Pr., 1992.

Saunders, Stephen. "Choosing High-Speed LANs." *Data Communications* 22 (14): 58–70 (September 21, 1993).

Sheldon, Tom. *LAN Times Encyclopedia of Networking*. Berkeley, Calif.: Osborne McGraw-Hill, 1994.

————. *Novell NetWare 386: The Complete Reference*. New York: McGraw-Hill, 1990.

Spinney, Byron. *Ethernet Pocket Guide: A Practical Guide to Designing, Installing and Troubleshooting Ethernet Networks*. Horsham, Pa.: Professional Press Books, 1992.

Stallings, William. *Networking Standards: A Guide to OSI, ISDN, LAN and MAN Standards*. Redwood City, Calif.: Addison-Wesley, 1993.

Stamper, David. *Local Area Networks*. Redwood City, Calif.: Benjamin/Cummings, 1994.

Taschek, John. "Network the Power of Your Best Ally: Information." *PC-Computing* 7 (1): 274–78 (January 1994).

Thompson, M. Keith, and Kimberly Maxwell. "Connectivity: Building Workgroup Solutions: Networking CD-ROMs." *PC Magazine* 9 (4): 237+ (February 27, 1990).

"Windows Remote-Control Software: Reaching beyond Your Grasp (Product Comparison)." *InfoWorld* 17 (8): 66–82 (February 20, 1995).

Magazines

The following magazines provide information on CD-ROM networking from time to time.

Byte
P.O. Box 555
Hightstown, NJ 08520
(800) 257-9402

Campus-Wide Information Systems (CWIS)
MCB University Press
60/62 Toller Ln.
Bradford, West Yorkshire
England BD8 9BY
(44) 01274-777700
(800) 633-4931

CD-ROM News Extra
Pemberton Press
462 Danbury Rd.
Wilton, CT 06897-2126
(800) 248-8466,
(203) 761-1466
Fax: (203) 761-1444

CD-ROM Professional
Pemberton Press, Inc.
l l Tannery Ln.
Weston, CT 06883
(203) 227-8466
Fax: (203) 222-0122

CD-ROM World
Meckler Corp.
11 Ferry Ln. West
Westport, CT 06880
(203) 226-6967

Communications News
2504 Tamiami Trail North
Nokomis, FL 34275-9987
(813) 966-9521

Communications Week
P.O. Box 1094
Skokie, IL 60076
(708) 647-6834
Fax: (708) 647-6838

Computers in Libraries
Meckler Corp.
11 Ferry Ln. West
Westport, CT 06880
(203) 226-6967

Data Communications
1221 Avenue of the Americas
New York, NY 10020
(800) 525-5003

Information Today
143 Old Marlton Pike
Medford, NJ 08055
(609) 654-6266

InfoWorld
155 Bovet Rd., Suite 800
San Mateo, CA 94402
(415) 572-7341

Interoperability
600 Harrison St.
San Francisco, CA 94107
(415) 905-2200
Fax: (415) 905-2234

LAN: The Network Solutions Magazine
600 Harrison St.
San Francisco, CA 94107
(415) 905-2200
Fax: (415) 905-2234

LAN Times
P.O. Box 652
Highstown, NJ 08520-0652
(800) 525-5003

Library Hi Tech
P.O. Box 1808
Ann Arbor, MI 48106
(800) 678-2435

NetWare News
P.O. Box 17868
Irvine, CA 92713
Fax: (714) 262-0164

Network Management
1421 South Sheridan
Tulsa, OK 74112
(918) 831-9424

Network World
161 Worcester Rd.
Framingham, MA 01701
(508) 875-6400
Fax: (508) 820-3467

New Media Magazine
P.O. Box 1771
Riverton, NJ 08077-7371
(609) 786-4430

Online
462 Danbury Rd.
Wilton, CT 06897
(203) 761-1466

PC Computing
P.O. Box 58229
Boulder, CO 80322
(800) 365-2770

PC Magazine
P.O. Box 54093
Boulder, CO 80322
(800) 289-0429

PC World
501 Second St.
San Francisco, CA 94107
(800) 234-3498,
(415) 243-0500
Fax: (415) 442-1891

PCWeek
P.O. Box 1767
Riverton, NJ 08077-9767
(609) 786-8230

Syllabus
1307 South Mary Ave., Suite 211
Sunnyvale, CA 94087
(408) 746-2000
Fax: (408) 746-2711

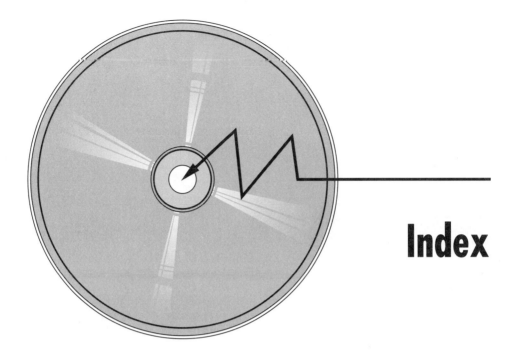

Index

Ahmed M. Elshami is systems librarian at Temple University Libraries and has solved numerous CD-ROM network problems. He is the author of *CD-ROM Technology for Information Managers* and *CD-ROM: An Annotated Bibliography,* as well as other publications.